America's Longest Siege

AMERICA'S LONGEST SIEGE

Charleston, Slavery, and the Slow March Toward Civil War

Joseph Kelly

THE OVERLOOK PRESS
NEW YORK, NY

This edition first published in hardcover in the United States in 2013 by
The Overlook Press, Peter Mayer Publishers, Inc.

141 Wooster Street
New York, NY 10012
www.overlookpress.com
For bulk and special sales, please contact sales@overlookny.com,
or write us at the above address

Cataloging-in-Publication Data is available from the Library of Congress

Book design and typeformatting by Bernard Schleifer

Manufactured in the United States of America
ISBN US: 978-1-59020-719-2

CONTENTS

||

The undated map above shows the defenses of Charleston Harbor at the
start of the Civil War. Fort Wagner was built later near the narrowest point
on Morris Island.

INTRODUCTION

No More Peace Forever

||

On a March afternoon midway through the American Civil War, the "rich and poor, white and black" people inhabiting Charleston, South Carolina, the birthplace of Secession, trudged behind the coffin of James Louis Petigru, defender of the Union. "All the interests and classes" of Charleston, scientists, judges, politicians, and especially "all the members of the Bar of this city" paid their last respect to this tattered remnant of the United States. As they slowly made their way from the house where the old lawyer died to the graveyard next to St. Michael's towering steeple, their faces expressed "the conviction that a great man had departed" from this world. The cold of winter did him in. Corpulent and debilitated by chronic bronchitis, Petigru knew by February that he was dying. He had no blood relations left in the city, and his own house in the heart of town had burned to the ground two years earlier in the great Charleston fire, so he faded in a borrowed room of an old friend's son, tinkering with his will before succumbing finally to the wintry cough.[1]

Charleston was hardly in a mourning mood. Fruit trees along the coast had been blooming for two weeks. The grass was "springing up everywhere," and the "most beautiful" lawns were growing on the sandbags that had been heaped up at the waterfront to protect the cannons that were protecting the city. The whiff of warmer days sweetened the breath of most of the white folks in the funeral cortege, and, while they listened with bowed heads to the "beautiful and touching" service, most minds probably drifted away from the venerable history of the

deceased to their own bright futures. The mourners might be forgiven
if they were not as sad as they tried to appear. The white people there
could not have been feeling much grief: a dignified respect, but not
much grief. They were burying a nagging annoyance, a naysayer, and
laid to rest with him was the last chill of doubt that the new Confederacy—the secession and rebellion and the nation then but two years
old—was neither just nor noble and should not long endure. Petigru
was a banner, a symbol, and Charlestonians took pride in the deference
they paid this frayed and faded relic of harmony between North and
South. While he was alive, the city had respected the "free expression
of his every thought," never molesting him, never muffling his acid
tongue. But their magnanimity had the taint of self-satisfaction, as if
Charleston held up Petigru and their forbearance of him as a proof of
their own virtue. Honoring this thorn plucked finally from their side
was a way of trumpeting their evenhandedness and reasonableness.
Their self-proclaimed generosity of spirit reminded Charlestonians of
the righteousness of their cause. Once the funeral was over, after the
men replaced their hats and the women had gratefully removed the
mask of solemnity from their faces, when all had turned their backs
on the grave and headed into the streets of the city, there would be
nothing to ponder but the brilliant spring sunshine and the brilliant
future facing the Confederate States of America. For old Petigru, the
last of the dissenters, the last Union man in the heart of the South, was
finally in the ground.[2]

No one was left to question the "positive good" theory of slavery,
the most destructive idea to come out of South Carolina's conservatism.
It was a relatively young idea in 1860, having been born barely forty
years earlier and entering its maturity no sooner than 1835. Like the
totalitarian ideologies of the twentieth century, the ascendancy of the
positive good theory required the parallel idea that political dissent is
evil, and so South Carolina strictly regulated speech, beginning in
1832, spreading such repression until the American South, by the
1840s and 1850s, was little better than a police state. Though only one
full generation of white southerners grew up under this regime, history has proven how much damage one generation can wreak.

In 1860, elder men and women could remember when times

were different, and the aged Petigru reminded his fellow Charlestonians of an older way of thinking. He was a Whig when there was no
longer a Whig party, and he belonged to the age when American statesmen from the South and the North tried to forge a common nation by
compromise and friendship, an age when the best minds of the South
openly regretted slavery and thought it would die a natural death in
the new republic by growing more anachronistic with each passing
generation. Petigru was a reliquary of what political discourse had been
before the rise of southern unanimity, and to see him on the street was
like looking at a museum curiosity, something that bemused but did
not influence the confident and unreflecting young.

In the Revolutionary era, dissent was not so isolated and impo-
tent. Just a month after the signing of the Declaration of Independence,
Henry Laurens, a merchant from Charleston, declared:

> I abhor Slavery, I was born in a Country where Slavery had been
> established by British Kings & Parliaments as well as by the Laws
> of that Country Ages before my existence. . . . In former days
> there was no combating the prejudices of Men supported by In-
> terest, the day I hope is approaching when from principles of
> gratitude as well as justice every Man will strive to be foremost in
> shewing his readiness to comply with the Golden Rule; . . . I am
> devising means for manumitting many of [my slaves] & for cut-
> ting off the entail of slavery.

Laurens knew that "great powers" opposed him, not only the "laws &
customs" of South Carolina, but his own and his countrymen's greed.
"I am not one of those," he said, "who dare trust in Providence for
defence & security of their own Liberty while they enslave & wish to
continue in Slavery, thousands who are as well intitled to freedom as
themselves."[3]

Unchecked greed had created slavery in Charleston almost from
the moment of its founding, in 1670, and no one then had any illusions
about it. Its earliest proponents knew slavery was a crime perpetrated
against a conquered people, and "the conquest of the earth," as Joseph
Conrad reminds us, "means the taking it away from those who have a

different complexion or slightly flatter noses than ourselves, [and] is not a pretty thing when you look into it too much . . . robbery with violence, aggravated murder on a great scale." The first English settlers of Carolina knew the stain that slavery put upon their souls, but they ignored their own moral compass in the face of staggering profits. Yet, as time passed with each new generation, as more whites and more blacks were born into slave society and grew up in it, as the institution was "creolized," it began to seem more and more natural. White men born into the slave system, whose wealth was dependent upon slavery but who were too genteel to see themselves as thieves, developed a paternalistic view of slavery, thinking of themselves as parents or custodians of the intellectual and moral development of the black people who had been degraded by earlier generations. Still, they understood that slavery was inimical to human nature, as the ideology of the American Revolution clearly indicated, and enlightened southerners looked forward to the time when this sin against liberty might be purged, when their black dependents might grow up and prove themselves worthy of self-determination. The contagion of liberty inspired patriots like Henry Laurens to imagine that the day might come sooner rather than later. He and other men of conscience knew that the "commerce between master and slave is despotism." Thomas Jefferson presciently confessed in his *Notes on the State of Virginia*, "I tremble for my country when I consider God is just, and his justice cannot sleep forever."

Few of South Carolina's aristocrats were ready to start manumitting their slaves, so Laurens knew that he was dissenting from the prevailing view. Nevertheless, this dissenter was a man of considerable influence. Laurens was the vice president of South Carolina when he declared his abhorrence of slavery; the following year he was president of the Continental Congress. He was the most prominent national politician south of Virginia, and one of the United States' five delegates at the Treaty of Paris, which finally ended the war. Nor was he alone. A sizeable and voluble minority agitated for emancipation-friendly legislation, a faction at first led by Laurens's own son, a colonel in the Continental Army, John Laurens. In the generation following the Revolution, prominent planters, respectable men of business, and influential politicians could openly dissent and even discuss how to eradicate slavery in the chambers of government. They had many fellow travelers: before about 1820, no one in Charleston was willing to argue that slavery was a public good. And yet, not a single delegate to the 1860 Secession Convention in Charleston believed that slavery was evil. A remarkable consensus.

One of the many bon mots attributed to the irascible Petigru was occasioned by this assemblage of men who were so uniform in their opinions. He was in Columbia on business, and Petigru happened to be walking past the Baptist church where the Secession Convention was meeting when a stranger stopped him in the street to ask directions to the insane asylum. Petigru pointed to the convention hall and quipped, "I think you will find the inmates yonder."

Even more remarkable than the ideological solidarity was how many in South Carolina agreed with the expediency of secession, a fearful step even for a staunch defender of slavery. The *New York Tribune* reported that if the election of delegates to the convention had been delayed just one week, the fever for secession would have begun to cool, and "'a positive Union party' would have developed itself in South Carolina." To understand how such a unanimity of public opinion could occur, especially where there had been disunity but a month earlier, and, by most accounts, would have been disunity again had the Secession Convention been delayed a month, we have to remember what a nineteenth-century, preindustrial southern city was like. The scale of even a large city like Charleston was far more human than, say, the New York or Boston of 1860 or even a larger town today. About seven thousand houses comprised the bulk of the Charleston's buildings, about a third of those made of brick. The total population, including the four working-class wards of the "Neck," which were annexed in the 1850s, was just about 40,000. Of those, 26,548 were "free white and colored," while 13,606 were slaves (almost 10 percent of the free population was not white). About 8,000 white males in Charleston were born in South Carolina; 732 were northerners, 1,771 came from Ireland, and 1,429 came from Germany.[4] Those figures might make Charleston seem somewhat cosmopolitan until we compare it to northern cities. New York, for example, had 383,000 foreign-born habitants, almost half of its residents. All of Charleston would hardly have constituted a neighborhood in New York City.

Charleston was almost Shakespearean, as if its streets were a stage and public opinion were forged in the open air. One can imagine Mark Antony carrying the bloody vestments of Caesar and asking the plebeians to lend their ears. Take this anecdote, for example. A slave, Nicholas, had been sentenced to death for deadly assault. While awaiting execution, he led a massive jailbreak of three dozen black inmates armed with an ax and sledgehammers. After most of the escapees had been recaptured, a white mob, suspecting a black church was behind the incident, gathered on the steps of city hall demanding vengeance from the mayor. Petigru's law office was just down the street, and, hearing the commotion, he hurried to the scene, "mounted the high steps of city hall," and with a speech worthy of one of Shakespeare's heroes, faced down the crowd. He reasoned with them, eventually cooling the heat of anger with the promise of an investigation. A citizen's committee would look into the matter, and if it were proved that the black church was seditious, Petigru pledged to go with the crowd himself and burn it down. But if the church were proved to be innocent, the mob could burn it, he warned them, only "over my dead body." This appeal to reason, delivered with a technique Petigru had sharpened before juries in the courts of law, persuaded the impulsive mob, which dispersed. Over the next few weeks, the committee did its patient work, and the church was saved.[5]

One can imagine how easily an idea might grip the minds of whites in Charleston and turn to indisputable *truth*, as if a mob, a crowd, a populace were a single organism able to feel emotions like the sting of insult and the pride of honor as one body. Especially when the men giving speeches from balconies were feeding the prejudices of the mob rather than opposing them, swifter than any disease of the body did pandemic of *opinion* circulate through the streets. What Petigru feared came about: the "passions of the mob" infused the "gentlemen" of the city—the men of learning and position—as much as it did "the rabble," and these gentlemen, infected with irrationality, further rallied the mobs.[6] He had good reason to worry. The private letters and journals of respectable Charlestonians in December 1860 record the euphoria that overwhelmed judgment and prudence. Public opinion became such an irresistible wave that no one, not even the eloquent barrister, could mount the steps of city hall and oppose the flooding tide. Petigru was reduced to grumbling like a crank.

On December 20, the delegates to the convention signed the Ordinance of Secession. Charleston exploded in celebration, led by the eager bells of St. Michael's mixing with the pealing of a dozen other church belfries. Petigru growled disingenuously to a passerby, "Where's the fire?"

"Mr. Petigru," the man responded with simple innocence, "there is no fire; those are the joy bells ringing in honor of the passage of the Ordinance of Secession."

"I tell you there is a fire," Petigru answered. "They have this day set a blazing torch to the temple of constitutional liberty and, please God, we shall have no more peace forever."[7]

One day not long after the secession, Petigru happened to be walking down Broad Street when a friend stopped him. "Mr. Petigru," the friend said, "these are times which require every man to define his position. You were a good soldier in the War of 1812; your captain told me so: where are you now?"

Petigru dropped his chin to his chest, a characteristic gesture, and thought about his words carefully. For a long time he didn't speak, and all the while they continued walking. Finally, "lifting up his head very quickly" and abandoning all attempt at wit he said abruptly: "I have seen the last happy day of my life."[8]

As all of Charleston knew and as more than one citizen attested, Petigru "considered the course of the State wrong in principle and fatal in its consequences. He would have prevented secession by any sacrifice it would have been in his power to have made. . . . He deplored the war; he considered us mad in attempting it." His apocalyptic bon mots circulated through the rumor mill, but they hardly dampened the enthusiasm for secession; by contrast, the shadow of his thoughts cast Charleston's obsession into greater brilliance. Petigru insulted the rector of St. Michael's Episcopal Church when the minister, in obvious accord with the sentiments of the community, declined to pray for the health of Abraham Lincoln.[9] Richest of all was Petigru's legendary remark, widely circulated in Charleston even today, that South Carolina was too small to be a republic and too large to be an insane asylum.

Petigru was the conscience of Charleston, the lone voice of reason among the self-congratulatory speech-makers, the fire-eaters, who in a haughty self-delusion considered themselves and their property, their *slaves*, to be so threatened by Abraham Lincoln. He wanted to demolish the hubris of those who thought they would easily defeat the North, if it came to war. Petigru told them time and again that they wove their winding-sheet. He was Charleston's Tiresias, and just as that seer testified to the king of Thebes his own guilty past and prophesized the suffering yet to come, Petigru foresaw what would become of his beloved city.

But Charleston didn't listen. Instead, all together, the citizens endured him the way a family puts up with its peculiar, annoying uncle. They decided not to take him too seriously. As one recent historian put it, Petigru was "assigned the role of admired eccentric—the exception who was so singular that he could be tolerated without fear." The diarist Emma Holmes summed up the city's view when she wrote, "We pity but cannot despise" him. Petigru, "one of our first lawyers and the pride of the So[uth] Ca[rolina] bar, is a Unionist, but he is quiet and does not meddle in politics." Or perhaps the citizens of Charleston, like Mary Chesnut, the most famous diarist of the Civil War, were more generous than Holmes: Petigru was "contrary to the prejudices of the people," but "he is as much respected as ever. Maybe his astounding pluck has raised him in the estimation of the people he flouts and contradicts on their tenderest points."[10] Petigru became the local crackpot, Charleston's Socrates, but in this case the state felt no need to execute the gadfly. Ineffectual as it was, such dissent could be tolerated. The city could afford to let it die of natural causes and pay tribute when it was gone.

Even General Pierre Gustave Toutant Beauregard attended Petigru's burial, and accompanying the general was his chief of staff, General Thomas Jordan; D. N. Ingraham, commodore of the Navy; and many of their officers, in their dress regalia, swords depending from their belts and clanking aristocratically, all lending romance to the bleak affair. This martial splendor bowed its head in poignant salute to Charleston's last Union man. The Union had been dead two years. The clumps of dirt rattling down upon Petigru's coffin were its coda, a nostalgic recollection of friendships with New York, with Boston, a reminder of mystic chords of memory that once bound southerners to their northern cousins, three generations of wrangling, quarreling, straining, reconciling, squabbling again about the fundamental division: *what to do about slavery?* Petigru was the last man in Charleston laboring and struggling to reconcile the divide. His aged, wheezing decline, the very sorrow of his final years of life, embodied the long anguish of union. Whether or not anyone felt it that afternoon, Charleston buried the last reminder of the struggle it had already given up. The world was left to the living, to those eager officers of the Confederate States of America, who, walking away from the graveside, donned their hats and mounted their horses with a singleness of purpose. Intent on battle, which is far less complicated than compromise and conciliation, they dispersed through the bracing sunlight to the various posts of their defense.

Siege was coming. Union forces already were gathering to the south, at the naval base they had established at Port Royal. General Robert E. Lee wanted Charleston defended "street by street and house by house as long as we have a foot of ground to stand upon," but no one thought it would come to that. The outer defenses were too powerful, too entrenched to need the inner defenses. In February Beauregard invited citizens to leave the city, and they paid him the compliment of ignoring the advice. But the siege was coming. In April, a month after Petigru's funeral, a fleet of nine ironclads would probe for weaknesses in the harbor's forts. In the summer, the Union army would invade Folly Island and then make its slow and arduous progress across the heavily defended Morris Island, performing the elaborate and inexorable investiture of Charleston. A gigantic cannon modified from a Parrott rifle and weighing over 16,000 pounds would be erected at the end of an improvised, "two and a half mile trestle roadway" in the hidden depths of a marsh, well beyond the sight not only of the city but of Confederate defenses, and in the middle of one hot August night the "Swamp Angel," as the Union troops called the gun, would hurl a 150-pound shell five miles across the harbor, further than any projectile had yet been thrown in human history. It burst like a meteor in the heart of Charleston, officially beginning the longest siege in

American history. Vicksburg suffered siege for forty-seven days before finally surrendering to Grant. Petersburg in Virginia held out for an amazing nine months. In the Crimean War, just ten years earlier, Sevastapol lasted eleven months. But shells would burst over Charleston for the next two Christmases, cratering the streets and falling through the roofs of houses, 545 days before the city, finally in ruins, surrendered. It was the longest siege in modern warfare until the Germans at Leningrad in World War II.[11]

But General Pierre Gustave Toutant Beauregard and the Confederate defenders and the citizens of Charleston could foresee none of that. Nor did they realize they were merely players in the final act of a longer drama, a three hundred years' war, the Enlightenment ideals of equality and liberty contesting with greed for the conscience of the South. Their fate had been determined by their fathers and their fathers' fathers. A remarkably small number of men set these events in motion, the oligarchs of Charleston, perhaps two or three dozen aristocratic families living along the swampy coast of the Carolina Lowcountry, who committed the original sin blotting American democracy, a sin atoned by the ruin of their city, so many dead, and so much racial suffering. Their mistake was age-old human greed, pride, the psychological pleasure of being the master of another man or of a hundred men, the old temptation to tally one's wealth in the number of limbs and straining backs tilling one's fields, for Ecclesiastes is right that there is nothing new under the sun. Not even Petigru foresaw this, that the broken glass and toppled masonry, the bombed-out buildings and the weeds growing in the rubble of his beloved city all might be glimpsed at its founding, when the first English planters arrived from Barbados, bringing with them a lust for quick wealth and no particular scruples about how they got it.

And yet, even in 1787, when slavery was enshrined in the United States Constitution, Charleston's eventual humiliation, defeat, and destruction were not assured. Fate might be avoided. Reform was still possible. In the generation following the Revolution, plenty of people dissented from the self-serving ideology of slavery, and even conservative Charleston was drifting toward liberty. The critical turn came in turbulent 1822, when, supposedly, hundreds of slaves led by the infamous, remarkable Denmark Vesey threatened to slaughter whites, put the city to the torch, steal a fleet of ships, and escape to Haiti. Then the flame of universal liberty flickered low.

Yet even then, in 1822, the calamity of civil war might have been avoided. Not until 1835 did Charleston seal its fate, when the slaveocracy completely closed the city to dissent. Not until then did men openly deny the Declaration of Independence, that *all* men were created equal. The sinews of the southern heart were twisted by the art of John C. Calhoun, its brain forged by his ringing hammer. In the smithy of South Carolina was forged the siege cannon of a new southern orthodoxy. Sapper lines were mined, stretching from Charleston to all the southern states. Conscience became a crime, and the ideological machinery laid siege to the mind of the South. It is impossible to point to dates in this kind of ideological conflict, to identify the exact moment of surrender, but by the 1840s this siege was won. Only then was the South's epitaph graven on stone.

There was no hope really for the last generation, the lost generation. The young men who flocked to the gray uniform and the young women who urged them on were acting out a fate determined not by themselves, nor by the signing of the Ordinance of Secession, nor even in 1861 by the violent attack on the flag of the United States flying over Fort Sumter. By the time Lincoln was elected, nearly every white man and woman in South Carolina was condemned to believe that slavery was positively good and, stranger yet, that the abolition of slavery was absolutely evil. They could hardly believe otherwise, and then the conflagration was sealed.

The history of Charleston is tragic. It follows the classic formula laid down by the Greeks more than two thousand years ago. What the citizens buried with Petigru was not a chance of salvation, for by then it was too late, but merely a chance for self-understanding. Charleston dug its grave in the 1830s, and in 1863 it was merely falling in. Once, it had been the jewel of the Southern Seaboard, one of the finest and most important cities of the nation, a rival to Philadelphia and New York and Boston. But its devotion to slavery sealed its sentence, and the Union's siege of Charleston and all the Civil War's dead, North and South, white and black, were the playing out of its tragic flaw.

1

THE STONO REBELLION

||

On September 9, 1739, near a bridge over the Stono River and over-looking a wide, treeless marsh just a few miles south of what was then called Charles Town, a group of slaves attacked a store, stole "a pretty many small Arms and Powder," decapitated the two white men there, and left their heads staring off the porch. The rebel slaves marched south along today's U.S. Highway 17 and at plantations along the way burned houses, killed the slave owners, and gathered more to their ranks until they numbered somewhere between sixty and a hundred, a motley, euphoric battalion. They killed white men, white women, even white children at the isolated farms, but they were not indiscriminate. They spared a certain Mr. Wallace, who owned a tavern on the road to Savannah, because "he was a good Man and kind to his Slaves."[1]

The whites hastily gathered their militia and caught the little troop of blacks about twenty miles down the road, at the next river, the Edisto, near the Jacksonboro Ferry. The well-armed militia attacked. Fourteen rebels were killed in the first volley, and as many as three dozen, realizing they were outgunned, fled to the woods. The militia-men strolled among the wounded, and when they found survivors moaning in the dirt they interrogated them, then shot them again unmercifully. The rebels in the woods were hunted down and executed without trial. The militiamen cut off their heads, about forty in all, and stuck these gruesome, rotting symbols on mileposts to terrorize the local black population.

To most in Carolina, the uprising came as no surprise. It was a local incident in a global struggle between European powers. The king of Spain had invited English slaves to flee their miserable lives in Carolina and find sanctuary in Florida, and the advertisements in the *South Carolina Gazette* were dominated each week by notices of runaways. The problem rose to a crisis in 1739, as relations deteriorated between mother countries. More than one slave conspiracy was foiled and more than one plot to escape to St. Augustine succeeded in the months before the Stono Rebellion. Frustrated slave owners remonstrated with the Spanish authorities, but runaway slaves were not returned, and then came the terrifying Stono Rebellion.[2] Georgia and Carolina together outfitted an expedition under the command of Georgia's General Oglethorpe, who took his ragtag Rangers and various irregulars and a regiment of Carolina soldiers down to Florida. St. Augustine, which was then a town of about twenty-four hundred Indians, mulattoes, escaped slaves, Spanish colonials, and soldiers, was guarded by a tiny but formidable castle that enclosed about an acre's worth of parade ground. Like Charles Town, the town was situated on a peninsula protected from the sea by two barrier islands. Oglethorpe captured a makeshift outer defense-work called Moosa, or the "Negro" fort, left about 140 men in the area to harass the town, and proceeded with the bulk of his army to the barrier islands, which he easily captured. There, he began erecting batteries that would pin down the Spanish half-galleys and lob bombs into the castle.

Three commanders at the captured Negro fort squabbled over their defense. Captains McKay and McIntosh of Georgia regarded the enemy, bloated as they were by runaways and Indians, with contempt. Colonel Palmer of Carolina was less dismissive, and he kept his troops at the ready, positioned along a ditch outside the fort. For days and days the detachment skirmished with the town, and day after day the Georgians grew more and more complacent, sleeping till dawn, neglecting the most obvious precautionary tactics. The Spanish counterattack finally came in the predawn darkness and caught men half-dressed running for their weapons, confused, roused from sleep by terror, but hardly knowing what desperate act might save themselves. Colonel Palmer tried to muster a defense, but he might as well have commanded a scramble of rats rousted from a hiding place. The Carolinians camped outside provided a flanking fire, but it was all too feeble, and once the fort was breached they could do little more than listen to the sounds of hand-to-hand combat and inevitable slaughter. Over the sides of the fort came the surviving English, who dashed into the ditch, only to find the company there abandoning their position for the woods. Colonel Palmer bravely held his ground, in the end commanding only two stalwart Rangers, but even these headed for the woods when Palmer was shot. Bleeding from his mouth, he reloaded his gun and turned again to face the enemy, crying, "Huzza my Lads! The Day's our own, I have been in many Battles and never lost one yet." But no one was left to see Palmer die. The Spanish force, about 450 men largely made up of "Negroes and Indians," marched back to St. Augustine "in great Triumph, shouting and firing . . . with the Prisoners and Colours that they had taken in the Fort, wearing in their Hats the Ears and private Parts of the Slain." Fifty English were killed and about twenty others were taken prisoner, including Captain McKay.[3]

The English slunk away from Florida, and instead of triumphant parades they met with accusations and intrigues that traveled all the way to London. It was a horrible ignominy and a sharp dose of reality: the colonists had been beaten in arms by a force largely made of slaves who had escaped from their own plantations. And while the Carolina legislature was preparing its report of the debacle the next summer, a fire swept through Charles Town. In the close-built town with so many wooden structures and so many kitchen fires, conflagrations were always a lurking danger, but this one proved particularly difficult to fight, and it destroyed "about 300 Dwelling Houses, besides a greater number of Store Houses & some of the Wharfs." Suspicious eyes were turned on the slaves, for it would take little for one cook or blacksmith to do more damage to the city than a warship. No culprits were discovered, but whites were all the more uneasy as they sifted through the ruins, kicked the remaining boards down into the ashes, and began thinking about building again.[4]

The Stono Rebellion, the invasion of Florida, and the Charles Town fire all reminded British colonists of something they had nearly forgotten. Blacks loved "liberty as much as other men," and for many Africans in America, *live free or die* was an urgent choice. "Liberty!" had been the battle cry of the rebelling slaves at Stono. With unabashed clarity the Commons House of Assembly reported that the battle at Jacksonboro Ferry was as fierce as one might suppose when "one fought for liberty and life, the other for their country and everything that was dear to them." In the very next year, black soldiers from Florida invaded Georgia, and, though they were turned back at the Battle of Bloody Marsh, the invasion brought home the danger that slavery posed to every white in Carolina. Blacks were capable of acting the way whites hoped they themselves would have acted had someone enslaved them. Insurrection was a natural and even *manly* reaction to being enslaved. Slavery was, in essence, a permanent state of war between one people wanting "liberty and life" and another people who wanted to steal their labor.[5]

It was all too clear who were the thieves in this economy. Just after the Rebellion, George Whitefield, the most influential of the itinerant, Great Awakening preachers who ever came to Charles Town, wrote an open letter *To the Inhabitants of Maryland, Virginia, North and South-Carolina, concerning their Negroes*. Whitefield had seen plantation life, and it appalled him. It was a sin to "encourage . . . perpetual war" between nations in Africa in order to supply America with prisoners, and boldly he told southerners that "it is sinful . . . to use [slaves] worse than brutes." Plantation owners treated dogs and horses better than they treated their human chattel, and Whitefield excoriated the frequent use of the lash and blade. It was God who made "their own slaves" rise up "in arms against them." "God first generally corrects us with whips," he warned readers, and "if that will not do, he must chastise us with scorpions." Whitefield stated outright what all of the English colonies had been repressing: "Although I pray God the slaves may never be permitted to get the upper hand, yet should such a thing be permitted by Providence, all good men must acknowledge the judgment would be just."[6]

Given the history of South Carolina, it should not have been surprising to find God displeased. In August 1669, three ships set out from England, touched briefly in Ireland, and then headed for Barbados, the British sugar colony near the coast of Venezuela, which they reached in October, the last stop on the way to the coastal region they called "Carolina." In April of the following year, after a journey of more than seven months, ninety-three people came ashore on a little peninsular bluff around a bend in a river they dubbed Ashley, well-hidden from Spanish and French raiders, who already, with their own Indian allies, were stalking the settlers. The English set up their cannons, built a palisade, and then got down to work.[7]

This was no voyage of discovery. The colonists were not zealots building a New Jerusalem. They were not political exiles looking for sanctuary. Nor were they land-hungry farmers from an overpopulated Europe looking to set up self-sustaining homesteads.[8] This was the seventeenth century's version of big business. Carolina was settled by the type of colonist already in Barbados: hard-drinking, hardworking, hardhearted fortune seekers. According to one contemporary observer, they were "the vilest race of men upon the earth," with "neither honor, nor honesty, nor religion enough to entitle them to any tolerable character." Only twenty-nine men were free, while sixty-three were bondsmen so desperate that they had consented to be temporary slaves. The richest was a minor aristocrat from Warwickshire, Stephen Bull, whose nine indentured servants entitled him to 1,050 acres of Indian land. Each new season brought more people, bonded and free, mostly from the West Indies. Their only goal was profit, and the surest way to make money was to set up a system that mimicked the sugar plantations of Barbados. They tried tobacco, "silk, wine, olives, indigo, and figs," but each failed in the strange soil.[9] So in order to make money in its first decades, the Carolina colony was little more than organized robbery of neighboring Indians. Its first exports were entirely unsustainable: lumber, tar and pitch, furs.

In 1670, slavery was a relatively new concept to the English. When Shakespeare wrote *Othello, the Moor of Venice,* in about 1600, England had no direct experience of slaves. Accounts came secondhand, and the English regarded slavery as synonymous with captivity, as the jurist Edward Coke explained to Shakespeare's contemporaries: "It was ordained by the Constitution of Nations . . . that he that was taken in Battle should remain Bond to his taker for ever, and he to do with him, [and] all that should come of him, his Will and Pleasure, as with his Beast, or any other Cattle." Such a loss of liberty was equivalent to a loss of humanity, something to which the English would not even subject the Irish, who, though papists, were at least Christians. Mohammedans, on the other hand, were at "ceaseless" war with Christians, and just as Turks and Moors sold their Christian captives into the "verie worst manner of bondmanship and slaverie," so could Christians take away the liberty of Muslims.[10]

So the English were not troubled when the Spanish and the Portuguese started kidnapping Africans to work in their tropical colonies. Hadn't the slaves been captured in wars? Maybe they weren't Muslims, but they were heathens and so in a sort of constant state of enmity with Christians. By the 1640s, when the English colonies in Virginia and Barbados were looking for a cheap labor force, it was inconvenient to look too deeply into the matter. Other European countries were taking captives from Africa to work in their colonies—why not England?

Native Americans were a type of pagan, and so within a year the Carolina colonists started harvesting them just as they harvested American trees to make tar and pitch. They armed the Westos, who made war on other local tribes, including Carolina's erstwhile friends the Cusabos, and sold their captives to the English. By 1680, ten years after its founding, the colony made war on the Westos, reclaiming dubious debts in the form of prisoners of war. Colonel Moore, marching with the Yemassee Indians against Spain's St. Augustine colony in Florida in 1703, netted a thousand Indian captives, most of whom were shipped to the northern colonies of New York, Connecticut, and Rhode Island. The English learned to prefer women and children, because the men tended to rebel or escape or refuse to work. Consequently, male captives often were killed outright, sometimes "burnt most barbarously," the necessary waste product of the growing industries, which denuded the coast of forests and Indians. But thirty years into the settlement, whites still had penetrated hardly more than twenty-five miles from their original site. Beyond this limit, of course, white traders lived in Indian country and channeled a steady stream of furs and deerskins to the coast. But compared with the Massachusetts colony, New York, or even the difficult Virginia colony, Carolina was slow getting started.

The population of the whole colony was about six thousand, and its town, Charles Town, had only about twelve hundred, half of whom were slaves.[11]

Right around the turn of the century they discovered the crop that saved the colony: rice. Small, yeomen farmers cannot really produce rice. Tidal swamps and marshes have to be drained, dikes heaped up out of the mud of river bottoms, giant trunk gates installed to let the freshwater on the outgoing tide sluice into the fields and to close out the brackish incoming tides. It was backbreaking, miserable, dangerous work, and the white indentured servants that the free colonists had brought from England and Ireland simply would not do it: only people threatened by the whip would submit to this type of labor. So around 1700, Charles Town started importing more slaves than it exported. Nearly four hundred thousand pounds of rice shipped out of Charles Town Harbor, and that number would quadruple in the next decade and then quadruple again. Money flowed back to the town. In 1701, the colonists began construction on a seawall along the banks of the Cooper River. By 1704 a moat, a barricade studded with seven armed bastions, and two drawbridges enclosed the town's eighty acres. Two wharves, one at the end of Tradd Street and the other at the end of Queen, extended far into the bay, where dockworkers loaded the rice, packed in barrels, onto oceangoing boats. In 1700, more than eighty vessels were clearing the harbor annually. By 1706, thirty-five hundred people filled a town of 250 dwellings, which provided a livelihood for five hundred white men. Shoppers now could find fine furniture and cookware, "silver tobacco boxes, silver tankards and silver-headed canes," while the wives of richer men had begun to collect all sorts of jewelry. A portraitist was painting the leading townsmen.

The first map of the city, Edward Crisp's 1711 survey, shows four churches—Anglican, Huguenot, Independent, and Anabaptist—as well as a Quaker meeting house, fifteen mansions, and ten nearby farms outside the walls. Planters built handsome houses in the Barbadian style, with broad porches (called piazzas) and gardens; they collected horses for pleasure; the slave hovels were replaced with the permanent, thatched clay huts distinctive of African villages on the Gold Coast. Between 1690 and 1710, the number of slaves in Carolina exploded from fifteen hundred souls to forty-one hundred, and between 1710 and 1720 their numbers tripled. Merchants imported Africans mostly from Angola, nearly twenty thousand people in ten years. There were setbacks: fires, plagues, hurricanes. Most notably, in 1715 a massive Indian rebellion led by the Yemassee nearly wiped out the colony, before the tide was turned by an alliance between the English and the Cherokee. Nevertheless, by the 1730s, with new rice markets opened in Europe, Charles Town was a booming, singular colonial city. The price of rice nearly doubled between 1732 and 1738, and all the while pitch, tar, and furs kept selling at a brisk rate. By 1735, "over 500 ocean-going ships and hundreds of smaller craft" traded their cargoes in Charles Town each year. The town was full of money, and its citizens bought beer from Bristol, cheese from Rhode Island, wine from Lisbon, eastern spices, hats, stockings, knee garters, wig powder, paper, books—all the goods of civilization. From their Broad Street shop, Sarah and Lucy Weaver sold the latest fancy dresses from London. A public school was opened. The city overran its fortifications. The western "line" was dismantled, and the old moat and drawbridge became the new center of town, the intersection of Broad and Meeting Streets. Property values doubled, then doubled again, even while the city ballooned in size, from the Cooper River all the way across the peninsula to the Ashley River, a city now of thirty-three intersecting streets.[12]

A protégé of Benjamin Franklin, Lewis Timothy, operated a printing press in 1733, an outlet for Charles Town's buzzing intellectual activity. In the columns of the *South Carolina Gazette*, women called for rights equal to those of men, sex was candidly discussed, even interracial sex, indicating that the great racial divide between blacks and whites had not yet fully established itself. If some contributors condemned miscegenation, it was clear that the practice was widespread enough to merit frequent censure. Some contributors, surprisingly enough, openly defended interracial unions: "Kiss black or white, why need it trouble you? / Of all things that make us truly blest, / Is not that dear variety the best?"[13]

In the 1730s Charles Town began to manifest a strange demographic pattern that would, by the 1770s, lead visitors to comment almost universally on how many of its citizens were rich. By the end of the colonial period more than a quarter of the white population had estates worth more than a £1,000, which was a considerable fortune. More than two-fifths of the white population could afford a genteel lifestyle—that's more than double the American standard of the day. Because the region had so few free laborers, it turned into a society of the rich and the very poor. The vast majority of the poor were slaves, who were beneath the notice of white visitors, so it seemed to whites that Charles Town was "a country of Gentry," as one resident boasted later. "We have no such thing as a Common People among us."[14]

The gentry had plenty to do. Horse racing became a standard entertainment, and a track was laid out for the new Jockey Club just outside of town. America's first theater opened its doors on Queen Street, lately Dock Street, in 1736, playing the bawdy, raucous fare that did not do so well in the soberer towns of New England. Local musicians provided concerts and played at numerous balls. The rich and the not-so-rich alike, elbow to elbow at round tables, could dine on game, salted fish, and puddings at the taverns, which also served the ubiquitous "rum-based 'slings,' 'flipps,' and 'toddies.'" Coffeehouses catered to a tonier clientele, but even there the class frontiers blurred, and shopkeepers and laborers could converse on equal terms with merchants and planters. Inns offered billiards and shuffleboard, and the affluent held dinner parties in the upper rooms of Shepherd's Tavern at the corner of Broad and Church Streets. Largely excluded from these affairs, women up and down the Atlantic Seaboard were, by the 1720s, enjoying tea parties, at which they perfected the arts of public conversation. Gentlemen gathered at the meetings of the Laughing Club and Smoking Club. The Friday-night Club was a bit tame, seasoned as it was with older gentlemen, but the Monday-night Club offered "cards, feasting and indifferent wines." Eighteenth-century colonial society was particularly fond of cards, so much so that the card table became "the altar of sociability," and more card tables survive today than any other type of colonial furniture.[15]

Such prosperity drifted people away from the notion that slavery was justified by the rules of war. Racial justifications were just beginning to arise. This is not to say that racial prejudice did not exist before the 1730s. The seeds of racism were planted in the English from the very start, when West Africans first were shown around Queen Mary's court in 1554. Blackness, unfortunately, already symbolized sin in the iconography of Christians, and the English were all too ready to believe that black Africans were the cursed descendants of Noah's son, Ham, and that their skin bore the mark of God's wrath. Scientific explanations were no better and perhaps worse, because they linked Africans to the "orang-outang" or chimpanzee, sometimes through tales of sex between the species. Many English, including scientists, believed that Africans and apes were possessed of sexual largesse and that they squandered their fortunes on each other. Voltaire lampooned this notion in his blockbuster novel *Candide*, so the belief must have been current among Europeans as late as 1759.

In retrospect, we now know that colonizers tend to foist onto "natives" the frailties they cannot themselves own up to, especially natural human impulses like sex and laziness. The English expected to find sin, sex, and rapine in Africa, so they did find these things, and when natives appeared in English plays and paintings and novels, they symbolized what most disturbed the English about their own secret impulses. Shakespeare's half-human monster, Caliban, is an early example of a tendency that manifested itself as late as Joseph Conrad's *Heart of Darkness* and Edgar Rice Burroughs's *Tarzan*. It helped that the Africans practiced strange, heathenish religions, for it was easier to make brutes and devils of people who lived outside the pale of Christianity.[16]

From their first encounters with Africans, then, the English were prejudiced. But the racial slavery in the United States of the 1800s did not exist in early colonial America. Early laws refer to slaves as "heathens" and to the English as "Christians." To baptize slaves obviously entangled owners in a sticky contradiction, and, consequently, early attempts to proselytize slaves necessitated embarrassing legal stipulations. The Fundamental Constitutions of the 1670 settlement at Charles Town, for example, had to indicate that if a slave converted to Christianity, he still remained "in the same State and Condition he was in before."[17] Few wanted to think of themselves as enslaving fellow Christians, so the English discouraged missionary work.

Even so, religion was never the final indicator of slave status. The English saw savagery in "other cultural qualities—the strangeness of [the Africans'] language, gestures, eating habits, and so on." Skin color was only one marker of difference and degradation, and hardly the crucial one. But within a few years, the terrible conditions under which the slaves lived was bound to degrade the black men and women who suffered it; in the eyes of the English it became all too easy to think of Africans as *racially* degraded. By a sort of self-fulfilling prophecy, "the cycle of degradation was fully under way . . . once the engine of oppression was in full operation." Right around the time that Carolina began cultivating rice and importing Africans in great numbers, the laws begin referring not to "heathens" and "Christians" but to "blacks" and "whites." "Dark complexion became an independent rationale for enslavement." It was really around the 1690s that the English first began conceiving of themselves as "white." This is the start of what we might call a full-blown, state-supported *racist* ideology.[18] Around 1700, whites were beginning to think that blacks, by the very color of their skin, were unfit for liberty—but it would take over a hundred years for that view to become typical. Events in between mitigated against it—the Stono Rebellion, for instance, and then that colossal ideology-shaping Enlightened explosion: the American Revolution.

In 1739, every rotting, bleeding, black head stuck on a milepost around Charles Town reminded whites of the reality of slavery, that it was a crime imposed on free people, and so long as white Carolina kept replenishing its labor force with fresh "captives" from Africa, they could not evade for long the fundamental truth that they were at war—perpetually at war—with the majority of their fellow colonists. In 1739, the Commons House of Assembly referred to slaves as the "intestine enemy the most dreadful of Enemies," explicitly acknowledging this condition of permanent warfare. Whites improved the way they prosecuted the war against blacks, and at the same time they more effectively obscured the fact that slaves were, essentially, prisoners of war. The first strategy protected their lives, and it was easy enough to enact: in 1742 the legislature instituted a new, comprehensive slave code that tried to regulate the system to the greater safety of whites. Slaves could not leave their masters' premises without a written pass; consequently, it became illegal to teach slaves to write, because a slave who could write could forge a pass; any group of seven or more slaves on a highway required a white escort; a regular slave patrol was instituted and granted the power of searching any slave quarters and examining any plantation for compliance to the law. These were the easy measures.[19]

But the Stono Rebellion also triggered a contrary, ideological shift. George Whitefield's pamphlet thundering about the wrath of God reminded people that in this war, justice was on the side of the blacks. So if whites were going to go on owning slaves, they had to find a way to protect their consciences. They had to begin thinking in some terms that would take the concept of war out of slavery. The first stroke in this battle of the mind came from Alexander Garden, the pastor of the most important church in Charles Town, St. Philip's.

Garden and Whitefield were old enemies. Silver-tongued Whitefield was already something of a sensation in England when he followed John Wesley to America, and he had a personality more pleasing to Georgians and Carolinians, easygoing, less pompous, even democratic. He dressed in neat and clean clothes, but they were no plainer or fancier than the average man's. He carried himself through the muddy streets of Savannah (which were then but five years old) with "an unassuming youthfulness" (he was only twenty-four) that won over a motley crew of settlers, many of whom were debtors liberated from England's jails. He was a handsome man—almond-shaped eyes dominated his face, and a mouth like a sensuous Italian cherub's with full lips in perfect bow shape forming an easy smile. Zeal beamed from his features not sternly but like a sunbeam warming those he looked at. In conversation he spoke simply, without the slightest tinge of the superiority he might have claimed—that John Wesley *had* claimed— as the right of an Oxford graduate living among coarse pioneers. His preaching amazed. He hadn't the fiery, Bible-thumping oratory we today associate with evangelicals. Ben Franklin heard him speak in Philadelphia, and though the scientific-minded Deist was uninterested in Whitefield's subject, he had to admit that "every accent, every emphasis, every modulation of voice, was so perfectly well turned and well placed, that . . . one could not help being pleased with the discourse; a pleasure of much the same kind with that received from an excellent piece of musick." Whitefield believed that the true Christian will undergo a dramatic conversion experience, a "new birth," that manifests his faith, and so he was less perfunctory, less rehearsed, less ritualistic. He preached against what he called the "almost Christian," the "luke-warm" man whose "subtle hypocrisy" leads other men to damnation, for the way to heaven is narrow, not broad. He came to Charles Town for a week in the late summer of 1738, and Alexander Garden invited "The Seraph," as Whitefield was sometimes called, to preach from the pulpit of St. Philip's Church.[20]

Alexander Garden embodied what Whitefield deplored. He spent his life climbing the corporate ladder of the Anglican Church, rising like a replica of the biblical Pharisee. He was born in Scotland in 1685, went to university in Aberdeen, and he was ordained in 1712 and assigned to All Hallows parish at the Tower of London. He came to Charles Town in 1720, married in 1726, had five children, rose to the positions of rector of St. Philip's and "commissary" for South Carolina, which meant that he represented the bishop of London. His wealth increased with the colony's, and by the time he died in 1756, he owned twelve thousand acres of land on the Savannah River, numerous lots in Charles Town, four slaves, and a lot of silver. While he lived he enjoyed the "comfortable" and "urbane life" of Charles Town's gentry. He was so amazingly complacent in his position that he did not at first recognize any threat from George Whitefield, and Garden was pleased enough to convey his respects with gifts of tea, coffee, wine, cakes, "and other things proper" for Whitefield's first long Atlantic passage back to England.[21]

Two years later, Whitefield, newly ordained a priest, passed through Charles Town a second time. In the meantime he had become something of a bogeyman for Anglicans. Though officially a member of the church, he insisted too enthusiastically that man was saved by faith alone, and he published his contempt for the run-of-the-mill clergymen in both England and America. This time, he was received coolly at St. Philip's. Garden happened to be out of town, but his curate refused to extend Whitefield the courtesy of an invitation to preach from the city's most important pulpit. Whitefield was unfazed. He preached at the French Huguenot church, then at the Baptist church, then at the Independent church, and finally to a thronging crowd he preached at the Scots Presbyterian church. He preached against dancing and card playing and against the complacency of a comfortable and urbane clergy. Three months later Whitefield, though assigned to Georgia, came again to Charles Town to stir "the dry bones," because, God knows, the Reverend Garden wasn't doing it. [22]

Finally, the Reverend Garden saw that Whitefield's portraits of the "almost Christian" referred to himself. He demanded that Whitefield wait upon the commissary of South Carolina. Initially, Garden indulged the delusion that he had summoned Whitefield to test the man's orthodoxy. Being slow to anger, Garden would give the young man a chance to qualify his statements, and only then would he decide if Whitefield should or should not be rebuked. He hardly expected to be examined himself, but that's exactly what Whitefield did. The two clergymen got out their razors and proceeded to test each other's skill at splitting hairs. If faith preceded justification, but good works were the fruit of faith, might not works precede justification, or must justification precede works while it succeeded faith? No doubt these were important matters, but their theology obscured the real issue. The two men did not like each other, and they did not like the kind of sheep the other attracted to his flock. Would Whitefield quit criticizing his fellow clergymen? Whitefield would not. Would Garden start preaching against the decadent "assemblies and balls" in Charles Town? Garden would not. He saw no harm in them. Then Whitefield would continue to denounce the rector. Then Garden would forbid the missionary to preach.[23]

Technically, Garden was Whitefield's superior, but that authority was only good as long as Whitefield acknowledged it. Garden stood in the position of a man on a hill watching a flood rise from the river. In a fit of delusion, he deliberated whether or not to grant his permission to the rising waters of the Great Awakening. But even he must have suspected something was beyond his control when he saw the waves of communicants at the dissenting churches. People Garden had never seen near a church came to hear Whitefield speak. It was all well and good to have people come to church, but such popularity threatened the privileges of Anglicans. And the things those people did! Shaking ecstatic revelation! Shouting in spontaneous overflow of powerful feeling! Proclaiming to be born again! Worse were the things that Whitefield told them. The poor and dispossessed "could know Christ better than their unregenerate social betters"! The ignorant could preach better than ministers, so long as they had grace! And worst of all, men were all equal before God! That was true, of course, in a technical sense, but Whitefield must have known how inconvenient a doctrine it was to put into practice, especially in a place like Carolina, which made its fortune on the inequality of men. Wasn't it more prudent to leave equality to the afterlife? Garden had enough. He vehemently denounced Whitefield from the pulpit, sued Whitefield for libel, and challenged the reformer to name exactly who these degenerate clergymen were. In a pamphlet he published the most damaging (if illogical) of all possible accusations: Whitefield was sent by Pope Clement XII to "distract and confuse weak minds." When Whitefield declined to name the offending clergy, Garden's ecclesiastic court officially suppressed him. So when Whitefield published his open letter against slavery, Garden was ready and able to oppose him.[24]

Ironically, Garden's best argument came in the person of Whitefield's disciple, Carolina's own Hugh Bryan. When he was a child, during the Yemassee War, Bryan was captured by Indians, who kept him as a slave for a year before his master, eager to "repair relations with the English," released him. While a slave, Bryan's consolation had been a stray Bible, which sparked in him a lifelong yet agonized relationship to God, who by turns hid from Bryan, tortured him with silence, and rescued him. In the 1730s, Bryan was succeeding as a planter. He enjoyed the relative comfort of the big house but also the isolation of a backcountry plantation, twenty miles from the coast, the closest town, and church. In the summer of 1739, just before the Stono Rebellion, Whitefield's preaching excited Bryan's conscience to a crisis. He suffered a dark night of the soul and emerged in the dawning light born again.[25]

Bryan styled himself "a sinful, polluted, wretched, hell deserving creature" whose guilt had been canceled by God's "free gift." His subsequent correspondences are so encrusted with self-flagellating platitudes that all else is obscured, like the outline of a sunken ship whose hulk, long since rotted away, is preserved by the encrusted shells. His letters do not reveal intelligence. Bryan established a chapel on his property and began gathering about himself a small community of enthusiastic Christians. He hired a schoolmaster to instruct slaves in the Christian faith, which would have included how to read the Bible. Like Whitefield, Bryan was upset with the general state of sin he saw all around him in the life of the Carolina gentry, and even more disturbing was the way Alexander Garden was attacking God's own prophet. Bryan drafted a public letter asking what it would take for Carolina to repent its iniquities. When might the church repent its persecution of Whitefield? Filled with zeal, yet hesitant and nervous, he toyed with the letter until Whitefield could look it over, approve it, and tinker some more. He sent it to Timothy, who published it in the *South Carolina Gazette*.[26]

Almost immediately, Alexander Garden had Bryan thrown in jail, along with Whitefield and, for good measure, the printer Timothy. Whitefield paid bail and sailed to England, never to face his tribunal, but Bryan did not have that luxury. These were his people, the elite class of Carolina planters, and he criticized them not out of hate but love. He wasn't used to the humiliation of spirit and body that the prophet must endure, and the squalor of jail unnerved him. He was visibly chastened, and Garden deigned to forgive whom first he crushed. The charges were dropped.[27]

But once Bryan was back on his plantation, he began again to take his conversion seriously, and the alarming numbers of slaves worshipping side by side with whites at his Huspah Chapel gained a certain notoriety in the Commons House of Assembly in Charles Town. With memories of Stono still keen, whites felt threatened by such "frequent and great Assemblies of Negroes." Bryan warned his kinsman, the lieutenant governor of the colony, that unless its citizens repented, God would use the "Negroes" to destroy the city "by fire and sword" by the first day of April 1742. The lieutenant governor, William Bull Sr., was unimpressed, so Bryan, nearing the limits of his mental endurance, sent a journal full of his prophecies to Bull's son, William Jr., who presided over the Commons House of Assembly. The "Blasphemy and Nonsence . . . in [those] 20 Sheets of Paper close written" were read to the assembly. The assembly interpreted the journal as threat, not prophecy, and condemned Bryan as a traitor.[28]

Just before his arrest, Bryan's sanity snapped, and he wandered in the wilderness conversing with an "Angel of Light." He was observed wandering "in the woods barefooted and alone with his pen and Ink to write down his prophecies." He fancied that he had become a miracle worker, a latter-day Moses, and he got himself a rod from a tree specially shown to him by God; he marched to a river (the records don't say which one); and, commanding the waters to part, he starting "smiting, splashing and spluttering the Water about with [the rod], till he was quite up to his Chinn." The waters did not obey. Bryan's brother had to drag him out before he drowned. Despondent, he wandered home where he predicted he would die before dawn, but God forsook him again.[29]

His subsequent apology to the Commons House is the ranting of an insane megalomaniac. Despite his "Zeal for God," Bryan confessed his "Pride required Abasement," and so God deserted him just as God had deserted Saint Peter and "holy David." It turned out that his Angel of Light had actually been Satan, who finally appeared to Bryan "a Devil indeed; shewing his Rage." "My whole Life has been spent among you," he pleaded with the legislators. As terrible as God's desertion was, to be ostracized from his own people was more than Bryan could bear. Whatever might have been gained by punishment had already been freely given by this abject humiliation, and, satisfied with his harmlessness, society accepted Bryan within its ranks once again.[30] Anyone with the slightest pride of intellect would hardly want to be associated with a zealot like Bryan. His attack on slavery was only a part of his wider jeremiad against Charleston's libertine, anti-Puritan material culture, and it was all to easy to dismiss the former because it was so closely associated with the craziness of the other. This is not to say that the Great Awakening had little effect. In the eighteenth century both Methodists and Baptists found slavery incompatible with the holy life, and those reforming religions found plenty of adherents among the South's poorer whites. But Charleston's elites recoiled from zealotry, and they preferred the more Enlightened, reasonable, moderate, and convenient views of their religious leader, Alexander Garden, who penned a public rebuttal, *Six Letters to the Rev. Mr. George Whitefield*. It is, perhaps, the most important and neglected document regarding American

slavery, because it was the first argument for the ideology of paternalism that would domesticate slavery in America. Garden compared
the slave system favorably to more modern labor arrangements,
because the

> lives [of slaves] in general are more happy and comfortable in all
> temporal Respects (the point of Liberty only excepted) than the
> Lives of three fourths of the hired *farming* Servants, and Day
> Labourers either in *Scotland*, *Ireland*, or even many Parts of *England*,
> who not only labour *harder*, and fare *worse*, but have moreover
> the Care and Concern on their Minds how to provide for their
> Families; which *Slaves* are entirely exempted from, their Children
> being all provided for at the *Owner's* Charge.[31]

Garden had more sympathy for African Americans than many whites
in his day. He conceded to Whitefield that slave owners had neglected
the souls of their charges, and with some difficulty he erected his own
scheme for converting them to Christianity. After the Stono Rebellion,
he opened his own slave school in Charles Town, one better regulated
than Hugh Bryan's. He wanted each plantation to send one slave to
his school, and the graduates would return to their plantations as mis-
sionaries. The Society for the Propagation of the Gospel approved the
purchase of two boys, Andrew and Harry, to be Garden's first pupils.
Andrew proved unequal to the task, so he was sold for some pieces of
silver, which Garden used to buy books for Harry. Harry, apparently,
tended the fledgling school for nearly twenty years, but eventually he
went mad, whether naturally or driven to it by his equivocal position
in the slave apparatus we don't know.[32]

Garden believed that slaves in Carolina were generally well
treated, and so he personally disputed Whitefield's premise that slavery was inherently cruel. So much evidence—including testimony
available to Garden—proves the opposite that I need not review it
here. Yet Garden was a tolerably honest man. Other honest men would
repeat this mistake for hundreds of years, and so it deserves some
explanation. We must ask ourselves, what slaves did Garden observe?
Peter Wood's analysis of St. George parish, just inland from Charles

Town, gives some interesting clues to how most white men experienced slavery in South Carolina. Of 108 households, 90 contained fewer than twenty-four slaves, and exactly half of these supported fewer than ten people, white and black combined. Half the households in the parish, Wood estimates, consisted of five whites and two slaves. Most whites, then, experienced slavery in the close quarters of small farms or village houses, where the lives of whites and blacks would have been more intimately related. There's no evidence (other than anecdotal) one way or the other, but we might surmise that life was more tolerable for the slaves in these households, and most whites, therefore, might consider the institution somewhat benign, no worse than indentured servitude.

Blacks experienced slavery quite differently. Of the 108 households in St. George, only 17 were plantations with thirty or more slaves, but two-thirds of the black population lived on those plantations. More than half of those blacks lived on plantations with more than fifty slaves, farms that could accurately be called slave-labor camps. So, while most whites lived in a household where they outnumbered blacks about two to one, most blacks lived on plantations in which they outnumbered whites by a margin of up to thirteen to one.[33] Fewer than one in five whites observed slavery as it was experienced on the larger plantations by two-thirds of the blacks. The trend was more pronounced in the city of Charles Town where most whites encountered what we might call the atypical, domesticated version of slavery.

Even so, if Garden had any intellectual honesty, he must have acknowledged the backbreaking work squeezed from men and women knee-deep in murky, snake-infested water, scorched by the sun, threatened by alligators, with little rest or relief and encouraged by the lash. He must have had high thresholds of discomfort and despondency to think these slaves were "happy and comfortable." The answer to this puzzle is that discomfort and despondency did have a very high bar in Garden's estimate. He compared Carolina's slaves to the day laborers working in the fields of Ireland, Scotland, and England, and the emphasis should be put on the Irish, where future apologists for slavery would put it. Landless Irish peasants in 1740 had been cast into poverty by penal laws meant to create an ascendancy class of Anglo-Irish Anglicans, and they regularly starved or died of overwork or of exposure. It's a tough question to decide whether the *typical* landless Irish peasant had a life harder than the *typical* Carolina slave. To our eyes, it is like saying this man, whom I've whipped, is better off than this other, whom I've beaten with a stick. But to the typical Protestant American, Garden's logic was inescapable. Black American slaves were no worse off than Irish Catholics, and perhaps better off; no one would countenance repealing the Penal Laws, so no one should complain about the condition of black Americans. This formula would prove to be a powerful argument for the next ninety years, until Catholic emancipation was actually accomplished in 1829, when the Liberator, Daniel O'Connell, would become one of Parliament's most outspoken critics of American slavery.

What most damns Garden in our eyes is his disarmingly stupendous qualification, that the slave is "happy and comfortable in temporal Respects (the point of Liberty excepted only)." How could Garden not see that this point outweighed all others? How could he, a liberty-loving Englishman, not understand that without liberty no honest man can be happy and comfortable? The answer is the rotten root of Garden's benignity. "I know there must be a due *discipline*, or Rod of Correction exercis'd among Children," he explained, "and this may be, and often is misrepresented for Cruelty and bad Usage. I know also, that like Discipline and Correction must be observed among every Parcel of slaves; and which in like Manner, may be, and often is misrepresented in the same Light." The slave, according to Garden, is no warrior captured in battle; in fact, he is less a man than he is a child. Garden was the first American to begin articulating a new ideology of slavery, one that demanded *parental* compassion from whites, and for this he must be thought of as a liberalizing influence on the institution.[34] But this compassion came at a price. So long as one considered Africans to be an "intestine Enemy," at least that definition implicitly recognized the manhood of male slaves and their equal right to liberty, while in Garden's view the African was no better than a child and no less needy of supervision.

The Stono Rebellion and its aftermath proved to be the fulcrum of this ideological balance. Many felt that the "slave-as-enemy" mentality was perpetuated by the constant importation of slaves from

Africa. The leaders of the Stono rebels, after all, had once been free men in Angola. By contrast, blacks born into slavery were naturally more resigned to their fate. Also, enslaved blacks outnumbered whites in South Carolina by a margin of two to one—forty thousand slaves to twenty thousand Europeans[35]—a situation that often required whites to display unchristian cruelty to ensure their own dominion. That precarious state of security might be lessened if the proportions of blacks to whites changed. Couldn't the legislature encourage the immigration of white laborers? Maybe a great influx of white Europeans would change the whole character of slavery in the colony. Diminishing the proportion of slaves would lessen the threat of slave insurrection, which would in turn alleviate the need to terrorize slaves, and, surely, the less that whites terrified the slaves, the more likely whites might get into heaven. In effect, South Carolina tried to change slavery into a much smaller, domestic institution.

In what was probably its most important legislation, the colony effectively banned the slave trade in 1741, imposing stiff taxes on the importation of slaves from Africa and even stiffer taxes on slaves from other American colonies. Before the ban, more than half of the slaves along the Carolina coast were Africans who had been in America for less than ten years. By the late 1750s, most of the slaves on plantations around Charles Town had been born in South Carolina. Slaves were not dying as quickly as they had in earlier decades, and births began to outpace deaths. No one knows exactly why, though a couple of reasons seem logical enough. Maintaining rice fields was not as dangerous as digging rice fields out of marsh and swamp, and by the 1750s most of the tidal lands had already been reclaimed. Also, with the slave trade suspended, owners were more likely to attend to the well-being of their human chattel because births rather than importation became the main source of replenishing their labor force. Whatever the cause, Carolina slavery became more creole than African in the 1740s.

The white population went through this same demographic change. With each passing generation, the white population grew more resistant to the yellow fever that periodically decimated their numbers, largely because yellow fever is less virulent in children than in adults, and once you survived the disease you were resistant for life.

White natives died in fewer numbers than white immigrants, who were so vulnerable that near the mid-eighteenth century whites virtually quit immigrating to the Carolina coast. The land was occupied, Charles Town didn't offer much opportunity, and the climate was more dangerous than that in the other colonies. By the 1740s, the white population, like the black population, was expanding itself through birth rates rather than through immigration. By the time of the American Revolution, the white population of the Carolina coast was "overwhelmingly native born."[36]

The historian Robert Olwell credits the changing attitudes of whites to these demographic shifts. It's one thing to leave Barbados or even England and freely choose to live in a slave society. You'll have few illusions about the brutal nature of race relations. It is quite another to be born into it. One feels less responsible for it—in fact, one is less responsible for it. The slave economy seems less and less the effect of human decisions, maintained by active diligence, and more and more a fact of life, something (for good or ill) to be borne, like the climate. One might oppose the institution philosophically but acquiesce to its apparent inevitability, in which case the widest scope for moral action is reform, not abolition.

The slave code of 1742 reflects this creole attitude to slavery. It attempted to impose on cruel slave owners and overseers the need to treat slaves humanely. First and foremost, the slave code regulated the behavior of whites, not blacks, enacting laws that reflected the new way whites conceived of slavery. Owners had to provide slaves with adequate food and clothing, allow rest on Sundays, and work their slaves no than more fifteen hours on the other six days. Popular punishments like the cutting of tongues, the cutting off of ears and testicles, and scalding were prohibited by penalty of fine. Such was the light that the Enlightenment shone on South Carolina. Dim as it was, it marked a definite step away from the darkness of perpetual war with an intestine enemy. The state was trying to reproduce the slave of Alexander Garden's active imagination: happy, comfortable, and infantile.

2

THE GOOD SLAVE TRADER
||

June breezes filled the sails of the *Neptune* as she pressed hard to keep up with her escort. Henry Laurens, a twenty-three-year-old colonial who had just been fired from his job in London, paced the deck restlessly, urging the heavy-laden merchantman to keep up with King George's man-of-war, *Shoreham*, which was headed for the Carolina station. The year was 1747, and England had been at war with Spain since General James Oglethorpe, governor of Georgia, launched his ill-fated invasion of Florida seven years earlier. The conflict was swallowed by the global War of Austrian Succession, which renewed England's ancient rivalry with the French and made even the home waters of the English Channel dangerous to sail. Enemy ships patrolled the sea routes, and pirates prowled everywhere.[1]

Snug down in the hold of the *Neptune* lay Laurens's first cargo of goods, a trunk of knives and scissors and sundries, bought on credit in London.[2] Should the French or Spanish capture the ship, Laurens would be bankrupt almost before the start of his career—which would turn out to be one of the most important business careers in American history. His return to Charles Town (for that was the city of his birth and youth) must rank with Benjamin Franklin's more famous, impoverished, rowboat arrival in Philadelphia a quarter of a century earlier, a southern version of that iconic, self-made American career. No one on the *Neptune*, least of all Henry Laurens himself, could have guessed that in thirty years' time, the impecunious young son of the middle class would be president of the rebellious, united, thirteen American colonies.

Like Franklin, Laurens was a master of self-discipline. He was careful, even punctilious about his deportment; his dress was clean and neat, not flashy, and he was unusually sober. His legs were somewhat short for his body, with stout, well-developed calves.[3] He had the healthy, athletic musculature of a serious young Carolinian. He was a good horseman, and, as a colonial, he cultivated his physique in the outdoors. He knew how to handle a gun, though probably not a sword. We know from later portraits that his face was pleasing enough, perhaps even handsome in youth, if we erase the shapes of age from the paintings. He conveyed a sense of tolerant wariness. His eyes were shaped in an undisguised expression of sympathy, one of his main characteristics. But there was no nonsense about Henry Laurens, not in later life as a statesman nor as a young man of twenty-three. He always judged himself by a higher standard than he judged others, and in his own eyes he passed muster. Untroubled by inner conflict, Henry Laurens was certain of his place in God's universe.

Yet as he stood there on the *Neptune*, he had only just been fired from his first job. Laurens had spent the last three years of his life clerking for the greatest of the Carolina merchants, James Crokatt, even living with Crokatt's family in London, at the end of which term the partnership—which Laurens had every reason to expect, which had virtually been promised—was not offered. A hint of scandal surrounds this unexpected turn of events, but whatever it was about Laurens that offended Crokatt is lost to history, and all we know is that a much-disappointed Laurens took the first boat back to Charles Town, preferring to arrive in his hometown before the news did.

A lesser man would have been staggered, for a partnership with Crokatt came with a fabulous income and a privileged life in the capital of the Western world. When a man tired of London, Samuel Johnson quipped, he was tired of life. Bursting with a population over half a million, resplendent with the spires of hundreds of churches and St. Paul's great dome, the houses and factories and hospitals and colleges and prisons and shops of London crowded two miles deep and five miles long on the banks of the Thames. Plays at Covent Garden, pleasure gardens at Ranelagh and Vauxhall (forerunners of our amusement parks), coffeehouses, the zoo or "menagerie" at the Tower packed with exotic animals from as far as Sumatra, deer in Hyde Park and St.

James's, the cockfights, card games and dice, art galleries, prostitutes and public executions, wax works and museums and bull-baiting, the streets themselves were a pageant enough to dazzle a young man on the fast track to wealth. But this cushy and splendidly varied life was not to be. Instead, Laurens would husband this first modest cargo of knives and scissors and set up his own trading house in Charles Town. He would use his own contacts to grow the business. The Laurens name, the slow-won earnings of his father's generation, was reputable in Charles Town, and Henry could trade on that. *Optimum quod evenit*, he told himself, like Voltaire's Pangloss, the philosopher friend of Candide. Whatever happens, happens for the best, and Laurens used the long transatlantic voyage to talk himself into that most American of all virtues: optimism.[4]

The history of the Laurens clan exemplifies the American immigrant. In 1685 the Protestant Huguenots were expelled from France by the Catholic king Louis XIV, and among them was Henry's grandfather, André Laurens. Fleeing with whatever portion of his wealth would float across the water, André first stopped in London, where he married another refugee, then on to Belfast, and finally New York, where they set up in a ghetto of more than two hundred Huguenot families already thriving in the New World. When André's son, Jean, was about twenty years old and newly married, the clan pulled up roots again and headed south. To quote their own legend about those days, the Laurens family found itself marooned in a land that "was almost a wilderness."[5]

By 1716, Charles Town was hardly a wilderness, but the devastation of the Yemassee War might have made it seem so to a New Yorker. The young Jean—now anglicized to John—Laurens began as a saddler and gradually grew to be a modest merchant, which in those days was close to what we would call a supplier or middleman. When an exporter in London or Boston or New York or Barbados sent his goods to Carolina, he used a Charles Town merchant to distribute them locally, and this merchant in Charles Town in turn bought local products—rice, tar, pitch, and so on—and shipped them abroad, using merchants elsewhere to sell them. A typical transaction might take more than a year to complete, so merchants had to be like bankers, extending credit to local farmers, making deposits with overseas merchants, using bills of exchange among each other as a sort of currency, not that far from the way we draft checks. After the Yemassee War, old planters in Charles Town needed credit to rebuild their farms, and new planters hurried into debt to snatch up and develop land vacated by the Indians. Through most of the 1720s and '30s, trade flourished, and John Laurens, though never rising above the middle class, became a leading citizen of the city.[6] It testifies to the family's good reputation that James Crokatt took the twenty-year-old Henry on as a clerk, which seemed to secure for the family an alliance with the most important merchant in the lucrative Carolina trade.

Henry was as promising a youth as Charles Town could produce. He attended one of the many "free" schools that provided the basics of education. First and foremost these schools taught children to cherish their "liberty," to which whites in Charles Town were even more fanatically devoted than the typical eighteenth-century English gentleman. The prerequisite to liberty, they recognized, was financial independence. So, every merchant's child would be trained in the "skills necessary to safeguard the material base of freedom." Next to the economic imperative was the Enlightenment's devotion to reason, the faculty by which one's own erratic impulses were disciplined. Other traditional subjects were neglected, such as the classics, modern languages, and literature. Henry was always more serious than his fellow students. As a young man, he and his best friend, the wealthy Christopher Gadsden (who would later lead the Sons of Liberty in Charles Town), vowed to resist the pleasures that distracted their undistinguished peers. Whenever a party tended toward licentiousness, they vowed to leave together, fighting the powerful peer pressure of the moneyed class with a sense of their own nobler, smaller society. They encouraged each other "in every virtuous pursuit" and shunned "every path of vice and folly."[7]

It is likely that the fourteen-year-old Henry Laurens heard George Whitefield preach at St. Philip's, and those performances might have emboldened his own unorthodoxy. (The family had by this time moved their loyalties from the Huguenot Church to the Anglican

St. Philip's, which was the most important parish in South Carolina.) The part of the Athanasian Creed so dear to his father, that "this is the Catholic Faith, which except a man believe faithfully and firmly, he cannot be saved," troubled Henry. These "intolerant damnating tenets" (as Henry later called them) violated the boy's innate sense of mercy. Could God really consign humans to everlasting torture for not believing the complex doctrines of the trinity and the mysterious twofold nature—both human and divine—of Jesus?

"This can't be true," he whispered to himself as he sat in his family's boxlike pew at St. Philip's. "I cannot believe it."[8]

But neither did his beliefs conform to Whitefield's, which narrowed rather than broadened the gates of heaven. Laurens tended toward a belief in the universal salvation of man, that all men, no matter their creed or their deeds, were redeemed by Christ's sacrifice. Even as an adolescent, Henry had the intellectual courage of the *philosophes* of France and the Deists of America, trusting his own conscience and sense of natural rightness over established orthodoxy. Fiercely tolerant of all beliefs, he thought that no public institution should infringe on a man's right to his own conscience.[9] But his God was not the Deists' God. His Creator was no watchmaker, who set up natural laws and then sat back to observe them tick away. God intervened in the world. Public events and events in his own life, Laurens believed, revealed the hand of Providence. The title that comes closest to describing Laurens is *pietism*, a movement associated with John Wesley's Methodism and the German Moravians who settled in Carolina. Laurens's faith expressed itself in personal piety, private study of the Bible, relative simplicity and moderation in his tastes, tolerance of other religions, and a firm belief in the separation of church and state: evangelical and Enlightenment traits married in Laurens's heart.[10]

After the Stono Rebellion, South Carolina stood at a crossroads. What Thomas Paine at a later juncture said about America applied to Charleston in the 1740s. Paine, not yet thirty years old and facing a break with his parents' generation, declared that "the continent will feel itself like a man who continues putting off some unpleasant business from day to day, yet knows it must be done, hates to set about it, wishes it over, and is continually haunted with the thoughts of its necessity." So was the city of Charleston after the Stono Rebellion, and the young Henry Laurens had the resources to lead. His own childhood had coincided with the young, growing days of Charleston. Both standing now on the verge of maturity decided the fate of their careers. A relatively few men, for example, would determine whether Carolina would support Georgia in its ban on slavery. Would it fill the Indian country with small-holding white farmers, or would it tie its fate to the West Indian style of slave labor camps? If the Stono Rebellion taught them anything, it was this: slavery was a high-reward type of business, but it was also high risk. And there was another economy to consider, the balance of justice, for anyone who looked at the matter squarely could see that taking people from Africa and forcing them to work in the swamps of Carolina was a cruel enterprise. But that meant following logic and conscience—Enlightenment views of natural rights and Christian charity—to their inescapable conclusion.

Land appeared undramatically to the *Neptune*, like a thin mirage, a watery line of shadow lying on the horizon that only gradually solidified into trees, the semitropical palmettos and the dense, gnarled, sea-blown oaks that backed the surf of the Carolina coast. Nimble schooners raced each other to bring a pilot who would guide the *Neptune* through the channels and over the bar on the high tide of June 3, 1747. After eight weeks on the expansive ocean, it was like coming in from the outdoors. The barrier islands seemed to close behind them and shut out the troubles of the sea, while before Henry Laurens's eyes spread the tranquil harbor, the safety of forty guns at Fort Johnson inside the bay, and dozens of ships—single-masted sloops and schooners and ketches of the coastal trade, oceangoing and three-masted ships of two hundred and three hundred tons—asleep in the anchorages, Five Fathom Hole and Rebellion Road. To the left was the lazy, marsh-edged Ashley River, which, a dozen miles from the harbor and around a few sharp bends, narrowed quickly to a stream, an avenue for the big canoes or pettiaugers ferrying barrels of rice from the plantations. To the right was the grander and deeper Cooper River bustling with maritime traffic. Between the two rivers was the town.

Eight wharves or "bridges" extended into the Cooper River, and dozens of lighters hurried back and forth from the ships at anchor. A colorful row of three- and four-story buildings fronted the water for half a mile. From the distance, they presented an unbroken, prosperous, colorful facade to the *Neptune*, and as Laurens drew closer to Crokatt's Bridge (the pier owned by his recent employer), he could begin to make out the bustling wharf men, black and white, loading and unloading the freights, overseen by the well-dressed merchants, who, as the ship was nestled into its own berth, could be observed consulting their long bills of lading, counting the barrels and hogsheads and seachests coming ashore.

Sixty days on a deck rolling over the Atlantic make the solid platform of a planked wharf and the firm grip of ground feel like a return to the land of the living. The arrival of the *Neptune* would have been an event of some minor note to the colonial community. Even those who had shipped nothing on her could get the latest accounts from London, the latest prices, news of which ships had been taken by the French or Spanish, which cargoes were lost at sea and which had arrived in England. The wharf would have been swarmed with men, and surely Henry would not have gotten far before old friends of his father and perhaps some of his own recognized him. Such changes as three years would have made in the appearance of a young man would have been noted with good humor and genuine pleasure at Henry's unexpected arrival, for Charles Town was still small enough that everyone connected with trade knew each other intimately. But the expressions of pleasure on seeing Henry—Harry to his friends—would have been replaced quickly with something akin almost to embarrassment. Henry must have seen the troubled look come quickly into the faces. Maybe it was his younger brother, James, who told him, or it might have been any of a dozen men with business on the wharf: his father was dead.

John Laurens left to Henry the remnants of his business, an inventory of unsold goods that went on for miles: fiddle strings and Psalm books, buck knives, horse scissors, loaves of sugar, and yard after yard of every kind of fabric imaginable, from Irish linen to "Maple Silk in Skeins." But the times were poor for a young merchant to set up shop. The war ruined the Spanish trade and depressed the demand for rice so severely that ships were leaving port without cargoes. Charles Town was overstocked with European goods that no one had the money to buy. Henry opened "a Store on the Bay" to sell his father's stuff and his own recent cargo, but it was slow going. The bulk of the estate, valued at over £19,000, was doubtful accounts receivable, and Henry spent most his time trying to recover those debts. Ever the optimist, Laurens hoped times would mend "as they seem to be now at the worst," but all the hope and energy and determination in the world couldn't alter the markets.[11]

Business languished through the next hot summer of 1748. The feared yellow fever arrived in Charles Town in mid-August and began carrying away immigrants of the colony. But with the epidemic also came news of an armistice between England and France.[12] Just then, with the city exuberantly celebrating and just as eagerly looking forward to a resumption of the boom years of the 1730s, Laurens suddenly and unexpectedly abandoned his shop on the waterfront, assigned powers of attorney to his brother-in-law, and climbed aboard the *Charming Nancy*, a merchantman that was waiting for a good wind to carry it back to England.

Without the threat of piracy, the price of freight would soon drop, and it would not be long before Europe demanded cargoes of Carolina rice. And James Crokatt, acting as Carolina's agent at the English court, would soon secure a bounty, basically a state subsidy, for indigo, which was just beginning to be cultivated around Charles Town. England's burgeoning textile industry needed the dye made from indigo, and Carolina had the perfect climate for producing it. After a decade of hanging on, barely surviving, Lowcountry planters were eager to resume growing, and they needed workers. But standing in the way was the ban on importing slaves, the legacy of the Stono Rebellion.

The legislation of 1741 had not exactly banned the slave trade, but it imposed an import duty of £100 per adult slave, a tax of about 40 percent on the typical sale. One intention of the law was to shift the pattern of farming away from large plantations manned by black slaves to smaller yeomen farms of European Protestant stock, and a fund was established to give bounties to those who brought in white immigrants. To some extent, the slave trade also was obviated by the war, which ruined the demand for rice and thus the demand for new slaves.[13] But the poor economy also discouraged European immigration, so the long ban on the slave trade did nothing to shift the balance of labor from black to white and little to shift the plantation model to smaller farms. The new peace reopened the debate: on the one hand, the demand for labor was about to explode, and slaves came cheaper than Europe's poor; on the other hand were all the arguments against expanding slavery, including the danger of living in a perpetual state of war with one's working class.

The younger colony of Georgia was convulsed with the same debates. From its founding in 1732, Georgia prohibited slaves, but its proximity to South Carolina made it nearly impossible to enforce the prohibition. Georgia planters were jealous of the advantage Carolinians had just across the Savannah River. In fact, it was fairly typical for successful Carolina planters to buy up cheap land in Georgia, and these absentee farmers tried to reproduce the West Indian plantation system by smuggling their slaves across the river. "Slaveowners poured into Georgia from South Carolina," snatching up the best coastal land and pressing the government to lift the ban on slaves, which it eventually did, acquiescing to a de facto reality created by South Carolinians. When the ban was finally lifted, men like Henry Laurens rushed in and transformed Georgia into a replica of South Carolina.[14]

But the permanence of slavery was hardly assured. Fears of insurrection revived when the Boston and New York papers reported three uprisings the previous summer, all on slave ships. And in early 1749 a slave named Agrippa scared Charles Town with a reminder of the Stono Rebellion: he told his master that plantation slaves on the Cooper River "had plotted to seize the powder magazine in Charles Town, murder the white people, and flee in pettiaugers to St. Augustine" in Spanish Florida. The militia was mustered immediately, more than a dozen slaves and—significantly—half a dozen white collaborators were arrested. Whites in Charles Town felt they had dodged another Stono, until the governor finished his investigation and reported that the plot "is nothing but a Forgery hatched and contrived" by a few mischievous slaves.[15] The supposed rebels were freed two weeks after the first alarm had sounded.

Though the ban on the slave trade was still on the books, it seems that no one enforced it in the summer of 1749, because three cargoes arrived between June and October. We don't know how many slaves were imported, but we do know that by December 1, 1749, the tax had yielded £3,995. At the full tax rate of £100/slave, such a figure probably amounts to somewhere between thirty and forty slaves imported, but it is more likely that the treasurer, Jacob Motte, did not collect the full amount of tax on small cargoes but rather charged a small tax on larger cargoes, closer to four hundred slaves—either in anticipation of a repeal or as part of a political power play. It was regular practice for the Commons House to instruct the treasurer to act on legislation it meant to enact in its upcoming session. It is quite possible that the Commons House instructed Motte to collect the lower £10 tax on the purchase of each imported slave as early as the summer of 1749 in the expectation that Commons would lift the ban the following year, forcing the upper-house Council and governor to go along with a fait accompli.[16]

The slave tax was at the center of a power struggle between the Commons House on one side and the governor and the Council on the other. These bodies roughly corresponded to the British Houses of Parliament, with the smaller Council consisting of wealthy, naturally more conservative appointees, and the governor standing in for the king. In the middle decades of the eighteenth century, the Commons House gradually increased its powers at the expense of the Council and governor, largely through its control of revenues and expenses. In January 1750, the governor informed the House that "several German [immigrants] . . . have applied for land and the usual Bounty" but that the fund meant to encourage European immigration was bankrupt. The House already had formed an ad hoc committee to figure out "how the State of the said Fund at present is, and whether the Tax imposed on the Purchasers of Negroes imported may be rendered more useful to encourage the Accession hither, and settlement here, of Foreign Protestants."[17] The only way to make the tax generate any revenue was to reduce it, because the £100 tax was so high as to ban all trade. Presumably, this committee was entertaining the idea of lowering the tax tenfold, back to £10 per slave, which would amount to about a 4 percent levy on the sale of a typical male slave, who sold at about £250 currency. Carolina currency generally traded at about £7 to £1 sterling. The committee also suggested that the legislature pay the subsidy for European immigrants not in cash but in tax credits toward the purchase of imported slaves. Needless to say, such method of payment completely undermined the goal of discouraging the importation of blacks, so clearly a faction in the House was working hard to revert to the pre–Stono Rebellion plantation-style economy.

This presumption makes more sense when we consider that one of the six members of the Commons' ad hoc committee was George Austin. Austin came to Charles Town from Shropshire, England, around 1730, in the boom years, and he established a thriving merchant house. A "clever" man animated by "good humour," he enjoyed the reputation of having "one of the best Characters of any person" in the city.[18] Certainly he was rich. Much of his money had been made in the pre-Stono slave trade, and Austin had prospered enough in the boom to survive the bust.

The House approved the bill introduced by Austin's committee, but the Council rejected it, insisting that it was a disguised revenue bill. Other squabbles followed before the Commons, in one of its last decisions in that session, voted that the colony's treasurer should refuse "to issue any monies out of the Public Treasury arising by virtue of" the General Duty Law. In other words, it basically defunded the European immigration program. This was one of many battles in the long war between the Commons and Council that gradually led to the Commons's domination in South Carolina politics. Most crucial, of course, were the colony's purse strings, and the Commons House of Assembly, like its model, the House of Commons in Westminster, increasingly demanded all control of money bills. The moral merit of the high tax on slave imports and the moral evils of a low tax were held hostage to the exigencies of the Commons's long campaign against the Council.[19]

Even so, we know that a significant faction in the House opposed reopening the slave trade, and those men fought back against George Austin. On January 31, 1751, the Commons appointed a committee of seven, headed by John Dart, to study a number of laws, including the tax on slave imports. Dart presented the committee's report on February 8, and on the twenty-eighth the Commons began to debate it. The arguments lasted through the next morning, when the assembly resolved that the tax on slaves was to remain "the same as were imposed by the last law" at £100 per slave. But the decision to retain the ban on new slaves was clearly controversial because at the June session of the Commons, its final proceedings for the year, the tax bill was amended to exempt the importation of Negroes. We have no record of the speeches made in the Commons House, let alone the behind-the-scenes politicking, but quite a lot must be submerged from our view, forgotten and unrecorded. Who opposed the resumption of the slave trade, and for what reasons? Did they fear insurrection? Did many legislators hope that Europeans might immigrate in meaningful numbers during good economic times? Did anyone, remembering the words of George Whitefield, feel sympathy for the Africans or a sense of their own sinfulness for robbing others of their liberty? All we know of this debate is that the pro-slavery faction won. The bill that officially reduced the tax on purchasers of imported slaves was finally passed on June 11, 1751, and the governor ratified it three days later. A real chance at changing slavery in South Carolina would not come again for thirty years.

We don't know exactly what Henry Laurens thought about slavery in 1747, but all men of conscience and intelligence were forced to grapple with it. Henry was living in Charles Town during the Stono Rebellion. He had seen the heads of slaves stuck on the highway's mileposts. The colony's legislature, meeting in Charles Town, debated and enacted the ban on importing slaves just before Henry left for his clerkship in England. It is inconceivable that he had not read Whitefield's open letter and Garden's rebuttals. His father did business with Whitefield's disciple, the notorious Hugh Bryan. Furthermore, the Laurens family owned five people: Flora and her daughter, Chloe; another mother and child, Jenny and Lucy; and one man named Colonel. More than likely these were domestic servants who cooked meals, cleaned house, took care of the horse and chaise, and attended to the personal needs of the family. When he started his clerkship in England,

Henry himself owned a boy, Achilles, who probably acted as his manservant. But the Laurens family was fairly progressive in its view of the institution. Henry's father looked forward to the eventual downfall of slavery in America, an opposition that was not a light or trivial view but the settled conviction of a man of conscience. John Laurens passed on his opinion to at least one of his sons, James, who thanked God he never had money problems enough to tempt him to get into the very lucrative but morally questionable slave trade.[20] The default position, so to speak, for Henry Laurens, as it was for many whites in Charleston, would have been to dislike slavery and to condemn the slave trade. Nevertheless, when he crossed the Atlantic in the *Charming Nancy* he carried with him a proposal for partnership with George Austin, the old slave trader, and the blueprints for building a slave-trading empire. He was just waiting for Austin to get the Commons House to legalize it.

Laurens rode through England with two fine horses and a servant, a man of substance ready to conduct business on a grand scale. Austin's friend, Abel Lewis, welcomed Laurens "with great kindness" and introduced him to the influential Sir Hugh Brigges, a baron and lately the high sheriff of Shropshire. Brigges in turn recommended Laurens to his merchant contacts in Liverpool, Foster Cunliffe, Edward Trafford, and John Knight. Laurens rode off to Liverpool in the third week of January, met with each of his contacts, and tried to convince them to begin sending cargoes of African slaves to South Carolina. "I can venture to assure you," the young merchant told Cunliffe, "there is a prospect of good Sales for Negroes" in Charles Town, and the planters would be ready to remit their debts in rice and indigo. A month later he was in Bristol telling the merchants there that "Negroes [will] sell at a monstrous price."[21]

Laurens and Austin proposed that the English merchants send their ships to the west coast of Africa in what was called the "Guinea trade," where they would pick up their human cargo, then on to Charles Town where Austin and Laurens would handle the sales to planters, which typically would be made on credit of up to two years. Remittances would be made periodically, in bills of exchange when possible and otherwise in commodities; Laurens and Austin would accept the risk of default by the planters, and in case of their own failure the transactions would be insured. The empty slave ships would be laden in Charles Town with "such produce as to be had at the Season," typically rice, indigo, or furs sprinkled with lime to keep the worms out, and Austin and Laurens would pay the coast commission in Carolina. For all of that, they would skim for themselves 10 percent of the sales price of the slaves. These proposals had been written by Austin, who remained back in America, while the novice Laurens did little more than read from his script and look dependable, substantial, and industrious.[22]

Laurens's progress reports make chilling reading today. With horrifying banality they attend to the details of the business, betraying not the slightest hint of a moral issue. Yet Henry's brother James refused to import slaves, and even James Crokatt, the great Carolina merchant, had qualms about staining his hands. It is impossible to say with absolute confidence why Laurens made the decision to join Austin, but we can reconstruct a likely scenario. When he accepted George Austin's proposal of a partnership in December 1748, he was twenty-four years old, still a young man to be sure, but already he felt that his life's race was stuck in the blocks. His father was dead, and he was now the patriarch of the Laurens family; the fast track to the leading rank of merchants had been held before him, tantalizingly, for two years, before Crokatt cruelly withdrew it; other men of lesser talents and self-discipline might be content to start near the bottom, husbanding a few cargoes to profit, accumulating over the course of a decade the reputation, the vaporous and elusive weightiness, the corpulence and image of solidity that reassured creditors and so defined a great merchant. But a man of Laurens's ambition needed to get there more quickly than the normal man. Already his childhood friend Christopher Gadsden was near success, and though Gadsden was himself no ordinary man and Laurens never indicated any sign of jealousy, the example of his friend's imminent success must have pricked his pride. Laurens's own best prospect had been dashed by James Crokatt. Could he afford the luxury of looking deeply into justice when another opportunity had been cast before him, like a pearl, so to speak, in the middle of the road, waiting only to be picked up? He had to strike quickly—in the winter of 1749—if he was to rescue his future from mediocrity. If he didn't sell the slaves in Charles Town, there were others who would: Perry & Taylor, for instance, who had already contracted (Laurens discovered in Liverpool) to handle James Pardoe's cargo of slaves from Gambia. Slaves would come to Carolina. There was no doubt of it. George Austin and others had made sure that the Commons House lifted the ban. In the next couple of years, men would be made rich. The only decision Laurens had to make was whether or not he would be among them. It was probably not avarice so much as ambition, and ambition was no more sinister than the desire to be great according to the terms of commerce. Laurens was a young, talented, promising merchant. He wanted to be a great merchant. The slave trade provided a timely means to achieve that status. He chose this largeness of character, to be a great merchant, over another that would have made him a great man. There was no positive decision to do evil. He just evaded the more difficult route of moral courage.[23]

In the summer of 1751, Laurens handled the *Orrel*, coming from Gambia. After nearly two months of the middle passage, the unsteady legs of black men, women, boys, and girls stumbled onto a Charles Town wharf, their minds dulled to despair by their suffering, released at last from the putrid ship, stunned by the summer sun. Laurens described them in the *Gazette*, "a Cargo of healthy fine Slaves to be sold on Wednesday." Probably there was no auction. Prices were relatively uniform, so it seems more likely that the Africans were displayed in a pen, and in the bright hot afternoon buyers strolled among them and offered a price near or at the market value for those people they wanted. It took about thirty-six transactions to dispense with the lot, from Bernard Elliot's modest purchase of one girl (for £180) to John Cumyn Ball's acquisition of five men, two women, and two girls for £2,150. Most shoppers bought one or two slaves. The total sale brought in £19,332; the commission for Austin and Laurens amounted to £966, a relatively modest 5 percent profit after their expenses had been paid. The standard fee charged by a slave factor was 10 percent of the sales price, and from this share the factor paid coasting fees, loading fees, and other incidentals that generally totaled about 1.5 percent of the sale price. So a slave factor could expect to clear about £21 currency on every healthy male slave he sold.[24]

Between the boom years of 1751 and 1769, Laurens imported 7,601 human beings, though that counts only the living ones. We do not know how many died on the sixty-nine voyages he handled, but it was probably somewhere in the neighborhood of 10 percent, or 760. At least one voyage chartered by Laurens in 1755 went very bad, that of the *Emperor* captained by Charles Gwynn. Laurens predicted "a glorious sale of your Cargo. . . . Our Planters are in full spirits for purchasing Slaves & have almost all the money hoarded up for that purpose." Laurens had paid £7,100 sterling for the ship's "Cargo and outsett," and with slaves selling for an average of £33 sterling in Charles Town, he needed only about 215 captives to cover his initial investment. Had Gwynn been able to buy his full complement of 570 slaves in Africa, Austin and Laurens would have realized a profit of more than 100 percent, about £50,000 currency. But after months in Africa Captain Gwynn managed to buy only 370, and his bad luck continued when a gale diverted the ship from Carolina all the way down to Jamaica. When the weather relented and the hatches were finally broken open, body after lifeless body of emaciated, filthy Africans were passed wearily out into the sunlight and tossed overboard into the warm waters of the Caribbean, where they were undoubtedly torn apart by sharks trailing the slave ship. One hundred and twenty died, a mortality rate of over 30 percent. Those who survived were weakened and demoralized beyond description. Gwynn negotiated a sale with a local factor, and what was left of his ragged cargo brought in only about £28 sterling apiece, at least £5 fewer than they would have fetched in Charles Town. Laurens estimated his loss at £2,000 sterling for the whole affair. Nevertheless, he faced the catastrophe with his characteristic optimism. "What can't be cur'd must be submitted to," he reasoned, and he submitted "with chearfullness to [his] ill luck."[25]

A rough but conservative estimate of his lifetime net receipts for handling the slave trade is £161,521 currency. That's figured at the standard 10 percent fee charged by slave factors, assuming Laurens sold each person at a price of around £250, and subtracting the 1.5

percent that covered his expenses—"coasting fees, loading, etc."[26] This crude estimate assumes that Laurens was always a factor handling someone else's cargo at its destination point. It does not, then, figure in his losses on the *Emperor*, when he himself paid for the ship, but neither does it calculate the incredible profits he would have realized on any successful voyages that he chartered. We have no information indicating which of these sixty-nine cargoes might have been his own, but it is certainly fair to treat this figure as a *very* conservative estimate. Probably Laurens made many hundreds of thousands of pounds during this revival of the slave trade. By the late 1760s, he was one of the richest men in America.

Charles Town prospered along with him, ballooning to about eight thousand people by the early 1760s, half of those free and half slaves.[27] A new statehouse, with handsome chambers for the Council and Commons, was completed in 1756; the theater, which had been closed for seventeen years, reopened in 1754 to packed houses; the walls and bastions and cannon protecting the city were rebuilt and expanded; St. Philip's parish split in two, and the majestic St. Michael's was built across the street from the statehouse. Lieutenant Colonel Laurens (he fought the Cherokee in the French and Indian War) was elected to the Commons in 1757 and quickly became one of its most influential members, exhibiting "a reasonable conservatism and a comprehensive patriotism."[28] He had the shrewd merchant's bone-deep trust of law and order, which was needed for international business, and he sniffed suspiciously at anything that threatened to disrupt trade. The patriotism came partly from the almost universal American pride in liberty, whose other expression was abject shame at being bossed around.

Laurens hated England's tax policies—the imposition of stamps, for instance—but just as staunchly he insisted that Americans oppose them only by constitutional methods, which generally meant sending ineffectual petitions to London. His great childhood friend, Christopher Gadsden, led the mechanics of the city, who were more radical than either the planters or merchants during the Stamp Act crisis, and probably it was Gadsden who spurred the mob on a hunt for the hated stamps, which the governor had hidden at Fort Johnson on James Island. Laurens made no secret of his high regard for the royal governor, so a couple dozen men imperfectly disguised in slouch hats and sooted faces came to his house one night looking for information. Apparently, the mob was satisfied nearly immediately that Laurens was not hiding the stamps because they did not even search the house, and the somewhat embarrassed rowdies struggled to save face by trying to make Laurens swear that he didn't know where the stamps were. Laurens did know where they were, so he refused on principle to swear any oath. Then followed an hour of farcical interrogations at the point of sabers. Laurens, furious at the effrontery, named nearly twenty of his assailants (having seen through the crude disguises), ridiculed them for resorting to such unmanly methods, and challenged them singly to duels with a brace of pistols. The mob watered down the oath, diluted it again, insisting that they loved Laurens and if he would just swear to this new formula they could go on their way. Eventually even that game grew cold, and the mob slunk away, taking care not to trample any of the flower beds on their way back to the dark streets.[29]

By the time of these crises, Laurens had bought up Lowcountry indigo and rice plantations and undeveloped land in the Carolina backcountry: Mount Tacitus, Wambaw, Broughton Island, Wright's Savannah, New Hope, Turtle River, altogether about twenty thousand acres. In 1762 he bought a three-thousand-acre tract thirty miles up the Cooper River from Charles Town, which, in later years, would become his main residence.[30] But in the 1760s he was still a city dweller, and he bought a large property on the recently opened, fashionable suburb of Ansonboro on the Cooper River, just west of the older wharves. The somewhat plain-looking house he built on this suburban plot reflected Laurens's sober personality; nevertheless, it sported a huge dining room on the first floor and an equally spacious ballroom above; and Laurens employed an English gardener to tend his four-acre park, whose exotics reflected the networks of friends and colleagues Laurens had made in all reaches of the Atlantic. A founding patron of the Charles Town Library Society, Laurens made up for his lack of *belles lettres* by populating his own library with two hundred linear feet of books housed in glass-fronted, mahogany shelves. He married into one of the richest and oldest of Charles Town's family's, the Balls, and his wife, Eleanor, had many children, nearly one a year, though most died in infancy. When they moved to the Ansonboro mansion only three children came with them, the oldest being John, a child of ten years. John, or Jack as the family called him, was precocious, learning to draw at the age of three, and as an adolescent he earned the respect of noted physician and naturalist Alexander Garden, a close family friend in Charles Town. His scholarly acumen showed all the more dramatically when compared to his younger brother, Harry, a rough-and-tumble child who was, in his father's words, "a little thick-headed." The youngest brother, James, took after Jack: "healthy and clever."[31]

Eleanor Laurens died in 1770, shortly after giving birth to a daughter, Mary Eleanor, leaving Henry with three boys and two girls. That change accelerated his gradual retirement from commerce, and he devoted his labor to the raising of the boys. They moved to England in October 1771 in order to finish the boys' schooling. Laurens did not like Oxford and Cambridge because he thought they were "Semenaries of debauchery," and ultimately he placed John, who was then eighteen, and Harry in Geneva in June 1772. John studied "Greek, Latin, French, Italian . . . Belles Lettres . . . Physics, History, Geography, Mathematics, [science], Riding, Fencing, Drawing," and in preparation for legal studies, Civil Law. Henry must have approved the "enduring marks" of "stern republican virtue and jealous independence" that Geneva left upon his oldest son.[32]

The early 1770s provided Henry with a pause in his own life, allowing him finally after the bustle and hard work of the merchant's life the expansive leisure to travel, to reflect on life, attend to ideas, polish his own soul. He regarded the world complacently. His fortune, like Charleston's, was secure, and he could now afford some moral considerations. Vaguely he was troubled by slavery, troubled enough to get out of that dirty trade himself, but not troubled enough to discourage others from getting into it. That attitude reflected most of Charleston's white society: the slave trade was vaguely distasteful, but not bad enough to make any waves about it; likewise, slavery itself was considered unfortunate, but, like the fallen state of the world this side of

Eden, it was thought inevitable. Men like Henry Laurens who grew up with slavery did not consider much how his own efforts had restored the trade and flooded the colony with slaves just when the balance might have been tipped toward white settlement, like the New England colonies. With so much money being made, no one thought much about George Whitefield's old prophecies about God's justice. Alexander Garden's paternalism soothed the white conscience like a salve, and Henry Laurens prided himself on his progressive notions of kindness and mercy. His slaves were his dependents, a responsibility, and the light of reason showed him at least that he must discharge that responsibility with humanity, charity, mercy.

But if he had found a way to quiet his conscious, Henry Laurens had the good sense and honesty to plant the seed of a stronger challenge to the convenience of the status quo. The next generation, the boys rising to the winds of equality, liberty, and revolution that swept up and down the Atlantic Seaboard, bloomed in the sun and soil such as Henry Laurens made, and he was astonished by their flower.

3

WE THE PETTY TYRANTS

||

James Somerset, an African who was kidnapped by slavers at the age of eight, grew up to be the manservant of Charles Steuart, "the highest-ranking customs" officer in British America. Two years after Steuart retired to England in 1768, Somerset ran away and hid in the maze of narrow, winding streets in the poorer neighborhoods of London, eluding bounty hunters for fifty-six days until he was found and dragged to a ship at anchor in the Thames. Three Englishmen who had become his godparents petitioned the court to issue a writ of habeas corpus challenging the legality of his abduction. Granville Sharp, a young "self-educated Anglican fundamentalist," the prototype of later abolitionists, championed his case, and it was adjudicated by William, Lord Mansfield, chief justice of Great Britain. On June 22, 1772, Mansfield declared, essentially, that slavery did not exist on the empire's mainland, and any colonial slave standing on English soil magically became free. The Somerset case was splashed across the newspapers and ran through the coffeehouses and taverns of the capital, including the Carolina Coffee House, which served as the London headquarters for Charles Town's merchants. The *London Chronicle* reported approvingly that the blacks in Mansfield's courtroom "congratulated themselves upon the recovery of the rights of human nature, and their happy lot that permitted them to breathe the free air of England." Such metaphors were proliferating: the winds of change blew through the free air of England.[1]

But the Somerset decision did not alarm Laurens, who was living in England then, nor did he find anything shocking to his own beliefs. Strangely, he regarded the whole affair somewhat comically. When his own personal slave, Robert Scipio, "behav'd a little amiss one day," Laurens told him, "If [you] do not choose to stay with me, . . . go about [your] Business." In other words, he invited his slave to claim his freedom. Scipio decided to stay.[2]

We learn much about Laurens's view of slavery when, in March 1773, he composed what amounted to a parable of the good and bad overseers. Peter Nephew, who ran Lauren's New Hope plantation, "makes less Rice with more hand[s]," Laurens observed, but "treats my Negroes with Humanity." William Gambell, the overseer of his Broughton Island plantation, might make "twice as much Rice" but did so by "Cruelty towards those poor Creatures who look up to their Master as their Father, their Guardian, & Protector." Laurens sermonized with the self-assurance and authority of Jesus on the Mount: "I would rather be without Crops of Rice than gain the largest by one single Instance of Cruelty or Inhumanity." But neither would he have it said throughout Carolina that "Mr. Laurens wont allow his Overseer even to speak roughly to a Negro, [so] how can he expect any work to be done?" Honest men, he asserted, "will Aim at a Medium." Besides the moral issue, cruelty was bad business. Nine of Gambell's hands had run away, leaving him in a dilemma with the crops wanting to be picked.

The epithet "poor Creatures," pregnant with real sympathy, encapsulates the paternalistic ideology. Laurens believed that the slaves' material, intellectual, and moral poverty impressed "a reciprocal obligation upon the Master." Blacks were ill equipped to engage the world: that was self-evident to creoles like Henry Laurens. Children born in captivity, who breathed the atmosphere of servitude their whole lives, were prevented by law from getting an education, so it is no wonder that a man like Scipio might choose to remain Laurens's manservant rather than cast himself upon the fortune or misfortunes that waited in the uncertain streets of London's ghettos. And it might seem natural for a man like Laurens to think of himself as a surrogate father and protector of these perpetual dependents. Nevertheless, Laurens's frequent use of the formula, "those poor Creatures," betrays a knack for avoiding responsibility. Like many other creole whites, he considered slavery a fact of life, something to be borne like the harsh summer climate and swamp fevers, as if the slaves would, as Christ said of the poor, always be with us. Laurens did not imagine a world without slaves, despite the fact that in his early career certain men in South Carolina politics tried to wither slavery in favor of free white labor, and despite the fact that he helped resurrect the slave trade and brought new waves of captive Africans to Charles Town. The notion that he himself was at least partly responsible for the poverty of all slaves and directly responsible for the degradation of seventy-nine hundred and the deaths of hundreds of other men, women, and children never seemed to enter his head.

But Henry produced a greater imagination in his oldest son. John's studies in Geneva went beyond the practical education needed for commerce and made him far more learned and idealistic than his father. Neither father nor son knew which career John might choose. He was tempted to three: to be a minister, whose eloquence and goodness "commands the most solemn Silence and serious Attention from all his Audience"; to be a physician and naturalist, whose remedies might give "eminent Service to Mankind"; or to be a lawyer "who shines at the Bar, and overcomes Chicanery and Oppression, who pleads the Cause of helpless Widows and injur'd Orphans . . . [and] disperses Benefits to Multitudes." Unlike his father, John never worried much about making money, and one of his luxuries was a devil-may-care view that allowed him to indulge high principles, laziness, and romantic dreams of helping widows. The other common theme to his ambitions was the scalding desire to win "lasting Fame to himself." Ultimately, the hope of fame persuaded John to give up his more congenial study of natural history in favor of law.[3] Though it was no prerequisite to public service and statesmanship, studying law was then, as now, a logical and popular way to advance a political career in the American democracies. Starting as the son of a wealthy and prominent planter who moved among powerful men on both sides of the Atlantic, John had the potential to go even further than his father had. He inherited all of his father's intelligence, a large share of his industry, and none of his caution.

The times were made for incautious men. In December 1773, a band of patriots stole aboard three ships in Boston Harbor and tossed hundreds of crates of tea into the briny water, an ineloquent protest against the monopoly granted the East India Company and the tax that accompanied it. In retribution, Great Britain closed Boston Harbor until the tea and its tax were paid. Other "Intolerable" acts quickly followed, the worst of which dissolved representation in Massachusetts and brought the government under direct control of the crown. In reaction, the colonies convened the First Continental Congress in Philadelphia and decided to boycott all goods from Great Britain and all goods from the East India Company, no matter where they originated. It also "wholly" ended the slave trade, declaring that Americans would not "be concerned in it ourselves, nor will we hire our vessels, nor sell our commodities or manufactures to those who are concerned in it." Alarmed at the escalating crisis, Henry sailed back to Charles Town, while John began his law studies in London.

John was an excellent student in Geneva, but he let his impulses run too ardently for his father's liking. Socializing ran through his annual allowance too fast, and he was obliged, shamefacedly and penitently, to ask his father for more money. The pattern was repeated in London, where John caroused with other wealthy Carolinians, spent all of his money, and received a stinging rebuke from his father. A man of great sensibility, John felt the shame acutely. "The more I look into my Conduct," he confessed, "the more I despise what I was, the more I wish that a long Series of such Deportment, as I now, dares such an irresolute man, say, resolve upon, were already past, and had regained your Confidence." It seems he had the lawyer's gift of confounding unpleasant facts in soft syntax, but more plaintively, and childishly, he added:

> I supplicate Your Pardon, and Pity, how dare I ask to restore to your Esteem, Your Unworthy, tho much afflicted and penitent Son.[4]

He was twenty years old but pretty far from being a grown man, still dependent on his father's money and approval.

Meanwhile, events in America quickly brought the colonies to their Rubicon. On April 14, 1775, news of the crown's resolve to reduce the American possessions by force of arms reached Charles Town. On the nineteenth, British troops quartered in Boston tried to seize guns hidden in Concord, and the "shot heard round the world" opened the war in Massachusetts. The Second Continental Congress convened the next month and appointed George Washington commander in chief. Meanwhile, Henry was elected to South Carolina's First Provincial Congress, which met in January 1775, then again in June, when its president, Charles Pinckney, "a reluctant participant in the Revolution," resigned his office. South Carolina's Congress elected Laurens to preside over the government because, though he was naturally cautious and far more moderate than revolutionaries like Christopher Gadsden, he was also a staunch patriot. South Carolina cast the dice a week later when it passed its "Association," a pledge "to sacrifice our lives and fortunes in attempting to secure [America's] Freedom and Safety."[5]

Henry Laurens's conscience had to wander a labyrinth before it found the way clear to take up arms against his king. The twists and turns of his reasoning are worth mentioning because they illustrate his great talent for self-delusion. In a speech before Congress he declared himself "to be one of His Majesty's most dutiful and loyal subjects, willing at all times to do my utmost in defense of his person, crown and dignity." His oath to shoot musket balls at the soldiers whom George III sent to subjugate America was an expression of this loyalty, for the king had been duped by "a few wicked men." By killing redcoats, so his reasoning went, he fully hoped to restore "to his Majesty his undoubted right of reigning over a vast empire of freemen."[6] He realized that others in Congress thought he was "absurd," and so he must appear to us, though it illustrates a sincere belief among many patriots that they were not overthrowing their king so much as defending the liberty that was a right of all Englishmen. Henry was no republican favoring a new type of government, but a constitutional monarchist fighting to preserve rather than revolutionize the status quo.

Under Henry's leadership, the Patriots in South Carolina raised an army and campaigned in the Upcountry against Loyalists, and when the royal governor fled Charles Town, the Patriots found themselves in total control of the colony. In the midst of these portentous events, while Henry was prosecuting a war against his sovereign king, the puerile exploits of his son must have been doubly disappointing, especially when his spendthrift ways repeated that summer. It is not surprising, then, that when John asked his father's permission to give up his studies to serve his country with "Ardour in some inferior Station," Henry, considering his son's immaturity, forbade it. John must stay in England and continue studying the law.[7]

In October, Henry's role as the chief executive of South Carolina involved him in a dispute mixing public duty and private obligations. It was an odd sort of affair, worthy of note mainly because its antagonist, a young man just returned from London, would later father the famous abolitionist Angelina Grimké. Twenty-two-year-old law student John Faucheraud Grimké, who was intimate with the Laurens family, "a lad to whom" Laurens claimed "to have been as a father," brought with him from England, as was typical in colonial times, packets of letters addressed by friends and acquaintances to various people in the Carolinas. On the day that Grimké landed in Charles Town, Laurens went straight from a meeting of the Committee of Safety to congratulate the elder Grimké on his son's return. When he walked in the door, the elder Grimké hurried him into a parlor and tossed "a number of packets and letters . . . down upon a table."

"Here are letters which my son has brought directed to *suspected persons*, and has laid by," he said. "Will you take them to the Committee?"

Laurens was shocked. Though many patriots thought it was necessary to read private letters, and though the government had authorized a "Secrecy Committee" to do it, Laurens thought that breaking the seal on someone else's letter was a grave error. The term "suspected persons" was odious as well, for Laurens had long opposed the unequivocal labeling of men as friends or enemies of America. More than in any other colony, the conflict in South Carolina was a civil war, and often men of goodwill were punished and branded as traitors for a lack of zeal in the patriot's cause. As loath as he himself was to break his ties of loyalty to King George, Laurens could sympathize and respect others who sided with the Tories as a matter of conscience.

"I am not of any Committee that open letters," Laurens replied diffidently. "I am of the Council of Safety, and I have never interfered in such matters."

"To whom shall I *send* or *give* them?" Grimké replied.

"I really cannot tell you, sir," Laurens insisted. "I never concern myself in opening letters."

But letters were opened, apparently in error, and when the recipients of those letters accused the younger Grimké of betraying a confidence—a serious public charge—he demanded, in a written note, that Laurens admit that he was responsible for the offense. Either the reputation of Laurens or of Grimké must bear the opprobrium. Cautiously, Laurens refused to see Grimké when he came to call, and he returned Grimké's notes unread, for to acknowledge having seen their contents would require from Laurens either a confession or a challenge to a duel. But when Grimké published his side of the affair in the *General Gazette*, and when he accused Laurens of "relying on the security of his age" to avoid settling things on the field of honor, the head of state could ignore the matter no longer.

Laurens responded in the *Gazette* with a lengthy account of his side of the story, from which the dialogue above is extracted and which concluded with this unequivocal challenge:

"Tell young Mr. Grimke, Sir, that although it is true, I am an oldish man, and infirm, as he well knows, yet, if he will name his time, place and weapons, I will walk over the ground, at the very time, armed in proper sort, and if he dares to oppose my passage, he shall find that my age, though near thrice his own, shall not protect him."[8]

Laurens's abhorrence of dueling was well known in Charles Town, as was his maxim that he was brave enough to face any man's bullet but too much a coward to return fire. In addition to this, he explained in a letter to his son, he had lent the young Grimké money when they were both in England, and it was unseemly for the young man to fire on his creditor before he repaid the bill. Nevertheless, when they met one misty morning on James Island, Grimké leveled his pistol, aimed at Laurens, and pulled the trigger. The hammer "snapped" without firing. Facing Laurens, who still held a loaded gun, Grimké's resolve wavered, and he retreated three or four paces before his legs regained their courage. But Laurens, true to his principle, would not shoot, and that ended the affair.[9]

John had to read about this duel and the more portentous national events from afar. Threatened by Washington's cannon, the British evacuated Boston in March 1776. No one knew where they would land until they appeared just beyond the mouth of Charles Town's harbor in June. Henry had spent much of the preceding weeks riding a horse around the city's fortification, exhorting their greater preparation. A Patriot garrison on the tip of Sullivan's Island, led by William Moultrie, scored an unlikely victory against the British invasion force. John felt the sting of British violence as keenly as if he himself had been insulted and more keenly was ashamed that he was not at home exposing himself to the dangers of war. But Henry continued to forbid the twenty-two-year-old from abandoning his studies in London. "I feel like a Man avoiding the Service of his Country," John wrote to Henry, "because his Father tenderly commands him to be out of Danger." He asked his uncle James, "How can I disobey so fond a Father[?]" But he worried more about this question: "Is it not dishonor to stay" in England? John imagined that people were pointing at him, whispering about cowardice, so long as he tarried on the safe sidelines during his country's most trying crisis.[10]

John was as impetuous in love as he was in everything else, and his sense of honor led him to the altar in a hastened, secret ceremony meant to shield a young woman from the shame of unwed pregnancy. The stern morals of his father did not descend to the younger generation, for John had allowed or perhaps encouraged a romance to proceed to its natural, physical consummation. His bride was the daughter of William Manning, one of Henry's best friends in England, a fellow merchant who acted more or less as Henry's banker. The families had been connected for a few years. When John was in Geneva, Manning sent his ungovernable son to a school in that city, and Henry asked his oldest son to look out for the younger boy. By the time John moved to London, William Manning was acting as his surrogate father, and so John often came to his house and was entertained by his three daughters, and the mutual attraction between his youngest, Martha, and Henry's oldest son, was evident to all. The match was propitious. The Mannings were nearly as prominent in England as the Laurenses were in America. Martha's brother would later serve as a governor of the Bank of England, and William's grandson was Henry Cardinal Manning, the famous leader of English Catholics during Queen Victoria's reign.[11]

"Pity" compelled him to marry, John confided to his uncle (for he could not at first bear to tell his father). "Pity" was a cryptic word that hid whether he truly loved Martha Manning, but it conveyed well enough the heart of the affair. Only after the secretive ceremony would John tell Martha's father: he was afraid that William Manning might extract a promise that John stay in England for the duration of the war. Facing his own father was another story all together, and he mentioned it only casually, at the end of a substantive letter, when Martha was five months pregnant:

> Will you forgive me Sir for adding a Daughter in Law to your Family without first asking your Consent. I must reserve particulars 'till I have the pleasure of seeing you. My Wife Mr Manning's youngest Daughter promises soon to give you a Grand Child.

Clearly this hasty marriage was a greater offense to this father's code of behavior than his improvidence with his allowance, and he does ask for forgiveness, but John's tone has none of the abject dependency of his earlier confessions. Henry had warned his son against just this kind of failure, citing the example of one of John's old tutors, Henry Himeli, who had excluded himself "from the Company, Conversation & Esteem of his old friends, by an attachment to a Trumpery Woman who Travels with him & whose quality is doubtful." Perhaps sensing that his son might be driven by similar temptations, Henry amplified the point mercilessly. "The Love & friendship of Good Men," he complained, "of a whole Community, the prospect of Glory & future good Days, All, All, sacrificed upon the Knees of a little Freckled Faced ordinary Wench. Let other Men . . . take Heed." We do not know if Martha Manning had freckles, but something about her tempted John to risk all, all upon her knees. Retroactively both fathers approved the match.[12]

As many commentators have noted, an ideology of shame and honor dominated the minds of white men in eighteenth-century America, as it would dominate the American South in the following centuries. Such an ideology is almost feudal and trusts the keeping of order as much to the dueling fields as to the courts of law. In a more modern way of thinking, private conscience trumps public reputation: what you think about yourself means more than what others think of you. Henry the pietist prized his private relations to family and to God more than anything else. That is not to say Henry did not feel the pique of a public insult—as we have seen, he fought more than one duel. But Henry was clearly stepping toward the modern world, and anyone reading his letters will find a mind similar to our own. He was the prototype of the contemporary, American middle-class mentality, formed by the complex, commercial society in which the home is the final refuge from the world, where work in the outside world serves to support and is justified by the construction of a satisfactory domestic life. Certainly Henry knew the value of his public image, but this was a business calculation, for a merchant depended upon his reputation. Always, his own judgment about his conduct was more severe than anyone else's, and his true self unfolded behind the front door of his house. This domestic mentality determined his relations to his slaves, whom he treated as if they were children. It also infused his politics. When news of the Declaration of Independence reached Charles Town on August 2, 1776, Henry felt like a son cast "by the hand of violence out of a Father's House into the wide world . . . a new World & God only knows what sort of a World it will be." While the town's folk huzzaed the proclamation, Henry felt that the moment was "Serious[,] Important and Awful," and he wept for love of "the good old Country & for the people in it."[13]

John did not weep. He had hoped that America would declare her independence, as if he could never achieve his own proper stature as a man until the colonies came into their maturity by claiming their separate and equal station among the powers of the Earth. Henry bemoaned the public duties that forced him to neglect the domestic; John embraced those public obligations to the neglect of his private. He loved his country more than he loved his wife. It was not even a contest. Not long after the Declaration echoed in the streets of London, John, by this time as eager as a thoroughbred moments before a race, resolved to return to America with or without his father's permission.[14] Henry finally agreed anyway. Now that the breach with the king was irrevocable, Henry could not provide for his family in England. "You are of full Age," Henry wrote, "entitled to judge for your self . . . [which] side you may take."

This tardy permission pleased John, but something gratified him even more in his father's August 14 letter. Henry had recently visited his remote plantations, finding "the Best crop that ever was borne" and well over a thousand barrels of rice ready for shipment. But the war prevented that, and the best he could do was hide them from Spanish "Picaroons" and hope that "time & Vermin" would not devour them. His slaves, he thought, were safer. Though the British were offering freedom to the slaves of rebels, Henry reported that

> My Negroes [in Georgia] are strongly attached to me, so are all of mine in this Country, hitherto not one of them has attempted to desert on the contrary those who are more exposed hold themselves always ready to fly from the Enemy in case of a sudden descent.

We know better than Henry did how empty were the gestures of attachment and loyalty that a slave might offer to his paternalistic owner. Though clearly he had not heard of it yet, five of his Georgian slaves had already escaped to Florida.[15]

"I was born," Henry went on to say, "in a Country where Slavery had been established by British Kings & Parliaments as well as by the Laws of that Country Ages before my existence. . . . I am not the man who enslaved [his own Africans], they are indebted to English Men for that favour." Laurens insisted that "Acts of Parliament have established the Slave Trade in favour of the home residing English & almost totally prohibited the Americans from reaping any share of it." These premises do not deny his participation in slavery, nor even his work in the slave trade, which could not be forgotten even a dozen years after retiring from it. But Henry disowned responsibility for these institutions by suggesting that they were the inescapable conditions of life in South Carolina. "In former days," he continued, "there was no combating the prejudices of Men supported by Interest." By 1776, Laurens was able to forget that in former times the prejudices of men could be combated, that indeed some people did fight them, and that Laurens himself chose to support the prejudices. A quarter of a century after the fact, Laurens could repress in his own mind his role in lifting the legislative ban on the slave trade. Only after this forgetting, having fully insulated himself from its consequences, did he free his conscience.

It was a complex maneuver, but it was essential to men of conscience in the South, and Laurens was not alone in blaming American slavery on Great Britain. Jefferson had toyed with the idea as early as 1774, when a mild version of it appeared in *A Summary View of the Rights of British America*, his instructions to Virginia's delegation to the First Continental Congress. The Revolution itself gave greater scope to antislavery sentiments, not only in the northern states but deep into the South, for everyone recognized how it contradicted the self-evident truths avowed to in the Declaration of Independence, that all men were created equal and that all men had a natural right to liberty. Jefferson's own draft of the Declaration of Independence tried to cordon slavery off from the noble American experiment in representative government. His last and climactic grievance against George III read:

> he has waged cruel war against human nature itself, violating its most sacred rights of life & liberty in the persons of a distant people who never offended him, captivating and carrying them into slavery in another hemisphere, or to incur miserable death in their transportation thither, this piratical warfare, the opprobrium of *infidel* powers, is the warfare of the *Christian* king of Great Britain. determined to keep open a market where MEN should be bought & sold, he has prostituted his negative for suppressing every legislative attempt to prohibit or restrain this execrable commerce.

Pauline Maier asserts that this is "an accusation that one seeks in vain elsewhere in the literature on behalf of Independence." But it must have been in the air: Laurens was in Charles Town, not Philadelphia, during the debates about the Declaration, so it is unlikely that he knew what was said publicly and privately that led to the removal of this clause from the Declaration's final draft. Nevertheless, we know that when the Declaration's bold assertions arrived in Charles Town, they emboldened Henry into voicing notions that had been long percolating in his mind, notions that he knew would please his son.[16]

That the crown vetoed legislation restricting the slave trade would have been common knowledge to any South Carolinian of Laurens's generation and station. But for Laurens to complain about it in 1776 required him to forget his hopes a dozen years earlier that the king would veto just such a ban in South Carolina. Making King George the scapegoat for the entire practice of slavery gave men like Henry Laurens someone to blame other than themselves, and it gave men like John Laurens, who was romantically devoted to the goddess of Liberty, someone to blame other than their fathers.[17]

"You know my Dear Sir," Henry continued, "I abhor Slavery. . . . The day I hope is approaching when from principles of gratitude as well as justice every Man will strive to be foremost in shewing his readiness to comply with the Golden Rule." Henry was at this time the vice president of South Carolina, so his son must have been astonished to read that he was "devising means for manumitting many of [the slaves] & for cutting off the entail of Slavery." We don't know whether cutting of the entail meant preventing anyone from inheriting slaves or preventing new children born to slaves from inheriting the status of their parents, but either way, Henry knew that such a plan would deprive his own children, including John, "of so much [of their] Estate."[18]

John didn't care. He read his father's letter "with rapture," replying that "your desire of restoring the Rights of Men, to those wretched Mortals . . . coincides exactly with my Feelings upon that Subject." In fact, emancipation had become something of an idée fixe. John had been schooled in this issue by two of his English friends, young lawyers, John Bicknell and Thomas Day, who had collaborated on an antislavery poem, "The Dying Negro," in 1773. John introduced Day to a planter's son within his circle of Carolina friends, which occasioned a learned disputation on the immorality of slavery and the motives of slaveholders in America. Henry's admission about how slavery violated the Golden Rule probably came from Day's pamphlet. "I have scarcely ever met with a Native of the Southern Provinces or the W[est] Indies," John told his father, "who did not obstinately recur to the most absurd Arguments in support of Slavery." When challenged, his fellow southerners abandoned their rationalizations and came to the heart of the matter: "Without Slaves," they exclaimed, "how is it possible for us to be rich[?]"[19]

Henry understood the power of greed, for he felt it himself, and though he considered public laws based on white greed to be "difficulties," he did not think them "insuperable." Emancipation would be hard work, and Henry expected to "appear to many as a promoter not only of strange but of dangerous doctrines." Caution, then, was the order of the day, and he asked for John's "advice & assistance." Henry's caution against granting blacks their natural rights probably had a lot to do with politics and the art of the possible: he feared appearing to his fellows as strange and dangerous, which would reduce his effectiveness. John had no such scruples. Like the Romantics of the coming century, he welcomed the isolation borne of high purpose, and, like Lord Byron, "proud though in desolation . . . He would not yield dominion of his mind / To Spirits against whom his own rebelled." He agreed with his father that progress must be slow but only because "there may be danger in advancing such Men too suddenly to the Rights of Freemen." Since "we have sunk the Africans & their descendants below the Standard of Humanity," rendering them almost "incapable of that Blessing which equal Heaven bestow'd upon us all," he argued that emancipation must be approached gradually. He promised to study the matter deeply in the time left before his return to America. Father and son both displayed what we could call the *enlightened* version of paternalism: slaves were immature and in need of guidance, but only because generations of slavery had degraded them. Echoing the Declaration of Independence, both acknowledged that God had created *all* men equal, and that blacks had the same inalienable right to and capacity for liberty.[20]

To get back to Charles Town, John had to travel through Paris, then to Bordeaux, where he caught a ship to Haiti. He found passage on a schooner in the South Carolina navy, which outran two British ships to finally reach Charles Town in April 1777. Six years earlier, he had left America as an impetuous sixteen-year-old boy. Now he was one of the best-educated Americans, a husband and father eager to join the national cause. His father, Henry, he soon discovered, had been elected to the national Congress. The two men were not yet equals, but they considered each other intimate friends, and from later letters we know that they discussed the issue of slavery, though we don't know the details. Perhaps there were no details, for no definite plan for emancipation emerged until later, in more desperate days, and it seems likely that as they together headed north to Philadelphia in June, each attended by an enslaved valet, their talks were more philosophical than practical. In July, Henry took his seat in Congress, and John secured a place on Washington's staff, the general's fourth young aide-de-camp, which was expanded to five when the twenty-year-old Marquis de Lafayette arrived on the scene.

Washington referred to his young staffers as his "family," and the metaphor was telling: John Laurens, Alexander Hamilton, and especially Lafayette were, in the words of Joseph Ellis, surrogate sons; and it is clear in John's letters that he considered Alexander Hamilton and Lafayette as close as brothers. Hamilton, self-protective and diffident, found that John had stolen "into my affections without my consent."[21] Within a month, John distinguished himself, helping Washington rally the Americans in a losing battle at Brandywine, as Lafayette reported to John's real father. Henry, along with the rest of Congress, scurried out of Philadelphia just before the British took the city, escaping to Bristol, a "little Town covered by fugitives, [its] River by Vessels of War & Store Vessels & others from Philadelphia, [its] Roads choked by Carriages Horses & Waggons," where he scooped up the young Frenchman, who had been wounded in the battle, and conveyed him in his own carriage to Bethlehem. Lafayette extolled John's boldness, which poured pride into Henry's broth of apprehensions.[22]

While the campaign that autumn quickly turned John into a soldier, Henry was elected to succeed John Hancock as president of the Continental Congress, where he became Washington's greatest advocate, buoyed as he was by reports from his son. Together, for example, Henry and John Laurens were instrumental in defeating the supposed "Conway cabal," which connived to supplant Washington with General Horatio Gates. John's fierce love of Washington launched him into a duel with Charles Lee, who had sullied the general's honor in one of the interminable, petty squabbles among American officers. This duel and John's battlefield behavior, rashly exposing himself to "a blasting shower of balls," as one friend from Charles Town described it, established his reputation as a valuable officer but impetuous, even reckless, as if battles were duels and to duck one's head was as dishonorable as ducking a challenge.[23]

The Continentals weathered the winter of 1777–78 in Valley Forge, which slowly leached the strength of the young army. "Our truly Republican General," John told his father, "will set the Example of passing the Winter in a Hut himself." Hunger, cold, and disease stalked the wooden hovels, and to fill their dwindled ranks two Rhode Island battalions proposed enlisting slaves, who would be freed and their owners compensated. Washington approved the plan, the Rhode Island legislature approved the plan, and John Laurens saw in this precedent a way to begin emancipating blacks in South Carolina. "I would sollicit you," John asked his father, "to cede me a number of your able bodied men Slaves, instead of leaving me a fortune. . . . I would," he insisted, use that patrimony to "reinforce the Defenders of Liberty with a number of gallant Soldiers."[24]

Henry had just recovered from an attack of the gout, which confined him to bed in December and left him leaning on a cane in January. He was harassed by the duties of Congress, not the least of which was to supply the army in Valley Forge. He struggled daily against the "prompters & Actors, accomodators, Candle Snuffers, Shifters of Scenes & Mutes" who connived against Washington. In the midst of such worries, he did not like the looks of John's plan. Taking a dig at the young man's impulsiveness, he replied, "More time will be required for me to consider the propriety of your scheme for raising a black Regiment, than you seem to have taken for concerting the project." Nevertheless, he would comply "if after mature deliberation you will say it is reasonable." Henry did not think slaves would willingly exchange their "tolerable" and "comfortable" lot for the uncertain dangers of the army, predicting that at the first chance "they would flee into the woods." Not only that, but he had dropped hints of the scheme with certain men only to find that none approved the idea. But if John decided to go ahead, Henry would back him, and the first order of business would be to find "twenty more [white planters] to share the reproach of Quixotism & to carry it into respectable execution." At most, John could raise about forty troops from his own inheritance, if Henry gave him all the suitable men out of a population of around three hundred slaves. Probably to dampen John's enthusiasm, Henry suggested it would take about twelve hundred all mustered at once for the scheme to succeed, and he asked if John had "consulted your Gen.[eral Washington] on this head." Whatever were his motives, Henry was laying out a blueprint for how a minority of dissenters might act as the point of a wedge, or rather as a fulcrum on which public opinion might be shifted. The worst thing was to appear crazy, and Henry warned John that if the scheme failed, he "will be reduced to the ridiculous state of the Fox who had lost his Tail."[25]

John knew he would face the scorn and laughter of "that monster[,] popular Prejudice." But his "zeal for the public Service" strengthened him, and besides he burned with "ardent desire to assert the rights of humanity." But most of all, John, who cared very much what others thought of him, had entered into the select brotherhood of Washington's corps of officers, and he cared more for their good opinion than for anyone else's. Little did Henry know that John already had assembled the point of the wedge, the approval "of a few virtuous men." Alexander Hamilton was "conspicuous among the founding fathers for his fierce abolitionism," and he and John might have persuaded the Marquis de Lafayette, who had little direct experience of slavery, to join the cause, for after the war he became an ardent advocate of abolition. John expected another Frenchman, Lieutenant Colonel Louis de Fleury, to help him train and command the troops. Washington himself was "convinced that the numerous tribes of blacks in the Southern parts of the Continent offer a resource to us that should not be neglected." Washington's only objection was that the scheme would render John "less rich than he might be."[26]

Henry's response to this final plea suggests that he had been humoring John, hoping for the idea to fade away, for he inexplicably ignored the report about Washington's approbation and insisted "there is not a Man in America of your opinion." The tone of the letter restored Henry to his old position as patriarch: "You have filled six Pages on the Negro scheme," he scolded, "without approaching towards a Plan & Estimate__ & . . . you have totally overlooked every other subject on which I have addressed you in several late letters." Afraid that enthusiasm had blinded John to practical reality, Henry pointed out that "Wisdom dictates that I should rather oppose than barely not consent to" enlisting any of the family's slaves in the army. For good measure, he sent along another two "Camp Shirts" and "a piece of Scarlet Cloth," asking sarcastically, "why will you not be so kind as to take the very little [time] which is necessary to barely acknowledge the Receipt" of such gifts? His plea was reduced to a parent's final resource, guilt: "I should have thought . . . the idea of humouring an old & good friend, would have made a proper impression upon a Man of so much accuracy as I perceive you are when you transact business for or correspond with any body but poor me." This discouragement must have come as a shock to John, who until this point thought he had secured his father's cautious approval. "I renounce" the scheme, he cried, disdainfully, "as a thing which cannot be sanctified by your approbation." Dutifully, drily, he thanked his father for the camp shirts. But the scheme was not renounced. It percolated beneath the surface.[27]

When the British captured Savannah, everyone expected that the spring of 1779 would bring redcoats across the Savannah River into South Carolina, where fewer than twelve hundred Continentals opposed them. General Benjamin Lincoln begged Congress for more troops. The governor of South Carolina, John Rutledge, feared that the British were preparing to invade with fifteen thousand men and complained that the "grand Army" would send not "a ship, a Man, or a Musket." But Washington, his hands full in the mid-Atlantic states, had no troops to give. John Laurens floated the idea of black troops again, Washington approved it, and in early March John wrote his father asking him to bring the matter before Congress. With South Carolina facing an invasion, Henry readily agreed, this time writing himself to Washington that "had we Arms for 3000, such black Men as I could select in Carolina I should have no doubt of success in driving the British out of Georgia & subduing East Florida before the end of July."[28]

Alexander Hamilton fully endorsed the plan, as might be expected, and he sent a persuasive letter to John Jay, the New Yorker who succeeded Henry Laurens in the office of president. Hamilton must have been familiar with Henry's earlier objections when he wrote, "I foresee that this project will have to combat much opposition from prejudice and self-interest," especially since "an essential part of the plan is to give [the slaves] their freedom with their muskets." If the Americans didn't make such an offer, the British surely would, and so the United States would be served better by turning this weakness—the great numbers of slaves in South Carolina—into strength. A year earlier, Henry Laurens had argued that slaves were unfit to be soldiers, but Hamilton believed that "their natural faculties are probably as good as ours," and, echoing John, he insisted that their "habit of subordination" would suit them to the soldier's life. Hamilton suggested the black battalions would exempt South Carolina from mustering whites for Continental service, since so few white men lived in the state, while North Carolina and Virginia would supply another thirty-five hundred white troops to combat the British in the South.[29]

On March 25, 1779, a committee of five, including Henry Laurens, recommended that Congress authorize South Carolina and Georgia to raise black troops "for filling up the Continental Battalions of those States or for forming separate Corps to be commanded by White Officers." The South Carolina delegation concurred in the decision, knowing full well that it was a step in the direction of emancipation. It is remarkable that William Henry Drayton agreed to the proposal. Drayton's plantation was on the south side of Charles Town, west of the Ashley River, the part most vulnerable to a British invasion. Though an ardent revolutionary, he was also committed to the oligarchic government of South Carolina, suspicious of democracy and any leveling measures, and ideologically disposed to believe heartily in white supremacy. Yet he, too, urged South Carolina to arm three thousand slaves and free them upon the war's end. Compound this disinclination to benevolence toward the slaves with Drayton's ongoing personal enmity for Henry Laurens, and we can see how thoroughly the war opened minds to the unthinkable.[30] Had Drayton and Henry Laurens together gone down to South Carolina to promote the idea, the sight of these two in unity would have changed many minds.

But only John went, and he found Charles Town nearly in a panic because the British had begun their invasion and the American general Lincoln had positioned most of his troops in the distant Upcountry. Laurens arrived on the scene with a commission from Congress as lieutenant colonel, and he joined General William Moultrie, a local hero, who commanded about a thousand militia, all that stood between the British and Charles Town. Moultrie welcomed the arrival of such a seasoned Continental officer as John Laurens and put him in charge of the rear guard as the little amateur army retreated toward Charles Town. But the fiery Laurens was not suited to retreat, nor was he well-suited to nurture the resolve of citizen soldiers, and he bungled his assignment by boldly advancing across the Coosawhatchie River, where he met a superior force, got himself wounded in the right arm, and spooked Moultrie's skittish militia. The little defeat forced Moultrie to abandon his own lines and retreat all the way back to Charles Town, his only hope to hold the city long enough for the main force of Americans under Lincoln to rescue them.[31]

The British crossed the Ashley River northwest of the city and marched down the Neck of the peninsula to face the uncompleted fortifications at the city's edge. They occupied James Island across the harbor, carefully watched by Peter Timothy, the printer, who spied on them from the steeple of St. Michael's Church. The American military leaders—Moultrie, the Polish count Casimir Pulaski, and John Laurens—advised Governor John Rutledge and the Privy Council that they could hold out till General Lincoln arrived, when the two American forces could turn the tables on the British by attacking from two sides. But Governor Rutledge was not so sure. The Americans had about three thousand defenders in the city, but he imagined the British forces numbered seven or eight thousand. Rutledge offered the British a separate peace: South Carolina would become neutral and remain so till the hostilities ended, at which point it would share the fate of the other states, either independence or reabsorption into the Empire.[32]

Inadvertently, John Laurens's proposal for a black regiment played a significant role in these events. Though South Carolina's delegates to Congress had been persuaded of the necessity of raising an army from slaves, those under siege in Charles Town, who did not see the daily effort and difficulty with which Washington's army was sustained near Philadelphia, felt abandoned by the national government.

They had pleaded for Continental troops to defend the southern flank of the country, and instead of soldiers Congress sent Laurens with the instructions to muster three thousand of their own slaves. Should South Carolina remain loyal to a government so indifferent to its defense? Rutledge and the Privy Council rejected Laurens's proposal out of hand.

John was disgusted by such logic. He was an American first and a South Carolinian second, and to adopt neutrality for the duration of the war would betray his comrades in the Continental army. Death on the barricades was better. He wrote up his own version of the councils that led to Rutledge's notorious offer to take South Carolina out of the war, carefully delineating his opposition and disavowing any responsibility.[33] He was not alone. The Council was comprised of Charles Pinckney, Christopher Gadsden (planter, merchant, childhood friend of Henry Laurens), Thomas Ferguson (Gadsden's brother-in-law), John Edwards, John Neufville, Isaac Motte, Roger Smith, and John Parker. Five of these, Pinckney, Neufville, Motte, Smith, and Parker, supported Rutledge's offer to make Charles Town and South Carolina neutral. The others were as horrified as Laurens—Edwards even wept, decrying, "What! are we going to give up the town at last?"[34] We don't know if Gadsden, Edwards, and Ferguson supported the black regiment, but we have to regret that Rutledge, who could have enacted the measure by fiat at this moment of crisis, would rather surrender to the British than arm three thousand slaves. Had he and the Council been persuaded of its necessity, like Henry Laurens, William Drayton, John Huger, and the state's delegation to Congress had been persuaded, South Carolina would have taken a great and irrevocable step toward emancipation.

Rutledge escaped a fate worse than Benedict Arnold only because the negotiations for ignominious surrender dragged on so long that the slow-footed troops under General Lincoln finally arrived in the vicinity, and the British abandoned the siege lest they be pinched between the two American armies, the hunter turning prey. The Council considered the proposal to organize a black regiment again twelve days after the British withdrew, and again they formally rejected Washington's suggestion. So Laurens brought it to the legislature. As he reported to Alexander Hamilton, he harangued his colleagues, which was not the best method of persuasion but was consistent with his zeal and sense of righteousness, for he considered this step toward emancipation his duty as a citizen. Though the idea was unpopular, it garnered twelve or so of about seventy-two votes, a sizeable minority, including David Ramsay, a doctor originally from Pennsylvania who would later marry John's sister, Martha, and write a popular history of South Carolina. As Ramsay saw it, it was the large faction of planters who led the opposition because they "figured to themselves terrible consequences."[35]

Ramsay represented the dissenting minority that held the "firm belief that [there] will not be a slave in these states fifty years hence." His best friend and frequent correspondent was Benjamin Rush, who eventually founded the Pennsylvania Society for Promoting the Abolition of Slavery, and the two agreed that any inferiority exhibited by African Americans was artificially produced by slavery and therefore could not justify a policy of white supremacy. In 1786, Ramsay demonstrated that he was to the left of the liberal-minded Jefferson who believed blacks to be inherently inferior, explaining that "all mankind . . . [is] originally the same & only diversified by accidental circumstances."[36] We don't know who in the legislature joined Ramsay and Laurens, but clearly a faction in the statehouse transcended the economic interest of the planter class and supported the progressive view.

Frustrated in that attempt, John Laurens went north to plead with General Washington for more Continentals, and in November the general sent over three thousand North Carolinians and Virginians to the South Carolina theater of war, while Congress sent three frigates, the *Providence*, *Boston*, and *Queen of France*. Even with about a thousand Charles Town militia and some more from North Carolina, Lincoln knew he didn't have nearly enough men, especially when in early January 1780 a strange ship looking suspiciously like a troop transport was sighted off the coast of Charles Town and sailing south. Again John Laurens pressed the legislature to muster slaves, this time backed by General Lincoln's pleas, and enabled by his father, Henry, lately president of Congress, who had returned to Charles Town. The proposal was assigned to a committee that Henry chaired, and, ever the savvy politician, he engineered a compromise measure in which a thousand slaves would be recruited to help man artillery batteries and perform garrison duty; that is, they would not need to be trained in firearms and would not need to be issued muskets. But ultimately the Privy Council, that most conservative body, again rejected the notion of raising black regiments even "in the last extremity."[37]

The American frigates soon discovered British ships near Port Royal, just south of the city, and more at Tybee Island near Savannah and even captured a couple of sloops. From the British sailors General Lincoln learned that the English would soon launch another invasion from Georgia, this one huge compared to the previous year's. Henry reported that "we are preparing for the reception of a menaced attack by a very formidable force." By the morning of February 11, Lincoln knew that 150 ships carrying eight thousand soldiers under the command of Sir Henry Clinton, the supreme general of all British forces, had arrived in Savannah, and he dashed off a warning to Charles Town that an invasion of South Carolina would surely follow. He expected it to take a few weeks for the troops to march north, so he was taken by surprise when later that same day fifty ships appeared in the mouth of the North Edisto River, just twenty miles from Charles Town.[38]

Clinton landed at Johns Island and set off a panic in Charles Town. Refugees grabbed what they could and poured out of town on the western and northern roads. The state's legislature adjourned itself, and its last act was to put the "power to do everything necessary for the publick good, except the taking away the life of a citizen without a legal trial" into the hands of the governor, John Rutledge, who immediately began authorizing the measures Lincoln needed to defend the city. The city was well defended by nature against the methods of eighteenth-century warfare. Though the British could easily take the coastal islands, once they reached the edge of James Island they could do little more than look across the harbor at the city a couple of miles away. To assault the town, they needed to either capture the harbor, the front door to the city, so they could bring their powerful warships within cannon range; or bludgeon down the back door by marching down the peninsula and face the defensive wall that ran from the marshes on the Ashley River across to the Cooper in a jagged line. The maritime route required a tricky maneuver across the bar at the mouth of the harbor, which was guarded by Fort Moultrie on Sullivan's Island. General Lincoln also deployed his six frigates inside the harbor to oppose any approach from the sea. He was pretty confident that the sea approach was secure. Even should the city fall to a land attack on the Neck, the defenders could always escape across the Cooper River to the north so long as the Americans controlled the harbor.

A land attack would require the British to march inland from the sea islands, paralleling the southern bank of the Ashley River, flanking the city until they got behind it and found a way across to the peninsula's Neck. To prevent Clinton from ferrying troops across the river, Lincoln confiscated every private boat for forty miles up and down the coast. If Clinton wanted to cross the river on foot, he would have to go many miles further inland, to Bacon's Bridge, where the Ashley narrowed to a stream. Lincoln detached a strong guard to hold Bacon's Bridge. Finally, he set to work fixing the city lines, which, amazingly, were still in horrible repair. Lincoln wanted twelve hundred slaves and a week to strengthen the lines, but the state could manage only a few hundred. On every front, manpower was a problem. While North Carolina had generously sent a strong militia force, South Carolinians were slower to arrive, fearing a rumored outbreak of smallpox (which had swept through the city the previous fall) and stayed closer to home to protect against Indians and slave uprisings. Merchant sailors were pressed into naval service. Colonel Charles Cotesworth Pinckney, who commanded the garrison at Fort Moultrie, wanted 1,215 men, but he had to make do with 200, vowing to "make the best defense in my power with the number that may be allowed me."[39]

The British approached cautiously, apparently meaning to attack somewhere across the Ashley. It took a week and a half for them to occupy all of John's Island—even though the Americans offered little resistance—which allowed the British to take control of the Stono River, which gave them access to James Island, which fronted Charleston's harbor itself, and the mainland west of the Ashley. Any land assault across the Ashley River required control of the Stono, and capturing this inland waterway would be the first step in the Union's siege eighty years later. American cavalry kept Clinton's troops from jumping across the Stono to forage from the plantations on the mainland, so most of the British supplies were either carried in on barges or captured from the sea island plantations. The British major André tried to prevent looting, but General Clinton allowed it, declaring any abandoned farm was ipso facto the property of a rebel and liable to looting. In very little time Wadmalaw, Edisto, and Johns Islands were stripped bare, for most of the residents, rebels or not, had fled before the army's approach. Peter Timothy, the printer, perched atop the steeple of St. Michael's, spied the British ships outside the harbor and charted the army's progress across the islands by calculating the position of their campfires. Two weeks after they first landed, the British crossed the Stono onto James Island, the Americans retreating ahead of them and destroying the bridge that crossed the Wappoo Cut onto the mainland. From the edge of James Island, General Clinton could look across the harbor at the faces of the town's buildings. He heaped up a battery a mere nineteen hundred yards from the city and close enough for his twenty-four-pound and even bigger thirty-two-pound cannon to fire balls into Charles Town but that would have little military effect, and the purpose of the battery was to prevent the American ships from pounding his own troops as they marched up the west side of the river. The long and circuitous route inland across the Ashley River, and down the Neck still remained.[40]

In a week, Clinton had rebuilt the Wappoo Bridge. But then for some reason he stalled and waited for the navy to secure the harbor. While the weather opposed such a chance of crossing of the bar, unfortunately the timid American commodore, Abraham Whipple, withdrew the frigates back to anchorage closer to town, and when the winds finally blew from the southeast on March 20, the British ships crossed the bar. Clinton stalled some more, waiting for reinforcements from Georgia, who plundered their way overland to a rendezvous west of the Ashley River. On March 27, Timothy, peering still from the steeple of St. Michael's, observed more than thirty flatboats making their way up the Ashley, and two days later Clinton ferried the bulk of his force across the river at Drayton Hall plantation, meeting little resistance as they landed above the Neck of the peninsula. The next day they began their march toward the city, delayed only briefly by a skirmishing of rifle fire directed by men under the command of John Laurens. All day long the skirmishing went back and forth, as the Americans abandoned, recaptured, and lost a redoubt about a mile from the lines, but ultimately, as he planned to do, Laurens and his men fell back safely inside the lines by nightfall. At dusk Clinton camped his army just two miles away, already within range of their heavy cannon.[41]

The next morning, the British began the long, choreographed tightening of the siege: sap trenches stretching out from their lines a distance, from which massive trenches parallel to their lines were dug; this process was repeated two or three times until the besieging army could bring its artillery within a couple of hundred yards of the city's ramparts, blasting at such close range as to thoroughly demolish them. Once Sir Henry Clinton got a view of the city's lines, he remarked that they were "by no means contemptible." The Americans built a canal across the neck, eighteen feet wide and six feet deep, which they could fill or drain at will through sluices at the Cooper River. Only a narrow passage near the Ashley River made its way around this ditch, and this bit of high ground was protected by a half-moon battery. Then came two lines of abatis, sharpened stakes in X shapes, and beyond those the main curtain wall fronted by a deep ditch at the bottom of which were two rows of sharp wooden pickets. Two fortified redoubts anchored the parapet wall, and behind it all the "Hornwork," a double redoubt surrounding the gate to the city, protected King Street, the main artery that ran all the way down to the city's point.[42]

The digging of the first parallel, the construction of its batteries, the dragging of cannon in place, took the British about two weeks, all the while suffering the bombardment from the American lines. Clinton ordered his battery across the Ashley River to fire random shots into Charles Town, hitting several houses, terrifying and angering the inhabitants. On April 8, the British fleet, which had been anchored at Five Fathom Hole ever since it crossed the bar, raced past Fort Moultrie in single file, suffering minor damage on their way into Charles Town's harbor. This maneuver gave Clinton's troops access to the land east of the Cooper River: if he could close the Cooper River to American traffic, he would completely encircle the city and cut off the only chance of the garrison escaping. They had not yet accomplished this encirclement, but it began to appear inevitable that they would, and Clinton asked Lincoln to surrender. Lincoln declined.[43]

The British began firing their guns from the first parallel, about four hundred yards from the American lines, and they lobbed cannonballs into the city itself, setting fire to houses. John Rutledge, now dictator of South Carolina, slipped across the Cooper River on April 13, leaving the civilian leadership in the hands of Christopher Gadsden. A week later, as the British made successful forays east of the Cooper, Lincoln considered evacuating the Continental troops before it was too late, but Gadsden angrily opposed the idea, insisting that they fight to the end or surrender together with the militias and civilians, so Lincoln and his army stayed. Fort Moultrie fell on May 7. The city capitulated on the twelfth, and the British legions marched through the streets of Charleston, arrested its civilian leaders (who eventually were sent to prison in St. Augustine), and accepted the surrender of the five thousand defenders, including two thousand Continental troops and Lieutenant Colonel John Laurens. It was estimated the garrison needed about nine thousand men to be made invulnerable, so three thousand black troops would have come close to saving the city, but John Rutledge, now hiding out in the hinterlands, would not have it. Henry Laurens dutifully reported all this to Congress.[44]

Like Governor Rutledge, Henry had slipped across the Cooper River out of the city before the noose was tightened because Congress had charged him with a crucial duty—to secure a treaty and a loan from the Netherlands. He spent the entire spring moving up the East Coast looking for vessels going to Europe, a vain search that brought him, eventually, as far north as Philadelphia. Most of his possessions, including his Charles Town home, were in the hands of the British, so Henry found himself for the first time in thirty years in much reduced finances. But his discouragements were mitigated by a reunion with John, who also came to Philadelphia, but as a prisoner of war. It was common practice in the Revolution to "parole" captured soldiers, especially officers, which meant that the British allowed John Laurens to travel, on his honor, to Pennsylvania, which would be his prison until he was officially exchanged for a comparable British officer. This indulgence allowed John enough freedom to sail with Henry down the Delaware River as far as Fort Penn, where the son took his leave from the father, parting for the last time. Henry sailed on the *Mercury*, a sixty-two ton brigantine with a fourteen-man crew and the reputation as the fastest ship in America, but even so she was overtaken by the *Vestal* off the coast of Newfoundland and the Americans were captured. The British shut Henry up in the Tower of London, where he faced charges of treason. His mission to the Netherlands gave Great Britain an excuse to declare war on the Dutch Republic, which until that time had been a neutral country aiding the Americans with its commerce. And while the Dutch lost most engagements and some of its western islands to the British, John Adams eventually succeeded in securing the treaty and loan the Americans needed.[45]

John was officially exchanged, went to France to help Ben Franklin negotiate important aid from Louis XVI, and was back with Washington's army by September 1781, just in time for the final entrapment of Lord Cornwallis at Yorktown. Washington appointed Laurens to the delegation negotiating the surrender, and after a little haggling about whether the same shameful terms accorded the American garrison surrendering at Charles Town would prevail in Virginia, the capitulation was accomplished. Cornwallis was the constable of the Tower of London, and so he was, officially, Henry Laurens's jailer. John could not resist the irony of offering to exchange Cornwallis for Henry.[46]

Though Yorktown essentially ended any hopes the British had for suppressing the rebellion and regaining her possessions in America, it did not quite end the war. British garrisons still held New York and Charles Town, and in November John hastened home to join the army in South Carolina. He made his third and final attempt to raise a black regiment in January 1782. Nathaniel Greene, the Continental general in charge of the southern theater of operations, advocated the plan, recommending that the legislature arm slaves so he could take Charles Town back from the British. This final debate differed from the others because South Carolina was no longer in crisis. In 1779, defending Charles Town had been crucial to the strategic defense of the whole South. In 1780, the British were knocking at the door, and still South Carolina refused to arm slaves. By 1782, after Cornwallis had surrendered at Yorktown, retaking the city hardly mattered to military strategy. It was an isolated British toehold rather than a base of operations.

So there was little urgency to the notion this time around. Nevertheless, Laurens marshaled a surprisingly able minority of votes. This was an odd parliament, meeting in Jacksonboro, a little village of only a few houses not far from the spot where the old Stono Rebellion had been put down and just a little south of Charles Town. The gathering must have been consciously humble compared to the sumptuous meeting rooms occupied by the British in the city. Laurens was supported again by David Ramsay and also by Thomas Ferguson, who had been on the Privy Council back in 1779, when the proposal was first rejected. Sentiment ran so high in favor of the idea of arming slaves that Edward Rutledge, the erstwhile governor's brother, was "very much alarmed" that it would pass because he was "repeatedly told that a large party" had been mustered to support Laurens. But in the end the planters reasserted their will. The Rutledge brothers, John and Edward, along with Christopher Gadsden, Aedanus Burke, and another representative from Charles Town, Jacob Read, spoke against the measure and convinced a large majority that it was too dangerous. No record was kept of the public debate, either on the floor of the chamber or in the muddy streets of Jacksonboro, but when the vote was tallied, only fifteen or sixteen representatives still supported the bill, while about a hundred opposed it.[47]

Historians consistently use this majority to demonstrate how illiberal South Carolina was, even in the age of revolution. But that interpretation takes the vote out of context. While the small aristocracy of Lowcountry planters still dominated South Carolina politics, despite the increased democratization that the Revolution brought to the state, a solid minority asserted their opposition to slavery in the legislature, enough to find comfort in each other's company, to be assured that their dissent was not singular and outlandish. Logically enough, the arguments against slavery seemed to persuade those who had more experience of national politics, who were exposed to the more liberal views of their northern brethren. Their leader was the rising star of South Carolina—John Laurens.

But the same romantic heroism that fired John's zeal for human rights, no matter the consequences to his own or any other planters' fortune, also pricked the soldiers' lust for glory. In August 1782, not long before the British finally evacuated Charles Town, Laurens and his detachment of rangers came upon a party of redcoats apparently foraging for supplies in the country outside Charles Town. In his characteristic fashion, Laurens charged his men headlong into the scrape, but the strange luck that hung about him like a shield deflecting the mortal musket balls deserted him in the end. With the war over, in a meaningless skirmish near the Combahee River, John Laurens was killed, one of the very last casualties of the Revolution.

Henry was still in the Tower of London, a prisoner of England, when John Adams wrote from Paris informing him that Congress had selected him to help represent the United States in the peace treaty then being negotiated. Adams added these words:

> I know not how to mention, the melancholly Intelligence by this Vessell, which affects you so tenderly__ I feel for you, more than I can or ought to express.__ Our Country has lost its most promising Character.

It was the first Henry had heard of the events on the Combahee, and it marked the end of his commitment to public life. He played a desultory role in Paris, but he came back to South Carolina a deeply saddened man, indulging little of the joy that swelled his fellow countrymen at having won the war, and, unlike Adams and Franklin, Jefferson and Washington, he was not much interested anymore in forming the new nation. John had been his brilliant hope for the future. Probably, even Henry did not understand that John Laurens was the best hope for the new republic, the one man around whom a cadre of dissenters might rally. Slavery had been singed and burned by the fiery rhetoric of liberty, but it was far too strong for the timid or the tepid to oppose. John Laurens, the surrogate son of Washington and natural son of Henry, uncompromising in conviction, fearless, charismatic and shining with the brilliance of a polished sword should have led the friends of liberty against the planters'greed. Henry was too old, and he lacked the Romantic impulse to follow an unlikely cause. He retired to his plantation on the Cooper River, Mepkin, where, like the old and weary Candide of Voltaire's novel, he tended to his own garden.[48]

4

WE THE ARISTOCRATS

||

Inside the paneled walls and high, meditative windows of Pennsylvania's statehouse, an impressively large man rose from his chair, propping himself on his peg leg, to pronounce an unequivocal accusation against the slave trade. "The inhabitant of Georgia and S[outh] C[arolina]," Gouverneur Morris bellowed, "goes to the Coast of Africa, and in defiance of the most sacred laws of humanity tears away his fellow creatures from their dearest connections & damns [them] to the most cruel bondages."

It was a Wednesday, August 8, 1787, and summer heat percolated under the collars of those assembled in the hall. The windows were closed to the outside breezes to keep proceedings strictly secret from the public. Deliberations, debates, shifting alliances, compromises, insults, last-ditch stands—all that was said must stay in the room. Making law, the adage goes, is like making sausage, and it's best not to watch the ugly process. Oozing from the grinder of this hot summer was the United States Constitution.

August was ugly. Gouverneur Morris, a New Yorker transplanted to Pennsylvania, barely disguised his contempt for the delegates from the two southernmost states, South Carolina and Georgia, who sat huddled together around one desk on the room's far side to the left of General George Washington, who presided over the meetings.

Morris was a man more feared than admired. It was rumored that he had ruined his leg while jumping out the back window of a pretty young woman's bedroom just as her cuckolded husband came in the front door, and though the anecdote was mistaken, it accurately captures his rakish life. He really broke the leg in a carriage accident, and after the amputation a friend's wife eased his convalescence in a way that confirmed the gist of the rumors. Another apocryphal story has him swinging the wooden leg like a shillelagh in arching, threatening circles, warning off a revolutionary mob in Paris, while his free hand hung on to a lamppost. Trained for the New York bar at sixteen, the canny lawyer was known for his wit and whimsy, and only his good friends recognized the hard work and industry hidden behind the "facade of playboy indolence."[1]

Not many in the assembly were likely to suffer his lectures on morality. Some forty-odd men had come to Philadelphia, which, at forty thousand inhabitants, was then the largest and most important of the American cities. Practically no one was satisfied with the Articles of Confederation, which had governed—or rather failed to govern—the United States since the Revolution. Indeed, it might not even be proper to describe the American republic as a nation, given the frailty of the federal government and incoherence of its policies. The war left the individual states with huge problems, especially economic, that were nearly impossible to solve when approached from thirteen different directions. Everyone recognized the inadequacies of the Articles, and they came to Philadelphia ostensibly to shore them up, but nearly all of the delegates wanted to go beyond that mandate and write an entirely new constitution forming a stronger federal government.

Ultimately, Gouverneur Morris wanted to bestow upon the new government the power to regulate slavery, but the particular article upon which he was discoursing was the three-fifths rule: that representation in the House of Representatives shall be allotted according to the population of states, and that for the purposes of such allotments each slave would count as three-fifths of a free inhabitant. Morris pointed out that such a rule would give the white men in slave states "more votes in a Govt. instituted for protections of the rights of mankind, than the Citizen of P[ennsylvania] or N[ew] Jersey." South Carolina's 140,000 whites would be represented by five delegates in the House, while a state like Pennsylvania, which was settled by nearly three times as many whites, would send only eight delegates to the House.[2] The three-fifths rule would give southern states an incentive to import more slaves, because every 50,000 new slaves meant another representative in Congress. The "nefarious" institution of slavery horrified Morris, and it galled him that the national Constitution should penalize states that banned slavery.

"Domestic slavery," Morris insisted, "is the most prominent feature in the aristocratic countenance of the proposed Constitution." Making vassals of the poor "has ever been the favorite offspring of Aristocracy." This barb was aimed at the four men from South Carolina, for all were planters, and Charleston's planters were famous for their aristocratic airs. But Morris didn't stop there. The northern states, which had to sacrifice "every impulse of right . . . every impulse of humanity" to allow slavery in the first place, now, under the Constitution, would be obliged to defend the patrician, undemocratic southern states that were enfeebled by so many degraded and disgruntled laborers. It would be northern money and northern soldiers who would defend Georgia and South Carolina from Spain or England, should those powers see fit to invade the weak, southern flank of the United States. And if the slaves themselves ever rebelled, the southern gentlemen would turn to northern soldiers for relief.

On this point Morris echoed Massachusetts's Rufus King, who moments before had pointed out the irony of representing the slaves in Congress while simultaneously preventing Congress from taxing the rice and indigo that those slaves produced. As the Revolution had demonstrated, South Carolina and Georgia did not have enough white men to protect themselves. And now that ties to the mother country had been severed, it would have to be Pennsylvanians and New Yorkers who saved white South Carolinians and Georgians from their intestine enemy. South Carolina could import "fresh supplies of wretched Africans," which would "increase the danger of attack, and the difficulty of defence." Yet Congress could not tax the southern economy to pay for such protection, and so the northern states not only would supply the troops but also pay them! In essence, South Carolina and Georgia were choosing to pursue an aristocratic way of life that they could not sustain on their own, and the draft of the new constitution demanded that the free states subsidize this unnatural, undemocratic arrangement. "There was so much unreasonableness in all this," King pointed out, "that the people of the N(orthern) States could never be reconciled (to it)."

Laced through this speech was the rabid detestation of slavery kindled in many patriots during the Revolutionary era, the abhorrence felt by men like John Laurens. After King spoke, Roger Sherman of Connecticut agreed that "the slave-trade [was] iniquitous," voicing the views of other delegates, such as Benjamin Franklin. But no one expected anything like Morris's wrath and candor. "Domestic slavery," Morris asserted, "was the curse of heaven on the States where it prevailed. . . . [T]he moment you leave" a free state to enter a slave state, he explained, "the effects of the institution become visible." Start in New England or Pennsylvania, settled by free whites, where "every criterion of superior improvement" is on display, and "proceed Southw[ar]dly, & every step you take thro' [th]e great regions of slaves, presents a desert increasing with [th]e increasing proportion of these wretched beings." Morris hardly paused to allow the words to sink in before he thundered on: "Are [the slaves] men?" If so, "then make them Citizens & let them vote[.]" If you insist that slaves are property, he challenged the South Carolinians, then why should they be represented in Congress when "no other property," such as the valuable real estate in Philadelphia, was represented? It was shameful, he concluded, to "saddle posterity with such a Constitution." Morris proposed that only free inhabitants were to be represented in Congress, and Jonathan Dayton of New Jersey, eager that "his sentiments on [slavery] might appear whatever might be the fate of the amendment[,]" seconded the motion.[3]

Fifty-five men were credentialed to participate and vote in the convention. Most of them shared the sentiments of New Jersey's Jonathan Dayton. Almost certainly, the majority of the state delegations disliked slavery and found it inimical to American republicanism. Everyone knew it was evil. They knew it violated the basic principles articulated in the Declaration of Independence. Gouverneur Morris was more vehement and less decorous in his expressions, but essentially he spoke for a solid majority. And yet, the leader of South Carolina's delegation, John Rutledge, listened to the jeremiad complacently and untroubled, confident that he could bend the Constitution to his will.

Rutledge was the master of backroom deals. Legislators were not swayed by speeches but behind the scenes, over drinks, under the fog of tobacco smoke, and it was a poor politician who relied on his oratory on the floor of the convention. This well-bred Charlestonian jurist was slight, unobtrusive, undistinguished as a physical specimen, except in his red hair, which, before he became an exalted judge and politician, was long enough to be tied behind in a ponytail, a slight vain extravagance in his refined deportment. He was mid-height, three or four inches under six feet, and his face housed a high-bridged nose with arched nostrils, small flattened ears, a square chin, nothing too handsome nor too ugly, easily lost in a crowd. Only the eyes struck one with anything of his "quick Apprehension, sound Judgment [and] much sagacity." John Adams, who often opposed the more conservative Rutledge, dissented from this picture, seeing no "Keenness in his Eye. No depth in his countenance." But most people thought his eyes his most striking feature, "blue-gray—sharpshooter's eyes." He exhibited a type of eloquence, though it was neither his rapid-fire manner of speech nor his voice that stayed with someone. It was the force of argument, the inescapable logic of his reasoning.[4]

He might have had sharpshooter's eyes, but he was no sharpshooter. He did not know how to shoot a gun or shake a saber, an unusual lapse for a young man of great wealth raised in the militaristic and debonair Carolina Lowcountry, where a gentleman would expect to fight at least a couple of duels in his life. His uncle Andrew came to Charles Town in 1730, gleaming with the glamour that a degree from Dublin's Trinity College reflected in the colonial town. He was lawyer to one of the province's richest men, Colonel Hugh Hext, who conveniently died, leaving a widow to be wooed by the Irishman. But it turned out that Hext had left his fortune to his daughter, who was then only nine years old, so the new stepfather sent for his brother John, a doctor, who hurried to America where he stood first in line to marry the nine-year-old girl, which he did when she turned fourteen. He swore fidelity to her in the picturesque Christ Church, under the live oaks abutting the northern coast road, acquiring not only the girl but two houses in town and two plantations east of the Cooper River.[5]

Dr. John Rutledge is best remembered for inventing Officers' Punch, a drink "composed of cognac and East Indian aperitif, with a touch of spice." When he died he left a gap in the long phalanx of planter-class partiers. His heirs inherited over a hundred slaves, three plantations, and a mountain of debt, for Dr. Rutledge ate and drank and gave away more than his slaves made in rice and indigo.[6]

Uncle Andrew took command of his brother's oldest son, John, who was eleven, and began grooming him for the bar. John's play consisted of mock court, and he strutted the roles of prosecuting and defending barrister. He learned the classics. His mother scraped up enough credit to send him to England, where he was admitted to the Middle Temple; he was called to the English bar in 1760, returned to Charleston in January 1761 at the age of twenty-one, and, upon discovering the shocking truth of the family's finances, he hung out his shingle from a little room on the corner of Broad and Church Streets. His first client was Henry Laurens. Debt collection was the main business of the twenty or so lawyers who constituted the Charleston bar, and Rutledge excelled in it. At least in the early 1760s, while he put his mother's plantations back onto a businesslike footing, the family's main source of reliable income was his law practice, which blossomed quickly, a result of his sharp mind and his carefully prepared, persuasive speech. In the courtroom, his logic was perfect even if he spoke far too quickly.[7]

Breaking with genteel tradition that promoted a false air of indifference, Rutledge campaigned for a seat in the legislature, riding to all of the plantations in Christ Church parish, a long tongue of land between the inland swamps and ocean marshes just north of Charleston, canvassing for one of the two seats his uncle and his father had occupied in the 1740s. Though the district was six miles wide and twenty-six miles long, he only had to convince a few hundred voters. Property and other restrictions rendered elections in South Carolina a fairly friendly and neighborly affair among the landed gentry. The entire colony was divided into parishes, all but one of which touched the Atlantic coast, and these parishes each elected representatives to the Commons, forty-eight in all. The polling places were located along the coast in order to disenfranchise the Upcountry pioneers, and so the interests of the big planters dominated the legislature. It was entirely natural in South Carolina politics that John Rutledge should, essentially, inherit the family seat in the Commons House. The only remarkable thing was how early he laid claim to his inheritance.[8]

By the 1770s, the Rutledges were extremely wealthy, with the requisite plantations and city mansions and carriages and, of course, slaves, who generally constituted the largest capital investments of such families. Rutledge's showcase plantation, his country residence near Charleston, was called Stono, situated on the tidal marshes south of town almost on the spot where the Stono Rebellion began. But like Henry Laurens, he was really a city man, and most of the property he bought was in town, including a number of adjoining lots on Broad Street that became the site of the brick and slate-roofed mansion he lived in.[9]

Rutledge's national service began with the Stamp Act Congress in 1765, when he chaired a committee petitioning the House of Lords to defeat the odious tax. He was just twenty-six years old. Ten years later, during the Revolution, John attended the Continental Congress for two sessions until he came back to Charles Town to serve as president of South Carolina, an office he held until 1778. He was elected governor under a new state constitution in 1779, and, when the British laid siege to Charles Town in 1780, the legislature, knowing it was about to go on the run, gave Rutledge dictatorial powers. After the capital fell, he led the exiled government from the hinterland.

After the Revolution, Rutledge was not so rich. His plantations had been ruined by the war, and he did little to restore them. Nor did he resume his private law practice. Others, including his brother, Edward, made fortunes untangling the issues of property ownership that the war had complicated. Instead, John took the highest judicial seat in South Carolina, chief justice of the Court of Chancery, the supreme court of the land, and probably he was more gratified by his noble title, chancellor, than the $2,500 salary. Apparently, John and his wife, Elizabeth Grimké, used the disruptions of the Revolution as an opportunity to diminish their own connections to slavery, to the point of having no great personal stake in its continuance. No cache of his personal letters remains to reveal his own conscience, but we know that before the Revolution Rutledge "personally owned around sixty" slaves; in 1787, that number had fallen to twenty-eight; and when he died at the dawn of the next century, he owned one.[10]

Nevertheless, he was bred to Charleston's oligarchy of planters, merchants, and lawyers, who all made their money from the rice and indigo trade. The war had pushed that plantation system and the old and elegant class it supported to the edge of a cliff. Long after Cornwallis surrendered in Virginia, the British clung to their southern toehold in Charles Town, and most of the state's loyalists, refugees, and escaped slaves, unsure what their fate would be, crowded into the sanctuary of the peninsula, elbow to elbow with the soldiers who barely ventured beyond the battlements. Not until one day in October 1782, more than a year after Yorktown, did forty ships take advantage of an offshore wind and ebbing tide to ride over the bar. The fattened flanks of those vessels rode low in the water for they carried most of the British soldiers, thirty-seven hundred loyalist civilians, five thousand liberated slaves, and tons of stolen goods, including the bell from the tower of St. Michael's Church. The Continental army, encamped across the Ashley River, occupying the same ground from which the British had begun their siege two years earlier, monitored the parade of ships and eyed the depleted defenses of the city. In mid-December, the skeleton garrison of redcoats embarked from Gadsden's Wharf, like partiers slipping out in the predawn, leaving behind the quiet, littered streets that awaited sunlight and the Americans. Almost right away, the triumphant Carolinians changed the name from *Charles Town*, which smelt too much like the British crown, to the modern *Charleston*, a spelling that reflected the soft taste of the second syllable, like the vapor of wine, savored in the mouths of locals. Reclaiming homes long occupied and looted by the enemy is a messy business. Many Patriots owed money to Loyalists who had fled the city—would they have to repay them? Patriots were aggrieved that their property was plundered, from the fine wines and silver and the slaves of spacious mansions to the petty thefts suffered by the lower classes. Would they be compensated?

What reparations could they expect from the hated British and from American collaborators? The sorting out was convoluted, and it was made more so by the mood of revenge.

Among those negotiating the British withdrawal was John Rutledge's brother, Edward. The state's yeomen farmers and Charleston's white mechanics and artisans were shocked at the forgiving terms he allowed the British, especially the government's commitment to uphold the claims of English creditors. Debt would become the great social problem of the 1780s, and it worsened the divide between the aristocratic planters and the state's more humble citizens. The old elites—planters, merchants, and lawyers—wanted to prop up the credit system, and the best way to do that was to get the economy back to where it was before the war. Merchants wanted to sell slaves and luxury goods, and planters wanted to buy them, but they had no money. Credit could only come from England, and if South Carolina's courts allowed debtors to default on old loans, or if the legislature devalued those debts by issuing inflationary paper money, the British would withhold their credit and the whole plantation system would collapse. That is exactly what the nonelites wanted—to reboot the economy, forgiving old debts and starting again on terms that served the little man rather than the highly capitalized factory farms owned by planters.[11]

The war had ripened times for a wholesale change in the economy. Even before hostilities began, the Continental embargo compelled South Carolina to suspend the slave trade, and for the duration, from 1774 to 1782, practically no slaves were imported anywhere in the United States. Two-thirds of Georgia's slaves escaped or died during the war—about ten thousand. In South Carolina, about a fifth of the slaves, twenty-five thousand people, disappeared—many on British ships.[12] Even as late as 1790, when the new nation conducted its first census, whites outnumbered blacks in South Carolina by a considerable margin, almost three to two, and in 1782 the white majority would have been even higher. The war had set in motion the demographic reversal that South Carolina had tried and failed to manufacture after the Stono Rebellion fifty years earlier. In most of the country, the war's disruptions broke the habit, so to speak, of slave labor. The New England states abolished slavery just after the war, while the middle states abolished the foreign slave trade. Manumission, encouraged even as far south as Virginia, initiated an almost irresistible trend toward emancipation.

But Charleston's planters wanted slaves, so to the disgust of the rest of the country, South Carolina reopened the slave trade, and in the first year after the British evacuated Charleston, merchants imported and sold almost six thousand slaves, buying them on credit with interest rates as high as 50 percent. But the crops partially failed in 1784 and then again in 1785, producing a staggering deficit in trade. In 1784, for example, exports amounted to £400,000, while planters, for whom "the sight of a negroe yard was too great a temptation . . . to withstand," squandered nearly all of that money on new slaves; add to that expense the importation of necessities not manufactured in the state as well as the furniture, plates, and wines that Charleston's elites always bought, and South Carolina found itself in a precarious position.[13]

Democrats rose in Charleston, men who thought the Revolution was not just about which flag flew over the statehouse, and they challenged the prewar oligarchy of planters, merchants, and lawyers. In the first postwar election, two of thirteen wards were won by the democrats. The old oligarchy still controlled eleven wards and the new office of intendant or mayor, which was held by the lawyer and planter Richard Hutson, nicknamed Richard I by the pro-democratic faction. This faction's main organization was the Marine Anti-Britannic Society, whose name advertised its equating of the old oligarchy with Toryism, no matter the manifest patriotism of planters like John Rutledge, Henry Laurens, and Charles Cotesworth Pinckney. The friction nearly erupted in riots, as radicals demanded equality, refusing (as one planter snidely put it) "to fall back into ranks" after the war. The establishment maintained order with an iron fist and a new police force, whose clear purpose was to protect the rich from the poor. The climax came in the summer of 1784, when acid campaigns led to the reelection of the oligarchy: Hutson was reelected over Alexander Gillon (387 votes to 260), and the embittered and aggrieved opposition accurately claimed that "a few ambitious, avaricious, and designing families" snaked their way into power. That fewer than seven hundred people cast a ballot indicates how good South Carolina's conservatives were at suppressing votes.[14]

Before the Revolution, half a dozen families—the Rutledges, Pinckneys, Middletons, Draytons, and Gadsdens, for instance—dominated politics. Add ten or fifteen more names, and we would describe the entire ruling class of the colony. While petty squabbles and idiosyncratic loyalties divided this clique on particular issues, ideologically they comprised a solid wall of opinion. They bound themselves together through marriage. John Rutledge married the sister of James Grimké, one of John's friends at the Middle Temple in London, whose household in Charleston was "more of a home to John than [his mother's] Tradd Street house."[15] (This Grimké was the brother of John Faucheraud, against whom Henry Laurens had fought a duel.) Edward Rutledge married Henrietta Middleton, sister of Arthur Middleton, a signer of the Declaration of Independence. Charles Cotesworth Pinckney married Henrietta's sister, Sarah, and a third Middleton married Charles Drayton, brother of William Henry Drayton, a delegate to the Continental Congress. After the Revolution, young Charles Pinckney married Henry Laurens's daughter, Mary Eleanor, called Polly. A more incestuous cast of characters can hardly be imagined, and most historians agree that for thirty or forty years South Carolina was more or less ruled by a dynasty of Rutledges and Pinckneys.

In the minds of the oligarchy, prosperity meant owning half a dozen plantations, most of them in remote locations as far away as Georgia, little more than slave-labor camps that produced cash crops in abundance. After the Revolution, with their big houses fleeced by the British, many of their slaves liberated, and their farms neglected and overgrown, these planters eagerly sought to reproduce the world they knew before the war. They bought up wasteland that they hoped to develop with the labor of slaves, whom they bought on credit that was itself secured by the expectation of a return to the old economy. Charles Cotesworth Pinckney partnered with Edward Rutledge to buy two plantations that the state had confiscated from Tories; in partnership with Charles Drayton, he bought thousands of acres of swampland he hoped to reclaim for rice farms. The Pinckneys and Rutledges invested in the Santee Canal Company, hoping to open the Carolina Upcountry to the large-production, cash-crop farming that dominated the Low-country.[16] No matter the paternalistic attitude these men might adopt in their Charleston mansions (served by perhaps twenty slaves) or their showcase country homes near town: in reality most of their slaves worked on plantations remote from the city and under regimes that showed less humanity than a factory. Charleston's elite planters pursued an enterprise that was ruthlessly capitalistic, and they protected slavery so energetically in order to spread this industrial-type farming. They were true "robber barons," for the labor they stole sustained their aristocracy. They knew well that they were thieves. The young planters whom John Laurens hung out with threw up rationalizations like inexpert palisades until, pressed hard by logic, they burst out in exasperated candor: *Without slavery how could they be rich?* The planters did not want a state populated with a vast, more or less egalitarian society of small farmers on the New England model, nor did they look kindly upon the democratizing force of manufacturing that might have flourished in Charleston. Charles Cotesworth Pinckney was reported to have said that "as long as there was a single acre of swampland in South Carolina," he would work for the further importation of slaves, and this attitude, this support for gigantically capitalized farming, should be taken as typical of the rice and indigo barons of South Carolina.

The democrats were no particular friends to African Americans either, as an anecdote involving John Rutledge illustrates. The chancellor, being a second-generation immigrant from Ireland, belonged to the Sons of St. Patrick, which held its annual dinner on the saint's day in Thompson's City Tavern. In 1784, Rutledge found himself too ill to attend the dinner, so he sent a slave woman from his Broad Street home down to the tavern to deliver his regrets. The woman returned with the note still in hand, undelivered, complaining that William Thompson, the innkeeper and democratic activist, would not receive it. Outraged, Rutledge demanded an explanation; Thompson claimed the woman had been insolent and had asked not to deliver a note but to climb to the tavern's roof to watch a public celebration. Rutledge said he would believe his slave's version of events before he would believe Thompson's, an insult calculated to enrage Thompson, who thought the chancellor was acting like a "Lordling" talking down to "his wretched Vassal." Thompson boldly wrote a letter demanding an apology from Rutledge, an escalation that might have ended in a duel, except that planters would not so condescend to fight keepers of taverns. Rutledge invoked the privileges given to members of the state's House of Representatives, which was then in session. Rutledge's younger brother, Hugh, who was Speaker of the House, referred the matter to a committee chaired by Charles Cotesworth Pinckney, another lawyer and planter, who reported in Rutledge's favor. Thompson was made to apologize to the House (which had been vicariously insulted) but would not bring himself to apologize to Rutledge personally, and so they threw him in jail until the legislative session ended.[17]

The whole affair illustrates how the two main white political factions related to blacks. Rutledge acted as the paternal planter, treating his slave as an extension of his own household. Because the woman belonged to him, she demanded a high degree of respect from someone of Thompson's lowly station. Thompson and his inn were allied with the Anti-Britannic Society and all those hoping to demolish South Carolina's aristocracy. He resented how Rutledge demanded that he show deference and was damned if he was going to give any to a black woman, no matter who owned her. His leveling principles did not enlighten him to his brotherhood with most of South Carolina's working class, the black slaves. Thus the paternalistic Rutledge could tell himself that he treated blacks far better than his political rivals did, despite the fact that the rise of democrats would have weakened the plantation system and therefore benefited the slaves.

Whenever the slave trade became a flash point in South Carolina politics, gaps appeared in the phalanx of planters, shifting the balance of power. For example, Ralph Izard, perhaps the richest planter in Charleston, moved that the legislature stop importing slaves for three years. For many planters, suspending the slave trade was nothing but a temporary expediency, but always underlying such debates were the moral arguments against slavery. Everyone recognized that the key to solving the problem of slavery was to reduce the proportion of slaves in relation to the free population. South Carolinians knew this back in the 1740s, when they closed the trade and simultaneously subsidized the immigration of white Europeans. After the Revolution, northern slave states were able to emancipate their slaves because they had so few blacks compared to whites. A similar process was at work in the mid-Atlantic states, where the numbers of free citizens steadily increased in proportion to the slaves. If the slave trade had been closed in 1787, it would have triggered the inexorable, eventual demise of slavery, and many South Carolinians interpreted the debate this way, no matter the transient economic expediencies. Henry Laurens, for instance, believed that if he could only "prevail upon my fellow Citizens to prohibit further importation [of slaves], I should deem it progress equal to carrying all the outworks . . . and time will work manumission or a state equal to it."[18]

A small, potentially influential group of Charleston's elites dissented from slavery in the 1780s. After John Laurens was killed, the group circled round Dr. David Ramsay, a transplant from Pennsylvania and close friend of Pennsylvania's Benjamin Rush. We've already seen how Ramsay, while on the Privy Council and then at the Jacksonboro Congress, championed John Laurens's plan to arm and then emancipate three thousand African Americans during the Revolutionary War, which would have tripled the number of free people of color in South Carolina. About fifteen legislators supported that measure, including another privy councillor, Thomas Ferguson. "All mankind," Ramsay once told Thomas Jefferson, "is originally the same," no matter the apparent differences among the races. Ramsay's view derived from John Locke's *An Essay Concerning Human Understanding*, which offered to the world the famous Enlightenment idea that we are all born as blank slates and that the world of sensation that we grow up in writes upon our tablets. In other words, it was only "accidental circumstances" that diversified the races of men. Change the circumstances of life for American slaves, Ramsay told the less progressive Jefferson, and, given time, they will be equal to whites. During the war, this kind of reasoning led Ramsay to the radical conclusion that slaves running away from their plantations to the British was "the smallest of evils. . . . [I]t appears to me that we have no more right to make property of them than the enemy." Besides, "reducing their numbers would make room for white people," he told Benjamin Rush back in 1779. "To speak as a Christian," he candidly admitted, "I really fear some heavy judgment awaits us."[19]

We do not know how many men in Charleston subscribed to this view of the races, which followed on the logic of paternalism. Some men, such as William Henry Drayton, who also supported Laurens's black regiment, might have done so largely out of military expediency, just as others in 1785 might have supported the ban on importing slaves for economic reasons. But we know that at least some influential Charlestonians agreed with Ramsay. John Laurens had pressed the exact same Enlightenment ideas on his father, whose letters indicate that South Carolina's most influential national politician agreed. John Rutledge's biographer suggests that even he secretly recognized the inhumanity of slavery, though that argument seems to be based more on wishful thinking than on solid evidence. We do know that a number of Charlestonians who had studied at Princeton were strongly antislavery. Ramsay was the most prominent of these, but they also included Lewis Morris, son of one of New York's signers of the Declaration of Independence and nephew of Gouverneur Morris. Timothy Ford was another. These Princetonians worshipped together at the Independent Church in Charleston, so Ramsay's declaration that Christianity was incompatible with slavery might have followed some conversations among that church's congregants. Surprisingly, the old regime's candidate for mayor, Richard Hutson, who was another Princeton graduate and close friend of Ramsay's, also worshipped at the Independent Church, though we have no evidence that Hutson shared the antislavery views of his friends.[20]

Though this liberal enclave came from within Charleston's elite, it accepted and even promoted some democratic reforms, such as moving the state's capital away from the coast to the center of the state. But the louder cries for democratic reform frightened even these progressives. Christopher Gadsden, Henry Laurens's old friend who during the years leading up to the Revolution led the radical, liberty-loving mechanics, found the new political element too disruptive, and so he closed ranks with his fellow planters and merchants. Politics makes strange bedfellows indeed, and in the years after the Revolution, the Princeton men who were sympathetic and even committed to reforming slave society found themselves most at home among Charleston's planters, merchants, and lawyers. They often married into the oligarchy. Ramsay, for example, married Sabina Ellis, daughter of a wealthy Charleston merchant, in 1775, which made him rich enough to join the Privy Council in 1778, which was open only to men who possessed more than £10,000 free of debt.

Ramsay and Sabina settled into a Broad Street house, which made him neighbors with John Rutledge. Sabina died a year after they married, and Ramsay remained a bachelor throughout the Revolution, not marrying again until the spring of 1783, when a northern woman, Frances Witherspoon, a twenty-four-year old ten years his junior, charmed him during one of his stints in Congress, which was then meeting in Philadelphia. Frances was the daughter of Princeton's president, John Witherspoon, who shared the antislavery sentiments of that school's students. When Frances died, Ramsay married Martha Laurens, Henry's daughter and John's sister, which made him brother-in-law to Charles Pinckney, his fellow congressman. A small world indeed.[21]

In the 1784 election of state assemblymen Ramsay's 427 votes put him third among candidates representing the prestigious Charleston parishes of St. Michael's and St. Philip's, behind Henry Laurens but ahead of Charles Cotesworth Pinckney, Thomas Pinckney, and Edward Rutledge. When Ramsay spoke in favor of banning the slave trade in the legislative debates of 1785, his moral opposition to slavery would have been well-known to most South Carolinians, who at least paid lip service to that view.

Even General Pinckney, who became the spokesman for the old plantation system, did not defend the morality of slavery. He candidly confessed that he was motivated by money. South Carolina, Pinckney argued, could not support small white farmers. The land "was not capable of being cultivated by white men." Only black slaves could transform the "unhealthy" swamps of South Carolina into farms, which in turn would improve "the salubrity of the air."[22]

Surprisingly, Edward Rutledge, who had strongly opposed the black regiment in 1782, joined Ramsay in trying to ban the slave trade, championing the cause in the House with "an animated speech for the proposition." A hundred South Carolinians joined him by signing a petition to ban the slave trade, which was delivered to the House. The democrat Alexander Gillon argued that the ban should go into effect immediately rather than at the first of the new year, as the bill under debate provided, because a thousand more slaves could be imported from the West Indies in the months between passage of the bill and its enactment on January 1. On October 1, the ban barely failed by a vote of 47 in favor and 51 against.[23]

That was on a Saturday. On Sunday, four members of the legislature who were known to be opposed to the slave trade had arrived in town too late to participate in Saturday's debate and vote for the ban.[24] By Monday morning, more petitions from the interior arrived in Charleston, demanding a ban on slave importations. Despite General Pinckney's petulant objections, the House agreed to reopen the issue the following Thursday.[25]

On October 14, Edward Rutledge again took the floor of the legislature. "He was induced still to persevere," the *Gazette* reported, "not only from a hope that many gentlemen [who had voted against the ban] had altered their sentiments, but from . . . something in his constitution that powerfully stimulated him to persevere to the utmost in accomplishing any measure that had an obvious tendency to promote the public good." A reasonable consideration of the issue demanded that South Carolina suspend the "destructive importation" of slaves. He asked the members of the House to "view our present calamitous situation—our people generally discontent and clamorous—our resources for trade almost exhausted—loaded with a large foreign and domestic debt,—the government in a great measure at a stand—the streams of public justice stopped in their course, and the Majesty of our laws trampled under foot." What caused these calamities? A "burdensome debt" incurred to satisfy an "improvident weakness"—the Lowcountry's addiction to slaves. Edward Rutledge hoped that South Carolinians would not slip from "ruin to perdition, but unite as one man to effectuate the political salvation of their unhappy country." He disputed Pinckney's claim that only slaves could till the soil in South Carolina. The state was a healthy place if only its population would drink less alcohol. He spoke of slaves as another vice of luxury, like alcohol—less inebriating but just as addictive. Republican manliness demanded greater self-control and self-reliance.

Edward Rutledge should not be thought a great friend of the slaves. It should be noted that he wanted to suspend the slave trade lest the "people . . . pressed by their necessities . . . became refactory, and finally might be disposed to lay aside all subordination."[26] In other words, he worried that unless the legislature adopted progressive reforms like an end to the slave trade, the people would get so frustrated with a government that favored planters' interests that finally they would overthrow it. He feared a revolution that could lead to "a general distribution of property." He considered pervasive slavery to be a weakness, even a disease, that made republican society susceptible to leveling revolts.[27]

Feebly and defensively, Mr. Pringle rebutted Rutledge's moral argument: both the Romans and the Greeks used slaves. Why shouldn't Americans? David Ramsay rebutted Pringle, speaking at length in support of banning the slave trade—but strategically avoiding morality and relying instead entirely on economic reasons. After Ramsay, Judge Pendleton spoke about how slavery corrupted the white population of the state, and he suggested that the legislature take the opportunity that this economic crisis presented to dissolve the pre-Revolutionary plantation economy. "Gentlemen had argued," Pendleton began, "as if this country was every where a low swamp; this was not the case; the beautiful part of the state was the upper country, where negroes were scarce; whoever rode throughout it, must recollect with pleasure those beautiful scenes, in which nature aided by art, is always renewing her variegated appearance: he must remember [the] chearful, healthy appearance of the people, their well stocked farms, cultivated fields, . . . and their unremitting industry in improving their possessions. It was here," he argued, on the small farms free of slavery, that "true happiness might be justly said to exist, rather than in gratifying pernicious propensities after luxuries which disturb our repose, and cause a feverish anxiety, ever thirsting, and never satisfied: Let us rather imitate the simple and innocent manners of our ancestors, who were content in enjoying the hereditary blessings of providence, which are most congenial and conducive to health, peace, innocence and virtue."

Pendleton was mistaken about the "manners of our ancestors," for planters had indulged in slaves since 1700. His Edenic fantasy of free-labor farms looked a lot like Pennsylvania and other northern states, a comparison not lost on the many, many Carolinians who had seen the North during the war. Even as late as 1808, David Ramsay was envisioning this kind of a slave-free society settling the empty lands of South Carolina. The rise of cotton, Ramsay thought, would provide an alternative to the plantation system. Rice and indigo, he rightly pointed out, "required large capitals," because, in his assessment, "they could not be raised to any considerable purpose but by negroes." But cotton could be raised on smaller holdings worked by individual families, and so it might fill "the country with an independent, industrious yeomanry."[28]

When General Pinckney rose, as he inevitably did, to oppose banning the slave trade, the gallery clamored so loudly that the *Gazette* reporter could not hear what was said. In the end, Pinckney prevailed, and the ban failed again. The ban would have to wait another year and a half, at which time David Ramsay joked on the floor of the House "that every man [who] went to church last Sunday, and said his prayers, was bound by a spiritual obligation to refuse the importation of slaves. They had devoutly prayed not be led into temptation, and negroes were a temptation too great to be resisted." Not so hidden behind his jocular manner was the serious conviction that slavery was a symptom of a sick society. This time the ban prevailed, 74 for and 56 against.[29]

Thomas Jefferson congratulated Rutledge "on the laws of your state for suspending the importation of slaves, and for the glory you have justly acquired by endeavoring to prevent it for ever." "This abomination must have an end," Jefferson continued, "and there is a superior bench reserved in heaven for those who hasten it." This is a tantalizing letter. We do not know much about the inner mind of either Edward Rutledge or his brother John. Unlike so many other Founding Fathers, neither left great caches of letters. We have little evidence that suggests Edward shared the progressive, Enlightenment ideas of race we find in John Laurens and David Ramsay, or even the racist though antislavery thought of Jefferson. Back in 1782, it was Edward Rutledge who led the opposition to Laurens's plan to raise a black regiment. In 1775 he went so far as to introduce legislation in Congress that would have required George Washington "to discharge all the Negroes as well slaves as freemen in his Army." Even so, one historian believed that, twelve years later, his friendship with Jefferson had so moderated his views that, even if he still believed in slavery and white supremacy, Edward Rutledge at least recognized that the slave trade was evil.[30]

But neither Edward Rutledge nor David Ramsay represented South Carolina at the Constitutional Convention, nor did any of the democrats, like Alexander Gillon. The state legislature convened in March 1787 and elected another Pinckney—Thomas—to be governor, and he presided over the discussion about whom South Carolina should send to Philadelphia. "You are proposed by many," David Ramsay reported hopefully to Henry Laurens, but the old man had just recovered from one of his periodic attacks of gout, so he declined the honor when it was offered in March, and the legislature settled on just four delegates: John Rutledge (who was then chief justice), General Charles Cotesworth Pinckney (the governor's brother), Charles Pinckney (the general's cousin), and Pierce Butler (a superfluous son of an Irish baronet who had married into the Middleton family). This group was far more homogeneous even than the typical South Carolina delegation to Congress. Of course they were "men of wealth . . . chosen by men of wealth," since the very rich controlled the legislature.[31] All were planters; the three who really mattered, John Rutledge and the two Pinckneys, were lawyers as well. Most significantly, they were part of the minority in the House (which itself was an elite minority of South Carolina's citizens) who wanted to preserve the slave trade.

The Pinckneys' background mirrored the Rutledges'. Their progenitor, Thomas Pinckney, came to the colony in 1692 as a privateer or, as some evidence suggests, as a pirate, but being rumored to be a pirate did not ruin one's reputation in the seventeenth century. Thomas married well, used his stash and dowry to set up as a merchant, flourished, and within a few years bought a plantation on the Neck. He had three sons, Thomas (a ship's captain), Charles (a lawyer), and William (a merchant). Charles was the first native-born South Carolinian to study law in London, and he made the most of this advantage, landing a succession of public jobs, both elected and appointed, beginning with the South Carolina House of Commons in 1731. He bought an island on Port Royal Sound far south of Charleston, whence he received as an absentee owner status and yet more riches. By 1740 he was Speaker of the House, and he was among those enlightened legislators who discouraged the importation of slaves by encouraging the immigration of poor whites. He adopted his young nephew, also named Charles, and Uncle Charles sent the nephew to England to study, just a year before the birth of a natural son, whom he again called Charles, exasperating historians who need to keep them all straight. While this third Charles, whose middle name was Cotesworth, was growing up, his father pursued a succession of government appointments in England, almost up to his death in 1758. As a result, Charles Cotesworth lived in the mother country from the age of seven to twenty-three.[32]

The nephew Charles Pinckney eventually became one of the leading lawyers in South Carolina, and, though a reluctant convert to rebellion, he served the Revolution in a number of posts, including membership on the Privy Council that turned down John Laurens's plan to arm slaves in 1779. He was also a planter, the proprietor of the pleasant Snee Farm plantation just north of the city. His son, the fourth Charles Pinckney, demonstrated the family genius for law, though he studied in Charleston rather than England because he came of age during the rising tensions between the two countries.[33] The youngest Charles was barely twenty years old when he was elected to represent South Carolina in the Continental Congress in 1777.

The first Charles died in 1758. His natural son, Charles Cotesworth, who returned to Charleston in 1769, served on the Council of Safety with Henry Laurens in 1775, secured a commission in the Continental army, fought in many battles, and quickly rose to the rank of colonel, commanding the First South Carolina Regiment and Fort Moultrie at the time of its surrender in 1782. The soldier's life suited him. Though a lawyer, he was an outdoorsman who loved the hard life of the circuit when he was attorney general for the Camden,

Georgetown, and Cheraw districts. "Broad shouldered" and "inclined to stoutness," his biographer describes him, with a personality to fit: given to laughter, unruffled by off-color jokes, and a good teller of stories, his wide mouth and bushy eyebrows made him a friendly companion at dinner, and after dinner he was a brilliant intellect and conversationalist.[34]

The second Charles, the father of our young delegate, mortified his family by swearing loyalty to the crown when the British occupied Charles Town. This betrayal imperiled the Pinckney estate because the Jacksonboro Congress threatened to confiscate it in retribution. Cousin Charles Cotesworth, who was then a senior officer in the Continental army and a member of the assembly, tried to mitigate the penalty. By this time the youngest Charles, released from a prison ship in Charles Town Harbor at the war's end, was lingering in Philadelphia. Charles Cotesworth urged him to come home. It tells us something of the fourth Charles's immaturity that rather than defend his family's reputation and property in Charles Town, he sowed his "wild oats" in Philadelphia and planned a grand trip to Europe, as if all the events of the Revolution had merely interrupted a wealthy rake's progress, which he was eager to resume.[35] In a great stroke of luck to his fortunes, his father died in 1783, obviating the state's need to punish the estate. This self-serving attitude characterized the youngest Charles Pinckney all his life, and he wanted to use the Constitutional Convention as much to cement his own reputation as the wunderkind of the Founding Fathers as to improve the country. Historians do generally credit young Pinckney with initiating the impulse among congressmen for convening a special national assembly to rewrite the Articles of Confederation. But the history of the convention, mostly written through the hand of Madison, slandered Charles Pinckney—probably because he was an ass. On that point most of his contemporaries agree, from George Washington through his fellows on the South Carolina delegation. He was demonstrably vain; he womanized; he lied about his age so people would think he was the youngest delegate at the convention. When the South Carolina legislature designated its four representatives, young Charles desperately wanted to lead the delegation.[36]

But that honor was given instead to John Rutledge, who invited the other designees to dinner at his Broad Street mansion. After a sumptuous meal they settled down to business in the library, lounging under the stern spines of hundreds of law books. All four men were nationalists. States rights advocates like Rawlins Lowndes were outliers in South Carolina, and the Rutledges and Pinckneys, like most planters, were devoted to the new nationalism spreading across the continent. In addition to the emotional ties forged in war, they understood the absurdity of South Carolina opting out of the national enterprise. This is not to say that they did not see the danger of a powerful central government, and John Rutledge meant to instruct his fellow delegates about that threat. Given the tenor of the times, a powerful national government might undermine the plantation system of slavery upon which Charleston's wealth and society were founded. Charles Pinckney understood this as well as anyone. Under the weak Articles of Confederation, Thomas Jefferson had proposed banning slavery in the western territories into which the young nation was already expanding. Charles Pinckney defeated that measure, but the episode must have made it clear to him how precarious slavery was in the national scheme of things. Emancipation fever already was advancing down the coast from New England. Even mid-Atlantic states like Virginia expressed open hostility to slave labor. If they were going to preserve the old regime in South Carolina, the delegation had to prevent anything that would promote liberalizing the laws governing slavery. Even in the hurly-burly of local politics, protecting their narrow interests had proven relatively hard: witness the ban on the slave trade. Philadelphia would be more perilous. There, the pro-slavery faction would be tiny. Really only the three southernmost states, Georgia, South Carolina, and North Carolina, had a vested interest in promoting the health of slavery. All others wanted to see its decline, and many wanted to hurry that decline along. How could these four men from Charleston leverage their influence to protect slavery while still forging a strong national government?

Through the library windows the four delegates could see the evening light settle on "the rose-covered brick wall and, next door, the big yard covered with magnolia petals," while inside John Rutledge hatched a plot expressed with the suavity of the serpent in the Garden of Eden. It is easy to imagine a different course had South Carolina's convention delegation reflected the slight liberal majority in its own legislature. Had a man like Alexander Gillon, who represented the white working class or "mechanics," or a progressive thinker like David Ramsay gone to Philadelphia, the primary purpose of the delegates would not have been to protect the narrow interests of planters. Had John Laurens lived to influence his father, surely Henry Laurens would have gone to Philadelphia no matter his gout, and we know that Henry was susceptible to the moral suasion of northern delegates. Had South Carolina's delegation exhibited any interest in weaning the state from the antidemocratic, aristocratic status quo, they would have allowed certain changes in the national law—incremental changes well short of emancipation but definitely putting society on the road toward it. But the assembly had chosen John Rutledge and the Pinckneys, and John Rutledge was the most cunning parliamentarian in America.

He had to be shrewd. Charles Cotesworth Pinckney, though staunchly in favor of slavery, approached the convention as he approached a meeting of the state legislature, with no more strategy than the short-term give-and-take of lawmaking, an approach that responded to the crises of the moment. He wanted the new nation to take over South Carolina's wartime debt. He was suspicious of New Englanders and wanted to protect South Carolina's interests regarding commerce. In so much as he had an ideology, he distrusted democracy and liked things that had the perfume of aristocracy, though this was less a political philosophy than it was a lack of imagination. He saw no need to prepare himself for the great national debate. His young cousin was too much of a self-promoter to be relied upon. And Pierce Butler was no match for the nation's greatest statesmen. The preservation of slavery had to be the work of John Rutledge.[37]

John Rutledge arrived in Philadelphia by boat on March 18, 1787, and he stayed for the first three weeks of the convention at the magnificent new town house of a Pennsylvania delegate, James Wilson. The residence was flanked by gardens, and eight horses could find their comfort in the ample stables. Wilson's home was catty-corner from Robert Morris's house, where General George Washington was staying. When his wife arrived, Rutledge moved over to the Indian Queen Inn, where many other delegates were staying. Twenty-five Pennsylvania shillings paid for a room, a groom for a horse, and a "Negro servant."[38]

Deliberations officially began on May 25. On a Friday morning, snug inside the statehouse meeting room as rain rattled the windows, Robert Morris of Pennsylvania nominated George Washington to preside over the convention, John Rutledge seconded the nomination, and Washington was unanimously elected. The first few days were given to rules, the most significant of which was the rule of secrecy— no one was to divulge any of the debates until after the convention finished its work. Slavery did not come up for about a month, and then only as an aside in the debate about whether big states and little states should have an equal vote in the Senate. On that day, the convention met, as was its habit, at eleven in the morning, and after James Wilson of Pennsylvania and Oliver Ellsworth of Connecticut each gave very long speeches, James Madison, the future president and Jefferson's protégé, rose to deliver his opinion. "The states are divided into different interests not by their difference of size," he explained, "but principally . . . from their having or not having slaves. . . . [T]he great division of interests in the U[nited] States . . . lay between the Northern & Southern."[39] We are not entirely sure what exactly Madison meant when he said "Southern," for later debates would prove that Virginia was significantly different from what were already being called the "Deep" Southern states of Georgia, South Carolina, and North Carolina. Virginia's natural economic impulse was to end the slave trade, and this interest aligned it with the mid-Atlantic states. Virginia's delegates, like northerners, desired the gradual extinction of slavery. Quite likely, Madison meant that Virginia's *southern* border divided the nation more distinctly than anything else, for the economic interests of the three states farthest south fused them into a distinct unit.

Ten more delegates weighed in on the motion about the Senate, but no one responded to Madison's remark. That slavery caused the great divide among the states was a novel idea, one that hardly seemed apropos to balancing power in the new government. Perhaps Madison himself did not see how prescient was his remark, for he spoke a second time on the issue and did not again allude to slavery. But John Rutledge pondered Madison's argument as he sat silently throughout the long afternoon's debate. The idea was not novel to him. From the moment he was selected to represent South Carolina at the convention, he understood two things: that South Carolina had a great interest in defending its prerogatives regarding slavery and, because this was an interest of so small a minority, protections would be hard to secure in open debate. More than likely Madison's comment alarmed him, because Rutledge wanted above all else to avoid an open debate about slavery. To shine a light on the thing was to expose its defects. One could not justify it to a candid world, so it was best to keep it in the dark. Whatever was his thinking, it seems that Madison's speech told Rutledge that it was time to act—behind the scenes.

Perhaps he surveyed the room, watching the reaction on faces as Madison spoke, and something in the "corrugated and gnarled" face of Roger Sherman, who except for Benjamin Franklin was the oldest man in the room, indicated a susceptibility to a devil's bargain. Rutledge must have seen something in Sherman, because he invited this unlikeliest of allies to a private dinner. Just a few weeks earlier Sherman had voiced his disgust with Rutledge, who loved plays and loved racehorses and in so many ways conformed to the stereotype of the Charleston planter, the connoisseur of sophisticated pleasures. Sherman was a sour old man from Connecticut. He had been born to a cobbler and had spent his youth bending leather to the soles of other men's feet. Too poor for the extravagance of school, he had picked up the law where he could, a true autodidact, and for years had conformed his habits to an austere religion that ran in the grooves of his own severe habits. No drinking, no gambling, no going to the theater, "an old Puritan" in the words of John Adams. And he hated slavery. With his lank hair and limp collar, Sherman need hardly raise his guard against suave southern hospitality, for it would rub him the wrong way. He could not be persuaded by the glamour of Carolina's wealth. Rutledge, born to the aristocracy and schooled in Dublin and London, typically entertained with an exquisite table, polished silver, and viands of expensive European wines. But he was adaptable, and upon Sherman's accepting his invitation to dinner in his rooms at the Indian Queen, he shrewdly kept the fare simple and sober. He invited Sherman to say grace and then patiently endured the puritan's ten-minute thanksgiving. They ate. They talked. They agreed. Whether the compact was sealed with a handshake or something more subtle, we will never know, but as Rutledge's biographer put it without much exaggeration, on this particular warm June evening John Rutledge and his northern dinner guest decided "the fate of America."[40]

What they agreed to was this: if South Carolina backed Connecticut's interests in western land investments (specifically, in the Ohio Company), then Connecticut would vote with South Carolina on slavery.[41] It is not clear at all how Rutledge could have persuaded Sherman to agree: no matter what Connecticut got out of the deal, his conscience should have prevented Sherman from shaking hands with Rutledge. What could Rutledge have possibly said to Sherman that would have persuaded the northerner to support South Carolina? The only evidence we have is in the floor debate itself, and the debate suggests that Rutledge lied to Sherman.

As we have seen, Rutledge did not need to draw upon this bargain with Sherman for about five weeks, which was when Gouverneur Morris launched his first attack on the slave trade. In what must have been a surprise to all but the South Carolina and Connecticut delegations, Sherman helped deflect that assault, deflating Morris's dramatic motion that only "free" people should be counted for representation. Sherman insisted that "it was the freemen of the South[ern] States who were in fact to be represented according to the taxes paid by them, and the Negroes are only included in the Estimate of the taxes." Perhaps this view, voiced by a northerner, was very influential, or perhaps Sherman merely voiced what most already believed, but either way Morris's hope that slaves would not be counted toward representation in Congress failed. Only Dayton's New Jersey delegation voted with Morris. Even Morris's own Pennsylvania delegation voted against him. Most delegates probably thought as James Wilson of Pennsylvania did: Morris's "motion was premature." The three-fifths rule was a side issue, and slavery would be tackled more directly later in the convention.

The real debate came in two weeks, on August 21, when Luther Martin of Maryland proposed an amendment that would allow "a prohibition or tax on the importation of slaves," essentially giving to the national government the right to regulate the slave trade. This proposal was made all the more dramatic because Martin was one of the chief defenders of states' rights, one of the more cautious when it came to federal powers. In fact, he so disliked a strong national government that he advocated a mere reform of the Articles of Confederation rather than a wholesale rewriting of the Constitution, which was bound to put more power in a central government. For Martin to overthrow this principle and recommend that the federal government should have the power to prohibit the slave trade reflects how deep-seated was his conviction on this issue, a conviction that surely was cemented when he attended college at Princeton. Slavery "was inconsistent with the principles of the revolution." It was "dishonorable to the American character," Martin asserted, "to have such a feature in the Constitution."[42] Here finally the main issue was engaged. A nation founded on the principle that all men were created equal and acknowledging the God-given right to liberty could not and must not justify slavery. To say that slavery was "dishonorable to the American character" was just about the strongest language one could use: it questioned the honor and morality of the South Carolina delegation. Back home, most of Charleston's gentlemen would have demanded satisfaction either by a withdrawal of the insult or by pistols on a remote field in the mists of dawn.

Rutledge would never rise to such provocations as that. Dispassionately, he explained that "religion & humanity had nothing to do with this question." He refused to engage the ethical issue. On the contrary, he conceded the ethical point by insisting that "interest alone is the governing principle with Nations." Then he played the same card that General Pinckney had weeks earlier, the great bluff that he hoped no one would call. "The true question," he declared, "is whether the South[ern] States shall or shall not be parties to the Union." Clearly in this context, when Rutledge said "Southern States" he meant Georgia, South Carolina, and North Carolina only, and the implication was that these states would opt out of any federal government that presumed to regulate the slave trade.

Connecticut's Oliver Ellsworth took up Rutledge's point about ethics. "The morality or wisdom of slavery," he opined, "are considerations belonging to the States themselves." Sentiment in Connecticut was clearly against slavery, not only among the people but among their representatives as well. Why would Ellsworth suggest that the ethical question should be left to the states to answer? It all depended on what Rutledge told Sherman back at that dinner in the Indian Queen Inn. While we do not know what exactly transpired, Charles Cotesworth Pinckney gave a telling clue when he of all people stood up to say that South Carolina "may perhaps by degrees do of herself what is wished, as Virginia and Maryland have already done."[43] He was implying that South Carolina would probably follow the lead of the mid-Atlantic slave states in passing antislavery legislation. The likeliest explanation of Connecticut's cooperation, then, is that Rutledge used some version of this same argument when he talked to Sherman. He must have persuaded Sherman that if the *national* government left slavery alone, the *state* governments would gradually do away with it, but on various timetables appropriate to each. Even South Carolina, he must have intimated, could be trusted to do the morally correct thing, albeit on her own schedule. Sherman, in turn, tried to sway the rest of Connecticut's delegation, who found it convenient to be persuaded.

The convention adjourned for the night on Pinckney's hopeful note, leaving everyone to ponder the prospect of South Carolina following the lead of Virginia in enacting laws that eventually would dispose of slavery. But the next morning the Virginian, George Mason, exploded any idea that the issue would be resolved by avoidance. Mason was a more formidable opponent to South Carolina than Gouverneur Morris, at least on the issue of slavery, for he was a planter with an even greater claim to aristocracy than either Rutledge or Pinckney, being the fourth George Mason in one of Virginia's "First Families." His opulent plantation on the Potomac, Gunston Hall, sported elaborate gardens and four tree-lined avenues, each providing dramatic sight lines to the manor house, and, like a feudal manor, Gunston Hall was really a village that included enslaved "carpenters, coopers, sawyers, blacksmiths, tanners, curriers, shoemakers, spinners, weavers and knitters, and even a tiller." Four separate farms, each with its own overseer and slaves, grew corn, wheat, and tobacco as cash crops. Plump and stocky, Mason was the quintessential southern gentleman, bred to the world of the colonial gentry, well read in the vast private library of his uncle and schooled in the ideas of John Locke and other Enlightenment philosophers. Like John Laurens and Alexander Hamilton and David Ramsay, he recognized that slavery was an unequivocal evil that corrupted both victim and master. As early as 1765, when Laurens was eleven years old and Hamilton only ten, Mason attacked slavery in print, and in 1773 he was among those proposing that children of slave parents should be born free, "provided with training for useful employment, and colonized outside the state at maturity." This was probably the same sort of scheme that Henry Laurens contemplated in 1776—a gradual way of ending slavery without confiscating property from slave owners. In 1781, the Virginia legislature legalized the very thing John Laurens had been hoping to enact in South Carolina: black soldiers who fought on the Patriot side in the Revolution were granted their freedom. And in 1782, with Mason's approbation and support, Virginia made it fairly easy for individual owners to free their slaves. History regards Mason as the great defender of human rights, a reputation held aloft by the twin pillars of the Virginia Bill of Rights in 1776 and the Bill of Rights adopted as amendments to the federal Constitution in 1791. His views could not be so easily dismissed or skirted.[44]

Though Mason was more progressive than the typical Virginian, it is no distortion to take his views as representing the rising trend of ideology in the mid-Atlantic states, and it gave such men good reason to think in the 1780s that slavery would disappear within a couple of generations. In 1790, at the time of the first census, Virginia, with 292,000 slaves, held more people in bondage than the three southernmost states combined. When we add Maryland, which had about the same number of slaves as North and South Carolina, just over 100,000, it is easy to see how most people in the country would have thought that the more progressive attitudes in the mid-Atlantic states would ultimately prevail throughout the whole nation. In essence, the debate was an internecine argument among southerners, between Virginia, Maryland, and Delaware on one hand, and Georgia, South Carolina, and North Carolina on the other. Would the model of slavery that served the coastal regions of the Deep South determine national policy? Or would the more progressive model of the Upper South prevail, which allowed for the natural withering away of slavery?

Virginia was pursuing the ideas and acts that would have allowed slavery, which everyone recognized to be incompatible with American political philosophy, to follow its natural course to extinction. Ending the slave trade was the most obvious liberalizing measure. While that might do little to change the demographics of the coastal region, it would certainly retard the westward progress of slavery by raising the price of black men, women, and children and limiting the new supply to the natural birth rate of current slaves. The other obvious measure was to enable, encourage, or at least not discourage individual owners who wanted to free their slaves. Then, the practice of equality would grow naturally to meet the aspiration expressed in the Declaration of Independence, and social opprobrium eventually would compel owners to join the trend of manumission. An important part of such voluntary manumission would be to protect the population of free people of color from penal laws. George Mason, like John Laurens, wanted to build institutions such as grammar schools to prepare slaves for the responsibilities of freedom.[45]

So the constitutional debate over the slave trade was really a debate about whether or not to take the first step toward eliminating slavery. Mason unequivocally argued for the federal government's right to "prevent the increase in slavery." When he described slavery's defects, he spoke from experience: it produces "the most pernicious effect on manners," Mason insisted. "Every master of slaves is born a petty tyrant," while poor whites learn to despise labor for its association with slaves. What would the country look like, he asked, if it permitted the expansion of slavery, especially into the western lands not yet filled up with people? The migration of whites, "who really enrich & strengthen a Country," would be retarded, if the "Western people[, who] are already calling out for slaves" could import them "thro' S. Carolina and Georgia." It was in the general interest of the nation to prohibit the expansion of slavery, and the first thing the federal government needed to do to hinder that expansion was end the foreign slave trade. But there was the even more compelling argument of justice: slavery "bring[s] the judgment of heaven on a Country. As nations can not be rewarded or punished in the next world they must be in this. By an inevitable chain of causes & effects providence punishes national sins, by national calamities."[46]

Ellsworth drolly replied that never having owned slaves himself, he could not testify as to whether men such as Mason were made into petty tyrants. Madison did not record whether the joke struck home, if the wit of the man from Connecticut successfully trivialized the Virginian's declaration of conscience. But the Nutmeg State must be forever ashamed of the sophistry that followed. It was all well and good, Ellsworth argued, for Virginians to try to close the foreign slave trade— slaves were born and raised in the mid-Atlantic states more cheaply than they could be imported. But "sickly rice swamps" killed slaves before they could adequately reproduce themselves, and so states like South Carolina had to be allowed to import them. One would have thought the death rate in the rice swamps would have been an argument against slavery, but Ellsworth reasoned that if the convention were to consider the moral question at all, it would be forced to free all of the slaves, and since that obviously was not going to happen, it was best to ignore morality all together. He then returned to the argument provided by Rutledge: "As [white] population increases; poor laborers will be so plenty as to render slaves useless. Slavery in time will not be a speck in our Country." Natural economics would kill slavery, and so Ellsworth reasoned that the government need not do anything about it; in fact, the government could enact legislation encouraging it and still slavery would wither away.

The two Pinckneys were outraged by Mason's virulence. The Virginian was suggesting that they and their fellow Lowcountry planters were purveyors of evil, and such an accusation could not be left to stand. The younger Pinckney rose to defend his honor, claiming that if "slavery be wrong, it is justified by the example of the world." Ancient nations and modern, including both France and England, engaged in the practice that subjugated "one half of mankind." John Rutledge must have struggled to hide from his face his anger at Pinckney. The young firebrand had forgotten the game plan entirely, which was to convince the convention that South Carolina could be relied upon to slowly weaken the legal sanctions for slavery. Instead, here he was defending the institution, trying to convince this gathering of revolutionaries that what the old world practiced and sanctioned must be all right for America! Perhaps he gave his colleague a swift kick under the desk, for as Pinckney spoke he seemed to realize the tactical error, and he returned once again to the script, suggesting that it was likely that the southern states, including his own South Carolina, would abolish the trade themselves; that he himself would vote such an act.[47]

James Wilson of Pennsylvania, though a close friend of Rutledge's, tried to call the Carolina bluff, pointing out that it seemed unlikely that a federal ban on the slave trade would drive South Carolina out of the Union if she were, as Pinckney claimed, ready to abolish the trade herself. Nevertheless, General Charles Cotesworth Pinckney rose to reiterate that point: even if he and his cousin and John Rutledge were to try their best to persuade South Carolinians to ratify the Constitution, they would fail if the document outlawed the slave trade. In perhaps the only honest moment in the debate, Pinckney "thought himself bound to declare candidly he did not think S. Carolina would stop her importations of slaves in any short time, but only stop them occasionally as she now does." But by this time the votes were clear to him, and he felt the threat of opting out of the union would carry the day. Rutledge doubled down: South Carolina, North Carolina, and Georgia would abandon the Union and go it alone if they did not retain control over the slave trade. By this time no one could have been surprised when Sherman advised the other states to fold rather than play their hand to its end: "it was better to let the S[outhern] states import slaves" than see them leave the Union.

In retrospect, we know the threat of opting out was a bluff. South Carolinians were closely divided on the issue of the slave trade, and Wilson's insight was right on the mark: the perpetuation of the slave trade was dear to a faction—a dominant but minority faction—in South Carolina politics. It just so happened that all four members of the South Carolina delegation belonged to this faction. That Rutledge and Pinckney were bluffing cannot be disputed by any judicious reading of the documents. Later, in debate in Charleston, Charles Cotesworth

Pinckney admitted that the southern states "are so weak that by ourselves we could not form a union strong enough for the purpose of effectually protecting each other." Outside of a union with the northern states, the southern states could easily be invaded by England or Spain; they had too few white men to protect themselves, and too many slaves who would aid the enemy. Of course Pickney kept this opinion out of view in Philadelphia, and Connecticut, having made its deal with the devil, helped to make the bluff more credible.

Perhaps the most telling comment was Sherman's concluding remarks. We must not give the federal government control, he reasoned, because if Congress had the power to end the slave trade, "it would be its duty to exercise the power." The slave trade was so manifestly immoral that were he himself to have control over it, he would be forced by conscience to end it. Therefore, he figured, it was best to refuse the power all together.[48] History must commend New Hampshire, Pennsylvania, and Delaware for supporting Morris and Mason in demanding that the national government begin the work of ending slavery. Massachusetts, like Pontius Pilate, washed its hands of the matter by abstaining. The others, including the northern states of Connecticut and New Jersey and even Mason's own Virginia, voted with South Carolina.

Mason predicted that cause and effect would inevitably lead to national calamity. Probably he was thinking of either a slave insurrection or a foreign invasion of the Deep South. Even he did not foresee the Civil War. Nevertheless, when John Rutledge was able get a majority of the states to do the bidding of a minority faction in South Carolina politics, that fate was rendered all the more difficult to avoid. The final version of the Constitution was a supposed compromise: Congress could not interfere with the foreign slave trade until 1808. But that would give the South twenty years to expand the institution, to export the plantation system beyond the Atlantic coastal states into Kentucky, Tennessee, Mississippi, and Alabama. With slavery retreating in Virginia, the Carolina coast amounted to a beachhead, a solid foothold on the continent where wealthy men had enough power to withstand the ideology of Liberty. But they controlled hardly more territory than the slave parishes of the Lowcountry. The Carolina planters might have claimed the coastal regions of Georgia, but they were barely strong enough to command even the Upcountry of their own state. They were too weak yet to imprint the plantation way of life on the unsettled land to the west or on the next century. Left to the natural course of things, opinions like George Mason's would spread from Virginia. The logic and justice of manumission were inescapable. Charleston's oligarchy needed to construct a bulwark against the natural forces of change, and so trenches must be dug at the state lines and palisades erected. No one must be allowed to determine slave policy in South Carolina but the Lowcountry planters. They needed time to align their own state with the plantation system. Rutledge and the Pinckneys got their needed protections into the U.S. Constitution. No one from Pennsylvania or Massachusetts or even from Virginia would mess with their business. Now they had to get the state to ratify it.

When the delegates to South Carolina's ratifying convention met in Charleston in May of the next year, 1788, the Pinckneys dominated the debate, and their arguments more or less mirrored those made in Philadelphia. Charles Cotesworth Pinckney made a grand defense of the 1808 sunset clause on the slave trade—or rather on the state's absolute right to continue importing slaves till then. While the Congress would eventually assume the power to end the trade, "the general government can never emancipate" the slaves, he reassured the convention. Given the antislavery sentiment in the other states and Virginia's equivocation, Pinckney mused that, "on the whole," he did not think the terms were bad.[49]

But there is little indication that anyone in South Carolina needed to be reassured. Immediately after Pinckney sat down, David Ramsay, who personally hoped the slaves would be emancipated, stood up and issued a complete non sequitur: "Our delegates," he said rosily, have "made a most excellent bargain for us, by transferring an immense sum of Continental debt, which we were pledged to pay, upon the Eastern States."[50] Slavery, which was so passionately attacked and dispassionately defended in Philadelphia, was hardly a concern at the South Carolina ratifying convention. This could simply be explained away by a lack of anxiety, a belief that the Constitution solidly secured the pre-Revolutionary status quo. But the lack of interest even in the 1808 sunset clause seems to indicate that the issue was more important to Charles Cotesworth Pinckney than to other South Carolinians at the ratifying convention.

The ratifying convention was not a democratically elected body. The arcane rules of South Carolina politics dictated that the majority of the delegates were drawn from the coastal gentry, many "related by marriage or blood," such as the "Rutledge, Pinckney, Laurens, Manigault, Izard, Kinloch, Grimké, [and] Smith" families from Charleston. Among the delegates from the city were Charles Cotesworth Pinckney, Edward and Hugh Rutledge, and David Ramsay. Two of the seven delegates representing Christ Church were Charles Pinckney and John Rutledge. Four out of five of the state's white citizens lived inland from the coast, but they were represented by only 40 percent of the delegates at the convention.[51]

The few Upcountry delegates who represented most of the population were deferential to the planters and merchants and lawyers who ruled South Carolina. Their few speeches in the convention are laced with their sense of inferiority, their humility when arguing against the accomplished orators and statesmen of Charleston. By and large, they opposed ratifying the Constitution, because they feared it gave a distant government too much power. Significantly, they were not worried about Congress's power to regulate slavery. They were worried about the president becoming a king; they worried about freedom of religion; they worried about freedom of the press; they worried that the document contained no Bill of Rights. Patrick Dollard, whose Prince Frederick parish was just off the coast, indicated that his "constituents are highly alarmed" that the Constitution would re-create a "despotic aristocracy" that would threaten their newly established, "dear-bought rights and privileges."[52] His constituents were not so concerned with what the Constitution said about the old slave system of pre-Revolutionary South Carolina. They were consumed with what it said about individual liberties. This is not to imply that Dollard and other off-the-coast Carolinians would have been happy to see the Constitution abolish slavery. The radical views David Ramsay espoused were entertained by a small minority, and such dissent tended to come from the ranks of the elites, at least insomuch as we have any records of personal convictions today. But it seems Dollard would have dealt the slave trade for the Bill of Rights.

That is because slavery was not yet fixed in the minds of white South Carolinians as their chief "interest." The majority of Carolinians who opposed ratification believed the debate about the national government was the same as their own local debate about democratic versus oligarchic rule. They thought the Constitution protected the interests of the rich and not the poor. Their quarrel was not with northern or eastern tyranny: it was with the creditors and lawyers and with an economic and political system stacked against themselves. If there was a "sectional interest" at the convention, it belonged to the Lowcountry elites, who refused to share their political power. The obvious exception to this rule is Rawlins Lowndes, the most loquacious of the anti-ratification faction, who did worry about the balance of power between the "five Southern States" and the "nine Eastern ones."[53] But this balance was just one of his many worries about the new, stronger national government, and Lowndes was a coastal planter himself, one of the few who broke ranks, and so his concerns did not represent the populace.

The state's ratifying convention helped to define South Carolina's "interest" as the interest of the Lowcountry planters. Even so, slavery did not even preoccupy the minds of this oligarchy as much as it worried John Rutledge and Charles and Charles Cotesworth Pinckney. In one long speech Charles Pinckney lectured his fellow elites on the "striking . . . difference . . . between the inhabitants of the Northern and Southern States." Pinckney told his audience that he saw a cultural divide of "manners" at Maryland's northern border, essentially equivalent to the "slave" versus "free" division that Madison posited earlier. "The southern citizen beholds, with a kind of surprise," Pinckney, the seasoned traveler, explained, "the simple manners of the east. . . . [Easterners], in their turn, seem concerned at what they term the extravagance and dissipations of their southern friends," condemning the "unpardonable moral and political evil" of slavery. The fact that he had to make a case for this division of manners (rather than interests) indicates that it was a new concept in Charleston; and Pinckney only brought up this supposed divide to indicate that it was based more on ignorance and prejudice than on any real distinction between easterners and southerners. He attempted to dispel southern prejudice against northerners, extolling the northern system of small, proprietary farms, tilled by free men, as the Republican ideal, an image that echoed Judge Pendleton's vision of a slave-less settling of the Midlands and Upcountry of South Carolina.[54]

Robert Barnwell, a planter from the coastal Beaufort area, declared that the two great "interests" competing for influence in the new government were the carrying trade and the exporting business. These did map onto an eastern/southern regional divide, since southerners shipped their crops abroad in vessels owned by easterners. But, significantly, this distinction was not defined as "free" and "slave." Similarly, Pinckney argued that the real interests competing in the American government would be defined by three classes, not by two or three regions: commercial men; professional men; and farmers and mechanics.[55] He clumped the big plantation owner, who did not actually farm his own land, in the same group as the farmer and mechanic, an audacious rhetorical strategy given that the main divide in South Carolina politics was between the modest farmers and mechanics on one hand and the rich planters on the other. But whatever the details, slavery played a remarkably small part in the debate. Even the planters themselves did not define their interest as sectional, or the sections as "slave" versus "free."

But things were headed that way. For the first time in Charleston, one's position on slavery became a sort of litmus test of one's suitability for Congress. Under the new Constitution, South Carolina would send five men to the House of Representatives, and Charleston, which had traditionally dominated the state's congressional delegation, would command only one of those five. Three men competed for that seat: Alexander Gillon, the leader of the democratic-leaning faction of mechanics; William Laughton Smith, the son-in-law of Ralph Izard, one of the richest planters in the state; and David Ramsay, physician and by marriage allied to the great planting and merchant interests of the Laurens family. One might suppose that Ramsay, who had twice been chosen to represent the state in Congress, might have a leg up, at least on Smith, who was aligned with the same faction. Observers believed they were running neck and neck, when, just before the November election, a rumor began to circulate that if Ramsay were elected, he would "promote an emancipation of the Negroes in this state."[56] Ramsay clearly did favor emancipation. Even if he came around to the view that most whites held—that the swampy Lowcountry was better suited to the health of the black race than the white— he did not see that fact as a justification for plantation slavery. For instance, he told Benjamin Rush that he thought the coastal area should be settled and farmed by free blacks.[57] Such views had not prevented Charleston from sending Ramsay to Congress just three years earlier.

Ramsay's friends published a response to the rumors in the *Charleston Morning Post*. They could not claim that Ramsay supported slavery, so they retreated to what they considered defensible ground: the new Constitution prevented Congress from meddling in slavery for twenty years, so whether Ramsay was or was not for emancipation was irrelevant. Ralph Izard, Smith's father-in-law, asked Ramsay to state unequivocally "that he has never declared that he thought slavery ought to be abolished." This Ramsay could not do. Smith himself asked if a man born and bred in the North could be trusted to represent "the true political interests of this country." Ramsay refused to declare that "he will not . . . endeavor to procure the emancipation of the slaves." If Ramsay were elected to Congress, so Smith charged, he would not "endeavor to reconcile the Northern States, to slavery, to convince them that without slavery, this district must be abandoned and rendered a mere wilderness." This was the beachhead: the First Congressional District of South Carolina, where a politician must prove his bona fides on slavery. It must have seemed to men like Smith and Rutledge and Pinckney that Ramsay was more interested in reconciling the southerners to George Mason's view of slavery, since he had explained in his pro-ratification pamphlet how northerners thought "we [Carolinians] ought not to increase our exposure to that evil" by continuing in the slave trade. Calling slavery an "evil" was hardly radical: it was a moral adjudication typical in the Revolutionary era. No one seriously disputed it, and the only defense of slavery even as late as 1788 was that it was a necessary evil. Nevertheless, Ramsay's sympathy with the idea that slavery was indeed evil and the nation ought to take steps toward its eventual eradication made him vulnerable. One of the accusations against him was that he had received and distributed antislavery literature. Ramsay admitted to having received Thomas Clarkson's essays, printed in Philadelphia, arguing against the slave trade; he conceded that he had forwarded the essays to an unnamed gentleman but that he had done so without knowing the contents of the postal package. "My own copy," he said rather lamely, "I never read." As a personal defense, this rhetorical formula was about as forthright as Bill Clinton's admission that he had smoked marijuana but that he had not inhaled. All in all, Ramsay could not dispute Smith's conclusion: that he was "principled against slavery, and [that] it is idle for him to contradict what is universally known."[58]

Smith demolished him in the election: 600 votes to Ramsay's 191 (Gillon won 386 votes). If the votes truly had been divided almost equally before the exposé, then it seems that most voters did believe it was the job of Charleston's congressional representative to "endeavor to reconcile the Northern States, to slavery." But that majority was slim, for neither Gillon nor Ramsay could be relied upon to do so, and together they garnered 577 or 49 percent of the votes, and they carried majorities in four of the nine voting districts.[59] Nearly half the voters did not think that being principled *for* slavery was all that important. How many of those believed that the city's representative to Congress should enact laws conducive to the withering away of slavery we cannot know, but we must presume that many of Ramsay's supporters were fellow travelers. If the election were a referendum on emancipation, as Smith sought to make it, it is quite remarkable that 16 percent of the electorate still voted for Ramsay. In retrospect, we have to regret that John Laurens did not live to run for Congress; as a native Charlestonian and war hero, he would have been a much less vulnerable spokesman for the progressive view.

Unfortunately, the lesson Ramsay learned was that if one wanted to get elected in Charleston, one had to be sound on slavery. It did not occur to him to oppose slavery by leading this sizeable number of dissenters from a position outside of public office. Nor did he seek an alliance with Gillon, who was the political enemy of Ramsay's personal friends. Ramsay prized his position among Charleston's elites, and so after the election he began to moderate his views, inching closer to the reigning oligarchy's belief that slavery was necessary. As his biographer explains, in 1780 Ramsay promoted the idea that "free blacks" should farm the Lowcountry. Eight years later "he maintained that since the 'great part of the low country' could only be cultivated by black labor *'domestic slavery seemed to be forced on the Southern provinces.'*" He did not understand that his own acquiescence left the high ground undefended in Charleston. The next crisis needed a cadre of intelligent and committed dissenters because the pro-slavery forces rolled in the greatest siege engine in any ideological struggle: fear.[60]

5

THE DENMARK VESEY REBELLION

||

The man called Denmark Vesey was born on the Caribbean island of St. Thomas, a tiny Dutch colony of about eighty plantations, four thousand African slaves, and six hundred Europeans and free people of color. We do not know what his mother named him or the exact date of his birth, but it was probably around the time that the Stamp Act was brewing up trouble in the 1760s. More than likely, the boy worked in the sugarcane fields and slept in the rows of clay and wattle huts that resembled African villages for fourteen years until, one day in 1781, he was herded down to the docks and loaded with 390 other surplus slaves onto the Massachusetts brigantine *Prospect*.[1]

The captain of this well-armed vessel was Joseph Vesey, a Bermudan whose rum and slave trade with Charles Town merchants brought him into sympathy with the Patriot cause. For most of the war, Vesey sailed in various ships as an American privateer, but on this cruise he followed a side business of supplying slaves to the French colony of Saint-Domingue. With only about twenty-four thousand whites putting the lash to nearly four hundred thousand slaves on the immense sugar, coffee, and cotton plantations, this island was industrial farming at its worst: owners regarded slaves with little humanity, calculating them as just one cost of doing business, using them up in the tropical sun at appalling rates. The fourteen-year-old boy's sentence to this hell was reprieved when Vesey, taking notice of his "beauty, alertness and intelligence," made him his cabin boy. Vesey named the boy after Odysseus's son, Telemachus, and the newly minted "Telemaque" began his new life as an enslaved sailor on a slave ship, making at least one voyage to Africa before Vesey settled in Charleston as a merchant with a shop fronting the wharves on the Cooper River. For nearly twenty years, Telemaque lived with Vesey at his home at 281 King Street, where he grew into his role as Vesey's manservant, a job that broadened his education as he assisted in importing salt, gin, slaves, and other goods. He learned to read and write English handily, spoke French, and climbed to the top rung of the low ladder of slaves in South Carolina, one of those few glimpses we have of genius among all of the vast talent squandered by slavery.

According to tradition, Telemaque was "comely." One early biographer, Archibald Grimké, thought he was a mulatto, but Douglas Egerton more plausibly argues that he was fully black. "Nature gave him a royal body," Grimké wrote around 1900, "nobly planned and proportioned, and noted for its great strength. There was that in his countenance, which bespoke a mind within to match that body, a mind of uncommon native intelligence, force of will, and capacity to dominate others." He was "abrupt and crafty" in his interactions, "imperious," and his "heart was the heart of a lion."[2] This might be more legend than fact, but contemporary accounts did pay tribute to his natural capacity for leadership, and all agreed he was an exceptional man: careful, even vain in dress; larger than most men in physical size; literate; multilingual; a world traveler; larger than most slaves in self-possession and confidence as he went about the streets of Charleston doing Vesey's business.

Urban slavery was quite distinct from the plantation life that most blacks suffered in South Carolina. Under the Lowcountry plantation system, most slaves were given a set amount of work to do each day, measured in a unit called a "task," depending upon their capacity. For example, a young man might have one and a half tasks to complete in a day, while a pregnant woman had less than a full task. A slave's given task was challenging and took most of his or her day, six days a week, but it allowed at least a small degree of autonomy, because once your assigned task was completed, you enjoyed what we might call free time. Within that time, Lowcountry slaves developed a rich culture and cash economy. The economics were more diverse than one might think: slave families generally had small plots on which they grew their own vegetables, corn, even cotton, which they might use or sell. Progressive masters might allow slaves to run a store on plantation grounds, and the big house might supply itself from that store, putting pocket money into the hands of slaves. In addition to these more or less sanctioned exchanges was the black market, the unofficial and often illegal multiracial exchanges flourishing especially from boats on the rivers and creeks, which provided ready cash for slaves' wares that had been produced legitimately or pilfered from their masters.

This slim space for free activity in the countryside was expanded considerably in the city, where, Frederick Douglass observed, the slave "is almost a freeman, compared with a slave on the plantation. He is much better fed and clothed, and enjoys privileges altogether unknown to the slave on the plantation." No urban slave owner wanted his neighbors whispering about poorly fed servants or overhearing the cries of house slaves receiving a beating. No doubt such considerations fed the business of the workhouse, where city owners sent their slaves to be punished outside the family home, but even so Telemaque's life in the 1790s must have been far from what we commonly think of as the slave's experience. Many urban slaves turned a profit for their masters by hiring themselves out, either as unskilled laborers or skilled artisans. An owner might make "several hundred dollars" a year without the slightest effort on his own part, for this type of slave often paid for his own room and board, sometimes even negotiating the terms of his own hiring. "Bondsmen and women," one historian explains, "were able to move about, earn their own wages, accumulate property, and secure a measure" of independence. Black neighborhoods spotted the city—Coming Street, for instance, was a center of free black and slave housing, and sections of the Neck had virtually no whites. In addition to these urban slaves, the free black population of Charleston increased by 22 percent between 1790 and 1800, mostly through manumissions, and runaway slaves could melt into these communities, hire themselves out, and live quasi-free lives.[3] Telemaque moved within the circuit of this semiautonomous black economy, as he carried on Vesey's varied business as a merchant, and as Vesey's fortune grew so did Telemaque's independence.

Charleston's economy, so stagnant in the 1780s, thrived in the '90s, buoyed not only by the revival of the rice trade but the expansion of a new cash crop, cotton, for which Charleston served as a major depot. The coastal region produced "sea island" or "long staple" cotton, a variety more luxuriant and easier to weave than the "short staple" cotton grown in the inland soils. But Eli Whitney's cotton gin made short staple cotton economical, and the completion of the Santee Canal gave the city access to the newly developed farms in the Midlands of the state. South Carolina produced 1.5 million pounds of cotton in 1791; more than 20 million pounds in 1800; and ten years later more than 40 million pounds. Prosperity displayed itself across the city in the newly opened College of Charleston, fresh clean water piped in from Goose Creek, the concerts and fireworks and exotic animals put on for public amusement in the outdoor Vaux Hall Park on Broad Street. Silversmiths and more than sixty cabinetmakers found a ready market among the planters, who supported a vigorous trade in luxury goods and services during this second golden age for Charleston.[4]

The rise of cotton coincided with two apparently contradictory trajectories in American slavery. The first was a renewed pressure on the labor market, for even the surplus of slaves in mid-Atlantic states like Virginia could not supply the needs of eager cotton farmers. In a move that was highly controversial in South Carolina and roundly criticized by the rest of nation, including the other southern states, Charleston once again opened its ports to the African slave trade in 1803, just five years before Congress would ban it forever. Two years later, Governor Paul Hamilton, a Lowcountry planter, again called for an end to the trade, citing the familiar arguments of widespread indebtedness and the insecurity caused by a slave majority. Some South Carolina legislators echoed the complaints that were voiced around the country about the inhumanity of the trade, urging their fellows to overcome their greed and put justice ahead of profit. Twice as many in

South Carolina's House of Representatives voted to close the trade as voted to keep it open.[5]

But in the upper house, Senator William Smith from the Upcountry county of York led the fight to oppose the ban. Smith did not have the flash of phrase or gesture that distinguished so many others in this great age of American oratory, but he was effective nonetheless, getting fifteen other senators to vote with him, a majority of one, to keep the slave trade open. The following session, in 1806, was even more dramatic. "Let us . . . remove temptation from the eyes of our citizens," Governor Hamilton urged the legislature, and "cease to practice what every other state in the union discountenances." Everyone but two in the House voted to close the trade. Smith, who was by this time president of the Senate, once again led the fight to keep it open, prevailing finally when the bill failed on a vote of 16 to 16. Had just one senator been persuaded by the governor or by the moral pressure of so many commentators outside South Carolina, or had Smith himself not been so diligent in defending the trade, the wharves of Charleston would have been closed to African captives in 1806. Over fourteen thousand slaves came through Charleston in that year, which was about 96 percent of all slaves imported to the United States. In 1807, over twenty-one thousand were imported through South Carolina—95 percent of the national total. Charleston was the only place in the United States still willing to ignore the immorality of the slave trade, a small enclave unwilling to face the truths of liberty and equality on which the republic was founded. And even there, it was a small minority that leveraged disproportionate political power into a perpetuation of the slave trade, defeating a decided majority of South Carolina's politicians.[6]

David Ramsay had hoped cotton farming would populate the state with white yeomen farmers, diminishing the economy's reliance on slavery. In fact, it encouraged the opposite, and South Carolina exported slaves to settlers in Alabama and Mississippi. It exported whites also, and they took with them their ideology of paternalism. The historian Lacy Ford calls the Carolina Lowcountry a "beachhead" for paternalism, a way of thinking that invaded the nation in the late 1700s. Paternalism is sometimes described as the "domestication" of slavery, because, as Robert Olwell explains, the old patriarchal metaphor that relates a planter to a monarch and his slaves to distant subjects gave way to a new metaphor that infused itself in the minds of planters and made them think of themselves as the head of a family. Four "ideological propositions" distinguished paternalism from the crueler patriarchy: that slaves are as human as their masters; that the governance of slaves, just like the governance of children, should balance "affection and discipline"; that masters must be good stewards of the spiritual, moral, and intellectual development of their dependents; and that masters had a social responsibility to make sure that their neighbors did not tyrannize their slaves.[7]

Paternalism also requires whites to believe they have inherited a burden that is fundamentally temporary. A fifth ideological proposition of paternalism, then, is the belief that someday—perhaps not in one's own lifetime, but someday—slavery would disappear. The logic of the child metaphor requires an eventual change, for children grow up. Workers are not cogs in a machine but dependent persons infused by all of the innocence and malicious impetuosity we associate with children: thieving, loyal, simple in their virtues and vices alike, unschooled, developing their moral selves, on the path to moral maturity and the ability to tame and govern their own wild hearts. Implicit in paternalism is the belief that the slaves would and should eventually grow into adults. Private manumission was the logical sign of this belief. It was not just a reward for faithful, obedient service but the pinnacle of a long, apprentice-like climb toward financial and moral independency, and the freeing of even one or two slaves among one's scores or hundreds symbolized the evolutionary, progressive nature of the entire institution and demonstrated the good stewardship of the owner. The older, patriarchal ideology was wholly incompatible with republican principles, but paternalism, which posits a progressive rather than static view of slavery, allowed one to believe in natural rights like equality and liberty, and yet own slaves.[8]

In 1776, Henry Laurens promised to emancipate all of his own slaves, a liberal sentiment that redeemed his own sense of righteousness, but ultimately it only cost him the single, private, testamentary manumission of a favorite slave, a gesture too faint to affect public policy but enough to demonstrate his own belief in gradual emancipation, his allegiance to the angels' party, his credit for taking even a small step in the progress of American slaves. And so did the enlightened, private acts of thousands of others—in all sorts of liberal practices from manumissions to letting slaves participate in the money economy to refusing to break up families—dissolve white society's membership in the devil's party, at least in its own eyes. Even as slavery spread west in the early 1800s, the institution liberalized considerably.

White Americans recognized very astutely that private manumission, if left unregulated, would lead eventually to the natural death of slavery in a few generations. Many Founding Fathers built their complacency on this belief: they did not need to solve the slavery issue because it would solve itself, naturally withering under the sun of the American republic. Today's historians tend toward the other extreme, treating the perpetuation of slavery in the South as inevitably following on economic necessity. Greed magnified by capitalism naturally leads to exploitation, and we have seen how even a man of conscience such as Henry Laurens could reconcile himself to the deaths of hundreds of strangers transported in his ships and how easily he could ignore and disown the suffering of workers he owned, so long as they were sent out of his sight, to Georgia, for instance, in gangs supervised by overseers. There can be no doubt that the rise of cotton, facilitated by Whitney's invention, applied more economic pressure against liberty. Greed, after all, is powerful, and the final victims of the foreign slave trade were sacrificed to the cotton industry.

But more powerful is the humanity naturally inherent in most people, and we have also seen how much harder it is to be cruel to those one knows intimately, and perhaps, more important, how hard it is to be cruel in front of one's neighbors. If paternalism was a lie that whites told themselves to justify their dominion over blacks— and of course being based on a philosophy of racial superiority it *was* a lie—it also tended to magnify humanity the way capitalism magnifies inhumanity.

The impatient, incautious, emancipatory furor of John Laurens was the logical conclusion of his father's paternalism, and his scheme did not call for immediate abolition but rather for hurrying dependent slaves along the road to maturity. By arming three thousand slaves, drilling them as soldiers, training them in the discipline necessary for a military campaign, growing in their breasts the courage needed for battle, he would prepare them for freedom and citizenship, and they would prepare others. Thousands of other white owners in the Revolutionary period did the same thing, some with less and some with equal fervor, all on a smaller scale, when they manumitted their personal slaves. After the Revolution, only Massachusetts, New Hampshire, and Vermont enacted immediate emancipations. Other northern states adopted gradual policies, and as far south as Virginia great moral suasion, expressed for example by Baptist and Methodist ministers, urged private manumissions. Owners manumitted their slaves most often in those places where the proportion of slaves to whites was lowest—in the northern states of course but also in the mid-Atlantic and in the western portions of North Carolina, South Carolina, and Georgia. General Lafayette applied this kind of moral pressure to George Washington, urging him to safeguard his greatest legacy, his historical reputation, by sacrificing his lesser legacy, the slaves he could have willed to his heirs. "Manumission begets manumission," one contemporary observed, "they increase in geometrical proportion."[9]

Such liberal thinking progressed through the Revolutionary period, as most states liberalized their manumission laws. In 1782, Virginia allowed private manumissions for the first time in six decades. "By 1790, manumission was a slaveholder's prerogative throughout the South," except in North Carolina, where one had to get a county court's permission before freeing a slave, and even in North Carolina so many slaveholders ignored that mandate that the state had to pass new laws in 1788 and 1796 to prevent "divers persons, from religious motives" from continuing "to liberate their slaves." In the Upper South, "wholesale private emancipation released thousands from bondage." In Maryland, where manumissions went on unchecked through most of the antebellum period, slavery eroded at a remarkable pace. By and large, freed slaves migrated to Baltimore, joining a community of freed blacks that ballooned to about fifteen thousand by 1830, more than three times the number of slaves in that city. "The old rule of slavery for life," the historian Stephen Whitman notes,

"evolved towards slavery as a stage of life, ended by testamentary manumission, self-purchase, or flight." Private manumission proved so
popular that, allowed to follow its natural course, it would have eroded
slavery on its edges in Maryland, Delaware, Virginia, Kentucky, and
those edges would have crept ever closer to the absolute center of the
institution: Charleston. The free black community in Charleston increased a relatively modest 22 percent between 1790 and 1800—
mostly from manumissions.[10] Given the quasi-free status of many of
the city's slaves and the relative autonomy blacks enjoyed in certain
neighborhoods, Charleston was slowly becoming another Baltimore.

Telemaque's life reflected these dynamic changes. One fall day in 1799,
as he walked the streets of Charleston, he happened to buy an East
Bay Street lottery ticket, and in early November his number came up.
The erudite, mannered slave of a well-to-do, multiracial family won
$1,500. Immediately, he proposed to the Veseys that he buy his free-
dom, and considering his long and faithful service, they, like so many
others in their generation, acquiesced to his wish. On the last day of
the century, Telemaque handed his owners $600, and they signed the
deed that "manumitted, released and from the yoke of Servitude set
free and discharged a certain negro man named Telemaque."[11]

The newly freed man rented a house on Bull Street, on the edge
of the relatively prosperous neighborhood surrounding Coming
Street, where lived many successful "browns," or free mulattoes, who
often owned slaves themselves to cook and clean their homes. Free
black men plied any number of skilled and semiskilled trades, from
brick masons and butchers to bakers and barbers. Some few (twenty-
one in 1850) were professionals. Fewer than 20 percent of the free
blacks were unskilled laborers, and Telemaque, like most of his fellows,
took up a trade, carpentry in his case. Ironically, free people of color
tended to distance themselves from the ranks of slaves whence they
came, trying to secure their own status by contrasting their condition
to that of their less fortunate fellows. Fifty better-off free men of color
formed a fraternity, the Brown Fellowship Society, imitating the exclusive clubs of the white aristocracy and succeeding in establishing

not-so-subtle racial castes within the colored community, for no black men, only "colored," were allowed to join. Disgusted with such elitism, another group formed the Society of Free Dark Men, a benevolent organization not open to men of mixed race. It does not seem that the disease of exclusion ever really infected Telemaque, who associated equally with slaves long after he had become a free man.[12]

The speed with which private manumissions were changing southern society alarmed many whites, especially cotton farmers who were eager to reproduce the system that made so many rice planters wealthy before the Revolution. Simple racism even among opponents of slavery also contributed to a conservative backlash against the liberalizing trends, for many whites doubted whether they could live side by side with so many free blacks in peace. And the slave uprising in Saint-Domingue, led by the free black, Toussaint L'Ouverture, terrified many in the Carolina Lowcountry, where a black majority mirrored the demographics of that French colony. (Ironically, that slave rebellion increased Charleston's number of free blacks because many sought refuge in the city, which was still, in the 1790s, essentially a Caribbean town.) Just days after Telemaque secured his own freedom, South Carolina once again began restricting private manumissions, though its main motive was not unenlightnened. The government wanted to prevent pauperism. It was feared that cynical owners might free their older, unproductive slaves in order to escape the responsibility of caring for their aged workers. Beginning in 1800, the legislature required "that candidates for manumission prove their capacity for self-support before a court of magistrates and freeholders." Throughout the South, legislation after 1800 began to reflect anxieties about the widespread success of private manumissions, and conservative penal laws against free people of color began to creep back into society.[13]

Sometime in this period Telemaque's name changed again to a bastardized "Denmark." He entered the new century a free man of color in a society that was growing increasingly lax in its attitude toward blacks: even where legislation tried to thwart public opinion, everywhere public opinion grew more and more liberal. In North Carolina, for instance, Quakers conspicuously violated the manumission regulations, and they helped non-Quakers skirt the laws by acting as "trustees" of slaves, allowing those in their "trust" to live as free men and women. In Charleston, liberal owners also used trusts to free their favorite slaves, in effect if not in law, and support their independence. In one particularly instructive case in the 1840s, the famous lawyer James Louis Petigru helped legitimize one of these "trustee" families by securing them deeds of manumission from Philadelphia.[14] In Charleston, free black men sometimes bought their own wives and children, holding them in nominal bondage. Likewise, white men sometimes bought slaves they considered friends, making them virtually free. Liberal-minded people resorted to all sorts of subterfuge to circumvent the laws. Some masters treated slavery as an indentured servitude, promising to free their bondsmen after a period of faithful, industrious service. To the consternation of conservatives, even South Carolina's courts recognized the freedom of slaves if they had lived quasi-free lives for many years. One conservative 1812 petition near Orangeburg complained about "the general disposition of the people of the state to ameliorate the condition of the Slaves," arguing that the laxity of whites in enforcing penal laws allowed space for black men to mix with lower-class white women. Obviously, the attitudes of those white women must have been quite a bit more liberal than the law. Such conservative petitions are nearly ubiquitous, demonstrating how widely these kinds of quiet, unofficial acts of dissent had spread by the early 1800s.[15]

Denmark Vesey—for he had taken his former master's surname—ran his carpentry business out of the front room of his Bull Street home, prospered well enough to hire a few hands, effectively divorced his slave wife, and married again to a freed woman named Susan, who was almost thirty years younger than he. A couple of years later, Denmark joined the African Methodist Episcopal Church in Cows Alley in the black ghetto of Hampsted, on the northeast side of the city. Black Methodists outnumbered white Methodists in Charleston about ten to one, and in 1817 the high-handed manner with which the white reverend Anthony Senter spent money collected from his black congregants pushed them to rebellion. Nearly forty-four hundred blacks left the church overnight, and most found a home in one of the two brand-new all-black African Methodist Episcopal churches. In Philadelphia, a black or "African" church had branched off from Methodism just a few years earlier, when Richard Allen, disgusted with the racism practiced in the church to which he belonged, founded the African Methodist Episcopal Church. Allen ordained two black Charlestonians, Morris Brown and Henry Drayton, and they spread his movement to Charleston.[16] It is a testament to the relaxed attitude toward slavery in 1818 that white Charlestonians tolerated these unsupervised congregations.

Unsupervised, but not unsurveilled. Whites "routinely sat in the rear pews during Morris Brown's formal sermons," so, as one might surmise, the black minister walked a fine line between inspiring his congregation and appeasing the authorities. He avoided anything we might call liberation theology. Nevertheless, controversy found the church in its second year, when Richard Allen came to visit Charleston along with five other black bishops and ministers. They preached at one of the African churches, which so disturbed the city authorities that they sent in the city guard to break up the meeting. One hundred and forty black congregants spent the night in jail, and the following morning a paternalistic magistrate lectured them on the law. African Americans could attend church only during daylight hours, he reminded them, and only if they constituted a minority of the congregation; the city was willing to wave the second stipulation so long as at least one white person observed the church proceedings, but under no circumstances were blacks to gather, even for church, without a white person present. Allen defied even this concession the following Sunday, preaching in a private house, and the city guard again broke up the meeting, compelled the out-of-towners to return to Philadelphia, and sentenced local black churchmen either to a flogging of ten lashes or a $5 fine. Nevertheless, informal evening meetings continued outside the scrutiny of white authorities, in private homes like the Veseys', for Denmark's wife, Susan, was an enthusiastic member of the church. Apparently the old carpenter, skilled as he was in languages and a natural-born leader, began to preach.[17]

For four years the city either tolerated or failed to notice these meetings, until it all exploded in the summer of 1822. A slave named

Peter was idling one Saturday on the wharves when he happened to see a boat, either the *Liberty* or the *Sally*, which had recently arrived from Saint-Domingue, at anchor in the harbor and flying a flag with a revolutionary device and the number "96." If it had been a "76" he would not have wondered about it, but "96" made no sense until an acquaintance, William Paul, who happened to be at the pier, hinted that it was a reference to the Haitian Revolution, and this dark-skinned William followed up with some loose complaints about the conditions of the slaves in South Carolina. Peter was frightened. He didn't know exactly what to make of such talk but knew it was dangerous, and he hurried away. He mulled over the conversation before finally turning to an admired friend, a free man of color and member of the exclusive Brown Fellowship Society. William Penceel did exactly what whites expected an intermediary class of free blacks to do in such a situation: he told Peter to go to his master and repeat the conversation.[18]

But Peter's master, John Prioleau, was out of town, so the slave told his "mistress and young master," but they thought little of the story and did nothing for five days. Finally John Prioleau returned home and heard the tale. He sprang into action, dashing off a quick and alarming note to the city's intendant or mayor, James Hamilton Jr., which he gave to Peter to carry the several blocks to the mayor's Bull Street mansion while he himself marched to John Paul's grocery store. Prioleau ordered all of the male slaves associated with the establishment to be sent to the guardhouse. The Haitian Revolution had long been the bogeyman of Charleston's whites, and if there was even the hint of anything afoot, a man like Prioleau would take no chances.[19]

The intendant, thirty-five-year-old James Hamilton Jr., had spent his life looking for fights. His father was an Irish-born soldier in the Continental army: he headed the column of Continentals down King Street when they repossessed Charles Town after the British evacuation. He settled in South Carolina and married "a lively, wealthy young widow from Santee, Elizabeth Lynch Harleston." Elizabeth Lynch brought her pedigree and plantations and slaves to the marriage, and James built an "elegant" house at the corner of East Bay and Society Streets in the heart of the bustling waterfront, settling down to the siring of children and the squandering of money. He spent so much that he wasted the patrimony of his only son to survive infancy, James Jr., so the son was cast upon life with little more than his family name and his own devices. He studied law. He joined the army and marched around quite a bit during the War of 1812, almost getting into battles, learning the martial trade, and concluding that "war was a sport fit for the gods." He followed in his father's footsteps when he married a Charleston heiress, Elizabeth Heyward, who owned three coastal plantations along with two hundred slaves and $50,000 deposited in the Charleston branch of the Bank of the United States.[20]

Hamilton tried the planter's life at Callawassie, a rice plantation on Port Royal Sound near Beaufort, and his biographer describes "his attitude toward Negroes in general and the southern slave system in particular" as the "fairly typical view [of] the nineteenth-century planter." But this is to gloss over the point that in 1820, planters had a wide range of views of slavery, from actively working to eradicate it from American soil to accepting it as a necessary evil. We do not know exactly what Hamilton thought in 1819, but more than likely he did what other profiteers did: that is, he did not look into the question too keenly, for it was inconvenient to find oneself in the wrong. But planting did not suit him, and Hamilton took up the lawyer's life in Charleston. He partnered with one of the ablest young lawyers in the city, James Louis Petigru, which proved beneficial, because Hamilton himself, in the opinion of one friend, was "not fitted by nature or study" for a career in law, lacking the "peculiar talent" required to turn the "dry pages of the law in pursuit of precedents or principles." Principles got in the way of the aristocrat's pursuits, and Hamilton distinguished himself more as a "hot-headed" duelist than a jurist. He found that politics was his true calling, something more suited to the girth of his ego. In the tribal way of Charleston, Hamilton was elected to represent St. Philip's and St. Michael's parish, the most populous and well-represented district in the state.[21]

Hamilton threw his lot in with the nationalists, like William Drayton, Hugh Legaré, Joel Poinsett, and his law partner, Petigru, who dominated Charleston's public offices. To be a nationalist in 1820 meant two things: you supported national tariffs on imported goods as a means of streaming revenue into the federal government; and you favored spending that money on internal improvements, such as roads through the Appalachian Mountains to the western states. This point of view required Hamilton to "repudiate [a] strict construction" of the Constitution, and he vociferously defended the implied powers granted to Congress and rejected the states' rights protests as the whining of dinosaurs out of touch with the modern age.[22]

When he was elected intendant of Charleston, his profile rose even higher, and he saw opportunity in the alarmed note from John Prioleau on that mid-afternoon, May 30, 1822. He summoned the city wardens to a special meeting of the Council, and he sent his own note to the governor of the state, who lived just a few doors down on Bull Street. The Council met in Hamilton's office, where they listened to the slave Peter relate his tale yet a fourth time. They hardly credited the implication that a slave revolt was imminent but decided to examine William Paul to make sure. William, who was in the guardhouse, was brought before the Council, where he admitted to being at the wharf the previous Saturday, to seeing the schooner with the strange flag, to speaking with Peter, but he "flatly denied" any talk of insurrection. Hamilton thought that William's manner displayed "obvious indications of guilt," though his later account did not mention what those subtle indicators were or how the Council separated them from the natural fear any slave would feel being interrogated in such a way.[23]

William had good reason to be scared: whether innocent or guilty, the Council consigned him to the "black-hole" of the workhouse, where he was interrogated through the night by Captain Dove, a misnamed authority if ever there was one. Clearly the slave was psychologically terrorized, and, given the raison d'être of the workhouse it is reasonable to assume—as most historians have—that he was tortured. Hamilton practically admitted this, and William Paul would have assumed this treatment would continue until he told his tormentors what they wanted to hear. Not surprisingly, he offered up the names of two unlucky acquaintances: Mingo Harth and Peter Poyas.[24]

Hamilton had Harth and Poyas arrested, their possessions searched, and they themselves questioned by two wardens, who found nothing suspicious about them at all. Disbelieving Paul's trembling denunciation, the wardens released the two slaves and seem to have

been convinced the supposed insurrection was much ado about nothing, though they took the precaution of employing some other slaves
to spy on the released prisoners. The two narratives from which we
draw most of our information—one written by Intendant Hamilton
and another by the leaders of a special court he set up—both distorted
the events to justify their own vigilant actions, and so they gloss over
such dissensions among the principal white authorities. But odd details,
like the release of Harth and Poyas, seem to point to serious disagreements on the Council at this early stage of investigation. Governor
Thomas Bennett was skeptical from the beginning and grew more and
more doubtful.[25]

William Paul, still incarcerated in the "black-hole," was tortured
for a week. On June 8, Thomas Napier, one of the Council, interrogated him yet again. The councilman's patience was at an end, and he
told William that if he did not confess all he knew, he would "soon be
led forth to the scaffold" and summarily hanged. Finally, William
cracked, for his only hope now was to tell his tormentors what they
expected to hear, and he began to spin a tale of a complex, coordinated
insurrection. The historian Michael Johnson demonstrates how the
testimony in the official court records indicates that interrogators asked
their questions in such a way as to indicate the answers they expected
to hear, and answering such questions with a view to one's own self-
preservation is a skill well practiced by any subaltern in a slave society.
The official record did not record the questions, but they are fairly
easy to surmise, given the answers.[26]

Did he know of an extensive insurrection? Napier asked William a
final time.

Yes, William wearily assented, he did.

Who was the leader?

He didn't know the name, William said vaguely. The leader of
the insurrection was a conjurer who had a charm that made him
"invulnerable."

When were the slaves going to rise up?

What should William say? The pain of his beatings would have
throbbed still in his body, persuading him he had better say what
they wanted to hear. But what did they want to hear? He had to say

something credible. The rebellion would have to start on a Sunday, when the slaves had enough leisure to gather and launch such a thing. But did Napier expect an insurrection to be close at hand? William asserted that it was all to happen on the second Sunday in June, barely a week away.[27]

Napier had his doubts about the testimony, as did the Council, the governor, and even James Hamilton himself, but once such words were spoken aloud the duty of a public servant was clear, and they mobilized a defense, passing out live ammunition to the city guard, increasing everyone's wariness, and unleashing upon the city long trails of rumors among both whites and blacks. One of these rumors put Ned Bennett, one of Governor Bennett's slaves, near the heart of the conspiracy, and when he heard he was implicated, Ned boldly placed himself before the intendant, eager to be examined so he could put such rumors to rest. Taken aback, Hamilton questioned him perfunctorily and let him go on his way.[28]

One private citizen, Major John Wilson, dragooned his slave George into the intelligence trade. George, who enjoyed his master's "unbounded confidence," was a large, smart, mixed-race blacksmith and a class leader at the African church. Of course he heard talk among the blacks—the whole city was awash in talk. For example, Joe LaRoche, one of George's students, told him on Thursday the thirteenth that *he* had heard that some blacks were planning "a public disturbance" at midnight on the coming Sunday. Here was something, but George must have thought it was a meager offering because he waited till nearly 8:00 p.m. the next day to mention it to the major, who shot out the door of his Broad Street house and didn't slow until he came to Hamilton's house, where, out of breath, he told the intendant what George said about what Joe LaRoche said about what someone else had said.[29] Hamilton's doubts vanished in a moment of excited, reckless discovery. Here, he reasoned, was independent confirmation of William Paul's doubtful confessions, which had been extracted under the terror of imminent execution. It did not occur to Hamilton that all the hullabaloo of whites marching with loaded weapons in the streets might have created the rumors of insurrection, which then took on a life of their own. He shot off an alarm to Governor Bennett that warned him that slaves were about to rebel. An incredulous Bennett had no choice but to call out the officers of the militia, who were to meet at Hamilton's house at 10:00 p.m. In the meantime, the Council was summoned so they could interrogate George, who must have been a bit frightened by the serious frenzy that his casual information seemed to have triggered among the city's fathers. He found himself facing a very worried and expectant set of white faces.

What did he know about the insurrection?

Joe LaRoche had told him about it, he replied.

What did he tell you?

That Rolla Bennett had tried to recruit him, and that Joe was supposed to warn George to leave the city on Sunday night.

Rolla, the interrogators knew, belonged to the governor and lived in the Bennett mansion just down the street at the corner of Lynch and Bull Streets.

Had George himself spoken to Rolla?

He had.

What had Rolla told him?

At this point George seemed to understand the grave consequences of his statements, and he began to temporize. Rolla, he told the court, had "complained of his hard living."

Was that all?

He was "at something wrong," George offered vaguely. It was something that made George's own heart "so full that [he] wept."

Did he tell you in express words that he "intended to join in a rising to kill the whites"?

No, George said nervously. They could ask Joe LaRoche: Joe was there also and heard most of what Rolla said.

Did Rolla say anything definite about an insurrection?

He told George that something was "gone too far now to be stopped."

What did he mean by that? Did he mean an insurrection?

George didn't know. Rolla never said anything about an insurrection.

Never a word?

"We seemed to understand each other," George said evasively, "that [an insurrection] was in contemplation." The sophistication of phrases like "was in contemplation" seem to indicate that the recorded testimony was not a verbatim transcript of what the witness said, but rather the recorder's summary or paraphrase. However it was phrased, the questioner would not have liked this answer at all. Equivocation was of no help. *Was an uprising never mentioned at all?*

Oh, George said, Rolla told Joe all about it, and Joe told me.

And then in vivid detail and via hearsay the plan poured forth: it would commence at midnight on Sunday; their first target would be the Arsenal and powder magazine, "an Army of 4,000 men from James Island would land at South Bay, march up and . . . kill all the City Guard and then they would kill all the whites."[30]

Joe's own testimony before the court was even more salacious: "When we have done with the fellows," he reported Rolla as having said, "we know what to do with the wenches."

That statement played on the greatest fear in the breasts of white men, but it clearly contradicted George, who said that Rolla said that *all* the whites were to be killed. It should have alerted the authorities to the unreliability of the testimony. But when white women were threatened by hordes of rebel rapists, consistency mattered little to Intendant Hamilton. Nor could he be troubled by the absurdly large number of supposed rebels—four thousand slaves who were to gather on James Island, commandeer boats to cross over the water, and invade the city's harbor-front. At its height, the Stono Rebellion constituted sixty rebels. Joe's story resembled the fears of white Charlestonians, harbored in their minds ever since the Haitian Revolution, of a full-scale, well-coordinated slave rebellion, which eventually made its own way into the story. Joe reportedly embellished the tale by suggesting that soldiers from "St. Domingo and Africa would come over and cut up the white people."

Would Rolla even kill his own master, the governor?

"My Army," Rolla supposedly told Joe, "will first fix my old Buck, and then the Intendant."

This tidbit surely raised the eyebrows of Hamilton and Bennett, who were in the room as Joe testified. So they themselves were to be personally targeted.

"I then told him I would have nothing to do with him," Joe assured the two politicians.

You did not aid him in any way?

"He begged me to lend him my boat to go into the Country and hasten down the country negroes as he feared they would not come."

And you refused?

"I lent it to him," Joe admitted but quickly added that he told Rolla "to let it alone."

The white men must have been aghast at this intelligence, and Joe quickly saw his mistake, that he was implicating himself.

"He was going to Johns Island," he said, hastily revising the story, temporizing. "He went to Johns Island at Christmas, but then this business was not in train."

The questioner was not yet satisfied, for supposedly Rolla first asked Joe to join the rebellion in March, and here it was three months later.

"I felt it was a bad thing to disclose what a bosom friend had confided," Joe said, and the expressions on the faces of the white men must have persuaded him to continue: "that it was wicked to betray him." Only after he considered how many were to be killed was personal loyalty to Rolla "over balanced," and he saw that his "duty was to inform" the authorities.

"I refused to go to the meetings as Rolla wished," he offered to the Council, by way of excusing himself. He was afraid that if he went to the meetings, he would have to speak against the uprising, and then they would "make away with me to prevent me from betraying them."

This testimony naturally led to questions about the meetings and who attended them, and Joe must have seen that his narrative, which enlarged his own heroic loyalty as the tale grew, was going to require more and more detail.

"I don't know where the meetings were held," he said archly, "but I believe it was in Bull Street in which street Denmark Vesey lives." He then denounced two other slaves, Ned Bennett and Matthias.

What about this Denmark Vesey? If Hamilton was doing the questioning, he would be very interested here, because Vesey was his neighbor, and surely he knew the haughty carpenter who had bought his own freedom twenty years earlier.

"I know Denmark Vesey," Joe said, on solid ground again, and then he spun out a new chapter in the story that included Vesey's talk of a "large army from St. Domingo and Africa," bitterness toward whites, an illustrative metaphor about a wagon stuck in mud, and an avowal "that if we did not put our hand to the work and deliver ourselves, we should never come out of Slavery." George Wilson, who had been Joe's confidante, must have stared wide-eyed at this elaborate and incriminating story, for Joe had never mentioned Vesey before. This whole stream of detail seemed to have come from a valve turned on by the questioner, and before it was over Joe was talking about passwords and burning down the city and killing informers.[31]

Governor Bennett knew his own slaves—for Rolla and Ned both belonged to him—and he distrusted the testimony of this Joe LaRoche. As well he might, for Rolla Bennett, who bore the brunt of Joe's denunciations, had stolen Joe's wife, Amarctta, and though Joe claimed to be well rid of her, we can hardly credit his claim that he was Rolla's "bosom friend." Quite possibly he had a grudge against Rolla, and the tangled web he spun accidentally caught up Ned, Matthias, and Denmark Vesey, who were probably guilty of nothing more than some bold talk. But Hamilton did not see it this way. Unfolding before his very eyes was the event his whole life had prepared him for: a crisis that needed a man of action and violence.[32]

Governor Bennett and Intendant Hamilton were not exactly political rivals—Hamilton was not yet large enough a figure for that—but they differed in their views of slavery. Bennett "opposed the slave trade and advocated greater leniency in the criminal and slave codes." He owned more than fifty slaves, but he was not a planter: he made his fortune from lumber mills and was one of the few Charlestonians one might describe as an industrialist.[33] With the naming of his own slaves as ringleaders in a plot involving thousands, Bennett's lax and liberal attitude was discredited. I do not mean to suggest that Hamilton cynically orchestrated a scare, but it greatly benefited him to believe Joe's incredible story of a vast conspiracy—and to lead the forces to disrupt it.

On Sunday night Hamilton put the Hussars, the Light Infantry, the Neck Rangers, the Charleston Riflemen, and the City Guard all under Colonel Robert Y. Hayne's command, and they paraded the streets all night in a show of power and glory. By this time, everyone in the city knew what was going on, though the story still was conveyed by rumor and innuendo, for the newspapers would not publish anything. As Sunday night wore on, white families on the plantations outside town sat up through the late hours with loaded weapons, and overseers lit great bonfires. In the city all were tense as families refused to go to bed, afraid to sleep, and listened for signs of rebellion and the exciting, if consoling, sounds of the night patrols.[34]

Not a single black man made the slightest gesture toward rebellion. Hamilton credited the quiet to his show of force, but the more likely explanation is that no blacks ever conspired to rebel. Perhaps there was some loose talk, some dissatisfactions voiced, some approbation of Haiti's President Boyer, but the whole episode tells us more about the whites than about the blacks of Charleston. One can imagine the domestic slaves of Charleston watching all of this frenzied activity, knowing the sequel would be the rounding up of suspects, exile, and executions. They must have resolved to keep their heads down, profess their humble loyalties, and hope against hope that they were not suspected, for suspicion was but a hairbreadth from condemnation. A witch hunt every bit as bogus and deadly as that in Salem 130 years earlier was about to commence.

Hamilton established a Committee of Vigilance and Safety to explore "the causes and character of the existing disturbance, and [to bring] to light and punishment the suspected and guilty." Four special "Police Officers" were commissioned by the committee to conduct the raids, searches, and arrests. For the next two weeks, this Vigilance Committee searched and arrested, terrorized and interrogated thirty-one more people, one or two a day. Interrogations most likely took place in the workhouse. What is absolutely clear to us today but largely obscured by the documents is that the Vigilance Committee molded the testimony it gathered. The first of the arrests, on Monday the seventeenth, which must have been based on the testimony of the three cooperative witnesses (George, Joe, and Peter) and the one tortured witness (William), brought in ten unfortunates: Rolla, Ned, Batteau, and Matthias (all owned by the governor), and Mingo and Peter (the property of James Poyas), and four slaves of various owners, Amhurst, Stephen, Richard, and John. When Rolla was brought in for questioning, the governor was completely satisfied as to his innocence, but by then events were beyond his control.[35]

Hamilton convened a special "Court of Magistrates and Freeholders," an ad hoc body enabled by the slave code written after the Stono Rebellion to dispose of the suspected rebels with some semblance of regular justice. It was comprised of seven men headed by Lionel Kennedy and Thomas Parker. But by the time suspects were hauled before an officer of this court to give testimony in the presence of a "recorder," the Vigilance Committee had already terrorized them, probably roughed them up, and certainly rehearsed them several times until they knew what the committee wanted them to say. In at least some cases of which Governor Bennett had personal knowledge, the Vigilance Committee's methods of interrogation put words into the mouths of its victims.[36] This was not necessarily a purposeful deception; it merely reflected their belief that sorting out guilt from blacks' testimony was a less complex affair than sorting it out from whites', that hearsay was trustworthy when dealing with slaves, that torture and threats to execute blacks produced reliable confessions.

The court went through the motions of deposing the committee's victims, but even the court's officers led witnesses: for example, instead of asking if the witness knew of a conspiracy, the judge might ask, "Who were the conspirators?" The witnesses knew that the road to mercy lay in giving up some names, and so names were given up. Nevertheless, the vast majority of suspects resisted, professing their innocence (some all the way to the gallows)—only 23 of 131 detainees ever cooperated with the committee and court.[37]

From June 19 through June 27, the court held what it later would call trials, but really it just deposed men individually, judging who was guilty and who was not from this aggregate testimony. On the second day of the Vigilance Committee's terrorizing raids, just as the court's depositions were getting started, one white citizen published a cautionary tale in the *Courier*. He told the story of a supposed insurrection a dozen years earlier in the town of Edgefield near the Savannah River. A rumor of rebellion led a cavalryman, well into his cups and impatient for some action, to blow his trumpet. A troop of cavalry, leaping to the notion that the sound was a rebel call-to-arms, ranged across the country, finding no one but a terrified single slave crossing a field on the way home from work. This slave, who had neither weapon nor horn, was "whipped severely to extort a confession, and then, with his eyes bound, commanded to prepare for instant death from a sabre, which a horseman was in the act of sharpening beside him." At that point the slave remembered someone named Billy who might own a hunting horn. Billy, another slave, was found out as he slept in the midst of his family, obviously no part of an insurrection that night, but the incriminating horn, though full of cobwebs, was thought enough evidence to sentence him to death. Billy's master's imploring appeal to reason did not sway the court from its resolve. The innocent man was killed, and all idiots claimed an insurrection had been averted. The man who offered this story to the public was William Johnson Jr., and he was particularly threatening to Hamilton because he also happened to be a justice of the United States Supreme Court. After witnessing the commotion of all of the mustered patrols the previous Sunday, he wrote up the anecdote, put it in his pocket, and delivered it to the *Courier*'s office the following Thursday. Finding that the editor was at a bar, he left it with an employee, jotting down the suggestion that it had a "useful moral" that "might check the causes of agitation which were then operating upon the public mind." He hoped that it would be a "solemn warning to the fabricators of alarming rumours."[38]

Hamilton and the members of his court (whose existence was not yet even known to Johnson) were insulted. They thought that Justice Johnson insinuated they might be dishonest in exercising their prerogatives. "We must *require* you," they wrote to him, to publish a retraction in the *Courier*. Johnson almost did so, but "such a view of the humiliation to which [he] was submitting rushed upon [him]" that he could not bring himself to submit. Instead he offered "an indignant repulse." He would not be cowed by such bullies. Johnson was used to being a lone voice against a majority. As Jefferson's first appointee to the Supreme Court, he was a lone Republican among Federalists in John Marshall's court, and he so often differed from his colleagues that his biographer calls him "the First Dissenter." But the weight of public opinion pressed on him. The voluminous "confessions" discovered by Hamilton proved to most whites that there was truth behind the rumors of insurrection. Ultimately, Johnson conceded the propriety of Hamilton's actions, and the principle of dissent was defeated. In hindsight, he admitted, he should not have published his anecdote, and with his tail between his legs he protested that he never "intended to interfere with the state authorities." Fear reigned supreme, and the lesson was well learned: one must not criticize or otherwise "interfere" with vigilance committees and secret courts.[39]

The committee continued its lethal work, ultimately aiming at Denmark Vesey. Given Joe LaRoche's and William Paul's later denunciations, the committee should have targeted Vesey much earlier, but Hamilton's henchmen do not seem to have started looking for Vesey until June 19, two days after they arrested and interrogated Rolla, Ned, and the others. The delay in the hunt for Vesey suggests that the committee got his name from the ten suspects they arrested on the seventeenth and then fed testimony to Joe LaRoche (a cooperative witness) and William (who gave testimony after torture). If Joe really knew about Vesey from the start, as his recorded deposition supposedly indicates, he would have told Hamilton back on Friday the fourteenth, and Vesey would have been targeted much earlier. By the time the vigilantes started looking for him, Vesey had made himself scarce. Whether he was in hiding or merely keeping low, as all free and enslaved blacks knew to do by this point, is uncertain. But we do know that on Saturday night the twenty-second, in the midst of a pelting storm of rain, Frederick Wesner and Captain Dove of the city guard found him at the house of "one of his wives." By the following Thursday, the twenty-seventh, the committee had extracted testimony against him from five slaves, Frank, Adam, Pompey, Edwin, and Jesse Blackwood, and supposedly put him on trial.[40]

These witnesses were hardly reliable. Jesse Blackwood, arrested and interrogated, denounced Frank. Frank's owner, a Mr. Ferguson, surrendered him to the committee, and under interrogation Frank confirmed Blackwood's denunciation of two other slaves on Ferguson's plantation, John and Pompey. The very docility of his slaves, Ferguson concluded, was evidence of insurrection, for rumor had it that Vesey had instructed the rebels to "assume the most implicit obedience" to their masters. Mr. Ferguson went to the governor's house asking for help in arresting the inoffensive John and Pompey, but Governor Bennett refused, saying that "it would be a great pity those poor wretches should suffer upon [such] slight evidence." So Ferguson had John and Pompey "severely punished in the presence of the other negro men on the plantation." For four weeks John and Pompey professed their innocence until finally they broke down.[41] One must wonder what would have convinced men like Ferguson of someone's innocence when loyalty was construed evidence of guilt. Such was the testimony that condemned Denmark Vesey.

No doubt some of what these witnesses said about Vesey had a kernel of truth. Frank claimed that he heard Vesey complain that "the negroes situation was so bad that he did not know how they could endure it." It seems that throughout the black neighborhoods Vesey was known as a bold talker. According to Edwin, for instance, after the first raids on June 17, "everybody, even the women [said] . . . that they wondered that Monday Gell and Denmark Vesey were not taken up." Unless we are to suppose that "everybody, even the women" were in on the conspiracy, this reference could mean nothing more than that Vesey and Gell were well-known to complain about slavery, and that much seems likely to be true. But under the pressure imposed by the Vigilance Committee, such behavior metamorphosed into fantastic stories of mustering all the countryside for an invasion of the city and inviting Haitian armies to land in Carolina. Even so, at the time of his so-called trial Vesey seemed no more prominent to the investigators than any of the others they supposed to be guilty. He was not yet described as the mastermind.[42]

We have no record of what exactly Vesey said during his own interrogations and deposition, except that he denied his guilt all along. None of the accused have voices in the historical record: only the accusers. On the twenty-seventh, the court wrapped up its work by condemning Vesey and five others to death, and these six awaited their executions in crowded cells in the workhouse because there was not enough room to confine them individually. Governor Bennett was outraged by the whole proceeding: conducting the court sessions in secret and not allowing the accused to confront those providing evidence against them did not seem calculated to serve justice. Innocent men, some of them his own slaves to whose character he himself could attest, might be sent to the gallows. He formally asked the state's attorney general, Robert Y. Hayne, for an opinion about the proceedings. Anxiously he waited, for the guilty were scheduled to be hanged on July 2, just six days after the court handed down their sentence.

The militias were active the eve of the executions lest some desperate slaves attempt to break open the workhouse and free their supposed leaders, but all was quiet. Shortly after sunup on the hot and humid morning, the prisoners, chained in iron, were put into a cart for the two-mile trip to the gallows beyond the edge of town, and still Attorney General Hayne had offered no opinion. Giant crowds of blacks and whites surrounded the scaffold. The condemned were marched up to the platform. The hangman pulled the nooses tight. The trapdoors swung open, and the six men dropped into thin air before the silent crowd. Later, privately, Intendant Hamilton admitted that they "met their fate with the heroic fortitude of Martyrs."[43] But they were not martyrs for the cause of armed rebellion, as Hamilton thought. Ned, Rolla, and Batteau, all slaves belonging to Governor Bennett; Jesse Blackwood; and Denmark Vesey, a free black man, were the wretched victims of white fear sparked by rumor and enflamed by Hamilton.

Hayne's judicial opinion came the next day, too late to save anyone's life, but it would not have mattered anyway, for Hayne sided with Hamilton. He could easily have done otherwise. Many whites in South Carolina still thought progressively enough to seek greater, not less, justice for slaves. For example, in 1821, the legislature amended legal codes to make murdering a slave a capital crime, just as it was for murdering a white person. Two successive governors, including Bennett, endorsed this measure, reasoning that in God's eyes a black life was as precious as a white. But Hayne chose to scold the governor, explaining that "slaves are not entitled" to public trial nor had they the right to confront their accusers. Hamilton used terror to get people to confess—in fact, he bragged about doing so—but Hayne saw nothing

untoward in obtaining testimony that way, because he was less interested in discovering the truth than in preserving the caste distinction
between races. In his mind, slaves must not be granted as *privileges* the
unalienable *rights* that God gave to whites. His vindication of torture
and star chambers sparked a loose political affiliation that all Americans
would eventually come to rue. Hayne and Hamilton were then just
state politicians, but soon they would ride their popularity as the sav-
iors of Charleston to the U.S. House and Senate, and there they stoked
the engines of John C. Calhoun's political machine.[44]

The executions of Vesey and Rolla and the others did not end
the rumors, arrests, and convictions. Monday Gell had been in custody
since the twenty-seventh, the same day the court condemned its first
victims. The Vigilance Committee arrested Charles Drayton on the day
of the execution, and others in the following weeks. Michael Johnson
thinks that the public criticism of Hamilton actually spurred him to re-
double this reign of terror because the larger the conspiracy grew, the
less likely anyone was to challenge his methods. To find yet more conspirators would justify the previous executions, and in fact Hamilton
later claimed that much of the testimony *after* Vesey's execution confirmed the slight testimony that had condemned him.

The secret court reconvened to deal with this new wave of prisoners. This time, mindful of its vulnerability on procedural issues, the
court actually conducted hearings during which a prosecutor accused
a suspect, the accused submitted a plea of innocence or guilt, and witnesses were examined on the specific question of that innocence or
guilt. But these were still witch trials, held in secret and with no pro-
vision for defendants to meaningfully challenge their accusers: by mid-
August, twenty-six more men were condemned to die on the flimsiest
bits of unreliable testimony.

Much of that testimony came from Monday Gell and Charles
Drayton, who had professed their innocence throughout their own interrogation and "trial." But on July 9 the court found them and three
others guilty. In Hamilton's view, their impending executions gave the
committee "some prospect of the investigation closing." The trail of
informers petered out, no more conspirators were denounced, and,
though thousands were reputed to have been involved, Hamilton con-

tented himself with killing only five more, the last of eleven "ringleaders." These prisoners were dragged out of their cells to hear their death sentences read aloud. Then they were dragged back to a holding cell, at which point Charles Drayton, whom Hamilton described as "overwhelmed with terror," knowing that his only hope lay in confession, harangued Monday Gell, who himself began naming names. The flood of their words was interrupted only by the "arrival of the blacksmith," who hammered the irons to their ankles and hands. Then the turnkey led them each to their solitary cells. That night, in the loneliness of his dark cell, chained to the floor, contemplating the scaffold, perhaps imaging the hood that closed out his last view of the trees, feeling already the fibers of the taut rope that would tighten on his windpipe, Charles Drayton called for the warden of the workhouse. He needed to see the intendant, he said. He was ready to disclose all he knew about the conspiracy. The warden sent word to Hamilton, who, in the predawn darkness, walked the six blocks from his Bull Street home to the workhouse.[45]

As the morning light brightened the faces of the houses across Magazine Street, the warden ushered the intendant into Drayton's cell, where he found the prisoner "in a state of the most lamentable depression and panic," out of his mind with "the fear of death, and the consequences of an *hereafter*" should he die before confessing. Kennedy and Parker, the leaders of the court, claimed that Monday Gell, Drayton, and Harry Haig were given the "impression" that if they cooperated "they would ultimately have their lives spared." Drayton utterly and absolutely prostrated himself before the man who held the power of life and death. The conspiracy was extensive, he told Hamilton, far wider than Hamilton ever imagined. Drayton named some names. Monday Gell, he assured the intendant, knew of many more.[46]

Charles Drayton was a cook in John Drayton's town home, a relatively unimpressive man, but Monday Gell had the look of a leader. He was "very well-known" throughout Charleston, making harnesses in his own shop in Meeting Street. Though he was not a free man, Gell was one of those slaves living in quasi-freedom. He kept a "large proportion" of his profits for himself, and he could read and write "with great and equal facility." Hamilton ordered that Monday Gell be sequestered for twenty-four hours in the same cell as Drayton, inventing some pretext for bringing them together so as to keep Gell from suspecting their strategy.[47]

That precaution was somewhat absurd, since this bit of cleverness gave the two slaves a golden opportunity to get their stories straight. Both knew that informing on others was now their only hope of surviving this reign of terror, and they used their time well. On the tenth another slave, Perault Strohecker, also broke under interrogation, and he informed the committee that letters had been sent to Haiti asking for help from President Boyer. Then Harry Haig confessed. Hamilton's investigative acumen tingled with excitement, and it must have been with a keen sense of satisfaction that he brought Drayton and Gell back in front of the court on the thirteenth. It was much less upsetting to execute men whose confessions confirmed your wildest suspicions. Not that Hamilton ever doubted his belief that he was exploding a most dangerous and subversive insurrectionary organization, but their confessions would vindicate him in the eyes of all critics. Drayton and Gell told him all he wanted to hear, denouncing dozens of others, painting a fantastic scheme that easily justified all of the questionable measures that Hamilton had employed, from the arbitrary searches and detentions, beatings and executions, to the expensive and alarming mustering and arming of volunteer guardsmen.

Gell told them the ringleaders were the six men they already hanged on July 2, those and himself. And if we can assign any guilt to Gell we must do so here, for he fingered another living man, William Garner, who was arrested in Columbia in August after an extensive manhunt. Gell admitted to writing letters to Haiti, to asking President Boyer to help the rebels after they sailed from Charleston.[48]

He delivered to Hamilton the names of forty-two people "who were in the habit of visiting his shop" on Meeting Street, supposedly "for the purpose of combining and confederating in the intended insurrection." And so Hamilton launched yet a third round of raids, this one bigger than either of the previous two. When it all ended in mid-August, 131 people had been detained in the workhouse over a two-month period. Thirty-five were executed, nearly two dozen on one Friday late in July, at a gallows "on the lines" along the site of the old city wall. Twenty-one were sold into exile, probably to Caribbean colonies. One was sold beyond the borders of the state. The court recommended to the owners of nine other slaves that they sell their property into exile. The court acquitted twenty-seven, and the Committee of Vigilance released another two dozen from their cells without bringing them before the court. Twelve were deemed to be guilty but had their death sentences commuted because they testified against others. Six of those twelve were "star" witnesses who provided 90 percent of the testimony at the July trials, and the "superstars" were Monday Gell, Charles Drayton, and Perault Strohecker, who provided three-quarters of the testimony in July. Almost everyone against whom these three witnesses testified was convicted; only four men were convicted and sentenced to death without their testimony. All of these six star witnesses had their executions commuted and were sentenced instead to exile. Three others who testified for Hamilton were spared as well, including William Paul, who was the first to break down while facing the scaffold back in June.[49]

By late July, Hamilton was satisfied that they had squashed the whole insurrection by disposing of its leaders, but supposedly thousands of slaves on the outlying plantations had been recruited, so the minority white population of the Lowcountry remained alert and nervous. On July 15, in the midst of the second wave of arrests and trials, Thomas Bennett asked the secretary of war, John C. Calhoun, to send federal troops to the city, hoping that such a show of force would "tranquilize the public mind" while also demonstrating to the black population the hopelessness of rebellion. A week later Calhoun ordered an artillery company to sail from St. Augustine, and when they finally disembarked in mid-August at Fort Moultrie, they provided an emotional end to the entire episode.[50]

But the rebellion transformed the political climate, as if the white population had been brought through a fire that burned all liberal sentiment from their hearts. For instance, something had to be done about the African Church. Hamilton ransacked the church buildings and the homes of its leaders in a dogged search for evidence. To his credit, finding none, he did not trump up anything, and when he found a rumor about Reverend Morris Brown's involvement to be false, he dropped that line of inquiry. Nevertheless, the leaders of the African Methodist Episcopal Church could read the writing on the wall, and they "voluntarily dissolved" their congregation, a decision that Hamilton publicly approved. The city could no longer tolerate an independent black church, and the searches of its leaders efficiently frightened them into capitulation. Likewise, the white authorities reined in the lax attitudes that had allowed the growth of the quasi-free neighborhoods. Hamilton noted that the slaves at the heart of the conspiracy were those who enjoyed the most freedom: they "had no individual hardship to complain of, and were among the most humanely treated negroes in our city." The problem stemmed from the "misguided benevolence" of indulgent owners who allowed their slaves to achieve a level of comfort, dignity, education, and unsupervised leisure, giving them "the facilities for combining and confederating in such a scheme." The court explained that the rebels avoided recruiting domestic servants, because they might be loyal to their masters, so most of the recruits came from "Negroes hired or working out, such as Carters, Draymen, Sawyers, Porters, Labourers, Stevidores, Mechanics, those who worked in the lumber yards, and in short to those who had certain allotted hours at their own disposal." The killings and deportations of June and July constituted a pogrom of the quasi-free blacks of Charleston.[51]

The rebellion also cast a shadow of suspicion on the free people of color in Charleston. Only 8 free people of color, some called "black" and some called "col[ore]d," were brought before the court, a small proportion of the 131 examined. But the great leader, Denmark Vesey, the court explained, "being a free man encountered none of those obstacles which would have been in the way of a slave; his time was at his own disposal, and he could go wherever he pleased, without interruption; qualifications and advantages absolutely necessary for the Chief in a Conspiracy."[52]

All the bogeymen of conservative whites found their way into the Vesey Rebellion—Haiti, the African Methodist Episcopal Church, quasi-free blacks, even free blacks. Most odd, however, was the contention that northern congressmen caused the insurrection. In early 1819, Congressman James Tallmadge of New York moved that as a condition of statehood Missouri be barred from admitting any more slaves and that children of slaves then residing in Missouri would be freed upon reaching their twenty-fifth birthday. The debate lasted two years, and Hamilton insisted that those arguments produced "discontent and delusion" in Vesey's circle. The "wanton recklessness" of senators like New York's Rufus King deluded Charleston's slaves into thinking that "those beautiful propositions of civil and natural freedom" applied to them. The claim was nonsense, but it reveals Hamilton's greatest anxiety: the federal government's long-awaited, long-delayed taking up of the cause of justice.[53]

The votes on Missouri came down more or less along geographic lines, which meant that Tallmadge's amendment passed in the House but failed in the Senate, where southern states had more power. Nevertheless, it must be remembered that most of those who wanted Missouri to be a slave state wanted to get rid of slavery. For example, the *Charleston Courier* argued that the Missouri Question did not involve "an *extension of slavery*, that is, the multiplication of slaves in our country." Rather, the issue "concerns only the *diffusion* or the *concentration* of the slaves now in the country." In other words, by admitting Missouri as a slave state, the nation would dilute the number of slaves in other states. Not only in Charleston but all throughout the South, politicians and newspapers arguing for diffusion implicitly and often explicitly acknowledged the principle that slavery is evil and ought to gradually disappear. We might be tempted to dismiss this sort of reasoning as being disingenuous as John Rutledge's empty promise to Connecticut at the Constitutional Convention, except when we remember that it was written in Charleston for an audience of Charlestonians. Nearly all southerners still thought slavery was incompatible with a free republic. As William Freehling explains, "southern congressional speeches" on the Missouri Question demonstrated that even those who voted to extend slavery into that state were "set against . . . permanent slavery." Their opposition to the bill depended upon their umbrage with "outside impositions to end temporary slavery." They erected their opposition to Tallmadge's amendments on the constitutional principle that only the southern states themselves could set the timetable for the abolition of slavery. The federal government, they feared, would move too fast.[54]

"Only in South Carolina," Freehling points out, "did a southern leader advocate *perpetual* slavery." The man was William Smith, the same politician responsible for keeping the slave trade open in the United States to the very last possible moment. The Greek and Roman republics had slaves, he contended, and Jesus Christ sanctioned it, as did its benevolent practice in the South, where "no class of laboring people in any country upon the globe, excepting the United States, are better clothed, better fed, or more cheerful, or labor less." Black children play with white children, Smith pointed out, forming strong affections between the two that are never forgotten, "so much so, that in thousands of instances there is nothing but the shadow of slavery left." Another senator reminded Smith of Jefferson's famous opinion, that when he reflected that God was just he trembled for his country. Smith replied that Jefferson's observation "could not have been founded on facts." In the Revolutionary era, he explained, Jefferson, like "every American was filled with enthusiasm," but in later years, after the inebriating fumes of the Revolution dissipated, after his "mind became enlarged by reflection and informed by observation," he must have discarded "such sentiments." How else could one explain the fact that Mr. Jefferson still owned slaves?

Here was a radical, new interpretation of the nation's founding principles: grandiloquent statements asserting liberty and equality were nothing more than enthusiastic, unrealistic, irresponsible liberal rhetoric about "natural rights." It was true, Smith conceded, that the Declaration of Independence announced that *all* men were created equal and were endowed by their creator with rights to liberty and to pursue happiness. But no one with any common sense thought such self-evident universal truths applied to black people. If such "truths" applied to blacks, he asked the senators of northern states, "why did you not all emancipate your slaves [in 1776], and let them join you in the war? But we know this was not done. . . . [T]here was an universal [unspoken] consent, at that day, that these people . . . had no share in the body politic."[55] In other words, Smith began to contradict the notion that Jefferson's words were aspirational; that the Founding Fathers believed in the gradual abolition of slavery; that sometime in the nation's future equality and liberty would be applied to "all men." One could not use such principles to govern in the real world. Practical, common experience and a realistic view of human relations ought to direct American public policy, and the long experience of human history proved that slavery was permanent. Jefferson's truths were so much empty rhetoric self-evidently contradicted by the way whites treated blacks in every state of the Union. Real-world experience trumped idealistic principle.[56]

Smith's views were unique in Congress, but they had their effect in Charleston, where Hamilton made a villain of New York's Senator Rufus King. King hit the nail on its ideological head when he claimed that the main motive "for the admission of new states into the Union" was "the extension of the principles of our free government." If slavery were an inherited evil, as everyone in Congress but William Smith conceded, its continuance was only justified by the dangers of immediate emancipation. Then what was the logic of expanding it to Missouri? Or to the Arkansas territories? "Slavery," he opined, "unhappily exists within the United States. Enlightened men in the states where it is permitted, and every where, out of them, regret its existence among us, and seek for the means of limiting and mitigating it." This kind of talk, James Hamilton insisted, led to slave insurrections.[57]

Kennedy and Parker, the heads of the secret court, were a bit more circumspect. They suggested that "perhaps" Vesey "garbled and misrepresented" the "speeches in Congress." But their general message was the same as Hamilton's: talking about the natural rights of blacks leads to violent disruptions of the social order.[58] Thus began the promotion of perpetual slavery, for if one cannot talk about the natural rights of blacks, how can one gradually grant them?

Some whites and free African Americans had been trying to build institutions that would prepare slaves (and slave owners, for that matter) for their eventual self-determination—the AME church, for example. The quasi-free in Charleston were themselves pushing society toward more liberal attitudes and practices, taking advantage wherever white vigilance slackened. But as history slowly, naturally, liberalized southern society, and as the federal government began to gesture toward hastening it along, men like Hamilton who had no intention of watching slavery disappear realized that the old paternalism would no longer serve. The times required a frank avowal of *permanent* slavery, even if that avowal required one to repudiate the self-evident truths of the Declaration of Independence. The Denmark Vesey rebellion provided the trigger for Smith's idea of perpetual slavery to begin rooting itself, insidiously, almost unnoticed, in the minds of the white population. Hamilton used the politics of fear to roll back Charleston's liberal, lax, progressive notions about African Americans, and it started a back-lashing, neoconservative movement. Probably, very few people realized the tectonic drift set in motion by the Vesey affair, because in this case public policy was well ahead of ideology. Tainting liberalism as hopelessly romantic and idealistic, and outlawing talk about natural rights, moved the siege engines further into place.

Already in 1820 South Carolina forbade the immigration of free blacks into the state, but post-Vesey legislation instituted even more severe penal laws. Hamilton introduced a bill expelling all free blacks who had resided in the state less than five years, but the legislature amended that bill to only require that they pay a $50 tax. More controversial was a law requiring that black sailors be sequestered in the jail while their vessels were in port, that the ship's master pay the expenses of the jail, and that violations would result in the sailor being sold into slavery. A vibrant exchange of literature and ideas circulated among the Atlantic ports, and we know that much "incendiary" literature (such as that aroused by the Missouri Question) came into the hands of liberal Charlestonians, both black and white, from the hands of sailors. The several Negro Seaman Acts, as they came to be called, were a bold gambit to suppress speech, and, cloaked as they were in the sanctimony of security measures preventing another Vesey-type insurrection, they were unassailable in Charleston.[59]

The first challenge to the 1822 Negro Seamen Act came not in a local court but, ironically enough, in Justice William Johnson's federal circuit court. A Jamaican sailor was seized by vigilantes and hauled off to the jail, and the British consul protested to President John Quincy Adams. The vigilantes belonged to the South Carolina

Association, a group of leading citizens who organized after the Vesey Rebellion in order to police the city, exposing those who through laxity and liberal ideals ignored the laws regulating the colored community of Charleston. When such violations were pointed out, the Association's members would put themselves at the disposal of the sheriff as a sort of deputized posse. They did not go as far as the roaming bands of radical Islamists do today when they beat up violators of Sharia law, for the Association was made of honorable men—governors, ambassadors, scientists, lawyers, rich planters, bankers—who were above such things. But they professed such an inordinate love for law and order that they would take its enforcement into their own hands. Their express purpose was to make sure that the penal laws were enforced strictly and that no liberal public sentiment suffered those draconian rules to be ignored. In other words, the Association meant to intimidate whites more than blacks, and it reinforced in its members and bred in the community the kind of radical, reactionary ideology embodied by Hamilton. It discouraged and humiliated liberals, essentially labeling progressive thought and action as dangerous and even illegal. William Johnson was outraged. "Flagrant as the violations of [federal] law and constitution are under" the Negro Seaman Act, Johnson wrote to President Adams, "I stand alone almost in the little opposition that I am able to make to it." Almost alone: the state's attorney general was James Louis Petigru, who also thought the Negro Seaman Acts were unconstitutional, and so the law's advocate was the extralegal Association, which, Johnson reported, had "managed to carry with them the populace, and to muzzle the papers." Johnson ruled that the 1822 South Carolina Negro Seaman Act was unconstitutional. But jailers simply ignored Johnson's opinion, and the Association attacked Johnson in both the *Courier* and the radical *Mercury* in such vituperative and alarmist terms that the case pushed South Carolina "toward more militant sectionalism."[60]

States' righters consolidated for the first time and celebrated their anti-Union sentiments, all in defense of an institution that they ostensibly considered an inherited evil. Men such as Hamilton willingly sacrificed progressive policy and liberal opinion on the altar of security, which was erected within the sanctuary of public fear, fear raised and multiplied by a spurious overreaction to an invented conspiracy. To return to our metaphor of the military siege, Hamilton rolled the big guns into place and swung their muzzles toward the city. Using the fear he generated through the Vesey Rebellion, Hamilton leveraged the public into enacting and enforcing proslavery policy. Those policies violated the logic of their own paternalistic ideology, so the siege upon the mind of the South was not yet complete. It would take another dozen years for ideology to catch up to practice.

6

THE FIRST SECESSION

||

"**T**oday I have torn up my novels."

Thus began Angelina Grimké's dark night of the soul on January 10, 1828, when the aristocratic woman from Charleston was twenty-two years old. Even given the low reputation of novels in the early nineteenth century, her unequivocal judgment, sentence, and execution seems a bit extreme. But Grimké did not single out books: she also put "a great deal of [her] finery . . . out of the reach of anyone" by splitting open an ottoman, jamming these lace decorations and whatnot inside, and sewing up the seam again, a gesture less resolute than the tearing up of the novels but more deliberate and bizarre. Grimké had the zeal of a martyr, eager to "look like" a Christian so all the world would see that she was condemning it and its "trifling vanities." She believed that the world would hate her, but she also believed that the "shafts of ridicule" it hurled at her would place her "one step higher on an eminence," an ascension that comes through "humbling." She sought that paradoxical species of humility that fills the sufferer with an exalting, sweet sense of her own superiority. Two days later, a desire to plunder the ottoman took hold of her, and in "grief and shame" Grimké found "it hard to yield [to her Master] willingly."[1]

Grimké grew up Episcopalian, and in Charleston that church frowned on enthused Christians. To the horror of her family she converted to the more austere Presbyterianism, where her religious devotion flourished until a restive spirit sought a covenant yet more austere. Quakerism was so exacting that it was barely on the edge of respectability. Not long after her conversion to plain dress, a humbling comment sent Angelina into sobs, and she fled the dining room for the solitude of her bedroom. She cried a lot. Five days later, her older sister, Sarah, who was more a parent than a sibling, reprimanded her for being mean to their mother, and Angelina cried, and in the midst of reconciliation she "burst into a flood of tears" again. She cried in April; she cried in May; she cried in August and October, releasing the pressure of painful forces struggling in her soul.[2]

Privately, she doubted her own severity, but even so she could not contain it: she must spread it throughout the world. She so frightened her Sunday school pupils that one young, upset girl, ashamed at her own weakness, confessed to Angelina that she had "taken great pleasure in cultivating" geraniums. Grimké put an end to that sort of thing. Another student had amended her dress to an admirable plainness but found she couldn't give up her fancy hat, which she had recently bought, because she could not afford to buy a simpler one. Grimké obligingly annihilated its pretty parts, handing back to her disciple the meeker crown.[3]

Her diary is filled with the drama of tempting ribbons and the exquisite, nearly erotic surrender to the unquenchable demands of her Master. Pride battles humility, and it is almost pathetic to see how much energy and sincerity this bright, young, budding intellectual squandered on the clichéd and shallow struggles so typical to the zealous victim of the Second Great Awakening. Such emotional and intellectual energy could have been much better spent, as Virginia Woolf would remind us, on the study of Latin or Greek. And the modern reader can hardly help but root for the devil, hoping that some simple pleasure might save this brilliant soul from the scars of self-inflicted piety. Considering that within a decade Grimké would become Charleston's most effective and notorious emancipator, it is amazing how much this private drama of her soul squeezes out all notice of the public events staged outside her window.

Unnoticed by Grimké, the vice president of the United States rebelled against the president, and the state of South Carolina staged its first version of secession, a dress rehearsal for Civil War. History would repeat itself, first as farce and then as tragedy. The star of this particular comic opera was John C. Calhoun, who seemed the unlikeliest of South Carolinians to lead a fight against the national government.

John Caldwell Calhoun was born in the Carolina Upcountry the year John Laurens died. The English murdered one uncle during the Revolution, while another died at the Battle of Cowpens, and yet a third was imprisoned when the British took Charles Town. Nestled in the foothills of the Appalachians, the Calhoun house percolated with hatred of the British. John's mother was full of "intelligence and energy of character . . . strong will and temper," all traits the son inherited. His father, Patrick, an Irish immigrant, came to South Carolina via Virginia, traveling by wagon down along the eastern edge of the mountains, a good representative of the new, inland settler. In 1756, when he built his first rude cabin in Carolina, about seven thousand whites and three hundred slaves dotted the region that bordered on Oconee and Cherokee lands and the wild forests full of panthers and wolves. Within ten years his father was laying out towns and surveying claims, skilled work that led to his own accumulation of twelve hundred acres. They were stern Presbyterians, and throughout his life Calhoun would be known for his remarkable self-discipline, capacity for work, his disinterest in most things that the rest of us do for recreation.[4]

His contemporaries thought Calhoun burst upon the national scene "like Minerva from the head of Jove, fully grown and clothed in armor: a man every inch himself, and able to contend with any other man."[5] There's good reason for this myth. His childhood had very little formal education; his father died when he was twelve; when he was fourteen he had to go to work managing the family's plantation, supervising about thirty slaves; not until he was eighteen, when his older brothers sent him first to a two-room school near Abbeville and then on to Yale in 1802, did he begin his studies. After Yale, Calhoun read law in a Charleston firm. The abstemious, backcountry, "cast-iron" man complained of the "intemperance and debaucheries" of the city, and all his life, true to type, he looked down from the mountains with disapproval of the coast.[6]

But his arrival on the national scene was helped rather than hindered by these humble beginnings. The Calhouns were big fish in a small pond, but the small pond of the Upcountry was gaining more political clout every passing year. A light like Calhoun's might have gone unnoticed in sunny Charleston, but it shone brightly in the gloomy glens and hollows of the Appalachian foothills. He was elected to the state legislature in October 1808 at twenty-six years of age, and he held his own against the fancy intellects of Charleston, so it is no surprise that at the age of twenty-nine his neighbors elected him to Congress. In Washington, Calhoun found himself amid some of the most remarkable talent that ever went to Congress, all young men, including Daniel Webster of Massachusetts and Kentucky's Henry Clay. Calhoun's colleagues from South Carolina, William Lowndes and Langdon Cheves, were under thirty years old. Clay, though only thirty-four, was Speaker of the House. All were conscious that the torch of national authority had been passed to a new generation born after the Revolution, and Calhoun, whose pride yielded to no man, thought always about the historic dimensions of his generation. In his manner and speeches he conveyed a sense of his own apostolic righteousness, which began offending other politicians both at home (like William Smith, who would be a long-serving senator from South Carolina and lifelong enemy of Calhoun) and in the capital (like Richard Stockton, who right away "grumbled about being forced to endure Calhoun's 'lectures'").[7]

As regards slaves, Calhoun had little imagination. He followed in the paternalistic pattern bequeathed to him by the previous generation of Carolina's planters, inheriting their sense of responsibility over a "family" whose lowest dependent members were the chattel slaves. But he lacked the sense of embarrassment, the apologetic reflex of men like Henry Laurens, who sensed distinctly the hypocrisy of holding slaves while dancing around the Tree of Liberty. Most of the slaves who toiled in the Carolina Upcountry came from the Lowcountry. They were Americans, not Africans. Their parents had been slaves, and they were born into slavery. It was easier for men in Calhoun's generation to avoid the moral question, especially since western provinces of the South were on the make, trying to build their fortunes by the obvious method. This is not to say Calhoun did not know that slavery stole a person's unalienable right to liberty. The slave trade was only closed in 1808, when he was twenty-six, and he understood how evil it was. In 1816 he declared in Congress that he "felt ashamed" that it had been South Carolina that had railroaded the protections for the "odious traffic" through the Constitutional Convention of 1787.[8] But he never followed the logic of his own condemnation to its conclusion. He never expressed the wistful hope heard so often during and right after the Revolution that slavery would go away. Eventually, Calhoun was master of two plantations, Fort Hill and Cane Brake, populated by well over a hundred slaves. He was sometimes sensitive to selling slaves who were part of Fort Hill's greater "family," sometimes not. One favorite piece of property, Sawney, had been a boyhood friend, and in adulthood Calhoun allowed him some fields to grow his own cotton, a significant privilege, the exception that proves the rule of slave dependency. Calhoun fancied himself a responsible head of household, but his paternalism was not so well received by the slaves. Sawney's own children ran away. His daughter, Issy, tried to kill Calhoun's young son and burn down the big house. Punishment for running: a week in jail on bread and water followed by "30 lashes well laid on" by someone hired for the task. Punishment for stealing: being sold away from family and friends.[9] Even so, his biographer suggests that Calhoun "could not question the morality of slavery because he had grown up with it in the new nation, watched its expansion bring honor to his father and prosperity and republican civility to the upper country and unity to the entire state."[10] As we have seen, this formulation is not true: Calhoun had plenty of examples near to hand of people who questioned slavery. The question, then, is how someone so smart as Calhoun could manage to forget that slavery contradicted the principle of liberty. The simple answer is that it did not pay to be a dissenting minority, not if one thought his proper place was living among the state's elites.

Calhoun took a great step in that direction when he married Floride Colhoun, the eighteen-year-old daughter of his cousin (Calhoun was twenty-eight). The Colhouns owned a plantation, Bonneau Ferry, near Charleston, and were the richest of the extensive Calhoun clan. Instantly, the rising political star joined ranks with the Lowcountry culture and society. When most people think of John C. Calhoun, they imagine one of the late portraits, with the fanatical gray hair and the wild eyes of an Old Testament prophet, the mirror image of abolitionist John Brown's righteousness. But in 1811 he had a face that women might fall in love with, a serious Mr. Darcy kind of look about him, and just as his prickliness and frigidity among other men was legendary, so too was his charm among women.[11]

Calhoun was a nationalist, which meant he wanted to strengthen national defense and build infrastructure, especially roads over the Appalachians to the western states and territories. The federal government's only way to generate revenue was to tax imports, and even though such tariffs tended to favor manufacturing states over agricultural states by raising the price of European manufactured goods, Calhoun defied narrow sectional politics and supported tariffs in his early years in Congress. The government needed money if it was going to wage war, and in the winter of 1811–12, Calhoun and the other war hawks lectured Congress about how Great Britain trampled the nation's honor. Calhoun penned a Foreign Relations Committee report to Congress detailing grievances against England—impressed sailors, shipping seized in international waters, trouble fomented among the Indians—in a language that paralleled the reasoned prose of Jefferson's Declaration of Independence but differed in telling ways. Where Jefferson spoke of the United States claiming its "separate and equal station," Calhoun wrote about the American "*character* and station among the nations of the earth." Calhoun's personification of the country was a subtle but important shift: Jefferson wrote about securing rights; Calhoun wanted to "vindicate the rights *and honor* of the nation" and "*avenge* the wrongs" America had suffered.[12] It was as if the two countries were gentlemen, and the insulted party demanded satisfaction on the field of honor.

This kind of rhetoric carried the nation into the War of 1812, which might have been symbolized by the disaster of the British burning of the White House had not that other great nationalist, Andrew Jackson, rescued the war hawks with his sensational victory at New Orleans, which secured the United States' claim to the entire navigable Mississippi River region. In 1817, Calhoun rose to a cabinet position—secretary of war—under President Monroe, and he seemed on the road to the presidency. One of the great ironies of his life occurred in these years. Spain was then a decrepit European power at the center of a decaying empire, and its Florida territory was the refuge of runaway slaves, English provocateurs, and restive Indian nations. Friction with an ever-expanding population of American settlers grew to a fever, and Monroe and Calhoun sent General Jackson to the American border to set things right. But Jackson did more than that. Their instructions were ambiguous enough to allow Jackson to claim he was authorized to drive out the Spanish, which he promptly did, burning Indian villages and hanging English agents as he went, essentially conquering Florida and sparking an international incident. Monroe gathered his cabinet. What were they to do? Should they rein in the dangerous general? Calhoun, rightly concerned that a military officer had usurped civilian authority, suggested that they arrest him. Secretary of State John Quincy Adams analyzed the situation from a sophisticated, geopolitical vantage, and he realized that Jackson had done at a stroke what would take diplomacy generations to do: asserted the United States' manifest destiny to occupy the continent. Adams suggested they thank the general, which they did, and all came out of the secret cabinet meeting wearing smiles. Spain promptly offered to sell Florida to the United States, and for years Jackson thought it was Calhoun who had been his champion.

Adams beat Jackson in a race for the White House in 1824. Neither won a majority in the Electoral College, so the decision went to the House of Representatives, which chose Adams when Henry Clay exchanged his influence for the job of secretary of state. Jackson was outraged. Calhoun, who had been elected vice president, was likewise outraged, and from his first day in office he joined Jackson in opposing the administration, helping to make Adams's presidency dismal and ineffective. When Jackson won the 1828 election, he owed much to the support of Calhoun, who was again elected vice president.

During the transition, the issue of tariffs came up again, putting Calhoun in a bind. On the one hand, Calhoun had no problem with tariffs that promoted the "general welfare" of the nation, such as coastal forts and a robust standing army. But increasingly in South Carolina, tariffs were seen as promoting the *particular* welfare of one section (the mid-Atlantic manufacturing states) at the expense of another (the agricultural Deep South). The economy of South Carolina was in shambles. The price of cotton collapsed, plantation profits withered away, and the state was bleeding people who were leaving for fresh western lands. All was blamed on the tariff, which become the bête noire of radical states' righters. But Calhoun wanted to be president, and to get elected he would have to appeal to all sections or at least most sections of the country, especially Pennsylvania, so he supported tariffs much longer than other South Carolinians, eroding his support at home so much that, in 1827, he was forced finally to make an irrevocable decision. A 50 percent increase in the tariffs on woolens had been proposed in Congress, and when the Senate split evenly on the matter, Vice President Calhoun, as president of the Senate, had to cast the tie-breaking vote. To allow the tariff would shore up his standing in the big-population states of Pennsylvania, New York, and New Jersey, but it might kill him at home. He voted to defeat the tariff, his first timid step away from his ambition to be president and toward sectionalism. But what could he do? One could not become president without the support of his home state.

In the summer session of 1828, steep hikes in tariffs, most from 30 to 50 percent, were again proposed. Calhoun's strategy for opposition exemplified the worst of cynical politics. South Carolina would pretend to support the bill but amend it with even more tariffs specifically meant to harm the interests of New England. At the eleventh hour, with a bill so "obnoxious" to New Englanders, southern congressmen would reveal their hand, and the South and the East would oppose the bill and defeat it. The idea was to lay the blame on New England, but in the final tally this dissimulation—with which Calhoun colluded—blew up in the face of South Carolina's congressional delegation, for enough New Englanders voted for the bill to help it squeak by. Adams, of course, signed this "Tariff of Abominations" into law.

South Carolina erupted in protest. The state's House of Representatives appointed a special committee to plot its opposition against the despised law, and the committee appealed to the state's ablest statesman, John C. Calhoun. At this point, Calhoun did not seem to recognize that he had already crossed his Rubicon. Still harboring thoughts of the White House, he "was careful to project a moderate image" to the public, and he accepted his assignment on the condition that his authorship be kept secret. Then he retired to his study, a detached building on his lavish Fort Hill property, to write the most pernicious disquisition on the Constitution ever authored by an American statesman: the *South Carolina Exposition and Protest*.[13]

The *Exposition* first explains why the Tariff of 1828 so aggrieved South Carolina. The document is written in the boring prose of the academician, clearly the work of a student of economic theory. Calhoun's long, rambling disquisition invoked the laws of supply and demand to demonstrate, pretty accurately, that the "general competition of the world" as regards staple crops, especially cotton, compelled South Carolina "to sell low" when it exported. The oversupply of cotton explained the collapse in its price on the world market, and nothing could or should be done about these prices, Calhoun explained, as much to educate South Carolinians as anyone else, because the proper operation of the laws of free trade dictated prices of commodities. But the low price of cotton was not the root of South Carolina's problems. Planters were losing money because the tariffs forced them to pay unnaturally high prices for the means of production, compelling South Carolinians "to buy high." Manufacturers might have to "buy high" just as farmers did, but the tariff allowed them to sell high as well, effectively indemnifying them against the *burden* of the tariff. "By this very increased price" in manufactured goods, which was induced by the tariffs, "the fruits of [South Carolina's] toil and labour . . . are transferred from us to" the manufacturing states. The tariff system enabled the majority of the nation's citizens to rob the minority—and do it legally, because of the principle of majority rule.[14]

If this injustice takes center stage in the *Exposition*, lurking in the wings of every page is Calhoun's fear that the golden age of the plantations might end with his generation. Just give the planters "free trade with the world," Calhoun insisted, "and we would become . . . the most flourishing people on the globe." Unacknowledged in that encomium to free markets was that the state's economy depended on unfree labor. Calhoun does not seem to consider that the cost of cotton's production in America was kept artificially low by the constitutional protections of

slavery. For two generations, America's long-standing policy of protecting slave labor artificially depressed the cost of producing cotton
and so it artificially inflated the profits that went into the pockets of
planters. Calhoun essentially admitted as much in a fascinating thought
experiment. Suppose the South responded to the incentives offered
by the federal government's tax policies. Suppose it embraced manufacturing. If southerners built factories, the tariff could make them as
rich as their neighbors in Pennsylvania, and Calhoun had sufficient
imagination to envision factories sprouting up in Charleston and Savannah and Richmond. But he could imagine no one working in those
factories except slaves. In that case the southern factory owners would
have a competitive advantage, because slavery would artificially reduce
their costs of production, while northern manufacturers paid for labor
on the free market. The danger of the tariff was not that it would impoverish the South; Calhoun feared that it would force the South to pros-
per by developing manufacturing industries, which in turn would give
northerners the motive to eliminate the federal protections for unfree
labor. In a moment of almost unguarded frankness, Calhoun reasoned
that the North "would not tolerate" such an unfair advantage, and so
it would "make [war] on our labor."[15]

Almost unguarded because Calhoun was still careful to avoid the
word "slave." There are only "staple" states and "manufacturing"
states. Full candor would force one to concede that slavery violated the
fundamental right to own one's personal labor. In a word, Calhoun's
rhetoric reveals how slavery still embarrassed him and the most radical
southerners even as late as 1828. They could not discuss it frankly lest
they be forced to admit not only to the world but to themselves that
the whole "staple" system required one person to steal someone else's
labor, a form of protectionism that violated free trade.

Despite this evasion, the rhetoric of the *Exposition* reveals how the
discourse of slavery was beginning to shift away from avoidance and
apology toward a rhetoric reliant on reason, logic, even the kind of
arguments that might come from a social scientist. In 1828, Calhoun
still had to avoid the great truth: that slave labor was the theft of the
God-given rights to both liberty and equality. But once those principles
were omitted, all manner of recourse to deductive reasoning might be

pressed, and Calhoun's treatise ascends like the many-roomed mansion of truth from a colonnade of "universally conceded" principles about humanity: "Men ask not for burdens, but benefits"; "Exports and imports, allowing for the profit & loss of trade, must be equal in a series of years"; "irresponsible power is inconsistent with liberty and must corrupt those who exercise it"; "the governed should govern"; "as in all other cases of compact between parties having no common judges, each party has an equal right to judge for itself as well of infractions as the mode and measure of redress."[16]

This last "principle" brings us to the heart of the matter: how might the American republic prevent majorities from abusing minorities? The Constitution ought to do it, and so the *Exposition* supposedly proved that the tariff system, as currently practiced by Congress, was unconstitutional because it served not the "general welfare" but a particular interest. The Congress's power to raise money through tariffs was "abused by being converted into an instrument of rearing up the industry of one section of the country, on the ruins of another." Normally, the Supreme Court would strike down unconstitutional laws. But the Supreme Court dealt only with the letter of the law, and the issue in the Tariff of 1828 was not Congress's right to levy a tariff but the "motives of [the] legislature." In addition, this case concerned the balance of power between the federal and state governments, so, Calhoun' reasoned, the judicial department, which was itself a branch of the federal government, could be no arbiter between the parties.[17]

This second reason gave Calhoun the opportunity to carve out the constitutional theory that would become the basis of secession. The United States, so Calhoun reasoned, the great national power rising upon the global scene, the magnificent people embarking upon their manifest destiny, this historical experiment in republican self-governance was . . . a "joint stock company." The states were like individual people who invested in this company, and the Constitution was the contract by which they conglomerated. The draft of the *Exposition* exposes how important was this rhetorical maneuver, when Calhoun once wrote down the word "Constitution" but in a second thought struck it out and wrote "constitutional compact." The change is subtle but worthy of the masterful spin doctors of our own era, and this insidious metaphor began to worm its way into the southern consciousness: the federal government is nothing but a corporation; the Constitution is a contract joining individuals into that corporation. There is no "American" people sovereign over the United States. There are only various peoples separated by geography and separately exercising their sovereignty over their individual states. Ironically, Calhoun found himself trying to unweave those stitches he himself had sewn, the *national* pride and feelings fostered by a standing army and navy, by nationally funded projects like roads to the western states, and, more than anything else, by the sense of national *honor* he invoked during the War of 1812. All of these contributed to a belief that the *We the People* of the Constitution was a single sovereign entity—Americans.[18]

What should a minority interest in this joint stock company do, Calhoun asked, when a majority of investors united against it? It must "interpose" or veto the oppressive acts. Just as the Supreme Court's veto of legislation was not stated but merely implied in the Constitution, Calhoun cleverly discovered another implied power of veto, this one sagaciously bestowed on the states themselves. The obvious objection to this theory was this: if the framers intended to give states this power, why hadn't anyone noticed it before 1828? Calhoun reasoned that if this power lay unexposed like a buried treasure chest for forty years, "the fault is not [the framers'], but ours, in neglecting" to use it. Though he did not yet use the term, this veto would come to be called "nullification," and Calhoun, in a really original contribution to constitutional theory, thought it should work this way: if a state felt that some federal law violated the Constitution, it could unilaterally "interpose" or declare the law null and void. Calhoun suggested that the best mechanism by which a state might nullify a federal law would be through a special convention, since it was through special conventions that the sovereign people of each state ratified the Constitution in the first place. Such a mechanism would ensure the proper authority for the veto while also guarding against its frivolous use. If a state ever nullified a law, the other states could overrule the veto by amending the Constitution: three-quarters of the states could rewrite the Constitution to explicitly sanction the disputed law. For example, if South Carolina nullified the Tariff of 1828 because it was a "protective" policy, the rest of the states could overrule it by amending the "constitutional compact" to give Congress the unequivocal power to impose protective tariffs.[19]

Calhoun secretly delivered his *Exposition* to the Special Committee of the South Carolina House of Representatives in mid-December 1828, and by Christmas four thousand copies were circulating through the country. The South Carolina legislature did not formally adopt the *Exposition* for the simple reason that most of South Carolina's politicians disagreed with it. The pro-nullifiers lost state elections in 1829 and 1830, narrowly missing the numbers they needed to call a statewide convention on nullifying the tariff. The *Exposition* was meant to win moderates to a position that was still perceived as radical even in South Carolina.

But Calhoun and the special committee that commissioned the *Exposition* also meant to influence President Andrew Jackson and the citizens of the other southern and western states. Everywhere in the *Exposition* Calhoun seeks allies among the other "staple" states, trying to persuade whites wherever slavery reigned that they were part of a beleaguered minority exploited by the greed of the free states. Though the Tariff of 1828 harmed South Carolina more than any other state, though South Carolina's economy was most dominated by the plantation system, "the other staple States," by which he meant Virginia, North Carolina, and Georgia, were injured in the same way, and "the fate of one must be the fate of all." Calhoun labored to yoke the western states to this group. It was true that the high tariffs *helped* the new western states because the national treasury funded key roads across the mountains and navigation on the Mississippi, but even so, the *Exposition* argued, western industry was largely agrarian and so the West's subjugation will "certainly follow" the South's. Here, then, was the first articulation of that division that would lead to the Confederacy: North versus South, where the "South" includes Tennessee, Kentucky, and Missouri.[20] In 1828, this southern/western alliance was far from accomplished. Even the other southern states were disgusted by South Carolina's notion that it could nullify federal law. As for the new president, Andrew Jackson, the Tennessee gentleman, soldier, planter who had ousted the milquetoast Massachusetts intellectual, John Quincy Adams—the committee might have hoped to find a sympathetic audience at his reading lamp. Calhoun knew Jackson more intimately and could not have nurtured such illusions. When the president read the document, he exploded in fury.

Andrew Jackson was inaugurated in March 1829, just nine months before the *Exposition* was published, and many considered his ascent to the White House equivalent to a second American revolution. He succeeded John Quincy Adams, son of the patriot and former president, favorite son of Massachusetts, whose suavity and sophistication made him the opposite of all Jackson stood for. For instance, there was that cynical politician's bargain with Henry Clay. Jackson believed himself above low politics. He was born in the hills of Carolina, no stranger to Charleston, which had melancholy associations for him. His parents were Irish Presbyterians from County Antrim who settled in Carolina backcountry in 1765. Andrew was born just after they buried his father. At thirteen years old and surrounded by revolution, Andrew joined a Patriot militia. One older brother, Hugh, died at the Battle of Stono Ferry, just after the first British siege of Charles Town in 1779. Andrew and another brother, Robert, were captured when the British took Charleston in 1780. Both suffered the cruelties of captivity—disease and abuse. Robert died just as their mother, who had walked hundreds of miles to Charles Town, managed to secure their release. Elizabeth herself died not long after that, later tending to victims of cholera in the fetid prison ships until she herself succumbed. She was buried in Charles Town.

A frontier lawyer, operator of a general store, cotton farmer, plantation owner, militia colonel, U.S. Representative, state judge, fighter of duels, land speculator, Jackson embodied a new sort of American, the quintessential southwestern man. In the 1828 election, his alliances with New York's Martin Van Buren and South Carolina's Calhoun assured Jackson of a national backing, and his election is considered the start of the modern Democratic Party. The Democrats were populists, as demonstrated at Jackson's inauguration, when a crowd of common folk, arriving by "stagecoach, cart, and wagon, on horseback and on foot," a "swarm of locusts" dressed in "broadcloth and homespun, in finery and tatters, in coonskin cap and silk topper," crowded the White House, their muddy boots unmindful of the cushioned sofas and the seats of chairs while necks craned for a view of their hero, like

George Washington, the army's general taking his seat in the highest office of the land.[21]

Though the Calhouns and Jacksons shared frontier origins, John C. Calhoun, like the other scions of the Upcountry, had become as stern, patrician, and elitist as any Lowcountry planter, and he looked down his nose at this kind of mobocracy. Despite his nominal, temporary alliance with Jackson, and though both men were slaveholding plantation owners, South Carolina was a thousand miles away from Tennessee, as illustrated by one of the many scandals orbiting the new president. Jackson chose a protégé, Tennessee's Senator John Eaton, to be his secretary of war, one of the close advisers who would come to be called his "Kitchen" Cabinet. Eaton married a gorgeous, Washington boardinghouse proprietor with a dubious reputation, Peggy Timberlake. Calhoun's wife, Floride, whose fine Charleston breeding made her prudish and stuck-up, found it beneath her dignity to socialize with the secretary's wife. Jackson stamped with anger. His own wife, Rachel, had suffered similar gossipy opprobrium during the bitter election of 1828: ruthless enemies accused her of bigamy, a technically accurate indictment, since there had been some mix-up in divorce proceedings before she married her beloved Andrew, but the attacks smacked as much of class snobbery as anything else, as if the Jacksons weren't good enough for Washington society. Rachel died before her husband entered the White House, broken, in her husband's imagination, by the vicious scandalmongering. Peggy Eaton, "still one of the most beautiful women in Washington," provided him with a surrogate damsel whose honor he might protect.[22]

But the split between Jackson and his vice president went deeper than petticoats. They might have both been white supremacists, categorically believing that Native Americans and black Americans were inferior races. But, as one of the chief historians of the antebellum South, William Freehling, explains, they subscribed to different versions of supremacist ideology. Calhoun was old-school, and his ideas that an elite class of white men, leisured and educated and thus supposedly disinterested, ought to govern all others, including lower-class whites, derived from the eighteenth-century politics of Charleston, the kind of aristocratic attitude that had inspired John Rutledge's contempt of tavern keepers in the 1780s and had been enshrined in the state's successive constitutions. One might give all white men the vote, but only certified gentlemen could run for office. It mattered little that Calhoun was raised in an Upcountry traditionally jealous of Lowcountry planters: by the turn of the nineteenth century, Charleston's attitudes, along with the plantation system, had been spread across the entire state. In addition, Calhoun had made his mother-in-law's property near Pendleton his permanent residence in 1826, a five-hundred-acre estate overlooking the Seneca River, nearly in the shadow of the cool-aired mountains. Pendleton was the favorite summer refuge for many of Charleston's elite families, and Calhoun's residence there helped him to maintain his "cordial relationships" with the "Pinckneys, Hugers, and Gaillards," among others.[23] When Calhoun endorsed Floride's "important censorship" of Peggy Eaton (to use Calhoun's own words), he celebrated "a great victory . . . in favor of the morals of the country" and betrayed a great cultural divide between himself and the new kind of American represented by Jackson.[24]

Jackson thought the only meaningful class distinction was between whites and people of color. "His feelings toward slaves," his biographer, H. W. Brands, tells us, "fell between his feelings for children and for horses." The authoritarian general demanded absolute obedience. He once offered $10 "for every hundred lashes any person will give" one of his runaway slaves, "to the amount of three hundred." Those slaves who obeyed him were treated with some humanity.[25] This great gulf between the inferior races and whites meant that in Jackson's mind there could hardly be any real difference among whites themselves, no matter the disparities in their wealth. A poor man might have as great a claim to honor as a rich man, and Jackson was the first lowborn man to become president, a self-made planter, so Calhoun's instinctive sense of superiority was repugnant to him.

Where Jackson was open and frank to a fault, Calhoun was conniving, secretive, a duplicitous sort of politician whose ambition was someday to become president. So in 1828 he hid his authorship of the *Exposition* from public view because it was so radical that it would have disqualified him for the presidency in the eyes of most Americans—North, South, East, and West. Calhoun had backed Jackson in 1828 only because he himself had not yet built the national support he needed to be elected. He hoped the aged, ailing Jackson would be a one-term president and that he, Calhoun, would inherit the new party's endorsement. His great rival among Democrats was Martin Van Buren, the architect of Jackson's campaign, who adroitly stood on the sidelines when Calhoun's enemies first whispered the truth in the president's ear: Calhoun had *not* backed him in that secret cabinet meeting back in 1817, when Jackson had delivered Florida on a silver platter. "I had a right to believe that you were my sincere friend," Jackson, stunned by this news, wrote to Calhoun, "and until now never expected to have occasion to say in the language of Caesar, *et tu, Brute*."[26]

Meanwhile, the *Exposition* and the "Carolina doctrine" it articulated convulsed the U.S. Senate in one of its great debates. The legislation in question regarded the disposition of federal property in the western states—would the national government sell those lands near their value, thus bringing revenue into the treasury, or would it dispose of the land at near give-away prices to encourage the quick migration of settlers from the Atlantic Seaboard toward the West? Senator Robert Hayne, a protégé of Calhoun and the state's attorney general during the Vesey uprising, mustered South Carolina in the western ranks, arguing for a land giveaway in a not-so-subtle attempt to gain western support on the tariff question. Daniel Webster of Massachusetts smoked out this strategy, and he decided the time was ripe to tackle the Carolina doctrine.

Hayne's and Webster's subsequent speeches are legendary. Throughout January 1830, they held the Senate floor for hours at a time before packed galleries, each speech drawing further away from the land sale into the realm of ideology, and each response spiraling further from polite decorum. Calhoun presided over it all, necessarily silent, the gavel idle in his hand. At one point only, when Webster pointedly directed his remarks at the vice president, did Calhoun cut in.

Was the senator implying, Calhoun wanted to know, that the vice president had been inconsistent in his support of internal improvements?

No, Webster quickly assured him. Nothing of the sort.[27]

Legend has it that Calhoun passed notes to Hayne, giving him pointers in the states' rights argument, but even Calhoun's twentieth-century hagiographer, Charles M. Wiltse, thinks that unlikely. Neither Hayne nor Webster needed any help. Both were seasoned lawyers who had debated before the Supreme Court; they had rehearsed their constitutional arguments many times before; and each knew just when to pause and lower the voice, when to rail, when to fall silent. The battle of words had been advertised in the newspapers, each editor promoting his own champion like it was a heavyweight bout between Massachusetts and South Carolina. Spectators poured into Washington, crowded the gallery, and filled the aisles, eager to hear the great Webster not only rebut Hayne but refute the *Exposition*, whose authorship was still a mystery, and Webster did not disappoint.[28] But it was not the type of debate that is won or lost. It was ideological, and so the orators' success cannot be measured in Senate votes. If Webster got more accolades, Hayne's speeches helped develop a *southern* consciousness, promoting that aspect of identity in the minds not only of Carolinians but Virginians and Georgians.

Hayne did not do as well with westerners, at least not with General Jackson of Tennessee. Jackson exposed to public view his split with Calhoun and repudiated Hayne just a few months later at a newly invented Democratic feast day, the "Jefferson Day dinner." By this time, states' rights advocates had thoroughly co-opted Jefferson's name. The complexity of his political thought, including his very serious complaints about slavery, were smoothed into a states' rights banner that one might wave on holidays and wave all the more vigorously as the empty bottles grew into a pile. Martin Van Buren saw the trap being laid for the president, for, though the dinner was supposed to be harmonious and noncontroversial, with the slip of a word here or there everyone would be toasting nullification. The Pennsylvania delegation walked out en masse before the toasts began, smelling an antitariff taint to the ceremonies. Jackson stood his ground. He raised his glass at each of the twenty-four scheduled toasts and even more unscheduled, holding his liquor as well as anyone, drinking to the Declaration of Independence, to the purchase of Louisiana, to all manner of people and events and ideas associated with Thomas Jefferson. Some skated near the thin ice of nullification, but none ventured there. When it was all over, the president rose, his frail and aged frame still commanding the room as the general had commanded his legions. He raised his glass and, glowering at Calhoun, said, "Our *Federal* Union— *It must be preserved*."

Calhoun was "visibly disturbed" by this public repudiation of the Carolina doctrine, but he gathered his wits and offered the next toast: "The Union—next to our liberty most dear." He might have finished there, but by way of explanation he added, "May we always remember that it can only be preserved by distributing equally the benefits and the burthens of the Union." Van Buren went next and then more than seventy other spontaneous toasters, but the newspapers reported and remembered and debated the president's and the vice president's toasts, and it was not long before most saw the Jefferson Day dinner as an augury of the coming crisis. At any rate, it had "sealed [Calhoun's] fate with the president," severing finally any pretense of amity.[29]

By the early summer of 1830, the rift was pretty evident to everyone, even to Calhoun, who was among the last to acknowledge it. And it was clear that Congress was not going to reduce the tariff, nor would Andrew Jackson prompt it do so. In South Carolina, nearly every white believed that the tariff was unjustly oppressive to the South, especially to South Carolina, but they split almost violently over what to do about it. Two distinct parties formed, both committed to "states' rights," but the Union Party wanted to repeal the tariff using recognized constitutional methods, while the Free Trade Party wanted to nullify the tariff. Calhoun's *Exposition* actually made it fairly difficult to do that, because it suggested that a state convention was required, and only a two-thirds majority in the legislature could call a convention. The most important campaign issue in South Carolina's fall elections was whether a candidate would vote for or against calling a convention. Though his authorship of the *Exposition* was something of an open secret among the state's elite, Calhoun still kept himself offstage and left the leadership to men like James Hamilton and Barnwell Rhett. What frightened them most was that southerners might begin finally to act on the belief they had been professing for generations: that slavery was an evil visited upon

America, and that, were it possible to eradicate the institution, the nation would be all the better for it. William Preston, one of South Carolina's U.S. senators, predicted that the "slavery question will be the real issue." And the "slavery question" was not yet a North versus South debate. It was still a South versus South debate, as Charles Mercer, a congressman from Virginia, made clear when he introduced a bill in April 1830 to appropriate $50,000 annually to encourage whites to manumit their slaves and send them to colonize Africa.[30] Far more important to Hamilton and Rhett than any particular vote in Congress was the need to annihilate this kind of heterodoxy in the South and turn the region into a homogeneous ideological juggernaut.

This insight has been underappreciated in histories of the South: the Nullifiers did not fear that a national majority would tyrannize a regional minority so much as they feared that southerners themselves would continue drifting toward abolition. Especially in the Upper South, and most troubling in behemoth Virginia, white people—even important politicians like Henry Clay and James Madison—were actually devising schemes to eradicate slavery. The tariff was a slippery slope, Hamilton warned, and once the federal government established its power to issue a protective tax for "the general welfare," it would then naturally follow that the federal government could pay bounties for emancipated slaves and set up offices in Charleston to repatriate blacks to Africa. The South was already "infested" with "Yankee influence," he complained, so it was the Nullifiers' job to win the hearts and minds of the South.[31]

The 1830 electoral campaigns were nasty in South Carolina. The Nullifiers gave a dinner on the first of July in Charleston, ostensibly to honor two local congressmen, William Drayton (a known Unionist) and Robert Hayne (a Nullifier) for opposing the tariff in the last session. The celebration began at City Square, and six hundred people marched behind a band down Chalmers and Meeting Streets to the city hall, where a lavish meal was laid on tables set up in various rooms and galleries. "Six richly adorned canopies, composed of national banners interwoven with wreaths of evergreen" draped the room. "Twelve Corinthian pillars were erected round the room, gracefully festooned with variegated flowers and branches." On the south side of the main hall a giant eagle, its wings outspread, held a banner reading "State Rights" in its beak. Long speeches and toasts were punctuated by loud cheering, and, though banners touting "Liberty," "Union," and "the Constitution" hung at other points of the compass, the rally's real purpose was to fortify the radicals and ostracize those who opposed nullification.[32]

"Nothing is wanting to secure the success of our cause," Senator Hayne opined, "but *union at home*." Only "harmony of feeling and unity of action" will persuade "our oppressors . . . that we are *in earnest*." They would fail only if they "listened to the voice of those who have no common sympathies with us." Hayne's demand for unanimity bordered on rudeness, since William Drayton opposed nullification, and so James Hamilton began his oration on a more conciliatory note: "differences of opinion" such as Drayton's "we are bound not only to tolerate," he told his audience, which was half drunk already on words and wine, "but to treat with kindness and respect." But he left no doubt as to who wallowed in error when he predicted, somewhat too insistently, that "when South Carolina *does act*," that is, when the state does nullify the tariff, Drayton will join their ranks and "pour out his blood like water to the last drop in defense of this land." "We may well afford to tolerate dissent from our views," Hamilton cautioned his audience, though his was a strange species of tolerance, because he quickly added that "dissent should be accompanied by calumny and abuse." In his feverish peroration Hamilton called those who opposed nullification "cowards and slaves!" Nullification must not only win over the majority of voters, it must crush dissent until the state displayed unanimity to the rest of the nation. Already, nine-tenths of Carolinians were of the same mind, one reveler proclaimed. The pamphlet publishing these speeches concluded with these sentiments: "It is to be hoped that this exhibition of 'Public Opinion' will lead to reflection in the North, and to imitation in the South. Let the people of every Southern City do as Charleston has done—express their opinions and their feelings openly and fearlessly—and then there can be no doubt that our grievances will be redressed by a bloodless revolution."[33]

But there was no unanimity, even in Charleston. Two newspapers battled each other for the minds of Charleston's voters: the *Mercury* advanced the cause of the "Nullies," as they were unaffectionately dubbed by William Gilmore Simms, editor of the *City Gazette and Advertiser*, which promoted the Union. The two editors were about as diverse as Charleston, which hardly prized diversity, could produce. Pinckney came with a fine handle to his name: his father was Charles Pinckney, the younger of the cousins who helped draft the U.S. Constitution in 1787, and his mother was Henry Laurens's daughter, Mary Eleanor. He grew up in luxury, the consummate Lowcountry planter, on the family's farm just outside Charleston.

William Gilmore Simms was one of those rare types in nineteenth-century South Carolina: a self-made man who rose to national prominence largely on his talent and personal industry. His family, like Calhoun's and Jackson's, came from Ireland and migrated to South Carolina down along the mountains, settling in the Upcountry. Simms's grandfather eventually migrated to the city, where he set up shop as a millwright. William's father was keeping a tavern and grocery store when the boy was born in 1806. His mother was from a Charleston family, the Singletons, and her father possessed that almost unassailable bona fide of his generation: he was among those exiled and imprisoned in St. Augustine during the British occupation of the city in the Revolution. This mother died two years later, in childbirth, and his naturally happy, optimistic father was so distraught that he let his business die too, deposited his son with his mother-in-law, and headed west to start over. Among his adventures was service in the cavalry under Andrew Jackson at the Battle of New Orleans, but eventually he settled to a modest planter's life in Mississippi. The boy grew up an orphan, the life of a Dickens character, unschooled, and, in Simms's own retrospective, "with a heart craving love beyond all other possessions." When he was ten years old, William's uncle, who had been dispatched by his father and was then a stranger to William, visited Charleston and tried to kidnap the boy, only to be foiled when the child's screams brought the neighbors running.[34]

William and his grandmother were neither rich nor poor, but settled with sizable property—two houses (they rented one out), and twenty-five slaves (most of whom were also rented out and whose wages came back as family income)—that slowly dwindled under the grandmother's mismanagement. As a young lawyer Simms spent most of his energy on literature, editing a literary *Album* and then the *Southern Monthly Literary Gazette* when he was barely twenty years old and pouring forth from his brain as if gushing from a mountain spring an unbelievably prolific amount of verse, fiction, criticism, travelogues, all manner of writing. His first work noticed by the public was a poem memorializing Charles Cotesworth Pinckney, who died in 1825. By the early 1830s he was a promising, though not yet established writer, the father of a young girl (whose mother, Simms's youthful bride, had died), struggling to make his way in a rigidly hierarchical, almost caste society. He bought an interest in a dying newspaper, the *City Gazette*, and stepped into the realm of politics.[35]

Simms took on Pinckney, who was running for mayor as a Nullifier, and the battle between editors was vicious, reflecting the great public divide over nullification. Both the Nullifiers and the Unionists latched on to Andrew Jackson and tried to detach him from the other party, though clearly on that score Simms had the better argument: "Nullification," he reasoned, "will compel our *Venerable Jackson*" into "using the strong *Arm of Power* to reduce you and your deluded followers to submission." They were deluded because they failed to see that they were toying with treason and that Jackson would treat them so. Simms was vindicated when Pinckney lost the election, 838 to 754, which must have sobered Hamilton and Payne, because Unionists also put their men into the council seats for most of the wards in the city. This election is somewhat strange, because it seemed to repudiate nullification in the heart of plantation territory, but it must be remembered that Charleston harbored a still-significant population of anti-planter mechanics, and the ranks of planters themselves contained the most vociferous Union men, for Unionism was seen as a conservative position, while nullification was highly radical. The real hotbed of nullification was a little further south, around Beaufort, which had but one newspaper edited by the staunch Nullifier John A. Stuart. His influence, Simms thought, was dangerously unchecked by any opposition.[36]

Because it was radical, nullification was highly amenable to "mob psychology," a phenomenon that frightened even some of the leading Nullifiers, who deliberately tapped into this irresistible resource.[37] The

A Currier & Ives lithograph of the Confederate bombardment of Fort Sumter on April 12th, 1861, which started the Civil War

Left: George Whitefield (1714-1770), British preacher during the Great Awakening. After the Stono Rebellion, he warned South Carolina that God disapproved of American slavery.

Below: Edward Crisp's 1711 map of Charleston showing the street grid, fortified walls, and outlying farms

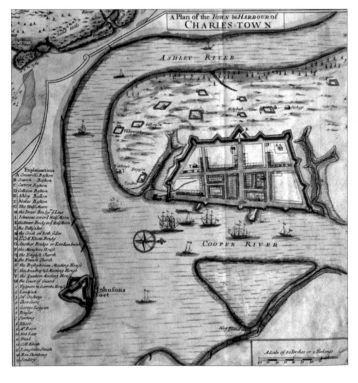

A view of the Charleston's waterfront circa 1776, with the steeple of St. Michael's church visible to the right of the ship. St. Michael's steeple was a lookout in both the Revolutionary War and the Civil War.

Below left: A 1784 etching of George Washington, Horatio Gates, John Paul Jones, Henry Laurens, and Benjamin Franklin. Charleston's Henry Laurens (1724-1792), a slave trader, was President of the Second Continental Congress and turned against slavery during the Revolution.

Below right: Colonel John Laurens (1754-1782). Son of Henry Laurens and Charleston's first abolitionist, John Laurens was killed in one of the last skirmishes of the Revolutionary War.

Charles Pinckney (1757-1824), delegate from South Carolina, advocated for a stronger national government and drafted an early version of the Constitution.

John Rutledge (1739-1800) led South Carolina's delegation to the Constitutional Convention in 1787.

Charles Cotesworth Pinckney (1746-1825), another South Carolina delegate to the Constitutional Convention, believed only African slaves could farm the Carolina Lowcountry.

Roger Sherman (1721-1793), delegate from Connecticut, hated slavery. Nevertheless, he made the devil's bargain with John Rutledge that protected slavery in the Constitution.

Henry Chandler Christy's 1940 painting of the signing of the Constitution, now hangs in the Capitol. Based on contemporary portraits, the figures are accurate. The two delegates on the left pointing towards George Washington are Charles Pinckney and Charles Cotesworth Pinckney. To the left of these is John Rutledge. Near them, Roger Sherman is the third from the left seated at the table.

This artist's rendering of a slave sale in Charleston, 1856, appeared in the *Illustrated London News*.

Left: Scenes like this from the Haitian Revolution fueled fears in Charleston when the supposed Denmark Vesey conspiracy of 1820 was uncovered through the testimony of tortured detainees.

Below: The Nat Turner Rebellion in 1831 began turning the entire South towards the slave ideology forged in Charleston.

John C. Calhoun (1782-1850), U. S. Representative, Senator, Secretary of War, Vice President, and often candidate for President, constructed the intellectual foundation for nullification and the "positive good" theory of slavery.

Right: William Gilmore Simms (1806-1870), Charleston novelist and editor, was an architect of Southern Nationalism.

Angelina Grimké (1805-1879), Charleston aristocrat and renowned abolitionist, was banished from her home city in the 1830s.

Left. John England (1786-1842), first Catholic Bishop of Charleston, was the papal legate to Haiti. An opponent of slavery, he was among the casualties of the South's new orthodoxy in the 1830s.

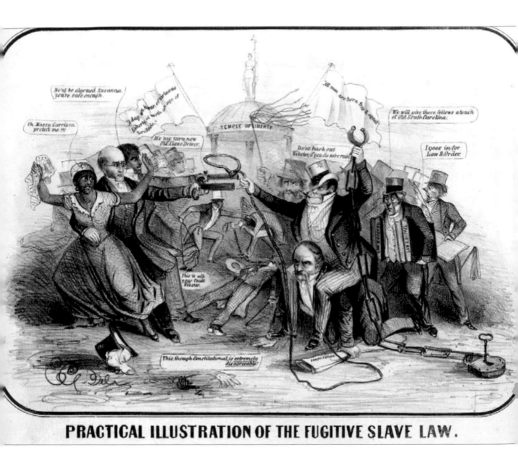

PRACTICAL ILLUSTRATION OF THE FUGITIVE SLAVE LAW.

An 1851 political cartoon, probably from Boston, critical of the Fugitive Slave Acts, which authorized federal agents to capture and return slaves who had escaped to free states. One figure on the right vows, "We will give these fellows a touch of South Carolina," an indication of that state's leadership among reactionaries.

James Hammond (1807-1864), U. S. Representative and Senator from South Carolina and early proponent of the "positive good" theory of slavery.

Below: Faithful slave Hector and the Indian-hunting dog Dugdale from William Gilmore Simms' novel, *The Yemassee.*

Woodlands, the plantation home of William Gilmore Simms.

The Democratic National Convention in Charleston in April 1860, at which the party split on the issue of slavery's expansion, assuring Lincoln's victory in November with a plurality of the vote.

Sic 'em, Buck! sic 'em! I wish poor old Hickory was alive. He'd bring 'em back in no time.

If we can only get them separated from the flock, we can pick their bones at our leisure.

VIRGINIA

LITTLE BO-PEEP AND HER FOOLISH SHEEP.

An 1861 political cartoon lampooning the decision of other southern states to follow South Carolina by seceding from the Union. Little Bo Peep represents the Union, and the lost sheep wander in a forest of palmetto trees (a symbol of South Carolina), where the European powers appear as wolves. Bo Peep wishes Old Hickory, Andrew Jackson, were still alive because Buck, President James Buchanan, cannot keep the flock together.

Left: Robert Barnwell Rhett (1800-1876), U. S. Representative and Senator from South Carolina and owner of the *Charleston Mercury* newspaper; one of the leading "fire-eaters" advocating secession.

Above: William Lowndes Yancey (1814-1863), another fire-eater born in South Carolina; representing Alabama at the 1860 Democratic National Convention, he led the southern split from the national party.

Left: General Pierre Gustave Toutant Beauregard (1818-1893), pictured here in *Harper's Weekly* shortly after he presided over the bombardment of Fort Sumter

A January 1863 illustration of the Confederates fortifying their positions on James Island, near Charleston

Later depiction of the 54th Massachusetts Regiment assaulting the Confederate Fort Wagner on Morris Island, July 18, 1863

Photograph of U. S. artillery on Morris Island in July or August 1863. After the direct assault failed the Union laid siege to Fort Wagner.

Union Parrott rifle on Morris Island, similar to the "Swamp Angel" that launched the first shell five miles across the harbor and into Charleston, starting the siege of the city on August 22, 1863

Photograph of the ruins of Charleston after the city fell in February 1865. On the right is Secession or Institute Hall, where the Ordinance of Secession was proclaimed and signed. The Hall was destroyed by the 1861 fire, not by the Union's siege guns.

Below: Ceremony commemorating the raising of the American flag at Fort Sumter, exactly four years after the Union surrendered it to Confederate forces. Abraham Lincoln, who declined to attend the ceremony, was assassinated that night in Washington, DC.

populist rhetoric of the Nullifiers whipped lower-class whites into a heightened sense of victimhood, getting the commoner who did not own slaves to identify with the cause of the aggrieved plantation owner, turning the tariff, which was really anti-planter, into an anti-*southern* conspiracy. The speeches at the fourth of July dinner constantly harped on South Carolina's subjugation and its being reduced to the status of a colony, reflecting this cult of victimization. The Unionist Thomas Grimké (Angelina's brother) accused Hamilton, Hayne, and Calhoun of working to "convince [the voters] by argument, and persuade them by eloquence, that they have been insulted, injured, oppressed by their brethren" in the North. James Louis Petigru commented wryly that the Nullies told stories "that we are treated like slaves, that we are slaves in fact, that we are worse than slaves and made to go on all fours," a rhetoric of crisis "that seem[s] to me very odd, and make[s] me doubt whether I am not under some mental eclipse, since I can't see what is so plain to others."[38] These were the same tactics of fear and crisis that Hamilton had used to such great effect in the Denmark Vesey days. Unionists held their ground in the Charleston city election of 1830, but this inflammatory rhetoric began to work in the statewide election just a month later, in October. By that time, Petigru was "recognized as the leader of the Union party," and he resigned his office as attorney general in order to run for a state senate seat representing Charleston.[39]

The election was closely contested all over the state, and Petigru himself lost one of the closest races of all, garnering 49.5 percent of the vote. If just thirteen more voters out of more than twenty-five hundred had gone his way, he would have won his seat in the senate. A month later, Petigru was gratified by being elected to the House, taking the seat of his friend and fellow Union man, H. S. Legaré, who had been elected to replace him as attorney general. The whole state was nearly as balanced. The Nullifiers won a simple majority in the legislature, which allowed them to put James Hamilton Jr. into the governor's office and pass a number of resolutions: that the Constitution was a "compact," that states could nullify federal law, that all of the radical notions expounded in the *Exposition* were official state opinion. The resolutions vilified Unionism, suggesting that to oppose nullification was to be disloyal to the state. Nevertheless, the Unionists could claim a measure of victory because they prevented the Nullifiers from garnering a super-majority of two-thirds of the legislature, which was required to call a convention.[40]

But Petigru knew he was fighting a rearguard action, delaying rather than defeating the advance of nullification. In the city elections the next year, Unionists were "egregiously beaten." The barbecue was a time-honored campaigning tool used by both sides, but as governor, Hamilton "traveled around the state in a military carriage, resplendent in full uniform, presiding over parades, musters, and political rallies," commanding a "well-disciplined newspaper network, and a multitude of states' rights clubs spread throughout the state." Petigru complained that the Nullifiers bought votes with cash and drink, kidnapped people to vote for their candidates, tried "everything that was audacious." The Unionists were facing the first great political machine in South Carolina politics, "men who follow the craft of electioneering" with few "scruples of conscience." It was a new type of politics that "openly preferred" passion to reason, that exploited the basest appeals—fear of economic ruin and a sense of insult—"playing the part of patriots," "blustering and bawling," until they could draw more of the "fools into their circle."[41]

Hamilton understood this as well, and he craved the prestige that Calhoun would give to the Nullifiers if only he would show his true colors to the world. Would Calhoun align himself with the cause of perpetual slavery, or would he continue his quixotic quest for national office by equivocating? The pro-nullification *Columbia Telescope* challenged the vice president to declare himself, and the Unionist Simms was just as eager to force Calhoun into the open and called for him to do so. Calhoun realized he could evade no longer. Once again Calhoun retired to his study, and in the luxuriant comfort afforded by the stolen labor of the scores of slaves surrounding his quiet little retreat, he penned his famous "Fort Hill Address," published in the small-town *Pendleton Messenger* in early August. John C. Calhoun, vice president of the United States, constitutional scholar extraordinaire, the most prominent national politician ever produced by the state of South Carolina, declared himself for nullification. So potent was his reputation that this dramatic endorsement electrified the Nullies and doomed Unionism to oblivion. Calhoun legitimized a cause that most Carolinians just a couple of years earlier had considered too radical to associate with. The effect was felt immediately in Charleston's mayoral election: Henry Laurens Pinckney finally prevailed, bringing the Nullifiers into ascendancy in the most important district in the state.[42]

When Congress yet again failed to reduce the tariffs in the spring of 1832, the summer campaigns in South Carolina brought nullification to a fever pitch. At Hamilton's request, Calhoun again published his views, this time at greater length, in September, again in the *Pendleton Messenger*. Shot through with the familiar nullification arguments, the essay introduced a couple of new ideas that rankled Unionists like Petigru. One was that there was no such thing as the "American people." Another was this declaration: once South Carolina nullified the tariff, all citizens of the state would be obliged to obey. To choose allegiance to the United States over allegiance to South Carolina was, essentially, treason.[43]

Petigru responded to Calhoun's paper in a report and resolution to the Union and States' Rights convention, held in September. "*Nullification* in practice," he explained, "must produce a direct collision between the authorities of the States and those of the Union," ensnaring "the citizen between inconsistent duties." South Carolina, Petigru predicted, would outlaw dissent. Those who disagreed with nullification and remained loyal to the constitutional authority of the United States would be compelled by "penal laws" to give up their opinions, or at least to remain quiescent, failing either to act or even express those opinions.[44] This was the greatest danger: nullification would become a compulsory belief. Calhoun "has abandoned the old ground of each party judging for himself," Petigru complained, "and now stands altogether upon the allegiance—the exclusive and absolute allegiance of the citizen to the State."[45] Simms astutely detected these real motives: the Nullies were less interested in reducing the tariff than in consolidating their own power. The frenzy over the tariff was a lever by which they moved the people into unanimity.[46]

Even before the election, pro-nullification mobs intimidated dissenters with threats of violence, Unionists threatened to stand their ground, and the state nearly erupted in civil strife. "The turbulence," Petigru wrote to Hugh Legaré, who was then in Brussels, "far outdid anything you ever saw here." Charleston's Unionists habitually met at Seyle's meeting room between King and Meeting Streets, and each night a "disorderly mob" gathered outside; Petigru and his party armed themselves "with bludgeons" when they left for home. On one occasion, two leading Unionists, Joel Poinsett and William Drayton, were "both struck" by blows from the mob. On election day, the Nullifiers emptied the Poor House to get votes, paid others, and it was "scarcely possible to conceive of any [electoral] abuse that was not openly practiced." Petigru warned that, should the state enact nullification and encroach "on the liberty of the citizen," the "sword will be drawn [by Unionists] in good earnest." If it came to "an affair of force," Petigru vowed, he "must take [his] share," for he would not bow to coercion.[47]

A county's level of support or opposition to nullification could be predicted by the density of slaves living in its borders. The counties that had the lowest percentage of slaves had the highest percentage of Unionists. Those Lowcountry counties in which slaves constituted more than 65 percent of the population all voted for Nullifiers in 1832. Twenty-one counties were more than 40 percent black, and only three of those voted for Unionists. Unionists won three out of four counties with slave proportions below 33 percent. In Beaufort, where the slave density was very high, the Union Party had "melted away" entirely, with Unionists seeing little point even of fielding candidates. Petigru wished they had, if for no other reason than to show "there is a minority."[48]

While we must not equate Unionism in South Carolina with abolitionism, those who sought to progressively diminish slavery or at least liberalize manumission policy tended to live in these pockets of low slave density. So far as Union men went, Petigru was fairly typical. Based on the influence of Locke and Montesquieu, he was philosophically opposed to slavery, which he thought was dying out, and nothing could justify saving it. In practice, that philosophy meant he opposed expanding slavery into newly settled territories. Nevertheless, he owned a plantation on the Savannah River, where he looked a lot like the paternalists of the pre-Vesey generation. "When I took them," he once said, his slaves "were naked and destitute. Now there is hardly a one that has not a pig, at least, and with a few exceptions they can kill their own poultry when they please." He freed some of his own slaves and sponsored others in quasi freedom, and he represented many in their circuitous journeys to liberty.[49]

As we have seen, Hamilton misconstrued the views of these southerners as an infestation of "Yankee influence" that had already rooted in the mid-Atlantic. Maryland's slave population in 1830 was about 23 percent, and most counties had even lower concentrations. While the population in eastern Virginia was equally split between whites and blacks, in the western counties slaves were only about 14 percent of the population. About one-quarter of Kentucky's population was enslaved and only about 20 percent of Tennesseans. Even among the deeper southern states, South Carolina was nearly unique: besides South Carolina, slaves outnumbered free citizens only in Louisiana. Each southern state contained regions that were much less affected by the slave economy, where emancipation would hardly be disruptive: four counties in northern Alabama, for instance, had fewer than 10 percent slaves; likewise, eastern Tennessee was about 90 percent white. These low-slave-density regions pocked the entire South, where antislavery rhetoric might easily take root or already had taken root. Once South Carolina was solidly and unequivocally committed to preserving slavery, so Hamilton figured, it could be used as the fulcrum on which the rest of the South would be lifted. In other words, Hamilton saw that the ideological hegemony that nullification would bring to South Carolina could be used to eradicate dissent throughout the whole South. The attitude of slavery that was congenial to the Carolina Lowcountry plantations would become not only the *dominant* but the *only* view of slavery tolerated by the law. Both Hamilton and Calhoun knew that if slavery were to survive, there could be no chinks in the armor, no dissenters among the southern phalanx. The campaign for nullification in South Carolina was really meant to purge dissent.

It worked. Immediately after the Nullifiers secured their two-thirds majority in the October election, Governor James Hamilton called a special session of the legislature; days later, the legislature called for a state convention. The state convention, which Petigru called "the plain tool" of Hamilton,[50] nullified the federal tariffs of 1828 and 1832, authorized ten thousand guns to be purchased, and called up volunteers for military service. Calhoun resigned the vice presidency and took Hayne's seat in the U.S. Senate. Hayne took Hamilton's job as governor, and then Hayne appointed Hamilton to lead the newly mustered South Carolina army. It was a backroom deal that stunk as bad as the Clay/Adams agreement that stole the presidency from Jackson back in 1828, and Simms "uncovered [the] corrupt political bargain," but did so in vain, for by then nullification was so popular that few were outraged by such machinations. Fewer still remained loyal subscribers to Simms's *City Gazette*, which was plunging toward insolvency.[51]

Governor Hayne immediately proclaimed that he recognized "no allegiance paramount to that which the citizens of South Carolina owe to the State of their birth or adoption." Simms reported that the city was "in a state of excitement little short of phrensy," and he predicted "collision and bloodshed in our streets. . . . [N]othing but blood & free draughts of it too, can quench the exasperated & burning though half smothered fire, chafing with lava, fervor & fury in every bosom." Simms himself bought "a new & additional pair of pistols, suited to the use of slugs in the *generale melee*."[52]

The state was on the verge of civil war, and the victorious Nullifiers would not tolerate the existence of Unionism. They enacted a "test oath" that would require all officeholders and soldiers to swear that their allegiance to South Carolina preempted their allegiance to the United States. "A deep & deadly hostility & hate has been engendered in the bosoms of our party by the odious ordinance of that petty dictatorship, which has broken up all the bonds once sweet & sacred of our society." Simms stumped throughout the state, rallying the Unionists to continue their opposition, urging officeholders to resign before swearing their highest allegiance to the state of South Carolina.[53]

Disconsolate and defiant, the Union Party held a convention of its own in Columbia and issued a "Remonstrance and Protest" against the nullification convention. Largely penned by Petigru, the "Remonstrance" disputed Calhoun's notion that no "American" people existed and asserted that the Unionists would sooner fight than be "driven from the enjoyment of those inalienable rights which by inheritance belong to every American citizen." It assailed the new government for enacting a test oath of allegiance, which would "enslave all freemen of conscience." Nearly "one-half of the freemen of South Carolina," the Unionist minority, were disqualified from "every office, civil and military," on account of "an honest difference of opinion" with the majority party.[54]

Privately, Petigru complained that the new political correctness was the work of a few men who gained "an ascendency which gives them an absolute control over the weak minds of that numerous class who are afraid or ashamed to think for themselves."[55] There is much truth to his description. Men like Hamilton used the methods of popular politics to whip up support for nullification, and now that that political ideology had gained its majority, it was fast attempting to outlaw dissent. The Union Party's proclamation resisted this tyranny, and just days later Petigru was heartened by the actions of President Jackson.

On December 16, Jackson's proclamation arrived in South Carolina, and it sent a shiver of fear throughout the ranks of the Nullifiers, who until then thought that the slave-owning president might be a fellow traveler, sympathetic to their cause even if he couldn't openly support it. Quite the contrary. The whole justification for nullification was a delusion, the President sternly told South Carolinians, a false sense of oppression concocted "by men who are either deceived themselves or wish to deceive you." Jackson told the Nullifiers they were at the "brink of insurrection and treason." And if anyone had any illusions about his resolve to collect federal tariffs, five thousand muskets were on their way to Castle Pinckney, a fort in Charleston's harbor; two navy vessels were converging on the harbor; revenue cutters would meet ships outside the bar and collect the tariffs there. Jackson had the federal fort on Sullivan's Island surveyed and was prepared to muster a hundred thousand troops to invade South Carolina. His local informant, Joel Poinsett, urged a vigorous saber rattling to hearten the Unionists living in South Carolina, but he also cautioned against drawing first blood, which would play into the Nullifiers' hands by fulfilling the prophecy of victimhood. A bleeding Charleston would rally other southern states to South Carolina's side.[56]

Virginia made a few hesitant gestures at sympathy, as did Georgia, but by and large South Carolina was on its own. Calhoun, back in the Senate, climbed upon his soap box, declared South Carolina would sooner secede than capitulate to military despotism, and complained that Jackson was the true aggressor for threatening "to have our throats cut, and those of our wives and children." Really that was taking things too far because Jackson only meant to "strike at the head and demolish the monster." He explained himself more clearly to Carolina congressmen who called at the White House: "Please give my compliments to my friends in your state, and say to them, that if a single drop of blood shall be shed there in opposition to the laws of the United States, I will hang the first man I can lay my hand on engaged in such treasonable conduct, upon the first tree I can reach."[57] All knew the threat was real.

Hamilton, who by this time had donned the fancy epaulets of brigadier general, took Jackson very seriously, as did Calhoun, and both labored hard to "restrain their excited followers" lest they prick Jackson into action. The spirit of defiance they had raised from the grass roots turned out to be a wild horse, and "with no small difficulty" they barely hung on to the reins.[58] Luckily, the confrontation fizzled before the guns were ever primed. Congress passed a "Force Bill" authorizing the president to execute federal laws in South Carolina, even if it took an army to do so. There was no equivocation in Congress: armed defiance of the tariff was treason and would be treated accordingly. But Congress extended a convenient way for the Nullifiers to save face, passing an anemic, almost insultingly slow reduction of the tariff, which would take ten years to finally reach a level that was, in the Nullifiers' estimation, constitutionally justifiable. But the Tariff of 1833 was not *quite* insulting, and South Carolina's Nullification Convention that convened in March accepted these terms of surrender as honorable. Calhoun scurried home across frozen roads from Congress, where he had negotiated this "compromise" with Henry Clay, because he was afraid the radicals would refuse to surrender, and South Carolina would choose armed secession. But he needn't have worried because they surrendered before he ever made it back to Columbia.[59] Accepting the new law, South Carolina suspended its nullification of the tariff, and then in a gesture that to all the world stank of impotence, it nullified the Force Bill, knowing full well that no one would now try to execute it.

Most interpret these events as vindication for the Union and defeat for nullification, for the Nullifiers were exposed to be petty men posing as great. Jackson's biographer suggests that "the real victors were Jackson and the idea of Union."[60] Freehling suggests that the Nullifiers played their hand nearly to the end but finally were found to be bluffing. South Carolina threatened secession, Jackson threatened violence, South Carolina backed down, and the tariff legislation of 1833 did nothing more than allow the Nullifiers to retire from the field with a scrap of dignity. "Minority veto was finished," Freehling concludes.

So far as national politics goes, this view is accurate enough, but at home the Nullifiers scored an irreversible victory over dissent. The Union —and the plurality of ideologies, the give-and-take of compromise politics inherent in the republic, and the belief in a progressive, changeable society—were more important to Unionists than preserving the plantation economy and way of life. This openness was all the space emancipation would need, for wherever it could compete on a level playing field, emancipation beat slavery. It had Christian charity and American political philosophy on its side. The Nullifiers understood this, and so they worked diligently to prevent even a toehold gaining ground in South Carolina. The field must never be made level, because then emancipation would infect the South and spread everywhere. No unconstitutional usurpation by Congress would be required: eventually, the southern states themselves would, one by one, emancipate the slaves, until South Carolina was left alone, calcified in an anachronistic economy, ostracized by the moral outrage of all the other states, compelled to capitulate to those self-evident truths shouted to the world in 1776. To avoid that fate, no one could be allowed to dissent.

The Unionists understood that the new South Carolina had no place for them. At the height of the tension, Petigru had made up his mind: should the "Union be severed," he resolved "to quit the negro country."[61] Thoughts of exile were on the minds of all Unionists in 1833. Simms thought the test oath would drive his party to "emigration *en masse*." He imagined that the United States would have to provide some wilderness "to which we may carry such of our gods, goods & spirit of Independence, as in these troublous times may have been left."[62]

In the end neither Petigru nor Simms left. They made their accommodations, Petigru by attaining the status of bizarre eccentric, the anachronistic "last Union man" in Charleston on the eve of the Civil War. Simms, by a remarkable reversal, ended up leading the new South toward secession. But at least one Charlestonian did go into exile: Angelina Grimké. Back in April 1829, not long after Calhoun secretly penned the *Exposition*, Grimké had an epiphany, a sudden burst of clarity that shone with the light of revelation through an ordinary, everyday incident. As she was walking down a street in Charleston, she "saw before me a color'd woman who in much fear & vexation was vindicating herself to two white boys one about 18 & the other 15 who walked on each side of her."

Grimké overheard a snippet of their conversation: the younger boy saying, "I will have you tied up."

The black woman, seeing the sympathy and distress in Grimké's eyes, blurted out desparately, "Misses[!]"

In an instant Grimké understood that the white boys were escorting the slave to the Charleston workhouse, where white masters who were too delicate to whip their slaves themselves sent offenders for punishment, which consisted either of flogging or working the treadmill. In the whipping room, the wardens of the workhouse would chain a "recalcitrant" slave's feet to the floor, slip nooses over their hands, and hoist the arms upward with a crane, stretching the body out for the flogging. The walls were double-thick and sand-packed, but that was not enough to fully muffle the cries of the tormented.[63] "It seemed as though its doors were unbarred to me," Grimké wrote in her diary, and "the wretched lacerated inmates of its cold dark cells were presented to my view—night and day they were before me & yet my hands seemed bound as with chains of iron." She could do nothing for the poor woman.

"It appeared to me all the cruelty & unkindness & oppression which I had from my infancy seen exercised towards these poor creatures came back to my mind with as much force as tho' it was only yesterday," Grimké wrote. "None but those who learn from experience what it is to live in a land of Bondage can form any idea of the weight of exercise which is endured by those whose eyes are open to the enormities of Slavery & whose hearts are tendered so as to feel for these miserable creatures."[64]

Grimké was then twenty-four years old. She had all the advantages that wealth could give a Charleston woman—a splendid mansion in the town, plantations in the country, education, her father's library full of books, leisure, money. And she had all the disadvantages of her sex—which meant that she could walk down no avenue that might influence public policy. Her brother Thomas was an active and vociferous Union man, but Angelina could stand upon no street corner and argue against the Nullifiers. No publisher asked for her opinions. And of course she could run for no office. And yet when she saw this woman hauled off by two boys to the workhouse, she felt God was preparing her "for future usefulness," and her "soul trembled at the solemn tho[ugh]t of such a work being placed in my feeble & unworthy hands."[65] She did not yet know what that work might be, nor did she for many years. But this incident cemented in her mind the impossibility of making any accommodation to what was rapidly becoming the unassailable political correctness in her home city. If she could not speak out against slavery, neither could she abide it. In November she embarked on the nine-day voyage that brought her to Philadelphia.[66] She never lived again in Charleston.

7

THE POLICE STATE

||

The packet ship *Columbia* steamed into Charleston Harbor on its regular run from New York City on July 29, 1835, and delivered its mailbags to the U.S. Post Office, where it was discovered that they contained abolitionist tracts sent by the American Anti-Slavery Society to various recipients in the city. The Negro Seaman Acts were designed to prevent the private circulation of any literature dissenting from the pro-slavery viewpoint, but this was the first-ever direct mail campaign, and Alfred Huger, Charleston's postmaster, did not know how to handle the explosive material. He decided not to deliver it for the time being, and he set it aside.[1]

That night a mob gathered outside the Exchange Building in downtown Charleston, marched to the post office, tried the windows of the building, and, finding them locked, coolly deliberated what to do. Between the hours of 10:00 and 11:00 p.m., they pried open the windows, rifled the mail, and stole the offending material. Though clearly illegal, the theft was sanctioned by the South Carolina Association, which sent circulars out to other southern cities warning them to look out for "incendiary publications." The *Charleston Courier* characterized the abolitionist campaign as an "abuse of the U.S. mail," and it too approved the mob's activity, quoting at length a section of William Drayton's memoirs that described Patriots intercepting Tory mail during the Revolution. The *Courier* described the crowd as well ordered, but some among its outraged hundreds were unruly and denounced John England, Catholic bishop of Charleston, as harboring more abolitionist literature in his residence next to the cathedral, so they resolved to march to the Catholic seminary near the cathedral on Broad Street.

They would drag John England from his house and lynch him and afterward tear down the church buildings.[2]

The American Anti-Slavery Society was a new type of phenomenon in American politics. During the 1820s, most northern abolitionists, like their southern fellow travelers, favored a gradual amelioration of the slaves' condition so as not to disrupt society. The schemes varied—a gradual decrease in the proportion of slaves to freemen in the population, gradual private manumissions, the gradual purchase and freeing of slaves, gradual repatriation to Africa—but always they sketched out a slow process that gave the South time to adjust its economy. No one wanted to impoverish the slave owners. But on January 1, 1831, a man named William Garrison repudiated gradualism as timid, unjust, and absurd, and declared himself for the "immediate enfranchisement of our slave population." He founded *The Liberator*, a Boston weekly devoted to the cause, and he promised, "I am in earnest—I will not equivocate—I will not excuse—I will not retreat a single inch—AND I WILL BE HEARD." *The Liberator* exploded like a bomb. Garrison organized a cadre of preachers who began disseminating the new gospel of immediate emancipation and denouncing slave owners as the foulest villains. Crowds turned out to lynch these preachers, not only in the South, but in New York, Boston, and Philadelphia. The house of Lewis Tappan, who bankrolled the movement, was destroyed, and the Tappan store was saved only because Arthur Tappan armed his clerks in its defense. Many of those sympathetic to abolition argued against this new goal of immediate emancipation and Garrison's attack politics. Even Arthur Tappan split from Garrison's American Anti-Slavery Society and formed the American Union for the Relief and Improvement of the Colored Race, which held that "the peaceful abolition of slavery in the United States depends upon securing the concurrence of slaveholders, procured by an appeal to their human and Christian principles." To gradualists, Garrison's followers looked more like religious fanatics styling themselves after early Christian martyrs than serious social reformers, for they deliberately provoked slaveholders, which seemed to do little more than satisfy the agitators' sense of self-righteousness. In December 1833, the American Anti-Slavery Society declared that "the slaves ought instantly to be set free, and brought under the protection of the law." Furthermore, because slavery was sinful, slaveholders need not be compensated for their loss of property. Perhaps most radical was the society's conviction that free blacks should be accorded full citizenship and ought to be allowed to move in society equal to whites.[3]

It was easy for Charleston hotheads to link the Catholic bishop to Garrison: after all, the first number of *The Liberator* extolled John England's good friend, the Irishman Daniel O'Connell, who emancipated the Catholics of Ireland just a couple of years earlier. Quoting O'Connell, Garrison wrote that the American Declaration of Independence was "a lie . . . before God and man" and that the slave owners who professed it were hypocrites. "Where is the O'Connell of this republic," Garrison asked, and "who will plead for the EMANCIPATION" of American slaves? Many Charlestonians presumed that John England fit the bill.

The thirty-four-year-old England came to Charleston from Cork, Ireland, in 1820, and no immigrant since the Revolution had disembarked on the bustling piers along the Cooper River with better equipment to combat racial bigotry, to disprove the racist attitudes of whites with the solid facts of science, to persuade the city of the evils of slavery, to undermine the tyranny of Charleston's first families.

Growing up as a Catholic in Ireland taught John England how to fight for justice. He saw that the penal laws against Catholics barbarized "and then reproache[d] you with barbarism." Naturally, the "conduct of men who had been almost brutalized by oppression, too often leads the unreflecting to believe that they must have been originally barbarians." Twenty-three years before South Carolina outlawed teaching slaves to read, the British denied Irish Catholics a proper education and then "justif[ied] the oppression" of Catholics by pointing to their ignorance. Sometimes, John England observed, the British went so far as to "forge testimony to prove the pretended necessity of [oppression]."[4] We are all familiar with the Irish stereotype, for its benign version stumbles through the streets of Savannah and Chicago and New York every Saint Patrick's Day. Its malicious version can be found in the Yahoos of *Gulliver's Travels*: brutish, dirty, backstabbing, thieving, irrational, unteachable, promiscuous, semi-human creatures. When the English began colonizing Africa, their popular cartoons began to depict the Catholics of Ireland with the features they associated with black Africans—flat noses, sloped foreheads, wide lips—to emphasize their natural barbarity. Even as late as the 1860s, Matthew Arnold, who was a Celtophile, described the Irish race as naturally feminine, childlike, irrational, sentimental, sensuous, lazy, quick-witted, hot-tempered, unruly—nearly all of the stereotypes white southerners used to justify their dominion over blacks. We know today that racial stereotypes and even the "races" themselves are invented by culture. They have no basis in biology. So John England, with the benefit of his Enlightenment ideals and personal experience of oppression, knew that racial stereotypes were forgeries.

In 1781, when John England's father, Thomas, was a boy of about seventeen years, his father was thrown in jail, probably for debts since the "last remnant of their land and furniture" were taken from his wife and her five children. John's grandmother died from the stress and terror of the family's predicament, which left Thomas to provide for his two younger sisters and two younger brothers. He tried to make some money by teaching geometry in a "hedge" school, a clandestine institution conducted by native schoolteachers often outdoors (under the shelter of a hedge), but he was found out, arrested, and faced transportation as a virtual slave to the West Indies. The local Protestant bishop offered to drop the prosecution if Thomas would renounce Catholicism and become a Protestant schoolmaster. Instead, he fled to the mountains, where he lived in hiding until, in John England's own words, "The declaration of American Independence, and the successful resistance of the colonies, produced some mitigation of the persecutions which the Irish Catholics endured."[5]

Thomas England came down out of the mountains and put his geometry skills to work as a land surveyor, an opportunity open to Catholics only because the profession did not yet exist when the penal laws enumerated the jobs from which Catholics were barred. He prospered, got his father out of jail, met and married Honora Lordan, and, taking up the tobacco business, they settled in Cork City in 1785. John, their first son, was born a year later, followed by five brothers and four sisters in the next eleven years. Once his grandfather took him on a trip back to Tipperary, and the sixty-year-old man showed the nine-year-old John the cell that had been his home for four years.[6]

John was twelve in 1798 when the United Irishmen rose and fell in a revolution, like the Americans', based on Enlightenment ideas about natural rights, and the movement attracted the boy:

> Never, [John England later wrote] was there found more true patriotism than in the body of the Presbyterian Clergy [who founded the United Irishmen.] [T]hey loved the country, they took pity upon the oppressed Catholic, they were joined by many of the best, and bravest, and most virtuous lay-members of the established [Anglican] church, they gave the right hand of fellow-ship to Catholic, and they formed a brotherhood of Irishmen of all religious persuasions. . . . Their objects were simple, substan-tial, and just, and constitutional—to obtain a fair representation of the people in the House of Commons, and to put an end to persecution on the score of religion. The attainment of these objects would have healed the evils of the country, but would not have suited the views of the oligarchy which had long been the bane of the kingdom.

His sympathy for the oppressed and hatred of oligarchies put John in conflict with his own bishop, the timid Francis Moylan, who reminded the Roman Catholics of Cork of their "sacred" duty to exhibit "Loyalty to the Sovereign and respect for the constituted authorities" of Ire-land.[7]

England studied for two years to be a lawyer, and that would have been a choice profession for his mind was naturally inclined to logic and could divide, define, syllogize, induct and deduct, clarify and clas-sify as finely as a comb parts hairs. This was between 1800 and 1802, just seven years after the legal profession was opened to Catholics, and had he continued England would have found himself in a select group of talented and influential new Catholic lawyers. But he underwent a mysterious change of heart. His American friend and biographer,

William Read, says merely, a "voice which broke the slumbers of [youth] . . . spoke to the heart of the great apostle of this western world. He turned from the pursuits of temporal ambition, and consecrated his virgin prime to the service of the sanctuary." This calling was nothing like Saint Paul's blinding light. Looking back years later, England said his was a reluctant vocation: "On this day [October 11] I parted from my family to go whither I thought God had called me, but whither I had no other desire to go." He continued, "Should this [diary] be read by a stranger, let him pardon that weakness of our common nature, which then affected me, and does now after the lapse of three months." This passage is uncharacteristically personal, and never again does England allude to this chronic "weakness" that plagued him for at least twelve years. It does not seem to amount to a doubt of his vocation, but it does indicate that the priest's life felt unnatural to him, that he undertook it as a duty, and that he would have chosen for himself another life. It is not surprising, then, that England did not distinguish himself at the seminary in Carlow, nor, after his ordination, did his occasional sermon and the odd editorial in the *Cork Mercantile Chronicle* show much genius for controversy.[8]

But in September 1811, Daniel O'Connell came to Cork. O'Connell organized a local Catholic committee that petitioned King George III, who by this time was embarking on his last voyage into madness, to emancipate the Catholics of Ireland. Early in 1812 the committee began staging massive gatherings of Catholics and sympathetic Protestants called Cork Aggregate Meetings, which nurtured a political consciousness in the quiescent city. John England was one of those awakened to public life. He was twenty-five when he helped found the Association of Independent Roman Catholic Electors of the City of Cork, which was in essence a political machine, and already his skill in words must have been well-known to his fellow citizens, because the association elected him secretary. The city was 90 percent Catholic but was represented in Parliament by someone who opposed giving full political rights to Catholics, so the association started a civil rights movement. England took over the liberal newspaper, the *Cork Mercantile Chronicle*, and his attack on the crown's veto power over the appointments of Irish Catholic bishops brought him to O'Connell's attention.

O'Connell recruited him, and England soon became one of the strongest gears in O'Connell's machine. The two men found in each other a warm intellectual friendship that would last beyond England's emigration seven years later. England always championed the "cause of a People" against the interests of the aristocracy. Sounding like Martin Luther King Jr. in his "Letter from Birmingham Jail," England did not shy from agitation and chastised those who resisted Catholic emancipation on the grounds that it disturbed political and economic order. They "may as well expect to behold an ocean without an occasional ebullition of warm and animated feeling."[9]

In Ireland as in South Carolina, an aristocratic class of Anglican planters owned most of the land (the term "plantation" was used to describe the British colony in Ireland even before the settlement of Virginia). These owners leased their land in parcels of between one hundred and one thousand acres to middlemen, who further subdivided to the level of one-acre and half-acre holdings tilled by "bound" laborers, who had use of the land for a year or at the will of the middleman. Typically, the tenant would be supplied a thatch-roofed cabin, a right to "a portion of bog for turf" (which was burned for fuel), the right to graze a couple of sheep, and "the run of a pig." To pay the rent, the cash-poor laborer had "to work for the farmer" about two hundred days in a year. In a good year, his acre of land might produce six tons of potatoes, which might be sold for as much as £15, but much of this crop would go to feeding his own family, and good years could hardly be counted on. Potato farming was always a precarious venture, so the life of the bound laborer was grim. Worse off were the unbound laborers, who rented small plots (without cabins and grazing rights) at exorbitant rates and who made as little as 4 pence a day for their labor. Female workers made even less than the men. A contemporary described the typical cabin as having "a single room, a hole for a window with a board in it, the door generally off the hinges, a wicker-basket with a hole in the bottom or an old butter-tub stuck at one corner of the thatch for a chimney, the pig, as a matter of course, inside the cottage, and an extensive manufacture of manure . . . [taking place] on the floor." There would be a cast-iron pot for boiling, a bit of wood stuck to the wall for a table, tree stumps for chairs, and often nothing but straw and rags for beds. They ate potatoes and then more potatoes and hardly anything else. After 1815, milk became a dreamed-of luxury, the price of grazing a cow being beyond the means of the poor. England's newspaper attacked landlords, claiming he must defend the peasant "who had no other advocate but a free press." He excoriated this economic system as white slavery.[10]

One particular case stood out in his own mind. A young, pious, "previously blameless" man was persuaded by some local revolution-aries to rob a government arsenal. He succeeded in hiding the weapons, but was himself found out, tried, convicted, and sentenced to death. England heard the youth's confession but refused to absolve his sins because the condemned man would not reveal the cache of stolen arms, which would mean informing on his coconspirators and sending them to the gallows also. On the day of execution—sometime in August 1820—England came to the man's cell to offer to say mass.

"You will not give me Communion," the prisoner complained, "[because] I shall not restore the arms."

Late in the afternoon the prisoner was brought to the gallows, the noose was tightened to his neck, and all the while the young man kept his misery controlled. He bore himself with the silent nobility appro-priate to Irish political martyrs but burdened with the doubt—planted by England—that by protecting his friends he risked his own damna-tion. Around the terrible scene stood a strong military guard, splendid in their uniforms and weapons, to ensure order among the people, who sympathized with the rebel. Just at this moment John England stepped forward and said to the prisoner, "Stop, sir! you shall not go to hell for half an hour yet!"

The prisoner's fragile composure was shattered, and he cried, "How could you speak so to a dying man?"

England bellowed something about his duty and busied himself with getting a brief stay of execution.

They took the noose off the man's neck, and the priest and his charge retired to the prison cell, where, apparently finally broken by the weight of the experience, the man confessed where the guns were hidden. The priest forgave the weeping man his sins and sent him back to the gallows, where he must have displayed to the crowd something less than the composure of martyrs in the ballads.

So far as England was concerned, his work for the prisoner was well done, since the man was speedily sent to heaven. But what to do about the guns? He informed the authorities that he knew where the stolen arms were hidden, but he insisted he would not reveal their location unless amnesty was guaranteed for the "persons harboring them." The sheriff disingenuously replied that anyone hiding the guns should first surrender them and then apply for amnesty. England protested he would be violating "a most solemn obligation"—a promise made in the confessional.[11]

The episode is curious. England was unequivocal in his refusal to offer the convicted prisoner absolution unless he confessed where the guns were hidden. Whatever his sympathies with revolutionaries, apparently England, like Daniel O'Connell, abhorred and eschewed violence. But if England was unequivocal with the prisoner, he was equally adamant with the government. Unless granted amnesty for the other rebels, he would not restore the arms. The confession's casuistic formula must have been something of a ruse that England himself invented to relieve the prisoner's political and religious consciences at once. When the sheriff refused his terms, England was not much troubled that the arms stayed in rebel hands. "I have acted," he claimed, "for the public welfare and the peace of the country. The advice that I have given has been dictated by an honest motive."[12] He always had the greatest contempt for the institutions of the British government.

That contempt spilled onto Pope Pius VII when he agreed to the British crown's veto over appointments to the Irish Catholic Church in exchange for Britain's support of his restoration to the throne of the papal states. John England excoriated the pope's plan in the August 2, 1815, issue of the *Cork Mercantile Chronicle*, lighting a fuse that exploded in protests across Ireland, and O'Connell further stirred up anti-Vatican sentiment at a Dublin aggregate meeting. Not surprisingly, as one contemporary observed, "The [Irish] hierarchy rather feared [England's] influence and views, which were decidedly democratic," and so "nearly all the bishops in Ireland" sent a letter to Rome asking that England be appointed to a foreign see. John England agreed, stipulating only that he not be assigned to "any country where the British government exercised any control." He admired the United States for separating church and state, and he considered the American republic "an ideal example for the world to follow," so he was glad to be consecrated as the first bishop of Charleston in 1820, a new missionary diocese that included Florida, Georgia, and the two Carolinas. On the eve of his departure, Daniel O'Connell gave a "glowing and beautiful panegyric on [England's] public and private character, and [his] patriotic exertions in the cause of civil and religious liberty." O'Connell's biographer called England "the principal mover in the whole of this democratic insurrection against aristocratic pretensions in Cork" and "the guiding genius of the [anti-veto] movement."[13]

St. Mary's, the largest congregation in the Charleston diocese, was then under the interdict of the French-born bishop of Baltimore, whose main complaint was that the congregants would not accept the priest he chose for them, Fr. Clorivière, because he was an antirepublican royalist who had been kicked out of France by the Revolution. "If Clorivière were hated," the pope's emissary reported, "the reason is not hard to find. . . . There were nine leaders or trustees who opposed the French priest, most of them of lax lives, whose position in the social life of the city was that of tailors, carpenters, saloon-keepers, druggists; and all were imbued with a spirit of false democracy, which rebelled against any authority but their own." The spirit of democracy lit a fire in John England, who was happy to consort with tailors and carpenters, and it was not long before he and the Catholics of Charleston loved each other. A thousand Catholics then lived in Charleston, about 4 percent of the population, and thirty-six hundred Catholics lived in the entire diocese, the population of which was nearly one and a half million people. These few worshipped in only three church buildings—one in Charleston, one in Savannah, and one in Augusta. England immediately bought the Vauxhall Gardens on Broad Street and built a cathedral that he christened St. Finbar's after the church in Cork.[14]

He also restyled church government on the American model. He wrote a constitution that compared the Catholic dioceses to the individual American states, and bishops to governors. The Catholic

Church, he wrote, is a federation of many dioceses. Just as the president of the United States is bound to execute the federal laws of the Union, so is the pope bound to execute the laws of the Church. But within its boundaries, each diocese was able to legislate laws convenient to itself, so long as they did not contradict the federal law. In Charleston, that meant that pew rentals could be outlawed because they encouraged the aristocratic ethos of the Anglican Church. England favored passing a basket for voluntary contributions, which rendered priests dependent not on "one or two powerful [rich] persons" but on "the body of the people at large."[15]

On September 25, 1823, the Catholics of Charleston assembled in St. Finbar's Cathedral to hear the constitution read to them, one clause at a time, and they unanimously approved it. By late November, lay delegates from Beaufort, Camden, Georgetown, Pocotaligo, and Barnwell joined four representatives from Charleston for the first Catholic Convention, or congress, which met in St. Finbar's Cathedral. St. Finbar's was a wooden structure on a wide lawn on Broad Street, the city's main cross street. As the delegates assembled on the steps of St. Finbar's, they must have congratulated themselves on having risen so far in so short a time, for Catholics were not even allowed in South Carolina until after the Revolution. Two houses down toward King Street was the elegant mansion of John Rutledge's family. Next door was the meetinghouse of the prestigious St. Cecilia Society, the most exclusive club in Charleston. Across the street a fashionable neighborhood of Charleston's gentry reposed on the shady piazzas of their houses.[16]

Nevertheless, England's views of slavery put him at odds with Charleston society. The moment he stepped foot on the pier, he would have been surrounded by African Americans unloading the ships and bustling through the streets of Charleston, at least the business streets and the market. The coopers and rope-makers and ironworkers and teamsters clustered on East Bay and the waterfront were largely black freedmen. England had observed the effects of unfree labor and second-class citizenship in Ireland, Catholics deprived of their rights and privileges and then called inferior for it. England confided to his superiors in Rome, "The . . . priests whom I had as companions [when I first went to America] urged me to abandon the land which they styled 'the land of many horrors and no hope.'" The horrors, besides the frequent epidemics of yellow fever, were slavery, which England considered "the greatest moral evil that can desolate any part of the civilized world." When he finally saw it, England was disgusted by "the condition of the slaves" in America.[17]

But the Charleston Catholic church was a tiny minority in the Protestant South. Its few numbers made Catholics vulnerable, for, as the revolutionary generation died off, a reactionary movement of nativists, scared of the increasing numbers of Irish and German immigrants pouring into New York and Boston and Philadelphia, returned to the old English anti-Catholic bigotry. Anti-Catholic propaganda streamed in from England, where the cause of Catholic emancipation, renewed by O'Connell in the mid-1820s, had revived old prejudices. When John England arrived in Charleston in 1821, the generation of religious toleration in America was drawing to a close.

An Ursaline convent in Massachusetts was burned to the ground by a Protestant mob in the winter of 1834–35, at the exact time that John England was arranging for the arrival of Ursaline nuns to come to Charleston from Ireland. The nuns barely escaped alive. The rioters might have been encouraged by Lyman Beecher, the fiery Presbyterian preacher and father of future abolitionist Harriet Beecher Stowe. Beecher was in Massachusetts to raise support for Lane Seminary in Cincinnati, and he exhorted charity mainly by pouring into the ears of his listeners the threat of a popish empire in the West. The leaders of the riot, which was as much an anti-Irish race riot as a blow against Catholics, were brought to trial and acquitted in December 1834, which further demonstrated the extent of anti-Catholic sentiment in America. England estimated that as many as fifty sectarian periodicals published anti-Catholic propaganda each week, and besides these were the bulk of secular newspapers that betrayed a religious bias as well. Books like Scipio de' Ricci's *Female Convents. Secrets of Nunneries Disclosed*, published in 1834, directed much of their invective against convents. "The sole object of all monastic institutions in America," Ricci wrote, "is merely to proselyte youth of the influential classes of society, and especially females," by which means Roman priests "shall silently but effectually attain control of public affairs." This assessment was a villainized but nonetheless generally accurate view of the Ursalines. John England told the pope he wanted to bring the nuns to Charleston to educate mostly Protestant girls. This way, anti-Catholic "prejudices will be removed and many conversions will follow; or at least the way will be opened through the good ladies educated by the nuns to exercise a very powerful influence on the whole mass of society." England wanted to influence public affairs, but only to the degree that he might remove all prejudices against Catholics. This design was enough to frighten men like Ricci and Beecher and John Quincy Adams.[18]

Because of his outspoken defense of Catholicism, the anti-Catholic press targeted John England specially, reporting that the pope had commissioned him "to establish the Inquisition in the United States." John England, after all, was the Vatican's emissary to the Republic of Haiti, and the newspapers told their readers that the ultimate purpose of England's mission was to "facilitate the abolition of slavery of negroes in the South." Certainly his mission to Haiti hurt him in Charleston, for he treated the citizens of that nation as perfectly equal to whites in the eyes of God. There were the "700,000 inhabitants of [Haiti] & their descendants," whose condition always preyed on his mind. But through these seven hundred thousand England hoped to touch "a far larger portion [of blacks] spread through the West Indies, and perhaps a large district of Africa."[19] England believed that if he could establish normal relations between the Vatican and a black republic in Haiti, he would improve the condition of the newly freed slaves throughout the West Indies. And he probably hoped that the example of a pious and just black republic would undermine the foundation of slavery in the Americas: the ideology of white supremacy and black inferiority.

To this end, England established a school for "black girls [and] the poor white girls" of Charleston in 1831, taught by the Sisters of Charity. In the summer of 1835, England opened a school for free black boys. England wanted to provide a Catholic school for black members of the church, who until then were obliged to send their children to Protestant schools in the city, but England must also have believed that was taking a small step toward liberalizing the condition of blacks in the South. As he knew from experience in Ireland, the best way to refute racist ideology was to educate the persecuted. His grandfather, his father, and he himself in their own educated persons had given the lie to the racist stereotypes that justified the penal laws of Ireland. After fifteen years in America, after two years of negotiations on equal terms with blacks in Haiti, John England finally began the struggle for emancipation that had taken the Catholics in Ireland half a century to win. The first Irish Relief Act came in 1778, and Catholics did not win emancipation until 1829. It would probably take longer to free the blacks, for the penal laws of America were more severe than Ireland's. But one had to start somewhere, and John England began with a small school for "free children of colour."[20]

Two seminarians taught the boys, while the nuns continued teaching the girls. A month after admitting boys, eighty-four pupils crowded their schoolrooms. This success did not go unnoticed by the anti-Catholic elements in Charleston, who saw in England's school "the germ of [slave] insurrection." England was caught in a bind, for by the 1830s any progressive ideas about slavery were easily construed as treason to the state. In a letter to a good friend, he explained that "it would be mischievous to attempt an explanation" of his views of emancipation.[21] This phrase suggests much while averring little, but at the very least we can be sure that England's views on emancipation contradicted the political correctness enforced in South Carolina since the Nullification Crisis in 1833. Within this one school for free children of color were combined the twin paranoias of popish and abolitionist conspiracies. It would not take much to incite violence against the bishop, and the abolitionist tracts mailed to Charleston in the summer of 1835 gave the mob all the reason it needed.

The unruly crowd also was incensed by a rumor that one of Charleston's nuns was a black woman—a rumor that proved to be true. One of the three convents in Charleston was a community of French nuns, the Dames de la Retraite, who had come to Charleston from Philadelphia. They set up a school for the French Catholics in town and bothered Bishop England by doing unusual things like walking through the streets of Charleston in their habits and giving public lectures on literary topics not in English but in French. England did not know exactly how to handle their strong-willed leader, Madame Hery du Jarday, so he let her have her way, and in turn she conciliated the French among his laity. One of the nuns in the convent was a mulatto, and, though the mixed-race woman escaped John England's notice, she could not escape the vigilante eye of Charleston's bigots. Now the mob would tear down all the convents to be sure they rooted out the evil.[22]

Two Catholics among the mob at the post office alerted the Irish Volunteers, a Charleston militia unit, which hurried to defend their bishop. England was rousted out of bed and quickly apprised of the situation. He gathered the officers, made them swear to obey his own command, and then directed them to the best defenses of the church property. They would fight the mob on his order.[23]

But the mob never arrived. Either they got wind of the defense or dissolved under the discipline of a long walk, but England kept the volunteers at their posts for days. On the second day, England wrote a letter to the *Courier*:

> GENTLEMEN—Understanding that a report has been circulated, that I have received and retained one of the mischievous productions which have been sent hither from New York—and that this report is partially credited, I beg you will have the goodness to inform my fellow-citizens, through your columns, that I have not received, and consequently have not retained any such paper. . . . I will add, that I know no Carolinian who more sincerely deplores, more fully condemns, or more seriously reprobates the conduct of those men, who, by pouring them in upon us, are destroying our peace, and endangering our safety. Nor do I know a single Roman Catholic, clerical or lay, with whom I conversed upon the subject, who is not fully determined to use his best efforts to prevent the mischief of their interference.

Naturally England opposed the abolitionists, who he once remarked "were most bitter enemies also to the Catholics." The South could be liberalized only slowly, and the impetus for change would have to come from southerners themselves. He told Madame Hery that he could not permit the mulatto nun to remain in a religious community in

Charleston. Hery refused to expel her, but presumably the woman stopped teaching in the French school, since that broke one of South Carolina's penal laws. If John England recognized the irony that he was now on the side of the law—the exact law—that had sent his father into exile in the mountains of Tipperary, he did not acknowledge it.[24]

That night the abolitionist tracts were burned "publicly in the square under the guns of the citadel," a fiery intimidation of anyone sympathetic to abolition. But the following day, "several of the most respectable citizens of all religions sent to have their names enrolled" in the Irish Volunteers. Despite this show of support, it was clear that nothing short of closing the school for blacks, which was suspected to be an incendiary institution, would defuse the situation. Sectarian papers in Charleston earlier had denounced the school, and in the midst of this crisis a "committee of citizens" asked England to close it. England was obliged to send an explanation to the South Carolina Association, which supervised all schools for blacks. In the letter, which was published in the *Courier* and in his own paper, the *United States Catholic Miscellany*, England said that his "disposition is not to act in opposition to the wishes of any respectable portion of the community in regard to any political, civil or social subject, even under the permission of the law." But he would not stand for the Catholic prejudice. If the city council and the South Carolina Association meant to close *all* schools for blacks, he would "not be found backward in sacrificing my opinion to their advice." But if the Catholic school were singled out, he would refuse.[25]

England hoped to demonstrate to the community that Catholics were not incendiary, so he had to distance himself and his religion from abolitionism. Within a week, Charleston's storekeepers, many of whom were Catholic, resolved to boycott northern merchants who were known to be abolitionists. This measure was probably directed at the New York Tappan family. The same day, "a large overflowing meeting of citizens, comprising an ample representation of the property, respectability and intelligence of our community, assembled at the City Hall." They appointed a committee of twenty-one, including a Catholic, Captain James Lynah, which resolved to close all the schools for free blacks in Charleston, presumably on the grounds that educating free blacks would tend to aid an insurrection of slaves. England must have been disappointed, but at yet another public meeting during which "thanks were returned to those who closed the schools," England proudly found himself sitting "with the presiding magistrate in the most conspicuous place."[26]

Today's readers might be surprised by England's outrage at being accused of abolitionism, his sincerity in denouncing the "incendiaries," and his sense that he had handled the crisis successfully. His protestations in the *Courier* might seem to contradict his hopes for emancipation, but really they do not. Garrison's direct mail campaign forced those that the South Carolina Association suspected of abolitionism to declare themselves for or against emancipation. Those who quietly sympathized with abolition had to make a terrible decision: face the coercive mob or betray their conscience. England equivocated. He declared Garrison his enemy, but he refused to confess his own emancipatory principles, thereby leaving his fellow white Charlestonians to infer that he was pro-slavery. By abandoning his progressive reforms like the schools for blacks he could stay in the city, avoid bloodshed, and deflect from Catholics the charge of treason against the state.

The equivocation paid immediate dividends. That fall, England went to Columbia to give the benediction opening the new session of the state senate, and on the way there he shared a coach with three "intimate acquaintances," James Hamilton, Robert Hayne, and James Louis Petigru. "We were two to two in politics," England observed, because he and Petigru had been against nullification while Hayne and Hamilton were for it, but even so, "we were firm friends."[27] They discussed England's mission to Haiti, the upcoming campaign to get the legislature to charter the Ursalines, and surely they must have discussed the closing of the schools for free blacks in Charleston. But no matter their discordant views of slavery, it was a jolly party of friends. They could all get along, so long as the opponents of slavery thoroughly capitulated. England capitulated, and Catholics were assured of their ride in the carriage to Columbia.

Angelina Grimké, then living among Quakers in Philadelphia, read in the *Pennsylvanian* about the "bonfires" in her hometown of Charleston, the breaking into the post office, the burning of Garrison and Arthur Tappan in effigy, and she considered the mob action to be nothing short of an "insurrection." After her emotional conversion and move to Philadelphia in November 1829, Grimké found life within the Quaker community nearly as trying as life in Charleston. She involved herself in a number of religious squabbles, many deriving from her refusal to play the role of the retiring, mild, and obedient female communicant. All the while, her diary records an increasing opposition to slavery, which put her in advance even of the liberal attitudes of her congregation. As she read successive issues of *The Liberator* and other radical tracts, her interest in abolitionism increased and her devotion to Quakerism waned, because she thought that the Friends were taking no part in "the great moral reformation of the day."[28]

Garrison's religious zeal and rhetoric attracted Grimké. *The Liberator* never had a huge circulation, and most whites in the North and South viewed the editor as a radical-fringe fanatic and perhaps crazy. He raved about the apocalypse from *The Liberator*'s first issue, which prophesized, as George Whitefield had prophesied ninety years earlier, that Americans who countenanced slavery "must cease to expect the mercy of God—we must prepare for the coming judgment of Him who, as our charter acknowledges, made all men *free and equal!*'" Those few non-radicals into whose hands his paper strayed easily dismissed his forthright reading of Old Testament–like omens. Until Nat Turner.

On a Sunday afternoon in August 1831, in Southampton County, Virginia, just eight months after Garrison started publishing *The Liberator*, Nat Turner and a few of his followers shared dinner by the bank of a pond and decided finally to go on the rampage they had been planning for months. Armed with axes and hoes, they killed about sixty whites—many women and children—beheading many victims before being routed by the roused militias and slave patrols, whose own rampages against guilty and innocent blacks alike soon dwarfed the rebel outrages. The reports circulating around the nation emphasized Turner's religious fanaticism and his prophet-like status among fellow blacks. And if anyone doubted the connection between Garrison's religious, apocalyptic rhetoric and Turner's rebellion, *The Liberator* itself made the connection for them. On September 3, 1831, while

Turner was still hiding out in the swamps and the earth that was heaped on the graves of the dead was still raw, Garrison told his readers, "What we have long predicted . . . has commenced its fulfillment. The first step of the earthquake . . . has been made. . . . Read the account of the insurrection in Virginia, and say whether our prophecy be not fulfilled." This kind of religious rhetoric stank in the noses of most Americans with the odor of messianic egoism. It gave abolitionism a bad name, and men who cherished reason and logic, like John England, shrank from it.[29]

The Nat Turner Rebellion triggered the most "public, focused, and sustained discussion of slavery and emancipation that ever occurred in . . . [any] southern state." Should Virginia preserve slavery? Should the state gradually abolish it, as Thomas Jefferson Randolph proposed in a controversial motion before the legislature? Randolph, the grandson of Thomas Jefferson, asked that

> the select committee raised on slaves, free negroes, and [the Nat Turner Rebellion] . . . be instructed to inquire into the expediency of submitting to the vote of the qualified voters in the several towns, cities, boroughs, and counties of this commonwealth, the propriety of providing by law, that the children of all female slaves, who may be born in this state, on or after the 4th day of July, 1840, shall become the property of the commonwealth, males at the age of twenty-one years, and females at the age of eighteen, if detained by their owners within the limits of Virginia, until they shall respectively arrive at the ages aforesaid, to be hired out until the net sum arising therefrom, shall be sufficient to defray the expense of their removal, beyond the limits of the United States, and that said committee have leave to report by bill or otherwise.

It was not a bill to emancipate the slaves, but Randolph predicted that in eighty years it would abolish slavery in the state of Virginia and replace it with free labor. Ultimately, Randolph's motion was tabled, effectively closing the door on eradicating slavery from that state. And yet, the preamble of the final resolution regarding the Nat Turner

Rebellion still could not let go of the Enlightenment idea that Jefferson and other Founding Fathers cherished: the Virginia legislature pronounced itself "profoundly sensible of the great evils arising from the condition" of slaves and free blacks, and left open the notion that in some distant day the issue might be revisited.[30]

Nevertheless, it became evident that the pro-slavery conservatives viewed the truths of the Declaration of Independence as somewhat naive and hopelessly heedless of reality, the stuff of dreamers and idealists. Advocates of slavery considered themselves almost as scientists who derived their principles from "positive law, history, and experience," not from natural rights. The Preamble of the final Virginia legislation notwithstanding, the debate over Nat Turner's rebellion introduced the idea that slavery might not be evil at all. Those debates were open to the public, the galleries were filled, the newspapers full of reports, but it was a little book by Thomas Roderic Dew, *Abolition of Negro Slavery*, published just after the debates concluded, that framed further discussions not only of the Virginia debate but of the place of slavery in the American South. Dew, rector of the University of Virginia, began by lamenting the fact that the "excitement" stirred by Turner led to the legislative debate at all: he would have preferred to have waited a year or two until "the empire of reason could once more have been established." Clad in the drab robes of a scholarly logician, he pried apart the foundations of emancipation, demonstrating that the abolitionists' "arguments, in most cases, were of a wild and intemperate character, based upon false principles, and assumptions of the most vicious and alarming kind." In contrast, he himself gave the "vital question of abolition the most mature and intense consideration which we are capable of bestowing." He drew "a conclusion which seems to be sustained by facts and reasoning as irresistible as the demonstration of the mathematician." Those facts and that reasoning led him to an inevitable conclusion that repudiated almost all American rhetoric about slavery up to that day, but which was implicit in the policies of James Hamilton and the other Nullifiers: *slavery is good for blacks*. As absurdly self-serving as this conclusion seems to us today, Dew based it on a then-reputable analysis of political economy, which predicted that the cost of free labor in the North would fall below that of unfree labor in the South. Workers who could not feed themselves and their families would overthrow civilization. Dew thought that the only refuge for free and unfree workers alike in the modern world was the southern model of society, which alone could "guarantee republican liberties of the propertied, security for the propertyless, and stability for the state and society."[31]

By contrast, the rhetoric of the new abolitionists was idealistic, biblical, shrill, alarmist, apocalyptic, all tendencies that appealed to the sensitive, irrational anxieties of Angelina Grimké's intellectual life. Garrison's style approached the fervent, fanatical, spiritual narrative that Angelina Grimké was writing in her own diary, a story full of trials and gigantic sin and more gigantic surrender, and so she saw in Garrison the beacon she had long sought from God. In the summer of 1835, when so many rioted against his campaign, she feared he might be frightened into compromising his demand for immediate emancipation, so she determined to help fortify his soul. She would write him a letter. Theoretically, it was a private letter, but, as her subsequent confessions to her sister indicate, Grimké knew that this was the decisive moment of her life. Posting the letter and letting it slip out of her own hands to circulate in the world was equivalent to taking her own conscience, which had been hidden for so many years in the shadowed, Gothic cathedral of her soul, and plastering it on a billboard. For thirty years she had led an intensely private life, fighting an intensely private drama, eagerly awaiting a vocation from God, and she sensed that her long years of hesitance and preparation and the private drama of her life were all about to end. Even if she did not allow herself to acknowledge it consciously, she knew that Garrison would publish her letter.

And publish it he did, immediately, without so much as asking permission. "We cannot," Garrison wrote, "we dare not suppress it, nor the name of her who indited it. . . . It comes to us as the voice of an angel. . . . We publish it that our cruel assailants may perceive how heavenly is that temper, and how pure that principle, which they are branding as fanaticism and madness." Garrison predicted, "This letter will be read widely—attentively, *now*: it will be read with admiration and thanksgiving by *posterity*."[32]

Grimké's letter began by explaining how gratified she was that the intrepid abolitionist stood "firm in the midst of storm, determined to suffer and to die, rather than yield one inch." Grimké told Garrison that "the ground upon which you stand . . . is holy ground," and he "must never surrender it." As a southern aristocrat, Grimké possessed an authority none of Garrison's other contributors had, speaking "from what I have seen, and heard, and known in a land of slavery, where rests the darkness of Egypt." She did not develop the analogy but clearly implied that slave owners played the unenviable role of Pharaoh. For good measure, she accused them of the "sin of Sodom," no doubt a puritan's gratuitous sideswipe at the decadence of Charleston's wealthy. And to Garrison she assigned the role of prophet and martyr. Like the "first martyr who ever died," his suffering was part of God's design, for the persecution of the abolitionists was the "means which God has ordained for the accomplishment of this great end, EMANCIPATION." What if "*our* lives will be taken?" Grimké asked. "Yes!" she gloried in all capital letters, "LET IT COME." If Garrison was given pause by the enthusiasm with which Grimké invited not merely a metaphoric martyrdom but a real one, he gave no indication of it. Together, they welcomed the violence of the mob.[33]

Grimké had thought carefully about mobs and how they were used to eradicate dissent, how effective they were with men like John England, and how to combat them. It hardly mattered, she adroitly recognized, that the abolitionists' methods were perfectly legal—using the U.S. mail, for instance, to exercise their right of free speech. A "lawless breed of unprincipled men" could attack the abolitionists with impunity because those "too high in *Church* and State to *condescend* to mingle" with the mob "*secretly* approve and rejoice over their violent measures." The insight applied not just to Charleston's approval of those who broke into the post office, but even to the White House. Andrew Jackson instructed Amos Kendall, the postmaster general, to take down the names of any Charlestonians receiving the abolitionist mail and "have them exposed thru the Publick journals." Jackson wanted the "frowns of all good men" to chasten those who sympathized with abolitionists. In reality, as Jackson must have known, the mob would threaten all dissenters with vigilante violence, as it threatened Bishop John England. Mobs might lynch them, as it had elsewhere, and the president gave his tacit approval.[34]

It was not long before Grimké confronted a mob. The crowds that mingled in the narrow Philadelphia streets surrounding Pennsylvania Hall, where Grimké was preaching the gospel of abolition in the late spring of 1838, had accumulated all day long. By many accounts, most of the men and women thronging that quarter of the city were there only to see what would happen, subscribing neither to abolitionism nor to the pro-slavery views of the young rowdies who threw stones at the windows and howled so loud as to disrupt the proceedings inside. "Those voices," Grimké explained from the podium, putting herself in the role of the crucified Christ, "ought to awaken and call out our warmest sympathies. Deluded beings! 'they know not what they do.'"[35] No one in the crowded streets raised a disapproving hand or voice, so the stone throwers were emboldened by their belief that public opinion was behind them.

At the end of the day's convention, the women who were assembled inside the hall, both delegates and audience, black and white, proceeded out the doors of the building, clutching together arm in arm, hurrying to their homes and hotels. The thronging crowd—some reports put their numbers at twenty-five thousand—parted like the Red Sea to let them through. From somewhere, almost shyly, a first stone was thrown at them. Then another. The crowd did not disapprove. The young rowdy men were all the more incensed because white women walked arm in arm with black women. Though in fact they were huddled together for their safety, it would be falsely reported in unsympathetic newspapers that brazen amalgamations of "white dandies with spectacles, and black wenches,—and black dandies and white wenches" purposely flouted public taboos against miscegenation, hoping to incite the mob to violence. One abolitionist caught a stone in the head and was severely injured, but, miraculously, the rest made it to safety. Their tepid attempts at violence having gone unchecked, about thirty or forty men grew bolder and broke through the locked doors of the assembly hall, scattered whatever documents they could lay hold of, and lit a bonfire on the floor. The firemen, afraid to defy the rabble-rousers, watched the building burn to the ground.

But such violence must be borne quietly. Grimké's 1835 letter to Garrison outlined a plan for civil disobedience nearly a dozen years before Thoreau more famously theorized the strategy. "Let us . . . be prepared," she wrote, "for the enactment of laws even in our *Free* States, against Abolitionists." These they would resist, and the abolitionists must not try to escape the suffering they would surely endure as a consequence of breaking the law, but instead, by the example of their willingness "to suffer the loss of character, property—yea, and life itself," they would persuade even slave owners of the rightness of their cause.[36] In 1835, this scenario seemed likely. South Carolinians were calling on the northern states to write laws abrogating free speech. Some wanted the abolitionists extradited to southern states, where they would face prosecution and hostile juries, but in the end the northern states never did comply.

Grimké certainly suffered the loss of her character, a commodity of inestimable value in 1835. Despite all her courting of martyrdom, she felt the pain of this humiliation acutely:

> To have my name, not so much *my* name, as the name of Grimké associated with that of the despised Garrison, seemed like bringing disgrace upon my *family*, not myself alone. I felt as tho' the name had been tarnished in the eye of thousands who had before lovd & reverd it.

Her published letter confirmed the Quakers' disapproval of Grimké's radical nature. In her diary, she described her confrontation with Samuel Bettle, the "overseer of the Arch Street Meeting" of Quakers, which Grimké attended. Grimké had once been courted by Bettle's son, Edward, though the match ended unhappily. Bettle was "most exceedingly tried," wanted Grimké to write to Garrison to disapprove of his decision to publish the letter, and implored her to change "some of the expressions" in it. Garrison's introduction to the letter particularly incensed Bettle because it seemed the "ravings of a fanatic." The charge of fanaticism is particularly telling, because it became the ubiquitous label of abolitionists. Even Angelina's sister, Sarah, who was at times a partner in radical thought and always a great sympathizer, was shocked. The suffering engendered by Angelina's new "connection with the anti-slavery society," Sarah wrote in her own diary, was "another proof how dangerous it is to slight the clear convictions of Truth." Sarah's clear conviction at this point was that the abolitionists were wrong, and she thought that Angelina had "listened to the voice" of the devil. Sarah hoped her sister's suffering would teach her "obedience."[37]

Grimké *was* a fanatic. She had been writing this letter for seven years; her diary is chock-full of such over-the-top ravings. Only in 1835 did she think to plug slavery into the formula. Her biographers take this self-fashioning largely at face value. This is not to say Grimké's life did not have the stuff of heroism. Her determination is justly celebrated today, and, as her biographers rightly point out, she was steeled to the heroics by an exaggerated belief in her own righteousness and by her belief that the more she was scorned by men, the more God loved her. But Angelina Grimké was not made zealous by the righteous cause of abolition. She was a zealot who, after years of trying lesser things, finally found a cause equal to her temperament, "*a cause worth dying for.*"

The difference is important, not only to her contemporaries but to our understanding of the history of dissent in nineteenth-century America. Grimké's religiosity *was* irrational; her zealotry *did* lead her to bizarre beliefs. The young woman who in 1828, at the age of twenty-three, thought it "plain that Zion's King is about to take possession of our World," became the foolish, ridiculous soul who, as a middle-aged mother and celebrated teacher, expected Christ to end the world at 3:00 a.m. on October 12, 1843. She got dressed up to meet him. When no one descended from heaven, the preacher William Miller conceded that he must have had the date off by a year or so. Undaunted, Angelina prepared a second time for the Second Coming. Even when she was disappointed again, Angelina would not give up the apocalypse, believing fully "in the downfall of every earthly throne, the overthrow of every political government, the annihilation of every Ecclesiastical Establishment." Grimké's biographer interprets this sentiment as "an emotional response to a profound crisis in Angelina's life." But such "chiliastic rhetoric" characterizes all of Grimké's writing. She was disappointed when the world did not end and she had to return on the afternoon of October 12, 1843, to the questions of supper and housekeeping. Back in the days after the Stono Rebellion, the reformer Hugh Bryan smote the waters with his staff, expecting them to part, only to find himself drowning and laughed at. No one laughed at Nat Turner, but they all associated his crazy, religious, apocalyptic fantasies with the cause of abolition. No doubt Grimké's religious fanaticism seemed to her contemporaries to be cut from the same cloth.[38]

If Grimké's diary never mentioned slavery, it would be little more than the record of another intelligent woman stunted and tortured by the sexism and religiosity of the age. But of course it does mention slavery, nearly from its opening pages, and running parallel to the unfortunate spiritual drama is Grimké's gradual awakening, not to the problem of slavery (for she was clear about that from the beginning), but to the epic solution that would eventually consume the nation in a struggle of biblical magnitude. Grimké began her diary craving martyrdom, and she was lucky that five years later she found abolitionism, or the martyr's righteous sacrifice would have been squandered on the bullying elders of a small Quaker church on the fringes of society. The rhetorician Stephen Howard Browne thinks Grimké's great accomplishment was to transform northern ideology, making cataclysm seem a viable method of social change.[39] But doing so abandoned reason and logic to the new proponents of slavery. More important, it allowed these proponents to cast abolition in the mold of dangerous fanaticism, irresponsible idealism, and the romantic disposition to ignore scientific reason. Sensible men promoted slavery.

8

THE LOST GENERATION

||

"**O**n principle," the editor of the *Washington Globe* remarked in April 1833, "slavery has no advocates North or South of the Potomac." Granted, the *Globe* fiercely opposed Calhoun and nullification, but what it meant was that no one defended slavery *on principle*, only *on expediency*. "The present generation finds the evil entailed on it," the newspaper continued, and "in the course of time" the American people would be relieved of their "share in the misfortune." This categorical statement was something of an exaggeration, but it does catch the gist of public sentiment. As late as 1833, practically nobody advocated slavery, and public opinion everywhere but South Carolina still agreed with the Founding Fathers that slavery was an inherited evil.[1]

Historians have blamed the Virginian, Professor Thomas Dew, for inventing the "positive good" theory of slavery, for he first articulated a full-blown, complex argument explaining why a slave society was better than a free-labor society, and in the wake of the Nat Turner debates in the Virginia legislature, Dew's book circulated throughout the South. But perpetual slavery was patented in South Carolina, and in South Carolina it was fashioned into the central plank of a political movement. As the historian William Freehling put it, not until the 1850s did southerners in other states customarily proclaim that slavery *ought to be* perpetual. It took about fifteen years for South Carolina to foist this ideology on the rest of the southern states. The siege batteries were in place, and the long ideological bombardment began.[2]

||

Just after the direct mail crisis in the summer of 1835, Arthur P. Hayne wrote a letter to President Andrew Jackson that articulated the worries that plagued the brains of most of the Nullifiers. Literature advocating liberty would tap into a "restless feeling" about slavery, troubling the consciences of slave owners in the South and inspiring southern whites who did not own slaves to turn against the institution. Hayne was afraid of southerners who would convert to the cause of abolition, an army of Angelina Grimkés. Dissent would grow, and "Southerners would desert" slavery. Jackson, the Tennessean, did not worry much about it, but in South Carolina, where the Nullifiers already had swept away dissent, the issue of slave ideology in other states became the single most important political issue.[3]

Duff Green, the influential newspaper editor in Washington, DC, who was, essentially, John C. Calhoun's national press officer, understood that all the complaints coming out of Charleston about "incendiary" pamphlets stirring up a slave revolt were nonsense. Blacks hardly posed any danger at all, Nat Turner notwithstanding. The real danger came from the "morbid sensitivity" of southern whites, who, persuaded by the cause of abolition, would become "the voluntary instrument of their own ruin." "The gradual operation of public opinion," he explained, "would persuade us that slavery is a sin, a curse, an evil." From his post at South Carolina College in Columbia, Henry Nott wrote to his congressman, James Hammond, that, though Europe and the North were "against us," the more troubling fact was how "we stand at home." "Every town & every village," he conceded gloomily, "is full of northern people, many of whom are feebly with us & many in secret decidedly against us." The rural poor, he worried, "would on the ground of republicanism or religion either be inefficient friends or decided opponents" of perpetual slavery. Nott did not need to convince Representative Hammond, who already had sent a more strident letter to the *New York Evening Star* proposing a solution late in the summer of 1835. Fanatics, he wrote, "can be silenced in but one way—*Terror—death*."[4]

Soon after Hammond's unveiled threat, an unofficial delegation of town representatives called at the childhood home of Angelina Grimké. Angelina's mother let them in, sat them in the parlor, and gave them the customary gestures of hospitality while the awkward delegation waited for the right moment to bring up the subject of her daughter and the letter she had written to William Garrison's *The Liberator*. There was no delicate way to deliver their message, and though we have no record of their exact words, we can imagine their clumsiness as they explained to Mrs. Grimké that for Angelina's own sake she must write to her daughter and tell her never to return to Charleston. Angelina would be given no quarter where men like James Hammond flourished. In essence, Angelina Grimké was exiled by her native city.[5]

James Hammond, bizarre and brilliant, terrible and sentimental, knew something about terror. He had been practicing it for three years on his own recently acquired plantation, Silver Bluff, far up the rich swampland of the upper Savannah River. Hammond was not born to the Carolina aristocracy. His father was a Massachusetts stonemason who taught himself Latin, put himself through Dartmouth College, and came to Charleston to seek his fortune. He followed a series of disappointing careers, almost successes, and definite failures, including an academy in the Midlands and the South Carolina College in Columbia. His one great achievement was James, his oldest son, whom he "never doubted . . . was a genius." James got from his father the best education he could offer, and when he was a teenager James found for himself the Romantic poets, which led to dreams of medieval knights and castles. His education culminated in two years at the South Carolina College, where he lived a frat boy's life with the scions of the old Carolina aristocratic families. They all studied under Thomas Cooper, the political economist who worked hard to earn the epithet "Schoolmaster of States' Rights": two dozen of the signers of the Ordinance of Secession were his pupils. James felt himself intensely shy and intensely proud, longing for deep and intimate friendship but so fearful of any emotional dependence that he condemned himself to loneliness. Steeped in the poetry of Byron and Shelley, he made himself into a Romantic hero, a Childe Harold, cherishing that exultant loneliness even as it wounded him. Outwardly, he cultivated a reputation for being cold and calculating. Later in life, one observer described him as a "cold and chiseled classic beauty; his statuesque form and stately poise were antique in impressiveness."[6]

After college, Hammond studied law, which interested him little, so he threw his energy into editing a radical, pro-nullification newspaper. At the height of that controversy, Governor Robert Hayne commissioned him officer in charge of military preparedness of the Barnwell District, a job that discouraged the young man because he "could not find many volunteers" willing to march behind him in battle against President Andrew Jackson. Hammond had more encouragement in society. He was beautiful, vain, and charming, and he exerted a "powerful attraction" over women, who equally captivated him. Despite his libido and love of Lord Byron, he had no illusions about romance: marriage, he thought, "was an instrument of self-advancement." A portrait of the middle-aged Hammond still captured the features that seduced women: a fine nose and a delicate line of lips, soft and intelligent eyes, an amused and knowing look, as if he and the viewer conspired in a secret joke. But he was prone to spells of melancholy also, sorrowful as young Werther, while he lived in his younger days in a filthy, ill-kept bachelor's apartment in Columbia.

Hammond found his calling the way so many other intelligent and poor southern men did before him: at the age of twenty-four he married an heiress, a girl of sixteen who was so unattractive and awkward that no one but the bride believed he was moved by a genuine passion—least of all the bride's brother-in-law, the politically powerful Wade Hampton II, who recognized that Hammond was a gold digger and tried to frighten him away. But Hammond steadfastly pursued his quarry, which impressed her all the more. In December 1831, he and his bride took possession of her dowry, a neglected plantation called Silver Bluff, its best feature a high red clay cliff fronting the Savannah River not far from Augusta, Georgia. Along with an unprepossessing house, they owned 10,800 acres of swamp, of which nearly a thousand had been reclaimed and cultivated. The estate included a blacksmith, gin house, gristmill, lumberyard, all the usual things, and also typical were the 147 slaves who practically owned the place, used as they were to the lax rule of absentee landowners.[7]

It cleared barely $1,000 a year, but Hammond, who had never farmed a day in his life nor managed so many slaves, could make it pay. The first thing to do was whip the workers into shape. Discipline and efficiency, Hammond believed, were the answer to any problem. He watched how the field hands worked, and he saw waste everywhere in their slipshod, hasty jobs and idle hours in the long late afternoons. Under the "task" system, slaves had their given work for the day, however many acres to hoe for instance, and once they finished it they were more or less free to do what they wanted. Hammond found that his slaves were flying through their tasks, working too fast and without even breaking for lunch so they could get off the clock (so to speak) by mid-afternoon. That would not do at all. No one was trying to do a good job. All they wanted was to finish, and the farm suffered. So Hammond instituted a "gang" system, where the slaves, overseen by a supervisor, worked the fields from sunrise to sunset, with breaks, at a moderate pace, motivated not by the promise of free time but by fear of the whip.

Hammond needed the whip, for the slaves did not like the change. It robbed them of the small measure of independence they enjoyed, such as farming their own little plots, which was another thing Hammond did away with. No more personal gardens and away with the underground market of small-time entrepreneurs. Silver Bluff serviced steamboats plying the upper Savannah River, selling lumber to the vessels at a station below the bluff. Hammond approved the business but forbade any intercourse between his slaves and the lively river culture. Everything he did attempted to annihilate their independence. He forbade them to visit nearby farms. He found a vibrant religious culture among his slaves, who were in the habit of leading their own prayer meetings and conducting their own worship. No more of that. If anyone wanted to go to church, they could come to the white church and listen to the preaching of a white minister. In the words of his biographer, Drew Gilpin Faust, Hammond tried to destroy "the autonomy of the slave community, and bring its members under his direct and total domination." Nothing served domination better than the leather whip. For instance, when some slaves were "slow in returning to their work" after Christmas, the overseer "severely whipped" them. The tardy field hands, shocked by this violence, appealed to Hammond, who had them flogged again for impertinence.[8]

At the same time, Hammond relished his role as the head of this "family," pretending not only to the world but also to himself that he was a kind and just owner. Through his whole life, he avoided breaking up families, and he did not shirk his responsibility for the aged, unproductive slaves. He took a keen, professional interest in their diseases, becoming something of a physic himself and not stinting when he needed to hire more expert opinion. And he was appalled to discover that under his regime the infant mortality rate was nearly 75 percent. That was bad for business and embarrassing before his neighbors, a "melancholy" fact, to use his own word. In his first ten years as the "father" of this plantation family, seventy-three people were born and eighty-two people died. He had enough sense to scrutinize his own behavior in case that was the cause. Unfortunately, he thought the answer lay in better doctoring and not in better nutrition, for their diet consisted largely of "cornmeal, pork, and molasses." Faust points out that Hammond exercised no less wisdom than most nineteenth-century masters on that score, following the prevailing culture in the belief that "too rich or elaborate a diet" harmed slaves. Nevertheless, his regime's interdict on personal gardens must have robbed his slaves of vitamins, minerals, and proteins. Even so, Hammond measured his benevolence by effort, not effect, and, complacently, he fattened his ego on the strange fiction that he was kind to his slaves. And as the years went by, he literally fattened on the profits while his slaves wasted on poor rations.

Hammond burst upon the national scene when the House of Representatives debated the so-called gag rule, which was meant to suppress antislavery petitions sent to Congress. In its first session after the 1835 direct mail campaign, Congress received a number of petitions, as it was accustomed to doing, asking it to abolish slavery in the District of Columbia. Most members thought the Constitution barred Congress from doing much about slavery anyway, so to avoid unpleasant discussions, the House of Representatives for many years had received such petitions and promptly tabled them or entombed them in committees. But on December 18, 1835, after the direct mail campaign had died down and most congressmen thought they had avoided yet another discussion of slavery, James Hammond lit the fuse on a bomb.

Because they were based on the presumption that slavery is evil, all such petitions accuse southerners of being sinners, and such insults should not be allowed in the door of Congress. Hammond moved that the House refuse even to receive the petitions. Hammond's fellow representative from South Carolina, Francis Pickens, would not be found backward in his pique, and he spoke in support of Hammond's motion, not so much from injured pride as from a fear that abolitionism would spread and widen until the "moral power of the world" would force southerners to free their slaves.[9]

Hammond's mailbox filled with praise, nearly all from antiprogressives in South Carolina, and many of his correspondents predicted that the issue would lead to disunion, cheering Hammond in case it did. His old professor, Thomas Cooper, and Professor Beverley Tucker from the College of William and Mary were among these admirers, and Freehling argues persuasively that such schools bred the radicals of the rising generation who had little love for the United States. Likewise, Eugene Genovese touches on the largely unexplored topic of how deeply influential a few southern colleges were in disseminating among a few young southern elites what was a highly radical ideology in the 1820s; and how those elites then disseminated it among the electorate. That is exactly the process we saw in the nullification crisis in 1832, when a few committed men so manipulated politics that they transformed a radical minority position into the politically correct and only *legal* ideology in the state.[10]

On February 1, 1835, Caleb Cushing of Massachusetts, himself a freshman congressman, challenged Hammond by laying another petition before the House, signed by citizens of his state, asking Congress to abolish the slave trade and slavery in the District of Columbia. James Hammond had had enough. He immediately rose to "say at once what he had to say on this subject," painful as it was that "the truth should now be told." That "truth" was that slavery was good, not evil, and the South never intended to give up slavery. Gone was any pretense that the states themselves would figure out how to gradually do away with slavery. There would be no withering away. "We were born and bred under" a slave society, Hammond said, imagining that he was speaking aloud what South Carolinians had felt but had been too delicate to admit for half a century, "and will maintain [it] or die in [its] defence." South Carolina, Hammond strongly implied, had been lying to the rest of the country ever since John Rutledge hood-winked the delegates from Connecticut back at the Constitutional Convention in 1787, and it was time now to voice the "painful truth." "The camel loves the desert," he reasoned, "the reindeer seeks ever-lasting snows; the wild fowl gather to the waters; and the eagle wings his flight above the mountains." It was "equally the order of Provi-dence," he asserted, hiding the weakness of his logic behind the poetic analogies, "that slavery should exist among a planting people, beneath a southern sun." And it was just as natural that those slaves should be blacks, who were racially suited to servitude. Hammond repudiated the long-held American belief that blacks were "created equal" to whites but had been so long demoralized by slavery that they had to be prepared for freedom, and that preparation was slow and gradual. This was instead Dew's new idea forged in the debates over Nat Turner's rebellion. Slavery is good and it would be evil to end it. "The moment this House undertakes to legislate upon this subject," he ex-plained to his fellow congressmen, "it dissolves the Union. Should it be my fortune to have a seat upon this floor, I will abandon it the in-stant the first decisive step is taken. . . . I will go home to preach, and if I can, to practice, disunion, and civil war, if needs be. A revolution must ensue, and this republic sink in blood."[11]

What then could Jefferson and the entire revolutionary genera-tion have meant by that quaint phrase "all men are created equal"? Here Hammond deferred to Congressman Pickens, who told Congress that such idealistic musings are all well and good, but "the history of mankind proclaims that there is 'an elect and chosen few,' [who are] made the peculiar receptacles of the favors and blessings of an all-wise and all-pervading Providence." Such exploitation as one finds in slav-ery might seem unjust from an idealist's perspective, but there was no use denying the nature of humanity. "This is the world as we find it," Pickens said, fancying himself a realist, "and it is not for us to war upon destiny." If you try to apply the "abstract truth" of equality to the real world, he argued, "instead of its becoming a doctrine full of light and peace to a world sleeping in darkness and bondage, it becomes a doctrine of universal discord, confusion, and ruin. . . . [L]ike all other mere abstractions, it can have no actual existence."[12]

Hammond insisted that this supposedly realistic outlook was an age-old southern ideology, albeit one that southerners had felt obliged out of delicacy to leave unspoken until the abolitionists forced them to reveal it. And it is likely that he thought he was telling the truth, though history really indicates it was a new ideology entertained by so few southerners that it had no place even in South Carolina's politics before the Vesey Rebellion.

Also revealed by this devoted acolyte of slave society was an ugly and self-righteous race prejudice, which he expressed as realism confronting the romantic, idealistic naïveté of men like Jefferson. The abolitionists called for racial equality, including citizenship for all and voting rights for black men. Had Hammond been an honest student of southern history, he would know that this is exactly what men like John Laurens, steeped as they were in Enlightenment ideals, hoped for in the 1780s. Times had so changed by 1835 that Hammond felt he could demonstrate the abolitionists' evident absurdity merely by pointing out that they believed in racial equality. "Are we prepared to see [blacks] mingling in our legislation?" Hammond asked rhetorically, knowing full well that it would be the rare man in his Congress who would answer in the affirmative.

> Is any portion of this country [he continued] prepared to see them enter these halls and take their seats by our sides, in perfect equality with the white representatives of an Anglo-Saxon race—to see them fill that chair—to see them placed at the heads of your Departments; or to see, perhaps, some Othello, or Toussaint, or Boyer, gifted with genius and inspired by ambition, grasp the presidential wreath, and wield the destinies of this great republic?

No doubt Hammond spoke for most, north and south, when he proclaimed that "from such a picture I turn with irrepressible disgust."[13] By 1835, whites in America were consumed with a sense of their Anglo-Saxon-ness that was far more intense and essential to their self-identity than in any previous generation. Why that should be is far too complex a question to explore here, but it was clearly manifest in the schemes such as the Indian removal (then under way) and the black colonization movement. Even many of those with progressive ideas about slavery presumed the solution had to include the removal of blacks, for they considered it a given that the two races could not live side by side in peace as equals.

But Hammond took the notion of white supremacy to a level not contemplated by many: not only were whites by nature superior to blacks, but blacks were so inferior they were congenitally unsuited for liberty. Dependency was natural to blacks, and therefore slavery was good for them. "As a class," he boldly proclaimed, "there is not a happier, more contented race upon the face of the earth." American slaves were "lightly tasked, well clothed, well fed . . . their lives and persons protected by the law, all their sufferings alleviated by the kindest and most interested care, and their domestic affections cherished and maintained, at least so far as I have known, with conscientious delicacy." Remarkably, Hammond averred and believed "our slaves are a peaceful, kind-hearted, and affectionate race; satisfied with their lot, happy in their comforts, and devoted to their masters."[14]

Remarkable because so much evidence at Hammond's own plantation ran to the contrary. Numerous slaves ran away; and if Hammond became milder in his punishments as he aged, still his paternalism was predicated on the whip, as he well knew. More shocking to our own sensibilities than this wanton violence were his sexual conquests. He had wedded a girl of sixteen whom the world considered ugly, and all but the bride knew that he married for money. She spent her youth giving him children, with annual regularity, but she had little to do with the ardent fire of his sexual impulses. Those he spent on Sally, a seamstress he owned, who gave birth to a number of mixed-race children. When the bloom of youth faded from Sally, it blossomed in her daughter Louisa, and Hammond spent his sexual energy on her. But he was not exclusive. He initiated his white son, Harry, in the sexual exploitation of slaves, so that in the end he did not know which offspring were his children and which were his grandchildren.

Those sexual crimes were as much an indication of his attitude toward women as it was of his attitude toward blacks. From Hammond's point of view, his exploits were founded on serious emotional attachment, at least as much as one might have for a favorite horse or dog. When his wife found out about the infidelities she demanded that he sell the black women, but he refused even to the point of estrangement: such was his sentimentality that he would sooner be banned from his own house than betray his black dependents. In Hammond's mind, his white wife was herself a dependent: both women and blacks might be human beings but of a lesser sort than white men, and it was in the natural order of things that women, white or black, were put on the Earth to serve his sexual needs. His four nieces, Harriet, Catherine, Ann, and Caroline, the children of Wade Hampton, often visited the Hammonds at Silver Bluff. By this time, Hampton was reconciled to his brother-in-law, and when his own wife died, the girls' aunt served as a surrogate mother. When the oldest girl was about seventeen and the youngest twelve years old, Hammond encouraged a familiarity that quickly escalated from hugs and kisses to acts far more serious, everything—he confessed in his diary—short of sexual intercourse. He imagined the children were willing partners, even instigators, as they competed for his attention, "pressing their bodies almost into mine wreathing their limbs with mine." His hands could not resist their unresisting bodies, and his fingers explored their "most secret and sacred regions." When after two years of this behavior Catherine finally protested, bringing all to a sudden halt, and told her father what her uncle had been doing, Hammond faced a career-ending scandal. He was then governor of South Carolina, but Hampton had the power to demolish governors, which he promptly did through a quiet whisper campaign. In a stroke of good fortune for Hammond, his outraged brother-in-law had been for a long time a leader in abolishing the practice of duels, but Hammond was still frightened that his nephew might shoot him or cane him in the streets of Columbia like a criminal. Hammond admitted to his own self that he had erred, but he avoided the most serious of self-accusations by wondering, "Is it in flesh and blood to withstand" such temptations as offered by the girls? He imagined it was not; such irresistible cravings were in the nature of men; and so he assigned the lion's share of blame to the teenagers.[15]

Through a similar mental process Hammond could imagine that his slaves were content, though three out of four of their children died before they were five years old; though they constantly ran away; though they undermined his system of domination at every chance, carving for themselves whatever measure of autonomy they could from the edges of his surveillance; though he slept with the daughter of his mistress; though he kept his own children in bondage; though he resorted time and again to whipping them. The whipping gives us some insight into Hammond's mentality: he gave his overseers careful instructions that the tongue of the leather whip should not be more than an inch wide and that it should not be laid on with too much "severity" nor when "angry and excited." It should be resorted to only as a last resort of discipline, he explained. Thus he could tell himself he was a kind "father" of his slaves. Even so, slaves were so often flogged at Silver Bluff that Hammond earned a local reputation among whites as a severe master.[16]

But Hammond was a freshman congressman, a "radicalized arriviste" unknown beyond South Carolina before he hurled these rocks at congressional traditions. John C. Calhoun carried more weight. Like Henry Clay and Daniel Webster, Calhoun was one of the acknowledged titans of Congress. He was fifty-four years old and was beginning to take on the gaunt, emaciated look of his later years, the terrible and fiery prophet-like statesman we see in his most memorable images. His eyes were dark and seemed to have sunk back under the bony brow and rigid cheekbones. Not a trace of amiability was left in his face, which expressed to one contemporary observer "mind, energy, and malignity." He had become an angry man.[17]

But he spoke with the dispassionate, razor-sharp precision of a vivisectionist. His voice was reasonable and measured when he rose to speak on March 9, 1836. The Quakers of Philadelphia had sent a petition to the Senate asking Congress to abolish slavery in the District of Columbia, and James Buchanan, the future president who was then a senator from Pennsylvania, had proposed a compromise. Buchanan did not want to refuse to receive petitions because that seemed to violate the right "to petition the Government for a redress of grievances," which was protected by the First Amendment. The Senate would receive such petitions, but instead of referring them to a committee, as they had in the past, it would vote without debate to reject the petition. That way, the Senate could continue its long-standing gentleman's agreement of not discussing slavery, which certainly satisfied one of Calhoun's goals—to keep slavery out of national politics. But it violated another.

"The question now before the Senate is reduced to the single point," Calhoun explained: "are we bound to receive these petitions?" Receiving and then voting to reject petitions implied that the Senate could just as well vote to accept them, which tacitly acknowledged a power to legislate slavery. Calhoun insisted that the Senate must unequivocally disavow any such power. It was a question of jurisdiction. Congress had no authority to abolish slavery, neither in the states nor in the District of Columbia; thus it had no business receiving such petitions. Would the Senate "become the passive [receptacle] . . . of all that is frivolous, absurd, unconstitutional, immoral, and impious?" What if a "body of atheists . . . should ask the passage of a law denying the existence of the Almighty Being above us, the creator of all"? Would senators "take jurisdiction of it"? Calhoun need not wait for an answer. He knew the Senate would "instantly reject it with loathing."[18]

The self-evident frivolity or absurdity of the abolitionists was Calhoun's main theme. "We live in strange times," Calhoun quipped, when "there are Christians now more orthodox than the Bible." The abolitionists waged "a war of religious and political fanaticism," and "fanatic" became a pronoun reserved for them. But even such fanatics can eventually influence the masses. Though "public opinion at the North is not yet prepared" for abolition, "if the tide continues to roll on its turbid waves of folly and fanaticism," Calhoun warned, warming to his argument, abolitionists might begin to persuade people. Having failed in their attempts to use the U.S. mails as the vehicle of propaganda, they would use the Senate. "To this common centre the incendiary publications of the abolitionists would flow . . . to be . . . preserved among the public records. Here the subject of abolition would be agitated session after session, and . . . disseminated, in the guise of speeches, over the whole Union."[19]

Like Duff Green, Calhoun was not worried that "incendiary" literature might incite another Vesey Rebellion. He worried that if the nation openly debated slavery, eventually he would lose the argument. To allow debate on such petitions "compels us to sit in silence to witness the assaults on our character and institutions, or to engage in an endless contest in their defence. Such a contest," Calhoun confessed, "is beyond mortal endurance. We must, in the end, be humbled, degraded, broken down, and worn out."[20] Public opinion, which is so powerful in a republic, would swing toward abolition, and then there would be no perpetuating slavery.

The "we" Calhoun so subtly introduced into his speech referred to all white people of the South. He spoke as if all the slaveholding states held one opinion on the matter, or, rather, he tried to produce unanimity by pretending it existed. He knew that it did not. The border states were not yet with him. As Calhoun himself conceded, Senator Felix Grundy of Tennessee had spoken in favor of Buchanan's compromise. Worse yet, Henry Clay of Kentucky did not even think of himself as a southerner. "Southern" did not mean living in a slave state, but living where blacks outnumbered whites, mainly those coastal regions of the Deep South. The Kentuckian thought slavery was a terrible evil, and he wanted to end it by removing blacks, just as Indians were removed from regions east of the Mississippi. Calhoun knew he had to rally solidarity among the Henry Clays of the Senate, so he addressed himself especially to the "Senators from the slaveholding States, who most unfortunately have committed themselves to vote for receiving these incendiary petitions." Desperately, he tried to persuade them that "we all have a common interest": to perpetuate slavery forever. He was not yet so bold as Hammond to argue that slavery was positively good, but he did explain that "the relation which now exists between the two races in the slaveholding States, has existed for two centuries. It has grown with our growth and strengthened with our strength. . . . None other can be substituted." Any southerners who would be so base as to try to introduce some new relation between the races "would be traitors to our section, to ourselves, our families, and to posterity."[21] No one could deviate from the party line. Of course there was no way to enforce such a rule on all of the southern states—

at least not yet. But the siege was tightening. In the end, twelve south-ern senators backed Clay's ideas that a gradual diffusion of slavery away from Virginia, Maryland, and the District of Columbia was pos-sible, while only ten backed Calhoun. On March 14, only six senators ended up voting against Buchanan's compromise, none of them south-erners. Calhoun abstained.

Ironically enough, the first casualty of Calhoun's dictat was one of the radicals of 1832, Charleston's own Henry Laurens Pinckney, who founded the right-wing *Mercury*, the newspaper that had cham-pioned nullification before it was popular. This Pinckney, son of the Constitutional Convention delegate (Charles) and grandson of Henry Laurens, was instrumental in outlawing Unionism after the Nullifiers won their majority in the state legislature. He rode that victory all the way to Washington, being elected to represent Charleston on the wave that swept moderates out of public office. Once in the House of Rep-resentatives, Pinckney went along with the gentleman's agreement that buried all antislavery petitions in committee. But after the summer of 1835, what had been radical sounded like moderation, as men like Hammond took the floor. Pinckney was caught napping in 1836. He did not realize quickly enough that the freshman Hammond had forced a new, even more conservative orthodoxy on the state. Pinck-ney, by this time a veteran of the House, must have thought Hammond a bit naive and even dangerous to upset the tacit agreement to ignore the petitions. Little suspecting that Calhoun would back Hammond or that he would condemn those who dissented from the new orthodoxy as "traitors," Pinckney brokered a deal with New York's presidential candidate, Martin Van Buren. Ostensibly a compromise between the southern and northern branches of the Democratic Party, the compro-mise did little more than endorse the status quo: petitions would be received and promptly buried.[22]

Henry Wise from Virginia called Pinckney a traitor in so many words. Only an absolute refusal to receive petitions would disavow Congress's power to regulate slavery in the District of Columbia. Pinck-ney must have thought he could weather such extremist, partisan name-calling, especially when the House sustained his compromise by a vote of 117 to 68. Nearly 90 percent of the representatives from slaveholding states voted with Pinckney, and only a "sprinkling of Southern Oppositionists and Carolina extremists abstained or cast a protest vote."[23] But his vindication in the national theater cost him in Charleston. Calhoun endorsed Henry Wise: compromisers were "traitors." Pinckney could not withstand a break with Calhoun, and back home he faced an angry constituency. He tried to reason with the voters of Charleston, arguing that if receiving petitions and burying them in committee "be treason to the South, surely the inquiry may well be made, Why is it that no Southern Senator, or member, ever perceived it until now?" Southern congressmen had received and buried these "memorials" for years, without feeling any insult. "Where were all their zeal and fiery indignation, during all that time? And why is it that they have only been enkindled now?" But such protests made no difference to the grinding wheels of conservatism as they tightened their grip on Carolina politics. Pinckney, the archconservative Nullifier who had helped invent the no-compromise politics of coercive orthodoxy, thought that he had expressed "an honest difference of opinion with some of his colleagues, as to the best mode of proceeding in reference to the subject of slavery." But the rules had changed yet again in the summer of 1835. Pinckney stood alone in the siege lines of yesterday: Calhoun and Hammond and the rest of South Carolina had advanced to a new parallel. Pinckney lost his nomination for reelection and was reduced to telling everyone who would listen how loyal he really was: "the South has not a more devoted friend or faithful representative than myself," he simpered. "Upon that point I yield to no man."[24]

So the "gag rule" slept for a year. As was customary, petitions were received and buried in committee without discussion. But in early 1837, after Martin Van Buren had been elected president with significant (though eroding) southern support, Calhoun found another occasion to speak on the subject of petitions, and this time he delivered the most momentous speech ever heard in the United States Senate. Unequivocally, emphatically, dispassionately, with his famous logic and immense personal stature, John C. Calhoun advocated the new orthodoxy of South Carolina: that slavery was a positive good.

"Let me not be understood," he said, "as admitting even by implication that the existing relations between the two races in the slave-holding States is an evil—far otherwise; I hold it to be a good, as it has thus far proved itself to be to both [races], and will continue to prove so if not disturbed by the fell spirit of abolition." He was the first prominent American statesman ever to say this, and such was his stature and powers of persuasion that, when he finished speaking, the siege machinery so long tightening its circle on the southern mind could be said finally to have closed its lines. There was no escape. The endgame commenced.

"I appeal to facts," Calhoun reasoned. There was no need to dispute with the fanatical, apocalyptic religious rhetoric of the abolitionists, nor even the naive, idealistic rhetoric of the Declaration of Independence and all the Revolutionary thinkers. At every opportunity Calhoun called the abolitionists "fanatics," which is ubiquitous in the rhetoric of the late 1830s and after. Near death, in 1850, Calhoun still insisted that the ideological division of the South from the North that had widened since 1835 was not accomplished by southern "demagogues . . . excit[ing] discontent." Rather, the southerners argued *against* the "excitement" incited by the "blind fanatics." Charles M. Wiltse, Calhoun's sympathetic (and thus troubling) biographer in 1940, felt that in this speech, "The *theological absolutism* of the abolitionists was matched by an equally unyielding *logical absolutism* in the South."[25]

Calhoun would not discuss "slavery in the abstract," as did many northerners, but "slavery as existing." He would "speak freely" and from experience and the knowledge accumulated in all human history. "Never has yet existed," he asserted with shocking frankness for a man professing republican values, "a wealthy and civilized society in which one portion of the community did not, in point of fact, live on the labor of the other." In ancient times, the wealthy used "brute force and gross superstition" to gain and maintain their ascendancy. Modern times were hardly different: the capitalists of the present age use "artful fiscal contrivances" to rob the laboring class. "I may say with truth," Calhoun averred, surveying the great nations of the modern world, that in no country is "so much . . . left to the share of the laborer, and so little exacted from him, or where there is more kind attention to him in sickness or infirmities of age" than in the southern United States. "The sick, and the old and infirm slave" lords it over Europe's "forlorn and wretched . . . pauper in the poor house." American slave culture "forms the most solid and durable foundation on which to rear free and stable political institutions." Just look at the unrest fomented between "labor and capital" in the North for an edifying contrast to the somnolence of southern society. And if material and political security were not enough, consider the benefit to the Africans themselves. "Never before has the black race of Central Africa," he said, perfectly complacent in his utter ignorance of the subject, "from the dawn of history to the present day, attained a condition so civilized and so improved, not only physically, but morally and intellectually." American slavery must take the credit, for in "the course of a few generations . . . growing up under the fostering care of our institutions," the black race has been raised to "its present comparative civilized condition." "Instead of an evil, [slavery] is a good—a positive good."[26]

Calhoun did not present these as novel arguments, nor were they when a very short view was taken, for they had been pioneered in Charleston since the Vesey Rebellion. But taking the long view, these were strange ideas indeed, so strange that they had not even surfaced during the congressional debates over Missouri's admission to the Union just fifteen years earlier. And every point Calhoun made repudiated arguments made by prominent southerners in years past. Never in history has one class of people failed to exploit another? *So what,* the men of 1776 would have said. *A new historical age was born with the Revolution.* Here was Calhoun praising slavery for improving "virtue, intelligence, patriotism, courage, disinterestedness, and all the high qualities which adorn our nature," good habits forced upon the white "patriarchs" who command "the African race among us." Men like George Mason and Henry Laurens had worried and fretted that slavery degraded whites, making them petty, idle tyrants. Here Calhoun was claiming that slavery *raised* blacks from barbarism to the brink of civilization when all previous generations admitted that slavery degenerated the race, brutalizing independent people into the grooves of dependency.

This particular point in Calhoun's argument merits greater scrutiny because, even if it blithely dismisses African culture, it also asserts that black character is malleable and capable of improvement. Calhoun's speech brought blacks to the brink of civilization—to a late adolescence, so to speak. While paternalism had once predicted an eventual maturing of the black race until it was capable of citizenship, Calhoun had to justify *perpetual* slavery. He had to bring American slaves to a "comparative civilized condition" but no further. He did not explain why people who could be raised in a few generations from barbarity to the edge of civilization could not take that last final step. That would require a rationalization concocted by others.

For Calhoun, it was sufficient that equality, one of those "abstract" truths, was abhorrent: that was his justification for keeping blacks from moving into the full light of civilization. In 1830, the number of slaves living in South Carolina was 315,401, while only 265,784 whites resided there. The city of Charleston had roughly the same proportion, but some Lowcountry parishes had more than ten-to-one ratios of blacks to whites. In Colleton County, the hotbed of radical nullifiers, every white person was counterbalanced by fourteen slaves. Should blacks ever achieve a fully civilized state, Calhoun argued, "we would soon find the present condition of the two races reversed." Blacks, who held the majority, would partner with unscrupulous northerners to make slaves of the southern whites. In places like the Carolina Lowcountry, where so many blacks and so few whites lived, the stakes were too high to pursue emancipation.

But other regions of the South, where diffusion was easily contemplated, did not share Calhoun's urgency. On the floor of the Senate, Calhoun challenged Senator Rives of Virginia, "Did [he] not . . . consider [slavery] a good?"

"No," Senator Rives replied, unconcerned with being thought "soft" on slavery. It is "an evil in all circumstances," he continued, "though, in some [circumstances], it might be the lesser evil."

It was to such men that Calhoun aimed his remarks. He had to win over the majority of southerners who, thinking slavery was evil, would take no steps to protect it. Calhoun must "arouse the South to a due sense of [the] danger" felt already in South Carolina. In the North, abolitionists already had gotten hold of "the pulpit, . . . the schools, and to a considerable extent . . . the press." Grimké and Garrison were transforming the discourse about slavery. They were fighting a culture war, and Calhoun's strategy for fighting back was to stain abolition with the stigma of dangerous fanaticism. By contrast, slavery's proponents must calmly use reason, cite scientific and historical evidence, and appeal to experience in the real world over the facile attractions of idealism. In the age of Jefferson, those decrying slavery had cold, inescapable logic on their side—Enlightened reasoning disinterested by greed—while anyone so bold as to defend slavery did so illogically or apologetically, acknowledging all the while that their profits were ill-gotten. But the logic of Jefferson's self-evident truths never fully won the field. Now the abolitionists were forcing the issue into public discussion, but their apocalyptic visions abandoned the high ground of logic. Calhoun rushed in and planted his flag, appearing to be full of common sense and reason. Southerners were left to choose one of two positions: the wild-eyed fanatic or the rational, clear-thinking realist. Calhoun made it impossible to be both antislavery *and* reasonable.

Calhoun concluded his speech with a call for unity, or, rather a demand that southerners suppress anyone who dissented from the pro-slavery ideology: "All we want is concert," he said, "to lay aside all party differences, and unite with zeal and energy in repelling approaching dangers." The Nullifiers outlawed dissent in South Carolina; Calhoun insisted that that program must be reproduced all across the South. There must be no compromise. Everyone must profess the new belief in slavery's positive, perpetual goodness. Ultraconservatives, not the abolitionists, must seize control of "those great instruments by which the mind of the rising generation will be formed." Calhoun knew that, if the abolitionists had their way, American boys—even southern boys—born in 1830 would grow into men who thought that slavery was a sin, that slaveholders were sinners, and that the government ought to act on those beliefs. If the abolitionists could determine the terms of discourse, they would win the game. Calhoun could have little effect in the North, but surely he could manipulate the pulpits, schools, and newspapers of the South.

The case of Bishop John England demonstrates what the ascendancy of Calhoun's ideology did to men of conscience in the South. We have already seen how the coercive power of the South Carolina Association forced Bishop England to close his schools for blacks and abandon all attempts to liberalize southern society. Not long after Calhoun's speech, Bishop England found himself having to prove the loyalty of Catholics yet again. In 1839, Pope Gregory XVI, with an eye toward ending the slave trade between Africa and the Catholic colonies of Latin America, published a papal letter forbidding Catholics to have anything to do with the foreign slave trade. John England's political friend and mentor, the "Liberator" of Catholics in Ireland, Daniel O'Connell, used that letter to attack American slavery, decrying the sale of slaves from old states to new states, insisting that only a "hardness of heart" that did not mind "cruelty to the negroes" would allow it. It was not the first time he had attacked the South. Back in May 1835, just weeks before Charleston erupted with mobs burning mailbags and threatening to burn the Catholic cathedral, Daniel O'Connell gave a speech at the London Anti-Slavery Society in which he roared that "the star-spangled banner . . . was stained with Negro blood." Americans "refused their slaves even the blessings of education" and betrayed their own Declaration of Independence. He called slave owners "blasphemers of their God," and he charged that "the many Irishmen in the United States who were opposed to the emancipation of slaves" were "the objects of the curse of St. Patrick, who had banished all poisonous and venomous reptiles from the soil of Ireland." Here was a condemnation that put William Garrison to shame, and O'Connell's interpretation of the pope's 1839 letter again put John England in a vulnerable position.[27]

It was an election year, and John Forsyth, secretary of state for President Martin Van Buren, tried to stir up support for his senatorial campaign in Georgia by raising the specter of an abolitionist/Catholic conspiracy. He published a position paper in the *Augusta Constitutionalist* that called O'Connell ignorant, foolish, brutal, and, worse yet, insolent and insulting for meddling in American affairs. He detected a cabal made up of British agents, Irish politicians, the pope, and American abolitionists like "the late Rufus King and General Harrison" (the Whig candidate running for president against the Democrat incumbent, Martin Van Buren). Forsyth hoped that believing in the positive good of slavery would prove to be a sine qua non for candidates in Georgia. But Georgia resisted such politics of fear and helped elect William

Henry Harrison president. Being sound on slavery was not yet an absolute requirement for one's suitability for public office, at least not in Georgia. Charleston was a different story.[28]

John England could not afford to let Forsyth's anti-Catholic bigotry go unanswered. He refuted the notion of a conspiracy in his own paper, the *United States Catholic Miscellany*, intending above all else to prove that southern Catholics were "sound" on slavery. To do that, he had to persuade people that Daniel O'Connell and his fiery abolitionist rhetoric were not the typical Irish Catholic's view. On numerous occasions already, Bishop England had reproved O'Connell for his "assaults upon our planters." England assured his audience that he had seen firsthand the hypocrisy of the British abolitionists, who, while working to abolish "the slavery of the negroes in the West Indies," at the very same time riveted "the chains of the white slaves in Ireland, by continuing to enforce the penal laws against the Roman Catholics." So far as John England was concerned, the abolitionists everywhere had anti-Irish "bigotry where the heart should have been," and he refused "to be found . . . banded with [such] men."[29]

O'Connell, England explained, had misinterpreted the pope's letter. On the sinfulness of slave traders, Pope Gregory hardly minced words: they were "blinded by the lust of sinful gain," and the main point of his letter was, as John England said, to forbid Catholics from trading in African slaves. But O'Connell had failed to distinguish the *domestic* from the *foreign* slave trade: Gregory said nothing about forbidding Catholics to trade slaves within the United States. On this point, England was technically correct, but the pope's theme and tone also demonstrate that the Vatican thought slavery itself, let alone the slave trade, was incompatible with Christianity. Pope Gregory approved gradual emancipation and the liberal, progressive view of slavery, which John England subscribed to himself but was afraid to advertise too widely in Charleston: for example, the pope said that masters ought to be "prone to" manumitting their slaves. He endorsed the notion that historical progress leads to liberty, and he even noted approvingly that in "many [modern] Christian nations . . . no slaves can be held."[30]

Clearly, the official Catholic position on slavery was going to take some explaining if Catholics were to escape the accusation of "traitor," and England set out to do so in a series of articles in the *U.S. Catholic Miscellany*. Ostensibly, these articles were letters addressed to Forsyth, but William Henry Harrison was already elected, inaugurated, and dead of pneumonia before the series of eighteen "slave letters" ended in April 1841. They eventually comprised a 156-page book and narrated an erudite history of slavery in the Christian world, quoting long passages from church fathers like Saint Augustine and the Venerable Bede in their original Latin (supplied with England's translations), a magnificent display of history and canon law. Bundled together in a book, the dry scholarship is so tedious that the letters are nearly unreadable, but their thoroughness amply proves that slavery was ubiquitous in Hebrew and early Christian society. No sensible person could dispute it.

John England's time and energy petered out after about six months, and he suspended his work on the project in April 1841. His disquisitions had reached no further than the 1014 Battle of Clontarf at which the Irishman, Brian Boru, defeated the Vikings. For an honest history of slavery in the Christian world, this was far too early a moment to suspend one's narrative, for the intervening centuries saw slavery virtually disappear from western Europe. We must regret that England did not get around to writing a history of the seventeenth and eighteenth centuries, when the political doctrines that he so cherished, like the separation of church and state, freedom of conscience, political liberty, and equality under the law, were first theorized and put in practice. It is one thing to reconcile modern American slavery with Christianity in the ancient world. It would be quite another to treat it in the context of the United Irishmen or John England's own fight against the penal laws in Ireland. Because he left the later centuries out, readers were left with the impression that American slavery was continuous with all history.

England discussed contemporary slavery only briefly in order to separate contemporary planters from the sin of the slave trade. Slave owners in 1840, John England explained, "are in a different position from those who have been the former traders in the African market, who have thence brought away the negro and taken the money of the South for him whom they sold into slavery." American slave owners, he pointed out, "without their own choice, have been placed under the necessity of managing their property with a delicacy, a responsibility and perplexity, to which they who vilify us are strangers." This was the newly defunct paternalist ideal: slavery was an *inherited* evil. It completely mischaracterized men like Hamilton, Hayne, Hammond, and Calhoun, who so diligently worked to roll back the progressive reforms of southern society.[31] But at least England implied that slavery was evil, inherited or not. But by 1841, when he quit writing his unfinished letters on slavery, he was conscious that he believed in a doctrine that mainstream Charleston society had come to consider politically incorrect.

"I have been asked by many," he wrote in his conclusion to the letters, "a question which I may as well answer at once, viz.: Whether I am friendly to the existence or continuation of slavery?"

Here was the crux of the matter, the moment of truth, after eighteen lengthy letters that proved through a practical study of history that slavery was not un-Christian.

"I am not" friendly to slavery, he avowed unequivocally. But immediately he added, "I also see the impossibility of now abolishing it here." Like Pontius Pilate, he washed his hands of the matter: "When [slavery] can and ought to be abolished, is a question for the legislature and not for me." It was hardly a whisper of dissent. Never would John England have conceded so much in the fight to liberate Catholics in Ireland. Calhoun frightened him into silence, and to his eternal shame John England failed the blacks living in his diocese.[32]

Eight months later, while returning from a trip to Europe, England caught an "inflammation of the intestines," which one memoirist diagnosed as dysentery, and he suffered for four long painful months, his symptoms waxing and waning and finally killing him in early April 1842. The *Charleston Courier* celebrated his love of his adopted country, for he had been a "true friend and an able champion" of the South, "fearlessly throwing the weight of his character, influence and intellect, in favor of her much misunderstood and much reviled domestic institutions, and vindicating them both at home and abroad." This was his legacy. In the end, all thought him a good friend of perpetual slavery. The postscript to the Forsyth letters was forgotten, dwarfed by the massive historical narrative that vindicated slavery. Two years later, in 1844, a posthumous edition of the letters was printed as a monograph, and the postscript was suppressed altogether.[33] Not even his whisper could be heard.

Even though Calhoun and Hammond lost the gag-rule debate in Congress, they succeeded in establishing the positive good theory as political orthodoxy in South Carolina. "The politics of loyalty," one historian explained, in which dissenters are labeled traitors, "were also a form of social control, the strongest form of democratic social control short of undemocratic violence." Of course in Charleston the threat of vigilante violence was not far behind, should "mere words" prove insufficiently suppressive. "When faced with neighbors' withering hostility," William Freehling continued, "those tempted to dissent often instead demonstrate their soundness" on slavery. That's exactly what John England did.[34]

Catholics lagged behind the mainstream white Protestant churches. We've seen how the Anglican minister of St. Philip's first theorized paternalism back in the 1740s. Most southerners were Baptists and Methodists, and while these churches openly opposed slavery in the eighteenth century, they gradually reversed their doctrines to an unequivocal endorsement of the conservative, pro-slavery views ascending in the 1830s. The shift to pro-slavery doctrine became official for the Baptists in 1845, when the southern branch of the faith split from the northern on the issue of slavery. The Southern Methodists split in 1844, also over the issue of slavery.[35]

In addition to the pulpit, Calhoun wanted to control newspapers. Though he did not yet understand it, literature was probably even more important. While newspapers influenced opinion, imaginative literature had the power of changing people at the deeper level of belief. The most important change as regards journalism and literature was William Gilmore Simms's conversion to the positive good theory. When the Nullification Crisis boiled over in the early 1830s, Simms was editing the *City Gazette*, a pro-union paper. Though a young man, he was counted among Charleston's leaders in the pro-Jackson, anti-Calhoun faction of state politics, and he worked hard and long to save the Union, earning (among other things) the vitriolic hatred of the

Mercury and its editor, Henry Laurens Pinckney. But something happened to him when the Nullifiers won. By the time Unionism was outlawed, he had lost half of his subscribers. Heavily in debt, he sold his newspaper, retired from the political scene, and devoted himself entirely to his literary career. He spent the summer of 1832 in New York, where he met for the first time his longtime correspondent, James Lawson, who introduced him to that city's literary crowd. Still stinging from the reversals and failures at the hands of his native city, Simms immediately warmed to New York and its literary life, which welcomed him and published what he considered his masterpiece to date, an eighty-page romantic poem about a sea nymph who, after a series of fantastic adventures, chooses to pair herself with a mortal human.

We have very little evidence of what Simms thought about slavery before nullification, but what little we have suggests he conformed to the spirit of the age, which believed in the eventual emancipation of the slaves. "The time will come," he wrote in those days, "when the negro slave of Carolina will be raised to a condition, which will enable him to go forth out of bondage." He wrote his first, sustained analysis of slavery on that first trip to New York, just after he was exiled from Charleston politics. Mrs. Trollope, a British woman, toured the United States for a few years and, as was the fashion with so many Europeans, she wrote her impressions up in a popular book as if she were an anthropologist studying the strange exotic animal known as the American. Trollope had the perspective of an elitist aristocrat, who, insecure in the age of democracy, eagerly rattled off her snobbish complaints. Simms wrote a lengthy review in the prestigious *American Quarterly Review* that defended the democratic spirit and manners of his fellow nationals, and likewise he defended the nation's honor when he blasted her contempt for American slavery. "The notes on Slavery," he contended, "are full of errors, and scarcely deserve a mention. The details are many of them false— the lady knows nothing of the subject." Trollope displayed "the numerous gross absurdities into which a superficial and flippant writer is so likely to fall." Simms's review was republished in both the United States and England, and it must have done more than a little to ingratiate the old Union man to South Carolina's Nullifiers.[36]

Lawson urged Simms to stay in New York, and had he done so

we can imagine that his ideas and his work would have taken a turn more congenial to the modern American spirit, and schoolchildren today would be reading his stories when they read *The Scarlet Letter* and *The Last of the Mohicans*. But he came back south to the city that he thought hated him, relegating New York to annual summer visits. In 1833 he wrote two novels, *Guy Rivers* and *Martin Faber*, both published in New York, and their success with the public and with critics determined his future as a writer of fiction. "There is more acquaintance, displayed in these two volumes, with secret springs of human action," wrote one reviewer, "than in all the novels [James Fenimore] Cooper ever has written, or will ever write."[37]

Simms wrote his third novel, *The Yemassee*, between the summer of 1834 and May 1835; he sent the manuscript off to his publisher, Harper, not long before the abolitionists' direct mail campaign began, and its first edition sold out in three days.[38] Generally regarded as the best of all of the dozens of novels he wrote, *The Yemassee* tells the story of that tribe's war against the British back in 1715. The hero is the resourceful frontiersman Gabriel Harrison, whose real identity—the aristocratic, cavalier Lord Craven, governor of Carolina—is hidden from most characters and from readers until the very end. His faithful servant throughout the romance is Hector, an African slave, a selfless and brave servant entirely devoted to his master. Three racial groups collide: Native Americans, white Europeans, and Africans. Whites are unequivocally, unquestionably superior to both the "reds" and "blacks" (the text is preoccupied with these colors as racial markers, indicating that Simms subscribed to that hypersensitive racial self-identity most white Americans indulged in in the mid-nineteenth century).

Simms sympathized with the Indians. Half the novel is told from the point of view of the Yemassee chief, Sanutee, a complex, three-dimensional character who understands far better than any of his fellow tribesmen that his race is doomed to drown in the flood of Europeans invading America. Sanutee has little hope of winning his war. All his sound and fury is a way of shaking his fist at destiny. According to the novel, destiny or the nature of things or the natural course of history, whatever you want to call it, dictates that whites will ascend to dominance. Fatalistically, Sanutee decides to go down fighting rather than appease and accommodate the whites, and his refusal makes his half of the story tragic—tragic in the classical sense of that word.[39]

His son, Occonestoga, does not fight. He befriends the whites, aids them, tries to carve a place for Native Americans in this new world ruled by European settlers. But alcohol preys on his soul, and he dissipates into an unattractive, servile shadow of a man, suffering the contempt of his own father. According to one white character who clearly speaks for Simms, the Indians, being inferior to Europeans, "must become dependent. When this happens . . . they must become degraded, and sink into slavery and destitution."[40] The lesson is clear: dependency degrades a race until it becomes incapable of independent, manly action. This is the narrative that South Carolinians used to tell about Africans before the Vesey Rebellion: slavery degraded blacks, so they had to be prepared for freedom. Where, then, do the Africans fit in Simms's reckoning? Hector, after all, is perfectly servile, displaying the dependency so deplored by Simms and Sanutee in the drunken Indian, Occonestoga. What is so unattractive in Occonestoga is not degrading at all in Hector. Servility uplifts him, giving him an admirable and paradoxical nobility.

Simms presumes that the two inferior races (red and black) are essentially different—the Indians are unsuited to servility while the blacks are suited to it. When Hector's master offers him freedom at the end of the novel, the slave replies:

> I dam to hell, mossa, if I guine to be free! . . . 'Tis unpossible, mossa, and dere's no use to talk 'bout it. De ting aint right; and teny I know wha' kind of ting freedom is wid black man? Ha! you make Hector free, he come wuss more nor poor buckrah—he tief out of de shop—he get drunk and lie in de ditch—den, if sick come, he roll, he toss in de wet grass of de stable. You come in de morning, Hector dead—and, who know—he no take physic, he no hab parson—who know, I say, mossa, but de debble fine em'fore anybody else? No, mossa—you and Dugdale berry good company for Hector. I tank God he so good—I want no better. (II, 224–25)

The notion that Africans are racially suited for dependency betrays the ideology of paternalism even as it justifies perpetualism. The positive good theory of slavery is founded upon this very idea: that blacks, just as Hector indicates, are incapable of developing into independent, mature citizens. *The Yemassee* helped whites to *forget* that slavery degrades people and that African Americans were once like the noble Yemassee. The new myth governing slavery, as evident in Calhoun's speeches in the Senate, was that whites *raised* Africans out of a state of primitive barbarity. This new idea was the origin myth of slavery required by the positive good theory.

It is doubtful that Simms was conscious of the ideological significance of his depiction of the three American races in *The Yemassee*. Nevertheless, he was very conscious that his novels were constructing a new mythology that would bind the nation culturally as a distinct people from Europeans. "The modern Romance," Simms said in his 1853 preface to a new edition of *The Yemassee*, "is the substitute which the people of the present day offer for the ancient epic." And such epics as *The Yemassee* have a profounder function in society than the "domestic novel," which aims for realism in its depiction of ordinary lives. Romances, such as Sir Walter Scott's *Ivanhoe*, are "loftier" than novels, are almost poetry, seeking "for its adventures among the wild and wonderful." *The Yemassee*, Simms told his readers, is an "*American* romance," for "the material could have been furnished by no other country."[41] Like the epic, the romance formed the imagination of a people, providing them the myths of their own origins. Though he intended this romance and others he wrote to be read in the epic mode, to form that *American* imagination, it would really end up serving the separatist agenda of *southern* nationalism.

"The Southerner of the American Revolution owned slaves," Mark Twain tells us in his *Life on the Mississippi*. "So did the Southerner of the Civil War: but the former resembles the latter as an Englishman resembles a Frenchman. The change of character can be traced rather more easily to Sir Walter [Scott's] influence than to that of any other thing or person." What Twain meant was that books like *Ivanhoe*, tales of medieval chivalry and "the duel, the inflated speech, and the jejune romanticism of an absurd past that is dead" entranced the white southern consciousness and so divided it from the northern. Scott invented the "character of the Southerner—or Southron, according to Sir Walter's starchier way of phrasing it," along with its "bogus decorations" of a caste society "that made every gentleman in the South a Major or a Colonel, or a General or a Judge." Scott and his facile romanticism, Twain insisted, are "in great measure responsible" for the Civil War. Twain exaggerated. It took men like Simms to translate Scott's romanticism into "material [that] could have been furnished by no other country" than the American South. In the courts of government and public opinion, men like Calhoun promoted the positive good theory through reason and logic; ironically enough, Simms's irrational romanticism forged an even stronger support, for it influenced levels below the conscious self.

Simms followed *The Yemassee* with another success, *The Partisan*, a romance of the Revolution. But he never got out from under the debts he had earlier incurred, and it was not until he married for a second time that he found the leisure so conducive to writers. His bride was Chevillette Roach, whose British-born father owned two plantations in the Midlands on the banks of the Edisto River. Overnight, the newspaper editor, poet, novelist, critic became a planter. But we must not think Simms, who is a much more sympathetic figure than James Hammond, married for money. Writing to his New York friend, Lawson, Simms described his beloved as "young—just 18—a pale, pleasing girl—very gentle and amiable—with dark eyes & hair, sings sweetly & plays upon piano and guitar." He felt a sincere attraction, which seemed to grow through the summer of 1836. In June, he enlarged upon the "pleasing girl," mixing the acute observation skills of the accomplished novelist with the affection of the man in love. "She is a creature of heart entirely—very fond, devoted, artless—of nice, unobtrusive, but ever active sensibilities, and the very personification of truth and amiability." These virtues of her personality attracted him, not her money or her looks. "She is pretty—very pretty," he conceded, "but some of her features are defective. They do not harmonize." Her nose was "badly formed & rather large." Nevertheless, it was a face with which he'd fallen in love: an oval face, a mouth "well chiseled & sweet," fair skin, dark hair and eyes, high forehead. A small "but well & symmetrically made" figure, heightened by a "fine" bust, finished out the detailed description of the girl who had caught Simms's heart. They married in November 1836, and Simms's father-in-law installed the groom and bride at Woodlands, one of his two estates.[42]

The plantation diluted the acid of the long-standing debts, which, immoderate to a poor man, were of little account to the rich. Nor was Simms bothered by the eighty-mile distance from Charleston. They lived a short walk from Midway, a railroad station stop halfway between Charleston and Augusta, so a steady stream of literary and political luminaries visited the house. Often Simms, who thrived on having an audience, spun his rambling discourses and stories, during which he imitated the dialects of his various characters. Visitors listened more than they spoke, for Simms "could declaim only, not converse." Friends compared him to Dr. Johnson, though no Boswell sat at his elbow recording the wit. He grew fat. He took up cigars to quell his appetite. The house was large, brick, comfortable, massive enough to impress, which pleased Simms. All was plenty: food, talk, drink, ideas, good fellowship. He upholstered his library with ten thousand volumes, shelves stuffed fat like cushions. For Simms, who was no farmer, the planter's life was all leisure, or rather the life of the mind. When visitors took some exercise by strolling "the picturesque neighborhood," Simms lounged at home, his middle age having abandoned the exertions of his youth.[43]

Simms not only fancied himself the paternalistic master, but he lived the part as well. Unlike James Hammond, when Simms came into possession of his farm he made no changes in the way of life of the slaves, who were allowed those small measures of freedom that characterized creole slavery: the task system, personal plots for gardens, a small private economy (that included the big house buying its produce from the slaves), less surveillance, fewer restrictions. Sixty or seventy slaves lived in a cluster of cabins, "each with a plot of ground" for raising chickens and vegetables. William Cullen Bryant was one northern visitor to Woodlands who found slavery as practiced there "as harmless as it could be anywhere," even if the example did not dissuade him from his antislavery principles.[44]

Simms's own experience at Woodlands contributed to his second published treatment of slavery, again occasioned by his review of a travel narrative, this one by Harriet Martineau, an English writer whose two-year sojourn in the United States brought her to all corners of the young country. She examined all she saw as if the Americans were as exotic as the Polynesians, to paraphrase Simms. Martineau was a more formidable intellectual than Mrs. Trollope. Her *Society in America*, published in 1837, came on the heals of her wildly popular *Illustrations of Political Economy*, which was a sort of "idiot's guide" to the classic political economists Malthus, Ricardo, and Smith. *Society in America* criticized slavery at great length, and Simms carefully criticized its author:

> On the subject of American slavery, her detestation is avowed as being entertained long before entering the slave states; and so cordial is this detestation, that it is fed and fattened by everything she sees, and in sundry cases, we are sorry to add, at the expense of truth. I do not mean to say that she has wilfully related falsehoods. Not so—I think the book of Miss Martineau written in good faith throughout. But she was biased and bigoted on this subject to the last degree; and could neither believe the truth when it spoke in behalf of the slaveholders; nor doubt the falsehood, however gross, when it told in favor, or fell from the lips of the abolitionist.

As one example of Martineau's "bias" and "dogmatism," Simms cited the crisis of the mails that convulsed Charleston in 1835:

> We are told that the abolitionists sent no incendiary tracts among the slaves, and that they use no direct means towards promoting their objects in the slave states. [Martineau states that] "It is wholly untrue that [the abolitionists] insinuate their publications into the south."

Martineau confidently asserted that statement despite its being disputed by James Madison and Henry Clay, two southern opponents of slavery and proponents of colonization. "Here," Simms explained, "the lady undertakes to decide a question of veracity with singular composure, in favor of her friends [Boston abolitionists], and at the expense of the first names in our country."[45] Any moderate southerner reading Martineau and reading Simms could well judge who had the right facts of the case, and the argument for emancipation was thus discredited by the credible charge of "dogmatism." This was in 1837, just about the same time that Calhoun was turning the discourse of slavery upside down in the U. S. Senate. Simms, like Calhoun, used the irrationality of the abolitionists to claim the ground of reason for himself: slavery's advocates were realists; abolitionists were irrational fanatics who dwelt in the airy heights of ideals with no knowledge of the real world.

Even so, Simms's review of Martineau does not go so far as Calhoun did to insist upon the absolute goodness of American slavery. Like so many paternalists before him, Simms professed to believe in gradual emancipation, even if he believed that that day were conveniently situated in the distant future, after "long ages of preparation." Today, Simms unabashedly admitted, God had decreed that the slaveholder must "bestow upon [the slave] a fair proportion of the fruits of his labor," "improve [the slave's] mind," and raise "his condition to the level of his improved mind." Should all slave owners act on this principle, the day when slaves were ready for liberty would arrive sooner rather than later. And he had the humility to recognize that when the time came for a general emancipation, "it may be, that we [slave owners], like Pharaoh, will be loth to give [the slaves] up." But in his calculations, the time for such biblical analogies was still very far off. The abolitionists' Old Testament analogies were far in advance of the times, and Simms fell closer in line with Calhoun's orthodoxy by characterizing abolitionism as "wild fanaticism" and predicted a strong resistance to it among northerners based on their "good sense" and intelligence.[46]

Woodlands was situated in the Barnwell District, a section stretching from the Edisto River basin in the center of the state all the way to its western boundary at the Savannah River, where James Hammond's plantations were growing steadily larger. Inevitably, Simms came within the circuit of Hammond's influence, at first merely by way of agricultural advice, but it was not long before the older Hammond became Simms's friend and political mentor. The men had much in common. They both grew up relatively poor and outside Charleston's exclusive circle of elites, they made their first splash in the newspaper business, they became planters by virtue of their marriages. Their friendship began in about 1840 and grew steadily until Simms could be said to "dearly love" Hammond, even naming a son after him. Simms often rode over to Silver Bluff, where Hammond kept his house, and "there more punch was consumed and more political scheming indulged in."

Both were monumental intellects with monumental egos. Hammond was "the one man to whom Simms ever surrendered the floor in argument or conversation," one contemporary observed of a typical literary party at Woodlands. "They were foils to each other at every point."[47]

Foils socially but not politically. The two were at the center of what some considered a conspiracy to manipulate the South into secession, but more accurately would be called a movement. Calhoun's sister once wondered why South Carolina did not just "part peaceably at once" from the Union. Calhoun explained to her that making "two people of one" is "the most difficult process in the world." He was speaking of the political process, but his words make sense when applied to culture as well. Scheming with Hammond and Simms and Calhoun was Thomas Cooper, the old professor at the South Carolina College, and Cooper's favorite editor, E. W. Johnston, who once very aptly said, "We work on here, and make a doctrine popular."

It took a lot of cultural work before the positive good theory finished its siege on the minds of southerners. Sapping trenches had to be dug. New batteries put in place. New parallels constructed. Simms and Hammond especially realized that they had to create a new people. They had to give southerners the feeling that they were very different from northerners, and they had to make Virginians and Georgians and Tennesseans think they were culturally and even tribally connected to Carolinians and all the other slave states. In short, they were engaged in what we call today "nation-building," which is much more of a cultural job than political. Ultimately, the historian Freehling concludes that there was no real conspiracy to precipitate the South toward secession, at least not in the late 1830s and early 1840s. But there was a cultural movement, and Simms was leading it.

Simms's novels increasingly featured an emasculated version of the black slave, congenial and congenitally disposed toward dependency, a figure justifying not a progress toward freedom but permanent servitude. But his larger influence came through his editing various magazines, which not only gave him a wide readership on all manner of matters, from the arts to politics to science, but also provided a place to gather a cohort of southern intellectuals, men and women invited to contribute their talents much as Simms might invite them to the Woodlands, and through their good fellowship they created a sense of an awakened and vital southern mind. In May 1842, Simms became the editor of *Magnolia*, a literary magazine that recently moved from Savannah to Charleston. Only "through such a magazine," he thought, "could the South be awakened from its mental lethargy." The kind of contributor he was looking for was James Hammond, whose help he "took for granted." Hammond protested that a "want of Leisure" prevented his contributions, but Simms told him "that was out of the question." He must write an article on the South Carolina militia system, "pointing out its defects," or on "the [slave] Patrol Laws, as the military policy of the country,—which, by the way, needs great amendment." Very early in the project Simms reported that he was "rapidly accumulating about me, & in the cause of Southern Literature, a really able array of highly endowed and well educated men, who, without such an organ & an editor in whom they have confidence, would go to rust in our wilderness." He did not yet conceive of the project as serving secession: his promotion of *southern* letters was really meant to counterbalance the *northern* influence on American literature, almost the way South Carolina tried to leverage Congress through the Senate. The South has "been and remain[s] in literary bondage," Simms explained to John Tomlin, a would-be contributor to *Magnolia*, "but Southern pride would prompt the region to contribute its share to the erection of a national literature."[48]

Largely through his own connections and the prestige of his name and his personal gregariousness, Simms made a success of *Magnolia*. He secured a solid list of subscribers, easily enough to assure the magazine's financial security, and his wide-ranging friendships not only in the South but among crucial supporters in the North, who were willing to contribute articles for free, recruited a quality of work that surpassed anything else produced in the South, including its chief rival, the *Southern Literary Messenger*, and equaled the well-established magazines of the North. But its squabbling owners drove its finances into the ground, and after a year of accolades Simms bowed out of the *Magnolia*. "Without your aid," one friend told Simms, "the honor and pride of Southern Literature" would falter. The magazine folded up shop a month later.[49]

But through the next ten years Simms continued his editorial work from Charleston, first with the *Southern and Western Monthly Magazine and Review* and later the *Southern Quarterly Review*. Simms conceived the *Southern and Western* as a resurrection of *Magnolia*, but with "a more decidedly political complexion" that was reflected in its title: Simms, like his political counterparts, staked the southern claim to the American West, hoping to persuade the trans-Appalachian states that they belonged, culturally, to the South. In the magazine's first issue, Simms indicated that "our work simply proposes that justice should be done to the mind which fills our region," suggesting that nothing distinguished the western and southern states from each other, but that both suffered from "Northern literary dominance." Again, he gathered "about him a small but fairly capable group of Southern writers" who, in Simms's words, gave "to Southern opinion that tone & character which it is so desirable for the independence of the intellectual character of the country that it should possess." This same work was carried on till 1854 in Charleston's *Southern Quarterly Review*, albeit in a somewhat more scholarly and less popular fashion.[50]

One of the most prominent contributions to southern letters in these years was Hammond's pamphlet consisting of two open letters to the British abolitionist, Thomas Clarkson. Like almost all pro-slavery arguments, Hammond based his mid-1840s letters on a consideration of the facts on the ground—the "peculiarities in the operation of [the southern] social system, and special local as well as moral causes materially affecting it," circumstances not taken into account by the idealist abolitionists unfamiliar with the reality of the American South. He declared himself "one who conscientiously believes the domestic Slavery of these States to be not only an inexorable necessity for the present, but a moral and humane institution, productive of the greatest political and social advantages." Not surprisingly, Simms boosted Hammond's effort with a glowing review in the *Southern and Western*. "You are now so fairly enlisted & with so much eclat as the defender of the South," John C. Calhoun told Hammond, "that you will not be permitted to sheath your sword."[51]

If anyone doubts the power of cultural artifacts such as magazines and novels to move a people, to shift their ideological outlook on the world, they need only think of Harriet Beecher Stowe's *Uncle Tom's Cabin*. Hundreds of thousands of copies of the novel circulated throughout the United States, and the story of Uncle Tom's patient, saintly forbearance in the face of injustice and cruelty did more than anything else to enflame public opinion in the North against slavery. According to Frederick Douglass, the book lit "a million camp fires in front of the embattled hosts of slavery." One anecdote has Abraham Lincoln rising from his chair before a fire on a particularly cold and damp day in December 1862, when Stowe was ushered into the White House by William Seward. "So you're the little woman who wrote the book," President Lincoln said, bending to take her hand, "which started this great war." The story is probably apocryphal and belongs to a later generation, but its invention testifies to Stowe's effect on public opinion. She detonated a nuclear bomb in the culture war long ago started in Charleston, and any number of new-generation southerners raced to build their own. In the *Southern Literary Messenger* Simms wrote an unsigned review that disputed Stowe's depictions, especially regarding the murder of slaves and the separation of children from mothers, and he concluded that the novelist had become "the mouthpiece of a large and dangerous faction which if we do not put down with the pen, we may be compelled one day (God grant that day may never come!) to repel with the bayonet."[52]

Simms tried the pen over the bayonet. In 1852, in reaction to Stowe's novel, publishers in Charleston brought out a volume called *The Pro-Slavery Argument*, which consisted of four pieces, three of which were written by Thomas Dew (the originator of the positive good theory), James Hammond, and Simms (a reprinting of his review of Miss Martineau's book under the new title "The Morals of Slavery"). Right around the same time Simms was writing another in his series of Revolutionary romances, *The Sword and the Distaff*, which chronicled the British evacuation of Charleston in 1782. "It is probably as good an answer to Mrs. Stowe," he told Hammond, "as has been published." Hammond replied that Simms had "admirably defended our 'Institution' & elevated it in some respects."[53]

By the 1850s, the culture of the South had changed almost completely. When public education finally made its way to Charleston in the early 1850s, it was expressly designed to ensure the perpetuation of slavery. The free education of poor whites, for instance, was designed to help them feel and act superior to ignorant slaves; without such schooling, it was feared that working-class whites "could be marshaled against the planters." Charleston's curriculum full of practical science was borrowed from northern schools, but as a social institution Charleston High School reproduced the "cultural autonomy" that Simms pioneered, not only in his novels but in his histories.[54] This was the culture most southerners grew up in. By 1860, about three out of four white South Carolinians were born after 1830.[55] There was practically no one left in public life to tell them what life had been like before the positive good theory of slavery became political orthodoxy, not their teachers, the editors of their newspapers, their ministers, or even the books they read. Those who believed in gradualism had long since been cowed into silence or had pledged allegiance to the new orthodoxy. According to the biographer of Christopher Memminger, Charleston's chief proponent of public education, on the issue of slavery "a general consensus of support (if not absolute unanimity) prevailed among white people of the city, the state of South Carolina, and the Southern region after, say, 1830."[56]

He overstates the case somewhat. Unanimity in the city and state were only accomplished through the machinations of the Nullifiers. It took a while longer to spread this ideology across the whole South. Wildfires of political crises burned through the United States with almost inevitable regularity—the annexation of Texas, the Fugitive Slave Act, bleeding Kansas, Dred Scott, John Brown—and at the bottom of each controversy was the positive good theory of slavery. Each public debate was a lever by which the fire-eaters in South Carolina could move the rest of the South, until the election of Lincoln precipitated their final solution: secession.

Southern nationalists always attended to their repressive ideological agenda. South Carolina's secessionists feared the heterodoxy that Lincoln would bring to the South more than they feared federal legislation inimical to slavery. After all, as Lincoln often demonstrated, he had no objection to a constitutional amendment that explicitly forbade federal intervention in southern slavery. The radical advocates of states' rights did not fear direct federal intervention so much as they feared that the southern states themselves might someday outlaw slavery. They feared Lincoln would establish a southern wing of the Republican Party, at first recruited through the federal patronage and later encouraging antislavery thought in the non-slaveholding areas of the South, such as western Virginia. They had to suppress all dissent because they knew that in a republic such as the United States, slavery must eventually die of natural causes. So the natural course of American history had to be thwarted by constant, energetic action of eager, vigilant men.[57]

9

WAR

||

Showers watered fields of parched wheat and thirsty vegetable gardens
in late April 1860, and in the midst of this nourishing rain came a del-
uge of delegates to the 1860 National Democratic Convention, whom
the city welcomed with equal relish. The city's two hotels, the Mills
House and the Charleston, were brimming, and with other makeshift
arrangements the city could accommodate two thousand visitors. Private houses were accepting guests for a discounted $1 to $3 per day.
Cots were set up in Hibernian Hall, which became the headquarters of
the western states, Illinois, Ohio, Indiana, and Pennsylvania. The Tam-
many Hall faction of New York City roosted at the Mills House, while a
steamship, the SR *Spalding*, was berthed at Accommodation Wharf, the
"floating palace and headquarters" of the New England delegations.[1]

The city was on display. The delegates would convene at the spacious Institute Hall on Meeting Street, frescoed with cheap daubing
and a painting of three "improperly dressed women." In time to report
the proceedings, a new telegraph line to Mobile was completed. A new
rail line to Savannah brought delegates to town on its first day along
with five hundred other guests.

But these examples of technology hid the fact that the city and
even the state of South Carolina were dying. Unique among the states,
nearly 97 percent of the people living in South Carolina had been born
there. Far more people left South Carolina than came to live there, most
of those emigrants heading for Alabama, Mississippi, Louisiana, and
Texas, like the famous William Travis who died at the Alamo. The convention brought some of South Carolina's diaspora back to the old sod.[2]

One of these was William Lowndes Yancey, who was part of

Alabama's delegation. His father, who died early in the boy's life, was from South Carolina's Upcountry. Yancey's mother married a vehement, misogynistic abolitionist preacher whose abuse once took the form of nailing Yancey's mother into a room to prevent her escape from his dominion. Though Yancey's relationship to his stepfather was ambivalent and then hostile, the older man's intellectual connections brought young Yancey within the sphere of the preachers Lyman Beecher and Charles Finney. He was enrolled in Williams College in Massachusetts when the Nullification Crisis flared, and in the school's biweekly newspaper, like his Upcountry relatives, he sided unequivocally with President Jackson and federal power over state sovereignty. After graduating, he moved to the Greenville area of South Carolina to keep the books on his uncle's plantation, learning firsthand the profitability and glamour of the planter's life. The men in his family were staunch Union men, and in the aftermath of nullification, during the test oath debate, when South Carolina tinkered on the edge of armed civil war, Yancey condemned the idea of secession and a southern confederacy as treason. But like so many others, he converted in the late 1830s, probably influenced by the dowry a bride brought him: thirty-five slaves. In marriage Yancey was progressive. He deplored the enforced dependency of women and advocated their rights; ironically enough, he recognized and regretted that American law made them virtual slaves. Without breathing "the sharp and invigorating air of freedom," he reasoned, women "must languish like an exotic, and be reckoned but a beautiful flaw in nature." But he had no trouble with the laws forcing slavery on African Americans. He thought blacks were an inferior race and, like Calhoun, who became his hero, Yancey imagined that the lives of Africans were improved when they were captured and carried off to toil in America. In 1838 he joined the waves of South Carolina's emigrants flooding Alabama and building up there the kind of plantation system of farming that had saturated the lands of the East. It did not take long for him to reverse his politics, so that by the 1840s he was leading Alabama's anti-Union, states' rights radicals into a majority. By 1860, he was one of the triumvirate of fire-eaters leading the movement to secede and the only one who was a delegate to the convention. Stepping off the train and making his way to the Charleston Hotel, Yancey hardly looked the part of the "prince of the fire-eaters." Medium build, "bland" demeanor, square-faced, undemonstrative, open and honest looking, "no one would be likely to point him out in a group of gentlemen as the redoubtable Yancey," a correspondent from Cincinnati wrote, "who proposes according to common report to precipitate the cotton States into a revolution, dissolve the Union and build up a Southern empire."[3]

More radical even than Yancey was the titanic fire-eater from South Carolina, Robert Barnwell Rhett, who was born with the surname Smith. He descended from one of the aristocratic families of old Charleston and could quote his pedigree back to the Lords Proprietors of the seventeenth century. His father was an ineffectual planter near Beaufort, so Barnwell, as the boy was called, attended the relatively inexpensive Beaufort College, where he was for a time the pupil of James Louis Petigru, who began teaching there in 1811. By the time he was nineteen, his father had squandered the family's money, and Barnwell studied law, borrowing books and corresponding with his cousin, Thomas Grimké in Charleston. Despite these liberal tutors, the glamour of an old name and its promise of privilege attracted Barnwell to the anachronistic and aristocratic politics of the Lowcountry. He and his brothers abandoned the prosaic "Smith" for "Rhett" to cast the romance of glorious ancestors upon their generation. Tender and courteous with his own family, his children later described him as playful and full of laughter, kind to the poor, kind to women, though in his public life Rhett was "mercurial," quick-tempered, unfair and unflagging and uncompromising. Unlike Yancey, from his earliest career Rhett fought the federal tariffs and promoted nullification. As attorney general for the state, he defended the test oath in the court of appeals, arguing against his old mentors, Petigru and Grimké. His attitude toward slaves was unequivocal: masters should whip their property only when appropriate, and balance proper Christian firmness with mercy. He had no doubt about their suitability for freedom: "Of all the races of men, the negro race is the most inferior." As early as 1829 in an overheated speech he called for armed resistance, disunion, revolution; all the characteristics that marked him as a leader of the radical secessionists were in place already: a "didactic posture" when speaking, a tendency to "hyperbole and lack of proportion," an "intolerance of opposing viewpoints and the hint of contempt for those who disagreed," the use of ridicule to refute others, a "willingness to misrepresent opponents' arguments," a willful ignoring or distorting of "contrary facts." He insisted that to retain property rights in slaves was "to freemen [all that] is worth living for, is worth dying for." He was ahead of his time, and up until the eve of secession, though he held many high posts of government, many South Carolinians, even Simms and Hammond, considered him almost a crank. He labored harder than anyone else to turn the course of southern ideology. He and his son took over the *Charleston Mercury* in 1858 and made that paper, always reactionary and anti-federal, into a mere propagandist tool, diminishing its credibility with reasonable men as it exhorted all others to extremism.[4] Rhett refused to be a delegate to the Democratic convention, because he saw conventions as modes of compromise. Nevertheless, he hovered on the streets of Charleston, influencing whomever he could. One day he bumped into an old acquaintance from Congress, Colonel John Richardson, a delegate from Illinois and well-known supporter of Stephen Douglas.

Abandon popular sovereignty, Rhett urged him, "and we will give you the whole South for Douglas." Popular sovereignty—the idea that the white male resident population ought to decide if a territory became a free or slave state—was the single issue of the convention. Frederick Douglass and most northern delegates supported the concept, while most southerners wanted the federal government to guarantee the right to bring slaves into territories, no matter the majority opinion of residents. If the North held onto popular sovereignty, Rhett threatened, "the South leaves you—the Democratic Party will be divided—and Mr. Douglas defeated."

Richardson smiled uneasily and hurried away.[5]

The third man in the triumvirate, Edmund Ruffin, was a Virginian. Born in 1794, he briefly attended the College of William and Mary, spent some time in the state legislature, experimented in agriculture, and is credited with devising a system of fertilizing and crop rotation that would replenish the depleted tobacco farms of his native state. In the 1850s, he grew more radical, advocating southern nationalism and predicting that Civil War would commence with the election of a Republican president in 1868.

The fire-eaters followed the logic of the positive good theory of slavery all the way to its logical conclusions: slavery ought to spread from the South to the territories; the slave trade ought to be reopened; and an American empire should spread as far south as Nicaragua, those conquered lands being tilled by newly kidnapped Africans. Yancey's views were radical even among southerners, but he came from Alabama armed with the state's ultimatum: the Democratic Party must unequivocally support the right to expand slavery into the territories; Congress must guarantee this right, no matter the majority vote of white men in those territories; and Douglas, who had vowed to refuse the presidential nomination unless popular sovereignty was upheld, must not be elected as the party's candidate for president. If the majority of the delegates to the convention, who were northerners, Douglas men, and supporters of popular sovereignty, did not adopt the "Alabama platform," that state's delegates were prepared to walk out of the convention en masse. Yancey and Rhett and Ruffin all hoped that if it came to such a gesture that the whole South would follow Alabama. The collapse of the Democratic Party would assure a Republican victory in the November election, and a Republican victory would trigger a mass exodus from the Union. The dominoes were all lined up. It was up to Yancey to topple the first one.

The southerners looked strong, vibrant, and formidable to Murst Halstead, whose colorful journalistic account gives us the best picture of the convention. The southern oligarchy of slave owners sent representatives from its own rank, rich men capable and intelligent. All over the city men in "glossy black and fine linen," sweating in the damp heat of Charleston, puffing their cigars, toting their "ponderous gold-headed canes," whispered strategy, "talking about the Convention, and prophesying and wondering as to its actions." The buzz around the Mills House was like a barrel of molasses alive with flies, the Charleston Hotel sparking with fire.[6]

Douglas's supporters, virtually all from northern states, commanded a majority of the votes, and they were afraid if they abandoned popular sovereignty they would pay at the polls back home, for that principle of democracy was wildly popular in the North. They expected to win, even though they did not have the two-thirds majority needed for nominations. In 1856, when a majority candidate emerged (James Buchanan), the minority candidates (including, most significantly, Stephen Douglas) retired from the field, allowing the convention to unite behind the one man, and Douglas's supporters expected a similar courtesy to play out in 1860. But the southern states held 40 percent of the seats, and virtually every southerner stood against the principle of popular sovereignty, so they could prevent Douglas's nomination as long as they wanted. Many of these delegates hoped to deadlock the convention long enough for Douglas to surrender, leaving the convention to select a southerner, as it had in 1844 when the dark horse, slave-owning Tennessean James Polk, emerged the surprise nominee. Someone would have to blink, the northerners or the southerners, for the Democratic Party to survive as a national institution.[7]

There was a third way: destroy the Democratic Party. For days the pro-Douglas and anti-Douglas factions deadlocked, one not able to reach a two-thirds majority, the other not willing to surrender its minority power. And for days Yancey stayed strangely silent, choosing not to enter the fray. But on April 27, after the five long days of futile squabbling, Yancey decided his moment had come. Everyone knew what he was going to say, and the "perfect ovation" lasted for many minutes while Yancey waited patiently for it to subside, "wearing a genuinely good-humored smile, and looking as if nothing in the world could disturb the equanimity of his spirits." The "outside pressure" that the city of Charleston imposed on the chamber meant to squeeze it into Yancey's mold.[8]

Despite the intemperate nature of his words, Yancey's style was that of the lawyer, calculated and reasoning. He always meticulously prepared his speeches, though he spoke from notes rather than scripted sentences, hardly raising his soft tones above a conversational level, using little gesture, spicing his phrases with quick wit and the sharp barb of sarcasm, but always "calm, cool" and intense.[9] On this occasion, he spoke calmly and coolly, reassuring his audience that "there is no disunionist, that I know of, in the delegation from the State of Alabama. There is no disruptionist that I know of, and [no] factionists in our delegation." They were reasonable men come only to "hold up between us and your advancing columns of numbers that written instrument," the Constitution, "which your and our fathers made, and by the compact of which, you with your power were to respect us and our rights." The question was whether or not Congress would protect the southerners' right to bring slaves into the territories. Once a territory organized as a state, Yancey conceded, it might abolish slavery, but it could not do so while it was a territory, and the constitution submitted a territory to Congress as a condition of admission to the Union could not abolish slavery either. This was the issue, but it was merely symbolic, as Yancey himself explained. It was the last in a series of issues eroding the viability of slavery in the United States, and Yancey described the nation's drift, which, if unchecked, would carry the country to the complete eradication of slavery: the Missouri Compromise, which prevented the spread of slavery to most of the territory then held by the United States; the reception of abolitionist petitions in Congress; the lion's share of the spoils of the Mexican War going to the North; the admission of California as a free state; the banning of the sale of slaves in parts of the District of Columbia; the acceptance of popular sovereignty in Kansas.[10]

Only one great point lay under the surface of each of these crises. "The anti slavery sentiment is dominant at the North," Yancey explained, and "the slavery sentiment is dominant at the South." Abolition was so popular in the North that the Democratic delegates from northern states claimed they could not give up popular sovereignty, or they would lose every local election. But why was abolitionism ascendant in the North? "Believing [abolition] to be the common will of your people," Yancey lectured the northerners, "you hesitated, you trembled before its march, and you did not triumph over the young Hercules in his cradle, because you made no direct effort to do so." It was a failure of will, a moral weakness: "You acknowledged . . . that slavery was wrong." That was the heart of the matter, the cause of all problems: northern Democrats "gave up the real ground of battle, the key to success, when [they] acknowledged, what was the foundation of the antislavery sentiment, that slavery was wrong." Yancey seemed to have given up all chance of persuasion. He was haranguing the northerners in a theatrical spectacle meant for the consumption of southerners. "You acknowledged that [slavery] could not exist anywhere by the law of nature or by the law of God," he accused. "You yielded the whole question."[11] Was slavery forbidden by natural law? Or was it a positive good? Whether or not to allow slaves into the territories was merely the latest of a train of issues that boiled down to this one question: Was or was not slavery a positive good?

Yancey thought the answer was self-evident. Many of those in the convention chamber, he realized, had never encountered slavery before their present trip to Charleston. "I have no doubt, gentlemen, that each of you here enjoys most pleasantly, the hospitalities of this city—even such hospitalities as you pay for so magnificently." This reference to price gouging in the city triggered laughter from everyone. "I have no doubt of that," Yancey continued seriously when the laughing died down, "and I have no doubt that these sable people who wait upon you, who are slaves for life, and whose children are born slaves, and who descend to the heirs of their masters, are agreeable in their relations to you as an inferior class of beings, who are ready to contribute to your comfort, and whom you can command to contribute to your comfort." Take a lesson from that fact, Yancey instructed them, for "your relations towards [blacks] would be just the same in the Territories as they are here" in Charleston. If only northerners were more exposed to the benefits of white supremacy, they would embrace it. The Democratic Party must unite behind this all-important ideological principle. If northerners would just admit that slavery was good for blacks, southerners would "give you good servants for life and enable you to live comfortably." And slavery would prove good for whites as well: "we will take your poor white man and elevate him from the office of boot-black, and from other menial offices which belong to the highest order of civilization—we will elevate him to a place amongst the master race and put the negro race to do this dirty work which God designed they should do."[12] How could such a consummation be called evil?

Yancey was forty-five years old when he delivered this speech. He was only a boy of eight when Denmark Vesey supposedly plotted rebellion. He was eighteen when Nat Turner murdered so many whites, and barely twenty-one when John C. Calhoun first advocated the positive good theory in the U.S. Senate. He was among the earliest victims of Calhoun's ideological juggernaut. He had little opportunity to know that the positive good theory was younger than he was. He did not know that the narrative he offered to the Convention—that the abolitionists invented the notion that slavery was evil around 1830, and that northern politicians let the contagion grow from a tiny minority into a vast army of ideologues—was entirely false. Yet Yancey was not a liar. All witnesses attest to his sincerity, and we must conclude that after thirty years of the culture wars he, like so many others, forgot what life had been like before 1820. The southern delegates to the convention were unanimous in this cultural amnesia, as was Charleston itself.

"The fate of the party," Yancey concluded, "aye! and of the country itself" hung in the balance. Would the Democracy, as the Party called itself, uphold the minority rights of southerners, or would it back Douglas and popular sovereignty? By the time his speech raised its rhetoric to its majestic closing periods, the sun had gone down in the streets outside. The hall was illumined by gaslights. Warmth and splendor flickered about the shoulders of the crowd. "I make no threats," Yancey explained in quiet tones. "I am not authorised to do so." Then he proceeded to threaten: "such is the condition of the public mind at the South, that it cannot bear any longer any doubt as regards what is the position of this party on this great issue." The gallery, packed with Charleston's elite, showered applause onto the floor. The Democratic Party could unite behind Douglas and reap "the rewards of office and the distribution of the eighty millions [of federal revenue] annually." But to do so would "ask the people to vote for a party that ignores their rights, and dares not acknowledge them, in order to put and keep [itself] in office." Anyone advocating such a strategy "ought to be strung upon a political gallows higher than that ever erected for Haman." After so much meticulous argument and dry wit, this single gesture toward violence stunned the crowd, and Institute Hall exploded with applause from the floor of the chamber and from the gallery. Compromise was over. Yancey had thrown the gauntlet to the floor, and it rattled in the ears of the northern delegates.[13]

George Pugh of Cincinnati was quick to accept the challenge. If the Democrats were weak in the North, he countered, it was the intransigence of the South that made them unpopular. This novel insistence that slavery not only be defended, but that it must be expanded made the Democrats almost unelectable in the North, and now Yancey taunted them for their weakness. And now here in Charleston, where the northern delegates were overwhelmed, they were told they must "put their hands over their mouths" and swallow this further expansion of slavery. There was "no warrant in the Constitution" for this "peculiar protection of their peculiar property in the Territories." If Yancey and his fellow "Gentlemen of the South" thought Ohio would abandon popular sovereignty, capitulate to an ultimatum, and concede that slavery was a positive good, "You mistake us," he said: "we will not do it." Absolute silence filled the hall, for everyone knew that Pugh spoke for Stephen Douglas.[14]

Then everyone jumped to their feet, stood on the tables, spoke at once, screamed to be heard, and the president pounded his gavel, but no one could hear it. Gangs of delegates grappled with each other, until the president managed to eke out a vote to adjourn, well after ten o'clock, and everyone streamed out into a cold rain to continue their politicking. The following day was squandered on motions and countermotions and didn't adjourn till late at night again. The cold rain poured for days, pushing delegates indoors to caucus and horse-trade in front of fireplaces, the Douglas men promising federal appointments to anyone who would vote for their candidate. Inside the convention chamber the speeches dragged on, boring the spectators out of town, until finally the sun melted the rain clouds and a refreshing breeze blew through the city. On the seventh day, so many spectators had left the city that the gallery at Institute Hall was filled almost exclusively with South Carolinians, who watched as the convention voted in favor of popular sovereignty, 165 to 138. True to its word, Alabama's delegation walked out, followed by Mississippi, Louisiana, South Carolina, Florida, Texas, and Arkansas. Georgia followed the next day. North Carolina, Virginia, Maryland, and Kentucky "retired to consult."[15]

On the evening of the next day, the first of May, the bright, clear moon cast nets of silver into the live oaks along Meeting Street and a gleam of shining silver on the house fronts. This was eleven o'clock at night, and already the northern delegates had checked out of their hotels, leaving Charleston to revel in its victory. The Cincinnati correspondent heard a band playing and shouts and, following the music to the courthouse, he found a large crowd chanting Yancey's name. The Alabama delegate addressed the crowd, which "applauded with great enthusiasm" each "ultra sentiment" he uttered and cheered for the "Independent Southern Republic." When Yancey finished, the crowd paraded to the office of the *Charleston Mercury*, demanding to pay homage to the other great fire-eater, Robert Barnwell Rhett.[16]

Edmund Ruffin was not there, but his eager hope had come to pass. The only national political party had collapsed, splitting the Democratic vote, assuring that a Republican plurality at the polls would garner a majority in the Electoral College. And a Republican victory would inspire southern whites all across the South to fall in ranks behind the fire-eaters. Lincoln, of course, won the election in November 1860. A correspondent for the *Charleston Courier* reported that Lincoln's victory fulfilled "the hopes and anticipation of the majority of our community . . . inasmuch as it is believed it will tend to bring about the issue so much to be desired by all true hearted Southerners, viz: a Southern Confederacy." In Aiken, a torch-lit parade rode an effigy of Lincoln on a rail. Two slaves were made to carry the rail and then to hang the dummy from a scaffold, where it was lit afire amid "the cheers of the multitude." In Georgetown, slaves were ecstatic, thinking their liberator would sit in the White House. Boldly they sang,

> We'll fight for liberty
>   Till de Lord shall call us home;
> We'll soon be free
>   Till de Lord shall call us home.

Like most whites, they believed the lie that Barnwell Rhett was using to precipitate this crisis: that Abraham Lincoln would use the federal power to free the slaves. Lincoln had no such design: he meant to prevent the spread of slavery and was content to let South Carolina decide its fate in South Carolina. Nevertheless, these slaves in Georgetown were whipped for their audacity. The "Women of Charleston! Daughters of Carolina!" offered to buckle their sons and husbands into armor and send them into battle, not yet imagining anything less romantic than *Ivanhoe*. Charleston's militias were mustered and their muskets dusted off. One Charlestonian living in Philadelphia wrote that it was a pity that any "Conservative and Union men" still existed in the South because above the Mason-Dixon Line, he insisted, there was not "a single man . . . who does not consider slavery an evil." Most northerners, he reported, believed that "the South is merely playing the game of 'brag' in her threats of dissolution, and they do not hesitate to say that as soon as Lincoln is elected, the South will quiet down as submissively as inferiors should do always to their superiors."[17]

The General Assembly met in special session and immediately called for a Secession Convention, to convene in Columbia on December 17. The shrill calls for unity and the brandishing of terms like "true Southerner" as if they were bludgeons indicate that not everyone even in South Carolina was ready to leave the Union for the sake of preserving slavery, that some had to be threatened to toe the line. Those most eager to grasp the nettle were the richest planters along the coast, who had the most to lose if slavery died out even gradually. They still dominated the state's politics, and "the large majority [of delegates to the Secession Convention]—more than 100—were planters." Even by nineteenth-century standards, the Secession Convention was undemocratic and preponderantly aristocratic. Many delegates were lawyers. Fifty-six had been to the South Carolina College in Columbia, a hotbed of radical, southern nationalism. All together, they were a "wealthy, middle-aged, slaveholding, native-born group of planters and lawyers."[18]

One correspondent in Columbia believed that "if a true vote on the question could be taken, the majority of the people of S.C. would refuse to go out of the union." That letter-writer might have been thinking more wishfully than accurately, but he was not entirely off the mark. When the state convened delegates to consider the issue of secession, Charleston, the cauldron of southern separatism, selected nine "cooperationist" representatives (out of twenty-two). Cooperationists, while sympathetic to secession, were defined by their caution and did not want South Carolina to act rashly or alone. The *New York Tribune* reported that if the election of delegates to the convention had been delayed just one week, the fever for secession would have begun to cool, and "'a positive Union party' would have developed itself in South Carolina."[19] But it is hard to imagine that view was accurate.

The Union Party barely lost in the 1830s during the Nullification Crisis, but the loss was decisive because it delegitimized dissent, and by 1837 dissent was called treason. The Union men in the summer and fall of 1860 kept their heads low, and once Lincoln was elected there were very few with the courage of Petigru willing to stand before the wind. A generation had passed since John C. Calhoun demanded fealty to a positive good theory of slavery, since Angelina Grimké was exiled, since John England wrote his slave letters. No white person under thirty years old and not a single delegate to the Secession Convention believed, as so many in the Revolutionary days had believed, that slavery was evil.

The members convened on a Monday morning in the state capital, Columbia, and elected as their president D. F. Jamison, a delegate from Barnwell. There would be no debate. All already agreed that their "fixed determination," as Jamison told the assembly, was to "throw off a Government to which we have been accustomed." The "elections that sent us here," he continued, had already decided "that South Carolina must dissolve her connection with the [United States] as speedily as possible." By that evening, the delegates had unanimously declared that South Carolina should secede.[20]

Even so, Columbia was too cautious a city for the delegates, and they voted to reconvene the following day in Charleston, the birthplace of southern nationalism. The excuse for the move was a threatened smallpox epidemic, but the real reason was that political fever burned hotter on the coast. "Madness of ambition and wounded vanity," like a contagion, James Louis Petigru observed, was sickening the body politic.[21] The ambition belonged to the fire-eaters who hoped that noisy demonstrations in the streets of Charleston would steel the delegates in the chamber to their dangerous work. And the vanity was theirs as well, for men like Rhett, a U.S. senator and editor of the *Charleston Mercury*, the bellows of propaganda played upon the people's sense of honor, which the North had supposedly insulted by electing Lincoln.

The *Mercury* decried the "fetters" that the Union put upon the "brave limbs" of a "too long oppressed people." Lincoln's election threw down a gauntlet, and, fortified by the public demonstrations in

282 | | AMERICA'S LONGEST SIEGE

Charleston, the convention's delegates would not shrink from the challenge. On December 20, 1860, the delegates representing the white population of South Carolina (about 42 percent of the whole population) voted unanimously to secede from the United States of America. "A great Confederated Republic," the *Mercury* reported, "overwrought with arrogant and tyrannous oppressions, has fallen from its high estate among the nations of the earth. Conservative liberty has been vindicated. Mobocratic license has been stricken down." The phrase "Confederated Republic" was Newspeak for the "United States," emphasizing the southern belief that the country was a collection of closely associated independent nations. In earlier months, most South Carolinians were suspicious of this sort of rhetoric, as indicated by the fact that the *Mercury*'s readers numbered only about one sixth of those who read the more dignified and cautious *Charleston Courier*. But on December 21, 1861, the *Mercury* spoke for nearly all the white people.

The Ordinance of Secession was read aloud in Institute Hall, the very scene of the Democratic Party's implosion seven months earlier. "We, the people of South Carolina," it began,

> do declare and ordain . . . that the Ordinance adopted by us in Convention, on the twenty-third day of May, in the year of our Lord one thousand seven hundred and eighty-eight, whereby the Constitution of the United States of America was ratified, and also, all Acts and parts of Acts of the General Assembly of this State, ratifying amendments of the said Constitution, are hereby repealed; and that the union now subsisting between South Carolina and other States, under the name of "The United States of America," is hereby dissolved.

As the word "dissolved" hung in the air, "men could contain themselves no longer, and a shout that shook the very building, reverberating, long-continued, rose to Heaven, and ceased only with the loss of breath." Outside the building, "loud shouts of joy rent the air. The enthusiasm was unsurpassed. Old men went shouting down the streets. Cannon were fired, and bright triumph was depicted on every countenance." In conscious mimicry of the spirit of '76, crowds celebrated around the Liberty pole. Three thousand white people thronged "Secession" Hall that evening to witness the signing of the ordinance. The 169 delegates took two hours to put their names to the brief document, at which point it was read aloud again. That drama had no suspense. It was the kind of excitement that comes from doing something dangerous, momentous, but long-contemplated. In the center of the tumescence the delegates themselves, those who had enacted the will of the people, "proud, grave [and] silen[t] . . . waited the end with beating hearts."[22] The next day the banner headline in Rhett's *Mercury* echoed the final word of the ordinance: "Dissolved!"

The streets exploded with delirium "beyond the power of the pen" to describe. "The high, burning, bursting heart alone can realize it. A mighty voice of great thoughts and great emotions spoke from the mighty throat of one people as a unit." Without appreciating the irony, the *Mercury* appended to its enthusiastic report of this supposedly *universal* celebration: "Two of the negros who were proved to be interested in the late insurrectionary plot at Pine Level, Ala[bama] . . . have been hung." "Fetters" upon the "brave limbs" of "oppressed people," after all, are most odious when they are merely metaphoric. Real fetters were known by nearly half of Charleston's population, the African Americans, both free and enslaved, but hardly a man among the *Mercury*'s readers would have recognized the unintended irony. A day later, a parade of local white clubs, most of them paramilitary, marched to the space in front of the Mills House Hotel on Meeting Street. "The Washington Artillery, the Zonaves, the Palmetto Riflemen, the Cadet Riflemen, the Carolina Light Infantry, the Union Light Infantry, the German Fire Company, the Minute Men and the citizens generally" shot off fireworks, listened to bands playing the "Marseillaise" and the "Secession March," and then came speeches by various sententious dignitaries, beginning with the new governor of the state, the portly, square-faced Francis Wilkinson Pickens. Two days later, the *Mercury* declared that "the most impressive feature in the action of South Carolina is the concentrated unanimity of her people." This "concentrated" will, this "unity of purpose," convinced Charlestonians that they "*must* be right."[23] It was unthinkable that so many people in perfect agreement might be wrong.

The South had been patient. The South had suffered a long train of abuses, and, for as long as those evils had been sufferable, the South had endured them. But the election of Abraham Lincoln was the last straw. So sure was South Carolina about the rectitude of its cause that it consciously echoed the Declaration of Independence in its own Declaration of Immediate Causes Which Induce and Justify the Secession of South Carolina from the Federal Union. This document, much more lengthy than the Ordinance of Secession, was promulgated four days later, and in it the sovereign and independent nation of South Carolina carefully enumerated its grievances with her mother country. The *northern* states had repeatedly violated the Constitution, had refused to cooperate with the bounty hunters looking for fugitive slaves, and had, in fact, openly defied the clear mandate of the Constitution by actually *helping* slaves escape from the South. Could anyone deny that the northern states had treated the Constitution with contempt? Was not the present Black Republican administration "destructive" of every white man's "right of property in slaves"? The northern states had been violating the Constitution for years, and violating a part "so material to the compact," the constitutional protections of slavery, "that without it," Calhoun's generation believed, South Carolina would never have joined the Union back in 1787.

After the adoption of the Ordinance of Secession, in the midst of the delirium, all of South Carolina's anti-secessionists got in line behind the new republic, except for James Louis Petigru. Once the Union was dissolved, they instantly became ardent southern nationalists. Mary Chesnut, whose family was once split between secessionists and pro-Unionists, remembered "feeling a nervous dread and horror of this break with so great a power as U.S.A., but . . . was ready and willing." After secession was declared, "nobody could live" in South Carolina "unless he was a fire-eater." Factions instantly merged. Even those who had always been seceders recognized the strange hypnotic effect of total unanimity and were awed by the inevitable violence it led to. Come what would, Chesnut herself "wanted them to fight and stop talking. South Carolina . . . heated [it]self into a fever that only blood-letting could ever cure—it was the inevitable remedy."[24]

||

At eight o'clock on a Thursday night, crowds streamed through the streets of Charleston like storm water running to the harbor. They congregated at the Battery and on the wharves that gave a view across the dark bay to the giant American flag over Fort Sumter, near the gateway to the Atlantic. They expected a show of fireworks, cannonades and mortars firing from all the surrounding forts—Fort Johnson on James Island; Fort Moultrie on Sullivan's; the "floating battery," an ironclad barge moored near Mount Pleasant; Cumming's Battery—all in the hands of the new Confederate army and commanded by the dashing engineer from Louisiana, General Pierre Gustave Toutant Beauregard. Beyond their sight, a flurry of small boats rowing back and forth negotiated terms of a surrender, and rumors flew through the crowds. Eleven o'clock and no action. Midnight, and the guns were still cold. Most spectators returned to their homes, disappointed. But a few hearty and eager souls who kept vigil through the night were rewarded: just as the first gray of dawn appeared, something exploded out over the harbor, the first shot from a howitzer on James Island, and that signal triggered suddenly thousands as all the southern guns opened fire. Instantly the city was alive as people, wakened by the din, rushed back to the waterfront. More women than attended any gala in town flocked to the breezy promenade, all disappointed when the smoke cleared and showed the Stars and Stripes still flying over the fort.

It was all so romantic, and the editors of the *Courier* described it in terms more befitting one of Simms's novels than reality. "O! what a conflict raged in those heaving bosoms" of the ladies, "between love for husbands and sons, and love for our common mother, whose insulted honor and imperilled safety had called her faithful children to the ensanguined field." They might indulge such prose so long as the field was only metaphorically ensanguined. No one was hurt in the barrage—certainly no Confederate soldiers and remarkably no Union soldiers on the island fort.[25]

The editors of the *Courier* tried to "comprehend the nature of the work" and commenced with the bombardment, "the magnitude of the crisis" and "all its aspects, bearings and consequences." But they could not yet escape the foolish bravado of all those who had been making speeches for the last year:

We paused but it was not the pause of hesitation or doubt. We had long since made ourselves familiar with the dangers that darkened over our pathway, and had they been ten-fold greater we *would* have dared do what we have done, with the same steady courage and immovable resolution. We had marked out a way for our feet, and we would pursue this road let what may oppose our progress. This pathway was traced by the finger of honor, and Heaven's own light rests upon it.

Over at the offices of the *Mercury*, the Rhetts, "sure of success," were writing such foolishness as this: "brave men, fighting on their own soil, for their dearest rights, are invincible." They "rejoice[d]" that the "solemn reckoning with our enemies" was finally "at hand." It was all a play, "the opening drama of what, it is presumed, will be a most momentous military act," and they strutted their part of the Romantic hero. "It may be a drama of but a single act," the *Mercury* reported or rather hoped, because "the people of the North have rankling at their hearts no sense of wrong to be avenged."[26]

But this prediction, too, was foolish. President Lincoln immediately called up seventy thousand troops and convened a special session of Congress. A delegation from Virginia's Secession Convention asked the president what he would do, now that South Carolina had fired on the flag. They hoped he would back down, withdraw Union troops, and relinquish the federal government's claim on public property. But Lincoln expressed his resolve, and that was taken as a promise to "prosecute the war opened by the South Carolina secessionists with the utmost vigor, and never sleep until the revolution was fairly crushed out." Whatever disagreements there had been among northerners, the firing on Fort Sumter produced a "unanimity of sentiment." Ten thousand Pennsylvania and New York volunteers arrived by train to defend Washington. Ohio promised another ten thousand "for immediate service." Boston "tendered [the] services" of its second battalion. Kansas already was raising a regiment, and "General Robinson, one of the oldest citizens of Pittsburgh," volunteered. In Dover, New Hampshire, a "large and enthusiastic" crowd of citizens felt that, "without regard to political parties . . . the Government must be fully sustained." Three thousand people cheered on two companies of militia in Lawrence, Massachusetts. In Providence the banks immediately loaned the state $80,000 to outfit troops, and private citizens added their dollars. In Utica, New York, a "citizens corp" of three companies organized and offered their services to Lincoln. In Pittsburgh, "without regard to party," a monster meeting resolved to sustain the Union and "several companies" volunteered. In New Jersey, which alone among the northern states did not vote for Lincoln, "the feeling is universal for standing by the Union at all hazards." Wisconsin put the "military of the state on a war footing," and in Cincinnati, news of Sumter's fall "thoroughly aroused . . . the military spirit of the city." The governor of Maine promised that "the people of this State of all parties will rally with alacrity for the maintenance of the government, and the defense of the flag." All across the Union, from Maine to Kansas, the millions were outraged, and they began to hammer and weld, turn the wheel on the gears of a new and massive machine of war.[27] Just after the bombardment of Fort Sumter, some northerners published a pamphlet that reproduced Henry Laurens's 1776 letter to his son, John, immortalizing these words of dissent:

> I abhor Slavery. . . . [I]n former days there was no combating the prejudices of Men supported by Interest, the day I hope is approaching when from principles of gratitude as well as justice every Man will strive to be foremost in shewing his readiness to comply with the Golden Rule; . . . I am devising means for manumitting many of [my slaves] & for cutting off the entail of slavery.

"I am not one of those," Laurens continued, "who dare trust in Providence for defence & security of their own Liberty while they enslave & wish to continue in Slavery, thousands who are as well intitled to freedom as themselves." The northern pamphleteer who published this letter meant to provide "additional evidence against the Southern theory, that the same antagonism that now prevails between the North and South on the subject of Slavery, existed at the time of the American Revolution." Both "North and South," he insisted, "regarded [slavery], in the established formula of the day, as 'a social, political, and moral evil.'" Of course he was right, but this appeal to history could hardly penetrate the minds of southerners in the 1860s.[28]

All the while the armies battled in Virginia and west of the Appalachians, the Union slowly closed its grip on Charleston. In November 1861, Commodore Dupont of the Union navy captured Port Royal, a spacious bay fifty miles south of Charleston, and he commenced to erect a naval base there and a camp on Hilton Head Island, from which the army could stage an invasion. By November 1862, Thomas Wentworth Higgenson, a preacher from Massachusetts, arrived to take command of the 1st South Carolina Regiment of Volunteers, troops made up of escaped slaves from South Carolina and Florida. The first recruit he encountered had been wounded on a raiding mission. Colonel Higgenson asked him, "Did you think that was more than you bargained for, my man?" The wounded black soldier replied stoutly, "Dat's jess what I went for." Six months later came the Fifty-Fourth Massachusetts, a "first class regiment, both in drill, discipline, and physical condition" made up of black soldiers recruited in the North. They arrived on June 4, 1863, and were quickly paraded through the town of Beaufort, once a hotbed of secessionists but now captured by the Union, where they were cheered enthusiastically by the citizens and other soldiers who wanted "a look at the first black regiment from the North." The freed slaves or "contrabands" could not believe their eyes. James Henry Gooding, a corporal in the regiment and correspondent for Boston papers, reported that one of the free men said, "I nebber bleeve black Yankee comee here help culer men."[29]

The day after the Confederates abandoned Port Royal to the Union navy, General Robert E. Lee was put in charge of the southern coast, from South Carolina to Florida, a vast territory of innumerable barrier islands, inlets, marshes, river deltas, easily a thousand places where the Union might land its troops. Lee designed the grand defense: abandon the coastal edges that could be bombarded from the sea; fortify the inward waterways behind the shallow marshes, where the Union gunboats could not reach; build defenses across the spits of high ground that extended like gangways between the "impenetrable country," the swamps and jungles; and above all keep open the railroad running between Charleston and Savannah. The railroad was the key to defense. With all the marshes and inlets and swamps, the landing grounds consisted of innumerable peninsulas stretching their fingers toward the sea. The Confederates could station a few troops and maybe a battery on each, which could bottle up invaders for hours, stalling them long enough for reinforcements to shuttle up and down the railway from Savannah and Charleston to plug the hole, rushing fresh troops to the gap faster than the Union could land them.[30]

In the midst of Lee's frantic preparations, natural catastrophe swept through Charleston. A group of slaves were cooking behind a factory on East Bay Street that made window sashes and blinds, and sparks from their fire ignited the building just as a wind kicked up, blew to gale force, and spread the flames across the roofs of buildings and houses, a long, southwesterly swath of destruction through the heart of the city, which already was brimming with refugees from the barrier islands. Institute Hall, the site of both the ill-fated National Democratic Convention and then South Carolina's Secession Convention, was reduced to stumps of smoldering ashes along with 540 acres of residences, factories, and public buildings.[31]

As the rest of the waterfront slept at three in the morning on May 13, 1862, the crew of the side-paddled *Planter*, which rested at its berth moored to a Cooper River wharf, quietly and nervously readied the steam engines. The ship was useful to the Confederate defenses— laying torpedoes in the ship channels to ward off the Union blockaders, shuttling troops from coastal island to island, carrying supplies, transferring cannon. Though it could carry a thousand soldiers on its deck, it drew less than four feet of water, and so it was ideal for moving vital cargoes to various defensive posts along the inland rivers, creeks, and marshes, well out of sight and range of the Union's big gunships. The previous day, the *Planter* had been loaded with four cannon and two mortars from Coles Island, a marshy, inaccessible bit of land on which the Confederates had erected a battery to protect the mouth of the Stono River south of Charleston. The Confederates abandoned the post as indefensible, and the *Planter* meandered the long, backdoor route to Charleston's harbor, carrying away the guns. At dawn the next morning she would deliver them to Fort Ripley on the Cooper River. But for now, the tired officers were glad to tie up at the city-side wharf and sleep in their own beds for a change, leaving the steamship to the care of its enslaved crew.[32]

The wheelman and leader of the slaves was Robert Smalls, and he had been biding his time for months, waiting for just this sort of opportunity. He pulled the captain's coat over his own shoulders, donned his big floppy straw hat, and backed the *Planter* from the wharf and started on its slow course toward the mouth of the harbor. First it had to pass a sentinel at the waterfront. It was an unusual time to pull away from the dock, but the soldier thought he saw the boat's white captain at the helm. Smalls sheered close to the Atlantic Wharf, an arranged rendezvous, and a rowboat delivered Smalls's family and a few other slaves related to the crew, who were quickly hidden below deck. They steamed away from the peninsula out into the harbor, having to pass Castle Pinckney, Fort Ripley, Fort Johnson, and then the formidable Fort Sumter if they were to make it to freedom. If any of these posts raised an alarm they were done for, and Smalls and his crew resolved to blow the ship up before they would surrender, for to be caught was certain death anyway. At Castle Pinckney, Smalls blew the steam whistle's pass code, and they were waved on. Again at Fort Ripley and Fort Johnson, and finally, at around 4:15 a.m., they approached Fort Sumter, the gateway to the Atlantic Ocean. They came within hailing distance, the blank sixty-foot masonry wall with its threatening gun ports rising as if from the black waters. Smalls pulled the whistle: three shrill bursts and a long hissing sound, and then waited for a response. It seemed an eternity and still there was no reply.[33]

Robert Smalls was born in the heart of the most radical district in the state, near the coastal town of Beaufort just south of Charleston. His mother, Lydia, was a favorite house slave of Henry McKee; some speculate that McKee might have been Robert's father, though his biographer, Andrew Billingsley, thinks it unlikely, but whatever the relation between McKee and Smalls, the boy enjoyed the privileges that favoritism brought, including an education that stopped short of literacy. When he was twelve, Lydia persuaded McKee to send the boy to Charleston rather than to the plantation's fields, and Robert entered into the world of the quasi free, or what was left of that world in the 1840s. He waited tables at the Planter's Hotel for $5 a month, lit streetlamps, loaded and unloaded ships at the waterfront, thence to rigging ships, and finally he worked as a hand on ships plying the coastal trade. By the time he was a young man, Smalls was known as one of the best wheelmen or pilots skirting the coastal shoals from Charleston to Florida. He made $16 a month, $15 of which he remitted to McKee, but he used his contacts along the sea islands to run his own little supply business, carrying small private cargoes of vegetables and goods back and forth in the underground economy. Broad-shouldered, slim-waisted, just five foot five but confident and capable, the seventeen-year-old Smalls wooed a "merry" hotel maid with "sparkling" eyes, pretty curls, a "daring manner," and two children, the oldest of which was just three years younger than Smalls. They married, arranged to pay their masters $20 a month, and set up house on whatever they could garner above that.[34]

When the war started, Smalls was working as the wheelman on John Ferguson's *Planter*, whose red-cedar planking and frame of live oak could accommodate fourteen hundred bales of cotton, and its side wheels each had its own engine, which meant they could rotate in opposite directions and spin the boat around in place. Ferguson leased the boat to the Confederate navy for $100 a day, and three white officers came on board to command the crew of slaves. When the Federal navy took Hilton Head Island and Port Royal, about midway between Charleston and Savannah, and built a naval station, the *Planter* became an essential part of the feverish preparation for a Yankee invasion, supplying the far-flung batteries on remote marshy islands throughout the river deltas. As the man who knew those waters as well as any pilot, Smalls was crucial to these operations, and he understood the irony of doing such work for the Confederacy. Eagerly, fully mindful of the danger for his family and himself, he planned their bold race for freedom, which all hinged on the final signal from the blank and formidable face of Fort Sumter.

Finally it came. "Pass on by!"

Smalls throttled the engines forward.

Then a final shout over the walls of the fort: "Blow the damned Yankees to hell, or ring one of them in."

"Aye aye," Smalls shouted back, trying to sound like a white man.[35]

But when the boat failed to turn right, which would bring it past the battery on Morris Island, and instead steamed straight out to sea, someone finally figured out that something was wrong, and Fort Sumter signaled for the ship to halt. They flashed a signal to Morris Island to stop the ship, but still it steamed ahead, and before anyone decided to fire a cannon the swift *Planter* had made it through the Swash Channel across the bar and out of range.[36]

Outside the Confederate territory for the first time, Robert Smalls, his family, and crew were free. Out there in the Atlantic Ocean, in the predawn light, Smalls spied the Union ship *Onward*. He knew he probably looked like a blockade-runner, so they struck their Confederate colors, hoisted a bedsheet, and came alongside the gunship. A crew of Federal sailors scrambled aboard, and Robert Smalls, a free American, addressed himself to Lieutenant Nichols: "I thought this ship might be of some use to Uncle Abe."

Brimming with delight at the daring race to freedom, Nichols pulled down the white banner and ran the Federal ensign up the mast, and in just that amount of time Robert Smalls and his wife and children were citizens of the United States of America.[37]

The event had tremendous symbolic value on both sides of the war. The Charleston papers stomped and ranted and called for the speedy execution of the *Planter*'s officers, who were court-martialed by order of Robert E. Lee. The Confederates put a $4,000 bounty on Smalls's head and fantasized about what they would do to him if ever they got him back. Back up North, Smalls was a hero, giving the papers and magazines a rare victory in the first year of the war. Smalls and his crew were inducted into the United States Army, a privilege not yet accorded other black men. The *New York Tribune* pointed out with humility that "no small share of the naval glory of the war belongs to the race which we have forbidden to fight for us." Smalls's intelligence and daring were acknowledged by Admiral Dupont, who met him the day after the escape, and a congressman from New York recommended that the *Planter*'s wheelman be made military governor of South Carolina, once that state was conquered. In the meantime, he and the crew were granted half the value of the captured ship.[38]

But of even greater value than these symbolic triumphs was the knowledge that Smalls brought to the Federal navy, not only of the shallow and quirky inland waters, but of the Confederate defenses. For example, not only did he give to the Union the cargo of cannon and mortars lashed to the deck of the ship, which were precious enough to the depleted Confederates, but he told them that Coles Island had been abandoned. Dupont sent three ships into the Stono Sound, and, finding the approach undefended, Union troops were ferried up the river and landed at Johns Island, from which they launched their invasion of James Island, hoping to take Fort Johnson from the rear. If Fort Johnson fell to the Union forces, Charleston would soon follow, as had happened when the British laid siege to the city eighty years earlier. The governor and legislature of South Carolina passed a resolution: "Charleston should be defended at any cost of life and property. . . . [T]hey would prefer a repulse of the enemy with the entire city in ruins to an evacuation or surrender on any terms whatever."[39]

By this time, Lee had been called north to Richmond and replaced by General John C. Pemberton. The first battle leading to the siege of Charleston began under his command. Union troops began probing the city's defenses in the rainy, early summer days of 1862, at about the same time Lee was demonstrating his brilliance by outmaneuvering the Union general McClellan in the Peninsula Campaign in Virginia. By comparison to the Union's Army of the Potomac, whose one hundred thousand men were inching their way toward Richmond, the six thousand Union troops assaulting James Island were insignificant. Their target was an earthen fort called the Tower Battery near the village of Secessionville. But Secessionville was critical, and had the South lost the battle it would have lost Charleston, and the Confederacy would have collapsed like a house that had its central pillar chopped down. A tall observation tower gave the Confederate redoubt its name, and it was close enough to the city to be seen clearly from the steeple of St. Michael's, where Confederate lookouts kept an eye on the Union's movements.

The Confederacy's best defense in this case proved to be a conceited, blustering, rash Union general, John Benham. He was a somewhat vain man, who, when he arrived to take his post on Hilton Head

Island, paraded his "high feather[s] . . . like a spread eagle." He looked like a plump banker, with the front half of his head bald and the hair of the rest tightly coiffed in curls above his ears. Muttonchops held his jaw like the leathern straps of a helmet pulled tightly down on his head. He was rash, impetuous, too fond of liquor, and, unfortunately for the Michigan, Massachusetts, and New York regiments on James Island, too eager to whip the rebels. He ordered a nighttime assault on Tower Battery, the strength of which the Union pickets had not yet probed.

The Confederate fortification was pinched between two marshes, like the narrow part of an hourglass. Approaching the earthworks was a wide and open farm field with no cover but the low rows of cotton furrows, now weeded over, that funneled toward the open mouths of cannon.[40] On the Confederate side of Tower Battery, the land spread out again, opening toward the undefended backside of Fort Johnson, which faced the harbor. (It was from Fort Johnson that the first shot of the war was fired on Fort Sumter.) Wave after wave of blue-clad soldiers, most heading into their first battle, hurried through the predawn fog, their quick march beginning in wide lines that the marshes pinched together as they approached the Confederate battery. They hoped to reach the earthworks undetected, but Confederates were ready for them, and the four big guns roared with canister shot through the ranks, aiming almost blindly in the dark, drizzling, steamy dawn. Even in the dark they could not miss. One lieutenant later testified that a "shower of musket balls and discharges of grape and canister from their cannon seemed to mow our men down in swaths." It was an image that would become all too often repeated—fields of hay cut down by the arc of a scythe—but the cliché was especially apt, because the gruesome harvest took place in a tilled field, and the wounded, frightened living took what shelter they could in the furrowed ground. Screaming metal cut through arms and legs and chests and faces. The slaughter was horrendous. A few troops from Michigan managed to scramble through the ditch in front of the battery and scale the twenty-foot earthworks. Bayonets and musket fire clashed for a few brief moments inside the fort, but the Ninth South Carolina Battalion charged down the road from Secessionville and poured into the battery, beating back the Union troops. The assault was as valiant and futile as the Light Brigade's charge that Alfred Lord Tennyson immortalized seventeen years earlier: into the maw of death.[41]

In characteristic irony, two brothers fought on opposing sides. Alexander Campbell bore the colors for the Seventy-Ninth New York, while his brother, James, fought as a lieutenant in the Charleston Battalion. Similarly, two units of Irishmen fought against each other: the Irish-born soldiers of Massachusetts's Twenty-Eighth Regiment, part of the famous Irish Brigade; and the Irish Volunteers, composed mostly of Irish Americans native to Charleston. The Massachusetts men got the worse of the fight, but worst of all were the Michiganders. In angry hyperbole, one surviving soldier described Tower Battery as being as formidable as Gibraltar, and after the battle he wondered about his regiment: "Look! Where is the nine hundred now? Five or six hundred are crippled or sleep beneath the soil of the South." General Benham's subordinates had desperately pleaded against the attack, and they undertook it with no hope of success and fuming in anger at the general. But they followed orders. After the debacle, Benham was immediately relieved of duty, and the Union troops withdrew entirely from James Island to watch, wait, and bide their time.[42]

The *Charleston Mercury* gloated in triumph, interpreting the result as a vindication of the "patrician" over "proletarian." The good breeding of southerners vanquished the "superior numbers" of the "insolent," "beaten and crouching" invaders, who were motivated by "the lying promises of their officers" and "lust of unstinted plunder." Though "the blood of our best gentlemen has been freely spilled," the newspaper concluded, triumphantly, "Noblesse oblige!"[43]

In September 1862, Beauregard, out of favor with the Confederate government, was reappointed to command the defense of the South Carolina, Georgia, and Florida coasts. The city celebrated the return of their "Napoleon in gray," the general who had led the bombardment of Fort Sumter. A contemporary portrait still hangs today in Charleston's city hall depicting Beauregard in dress uniform, gold epaulets, sword, standing before a draped flag; in the background, a cannon is pointed toward Fort Sumter. His arms are folded, but the posture recalls Napoleon's own famous pose with hand half-buried in his tunic.[44]

The city had good reason for its confidence in Beauregard. No Union troops approached the city all through the fall of 1862, and the Confederates won some little victories. In the middle of the night on January 30, 1863, just before James Louis Petigru took to his deathbed, two ironclad Confederate gunboats "slipped quietly" out of Charleston harbor, greased for battle. In the predawn fog they came upon their first victim, the Union's wooden steamer, *Mercidita*, and with a single cannon shot pierced the Union ship's boiler and beat her into submission. They engaged the ironclad *Keystone State*, and after a brief exchange of cannon fire, they disabled the Union ship and killed twenty of its sailors, but the *Keystone State* was able to limp out to sea with one paddle wheel working. The battle took place just beyond the harbor's bar, on the edge of the ocean, and when the triumphant vessels returned to harbor, the Confederate batteries on Morris Island, Sullivan's Island, and Fort Sumter saluted them. News of victory reverberated around the harbor. The Confederate commodore Ingraham thought he had sunk a few ships, and, though his report would prove too optimistic, the Confederates had damaged a few and chased all nine Union ships away.

General Beauregard declared that the Union's blockade had been broken, and he ferried the Spanish and French consuls out to observe the empty ocean beyond the mouth of Charleston's harbor, while the government in Richmond sent official notices telling England that Ingraham had broken the blockade. Under the arcane rules of the sea, once a blockade was broken neutral countries were no longer obliged to honor it. The blockading country could not legally seize foreign ships again until it had successfully reestablished the blockade and re-informed international governments: the whole process could take weeks, and in the interim English and French and Spanish ships would have the right to sail unmolested in and out of Charleston. So the little victory might have had important consequences for the supply of war matériel. It certainly "inspirit[ed] the defenders of Charleston greatly," and the citizenry was electrified. The excitement in the streets nearly matched the heady celebrations that had followed Beauregard's conquest of Fort Sumter two years earlier. But ultimately, it became clear that reports exaggerated the victory. Though the Union vessels had retreated to their base at Port Royal, most were able to return to their posts by the end of the day, reinforced by more Union ironclads. England would not recognize that the blockade had been broken at all. Nevertheless, the engagement demonstrated the vulnerability of the Federals and contributed to the general optimism of the civilians.[45]

No other officer in either army was so adored as Charleston loved Beauregard, with his "melancholy," Louisiana eyes and "barely perceptible French accent." Back in 1861, he had accepted the surrender of the Union's Major Anderson and conducted that first engagement with a most gentlemanly regard for the enemy, allowing Major Anderson, on surrendering the fort, to salute the Union's flag "as honorable Testimony to the gallantry and fortitude with which [he] and his command had defended their post," a chivalric flair that pleased Charleston.[46] Hailing from New Orleans, a brilliant military engineer and a fine strategist, Beauregard was just beyond the prime of life, forty-three and white-haired but extraordinarily handsome.

The women all watched him. Isabella Cheves, after spying the town's chief celebrity, thought Beauregard surprisingly, disarmingly, delightfully shabby: "he is not a very short man, but immensely stout with immensely broad shoulders & long legs." Through the second winter of the war, the general and his officers thrilled the locals with romance and gallantry. They held a "grand review" at Fort Sumter. The fort sits on an artificial island in the mouth of Charleston's harbor, and the gentry were rowed across the cold gray water in the stiff winter wind, women in their finest dresses and "red noses" enjoying a supper and dancing and champagne. "Of course," one young woman wrote, "Gen. Beauregard . . . was the most marked object present," but "all the men looked so well in their uniforms." Despite the cold air in the castle-like fort, the dancing warmed officers and ladies alike. There could hardly be a grander excuse for a ball than the chance to pair a belle with a dashing officer: war and romance courted each other in the shadowy, early evenings of Petigru's last winter. Strict mores seemed to have been loosened, as they often are in wartime, and one old lady regretted that the dancers looked "like Lovers embracing." Young women, the old lady complained, were no longer demure, and they looked "over [their] Lovers shoulder to see the affect on the audience."[47]

298 || America's Longest Siege

About the same time that officers and ladies danced at Fort Sumter, a more solemn celebration was held under "the great gnarled oaks" of Hilton Head Island. Colonel Higgenson of the 1st South Carolina Volunteers woke to this greeting from one of his sergeants: "I tink myself happy, dis New Year's Day, for salute my own Cunnel. Dis day las' year I was servant to a Cunnel ob Secesh." By ten in the morning a multitude of "colored women, with gay handkerchiefs on their heads, and a sprinkling of men, with that peculiarly respectable look which these people always have on Sundays" was gathering in the groves. A white preacher, Mr. Fowler, offered a prayer, and then to the hushed crowd and the rows of black soldiers, a local doctor, W. H. Brisbane, read aloud the Emancipation Proclamation.

> Then followed an incident [wrote Colonel Higgenson] so simple, so touching, so utterly unexpected and startling, that I can scarcely believe it on recalling. . . . There suddenly arose, close beside the platform, a strong male voice (but rather cracked and elderly), into which two women's voices instantly blended, singing, as if by an impulse that could no more be repressed than the morning note of the song-sparrow.

> > My Country, 'tis of thee
> > Sweet land of liberty,
> > Of thee I sing!

> Firmly and irrepressibly the quavering voices sang on, verse after verse. . . . I never saw anything so electric; it made all other words cheap; it seemed the choked voice of a race at last unloosed. Nothing could be more wonderfully unconscious; art could not have dreamed of a tribute to the day of jubilee that should be so affecting; history will not believe it; and when I came to speak of it, after it was ended, tears were everywhere.

Back in Charleston, the dances went on.[48]

No matter his success in the ladies' parlors, P.G.T. Beauregard knew what he was doing when he went to war. He had fought in the Mexican-American War, helped plan the assault on Mexico City, and had been wounded in battle. He had commanded the Confederates to victory at the first Bull Run, having a horse shot out from under him. Transferred to the west, he fought Ulysses S. Grant at Shiloh in Tennessee in the spring of 1862. One could hardly find a more martial character, with "fire beneath" his composed features ready to explode "into an impassioned defense of the Southern cause."[49]

Despite the breathless enjoyment of the young women and the perennial caution of the old, Charleston in 1863 was not quite so foolish as it had been in December 1860, when everyone anticipated a quick little war. By 1863 the city had a better idea of how great a power was the United States of America. "The Enemy," one local observed, "still hover around our Coast," and the apocalyptic predictions of Petigru, visions of "no peace forever," had taken on some validity. On Christmas Eve, Jacob Schirmer, a barrel manufacturer, mused that "war with all its gloomy horrors" was "as dark and portentous as ever. . . . 'Tis true the Almighty in many instances have smiled upon our armies and recently almost every Victory has been in our favor, but Oh how terrible has been the loss of Life, How many have been called to mourn the life of those they loved and how many more even at this moment are suffering under anxious expectation of what is yet to be realized." No one in Charleston had been spared the death and impoverishment of war, so the romance of champagne and officers' uniforms and dances was made more potent by the sting of sacrifice. Schirmer, at least, felt chastened: "If [God] should help our Country with Peace and again grant us prosperity," he prayed, "[m]ay we receive it with humble hearts and be duly greatful [*sic*] for all his mercies."[50]

Most were still confident that God smiled on the Confederacy. Nearly all of the soldiers along the coast were South Carolinians defending their homes on their own grounds, men familiar with the creeks and swamps, the alligators, the semitropical climate, and all the dangers of the Carolina Lowcountry. Morale was high. Francis Middleton, a son in one of Charleston's oldest prominent families, was stationed near Pocotaligo, guarding the railroad linking the city to Savannah. Riding picket and camping nearly in view of Union tents, he thought the prospect of the spring campaign looked excellent. "Within the last two days," he wrote in February, "two regiments and Preston's battery of artillery have arrived here, and another regiment is expected to arrive in a day or two. With such a force, considering the impenetrable nature of the country, we are sanguine of holding the road against 12 or 15 thousand Yankees, at least sufficiently long to allow of reinforcements reaching us."[51]

Hadn't Charleston good reason to feel safe under Beauregard's care? Everyone knew how important the city was to the Confederacy. Robert E. Lee insisted that "the loss of Charleston would cut [the Confederacy] off almost entirely from communications with the rest of the world and close the only channel through which we can expect to get supplies from abroad, now almost our only dependence." Lee wanted it defended "street by street and house by house as long as we have a foot of ground to stand upon." But no one thought it would come to that. Since Beauregard's return, defenses were strengthened, troops in his department rose to thirty thousand, cannons were rumbling in on the railroads. Fort Sumter was crowded with forty-four guns; across the harbor, Fort Moultrie had twenty-one; and the batteries on Sullivan's and Morris Islands had another twelve between them. Charleston had such supreme confidence in the general's ability to repulse the enemy that when, as a precaution, Beauregard called for the women to evacuate the city, the citizenry ignored his suggestion.[52]

Peering from St. Michael's steeple, the Confederate lookouts watched the jaws of the machine slowly closing on Charleston's defenses. A couple of miles north of town a breastwork crossed the neck like a dog's collar and defended the city from a land invasion. They had learned the lesson taught by the British in 1780 and fortified the area west of the Ashley River where the redcoats had crossed the river. Both a train and a horse bridge crossed the Ashley in 1863, about a mile or so northwest of St. Michael's Church, but the approaches to these bridges were well defended. If the Union tried to come down the peninsula, they would have to start from deep in the state's interior, doing a long end around the defenses, and the lines on the Neck would stop them well beyond shelling range of Charleston. A small force on the Neck, like the few Greeks at Thermopylae who stopped the Persian hordes, could hold off ten thousand.[53] Along the eastern edge of the peninsula flows the broad and deep reaches of the Cooper River, the terminus of a web of inland rivers and canals, and in the nineteenth century this barrier was unbridgeable and untenable for an invasion of the city. There was little need to defend Charleston's eastern shore, so only a few batteries spotted the deepwater wharf area, and in the river itself only Castle Pinckney stood sentinel, a little fort on a little island garrisoned by a little force of infantry and artillerymen.

When the Union attacked they would come from the southwest, using the Stono River, the back door to Charleston Harbor, and James Island. The greatest defenses faced this direction. At the tip of the peninsula a grand park, White Point Gardens, fronted the water, where soldiers encamped amid rows of white tents and the cannon of another battery. Across the harbor, a series of entrenched lines, fortified batteries, and coastal forts described a half circle around the southwestern approaches to the city. The bulk of these forces filled the lines west of the Ashley River, a rigid series of hardened defenses broken only by the tidal streams and marshes, which were themselves very effective defenses. Any invaders trying to cut through marsh would quickly be mired to its hips in thick, black, pungent goo, the "pluff mud" of the Lowcountry. One line of defensive works ran overland from the Ashley River marshes on the right to the swift currents of the Wappoo River on the left. The all-important railroad to Savannah bisected this western line of defense, and up this railroad reinforcements would hurry to Charleston whenever the attack came. Parallel lines of Confederate defenses crossed the wide farm flats of James Island, one from the Wappoo River and another from the Stono, both terminating in the brackish marshes between James Island and the sandy barrier beach islands that face the Atlantic. Most of these fortifications would have been invisible even from the heights of St. Michael's, hidden in the dense foliage lining the western banks of the Ashley. The only indication of the extensive trenches and earthworks was the wooden tower rising twelve stories high from the trees on James Island, the lookout that marked the location of the critical Tower Battery that had been the site of the Battle of Secessionville a year earlier.[54]

The most impressive defenses were the forts guarding the channels into the harbor: Fort Moultrie, the front door to Charleston, famous in the Revolution for repelling a British fleet, stood guard at the tip of

Sullivan's Island. To the southwest were Fort Johnson on the harbor side of James Island and Battery Wagner on Morris Island closer to the sea. In the middle of it all, the brick walls of Fort Sumter seemed to rise from the waters. So long as these forts stayed in Confederate hands, no Union ship, they believed, would dare try to enter the harbor.[55]

In the spring of 1863, Charleston seemed impregnable still, and the citizenry still romanticized slave civilization, imagined the war in mythic terms, and fixed their minds behind the ideological breastworks of white supremacy. Nearly all of the regiments defending the city were from South Carolina. Many of the soldiers and most of the officers lived in or near the city. They were defending their homes. If they retreated, if Charleston fell, Union soldiers would occupy their houses. The muddy boots of Federal troops would tramp the floors of their own parlors and kitchens, and officers from Massachusetts and Michigan and New Jersey would sleep in their sheets. There was no doubt in anyone's mind about the rightness of their cause. They were the Israelites, and the Federals were Philistines; they were Greeks, and their enemies were Persians. They were fighting, they told themselves, to preserve civilization from barbarians.[56]

The barbarians were closing in. In April, one month after James Louis Petigru was buried, a fleet of ironclads steamed to the mouth of Charleston's harbor, eager to test the defenses of those impregable forts. Four monitors led the flagship, *New Ironsides*, "one of the most powerful warships existing" with its fourteen 11-inch guns, and trailing behind were four more monitors, each firing 15-inch guns out of their revolving turrets. Altogether the fleet had thirty-two heavy guns, including three new Parrott rifled cannon. They faced the seventy-six guns of the Confederate batteries, mostly in Fort Moultrie on the north side of the harbor and Fort Sumter on the south, but none of the Confederate guns matched the Union's for power. The ships lingered beyond the bar until three in the afternoon, when the tides were right, and they sailed in a line into the teeth of the forts, blasting away even as the Confederates blasted away. The *Weehawken* was damaged by a torpedo mine detonated from shore by a long line. The *Keokuk*, which had two revolving turrets, steamed to within nine hundred yards of Fort Sumter, a daring move that hurt her badly, for nineteen shots pierced her hull, and she limped away only to sink the next day near Morris Island. For an hour and a half the artillery dueled at close range, the Confederates firing over 2,200 times and hitting their mark 520 times before Admiral Dupont, on the *Ironsides*, signaled the withdrawal. The Union ships swam back out of the harbor. A direct sea-assault, the Union decided, was untenable: five of the eight monitors were so damaged as to require extensive repairs, and none had made it into the inner harbor; and the Confederates quickly improved the guns and the strength of the walls at Fort Sumter.[57]

So the Federals decided they needed to take a more gradual approach. They landed more than ten thousand infantry, four hundred artillerymen, as well as six hundred engineers on Folly Island, which the Confederates had already abandoned because it was exposed to the ocean. All that stood between these troops and Fort Sumter was a Confederate battery on Morris Island, a desolate, sandy island. In the darkness in the middle of a hot July night in 1863, the Confederate captain Charles T. Haskell Jr. heard the sound of chopping wood from Little Folly, and his scouting party discovered Union barges in the Folly River. As the sun rose on the morning of the tenth, just a week after the Army of Northern Virginia was defeated at Gettysburg, the Confederates on Morris Island found that across the swift narrow steam of Lighthouse Inlet the brush had been cut down and forty-seven cannon were pointed at them, while a squadron of monitors arrived from the sea, turned their turrets, and began firing right away, supporting an invasion of Connecticut regiments, which quickly overran the outlying rifle pits, and then, supported by troops from New York, Maine, New Hampshire, and Pennsylvania, captured Confederate battery after battery. Under a "broiling sun" the Confederates trudged in retreat through the sandy ground toward Battery Wagner, the formidable fort at the very end of Morris Island. By nine o'clock the Union held three-quarters of the island, all the while their progress clearly visible to lookouts on Fort Sumter, for Morris Island is barely above sea level and nothing taller than the small trees bent by sea winds obstructed the view. The blue-clad soldiers stopped only when they came within range of the guns on Battery Wagner. The next day they made their first assault. Peering through the dawn's twilight, the Confederates waiting high up on the curtain walls of the battery could hear but could not see the troops advancing along the beach until they emerged from the gloom of night just a hundred yards away, row after row of soldiers in a narrow column pinched between the surf on their right and impenetrable marsh on their left. Among the defenders in the fort was the Charleston Battalion, led by Major David Ramsay, the descendant of the Revolutionary-era dissenter, a "splendid" example of "heroic intrepidity." The assault was doomed: those Connecticut soldiers who briefly mounted the earthworks were abandoned and "left clinging for protection to the exterior slope of the parapet." The Union lost 436 men killed, wounded, or captured.[58]

The assault was renewed at dusk on July 18, supported by gunships and cannon moved onto Morris Island. Thousands of shells fell on the fort, and at dusk the Union troops ran in quick time up the beach, led by the black soldiers of Fifty-Fourth Massachusetts Regiment. When they got within a thousand yards of the fort, they lay down in the sand, waiting for reinforcements to come up, but after half an hour they were "ordered to rise up and charge on the works." It was a doomed assault. "The Rebels opened on us with grape and canister [and] a thousand muskets," one survivor wrote home, "mowing our men down by the hundreds." They "rushed to within twenty yards of the ditches," Corporal Gooding reported, "and, as might be expected of raw recruits, wavered." They had received "a tremendous fire right in [their] faces," but they pressed on and in their "second advance they gained the parapet," where they fought bayonet to bayonet with the enemy. The standard-bearer was shot there, and Colonel Shaw "seized the staff . . . and in less than a minute after" he was killed too. "When the men saw their gallant leader fall, they made a desperate effort to get him out, but they were either shot down, or reeled in the ditch below." The Union troops faced "murderous fire from the batteries of the fort," and it seemed the shells from their own gunboats were still bursting around them. They finally retreated "in very good order," winning the admiration of the white troops, who spoke highly of them for showing such "great bravery."[59]

One of the boats supplying the troops on Morris Island was none other than the *Planter*, whose pilot was still the resourceful Robert

Smalls. During one hazardous mission, the *Planter* was nearly sunk by a Confederate battery near Secessionville. The ship's captain, Nichols, hid in the coal bin while Robert Smalls steered it to safety. After the incident, General Gillmore dumped the white officer and promoted Smalls to captain of the *Planter*.[60]

On the ground, General Gillmore gave up the direct approach and began the arduous but less dangerous task of dragging in forty-one siege guns. The Fifty-Fourth Massachusetts did much of the sapping work, digging parallels of trenches in the sand ever closer to the fort. Some of them blew up when their spades hit "torpedoes" buried by the Confederates, early versions of land mines. There were no more grand assaults by infantry, no more massed columns of Union soldiers. The Federal guns, the most advanced weaponry in the world, with longer range and accuracy than ever before, settled into the long grind of shelling the Confederate positions from thousands of yards away, both from Morris Island and from the sea, while the Confederates hunkered down in their bombproof shelters, an impersonal kind of battle, a steady, unrelenting, mechanized sound and fury, the gears of a trap slowly closing. It became "an engineering operation." The men of the Fifty-Fourth cleared away the rifle pits near to Wagner, and when they took over rebel trenches they found terrible-looking pikes with strange hooks on them meant to impale soldiers making an assault. This captured trench became the last parallel besieging the fort. Eight-inch mortars were brought in as well as "sap rollers," which were gigantic "sand filled, wooden, woven basket[s]" nine feet long and four feet high, tipped forward with metal levers inch by inch while troops with axes and short shovels dug sapping trenches behind. But luckily, the artillery did the dirtiest work now. Those in the "last parallel" were rained upon by the fragments of shell bursting in the fort, but they huddled low until the barrage ended. Fifty-eight days after the Union troops first landed on Morris Island, the weary Confederate garrison abandoned the fort, and one of the last Confederate evacuees noted wryly that he was "afeared of hell no more, it can't touch Wagner." The Fifty-Fourth Massachusetts were among those who entered the dismal place. "The smell of Wagner is really sickening," Gooding noted, "dead men and mules are profuse, some exposed to the rays of the sun, and others being half buried by earth thrown over them by our shot and shell during the bombardment."[61]

Next was Fort Sumter, and its bombardment began on August 17, 1863. The building was quickly reduced to rubble, but it withstood a second bombardment lasting 41 days and over eighteen thousand rounds of shell, which didn't end till December 6, 1863, after eight of the Union's guns had burst. The heavy shelling of Fort Sumter was renewed twice, and over the course of twenty months, over forty-six thousand projectiles were fired at the tiny artificial island, about thirty-five hundred tons of metal and explosives. Altogether, the Union poured heavy fire into the fort for 117 days, but "steady and desultory" fire went on for 280 days, as if the white clouds of thunder and salt-peter became permanent features of Charleston's horizon. The echoing of cannon beat like a metronome, a *memento mori*, always haunting the city, noticeable only on those odd days when the guns did not fire and a strange cave of silence filled the ear.[62]

Early in the fighting, before the Confederates evacuated Fort Wagner, during the first bombardment of Fort Sumter, a Union engineer, Colonel Edward Sorrel, set out from the Union-held portion of Morris Island to tramp through the muddy marsh on the harbor side of the island, looking for a patch of ground less soggy than the surrounding muck. The engineers constructed a wooden trestlework road two and a half miles long that terminated in a newly constructed battery supporting the eight-and-a-quarter-ton modified, eight-inch Parrott rifle nicknamed "The Swamp Angel." The battery itself was an apt symbol of the Union war machine: "307 tons of timber, 28 tons of lumber, 812 tons of sand and sandbags, and 8,958 days of labor, broken down among the engineer officers, engineer soldiers, infantry soldiers, and horse teams" contributed to the construction, which a contemporary English journal described as "one of the most important engineering works done by either army." The gun deck supported "123 pounds per square foot," while the foundation, an ingenious system of counterweights that made it a floating island, supported "513 pounds per square foot." The Swamp Angel was mounted in place. The gunners of the Eleventh Maine Regiment could not see Charleston, so they sent a scout deeper into the marsh, who spied St. Michael's steeple and relayed aiming instructions back to the battery, the first time in history that artillery was directed by compass bearing. The city was more than four and a half miles away, farther than any gun in the world had fired effectively before. "The age of science," as Corporal Gooding put it, would prove the "oft boasted impregnability of the defences of Charleston to be all moonshine."[63]

At 1:30 in the morning on August 22 most of the city slept soundly. The distant rumbling thunder at Fort Sumter, constant then for five straight days, was by this time a familiar drumbeat of war. A British magazine illustrator, Frank Vizetelly, had a room at the Charleston Hotel but could not sleep, so in the humid, sticky air he pulled out a volume of *Les Misérables* and began reading the long account of Waterloo, when a meteor like "a phantom brigade of cavalry galloping in mid-air" whirred overhead, followed by "a crash, a deafening explosion in the very Street on which my apartment was situate." The Union guns had reached Charleston. Vizetelly leapt to his feet, ran out the door, heard a second whirring and explosion, and knew the truth, as did the "terrified gentlemen rushing about in the scantiest of costume." One patron of the hotel "was trotting to and fro with one boot on and the other in his hand," while others panicked and a squad of black men in a fire company extinguished the blazes. The next day the hotels emptied and residents and visitors alike either packed the refugee trains or relocated above Calhoun Street. Hurling the 150-pound charges four and a half miles had shifted the Swamp Angel out of position, and it took a full day to get it ready to fire again. The bombardment continued the next night: nineteen more shells delivered, aimed at St. Michael's Church steeple and bursting in the heart of the city, before all suddenly stopped. The Confederates did not know it, but the Parrott rifle burst, blowing out its back end and hurling the barrel forward into the sand. Beauregard protested the inhumanity of shelling the city, especially with little official warning, but General Gillmore of the Union forces upbraided him, citing "the well established principle, that the commander of a place attacked, but not invested, having its avenues of escape open and practicable, has no right to expect any notice of an intended bombardment, other than that which is given by the threatening attitude of his adversary." Beauregard should have long ago evacuated noncombatants from Charleston, Gillmore reasoned. For two and a half years the Union had threatened the city. They had been fighting on Morris Island for the last forty days. What more notice did the city need?[64]

The bombardment did not really start again until mid-November, when an average of nine or ten shells a night fell into the city, always aimed at the center marked by St. Michael's steeple, and forcing a slow exodus away from the harbor. Beauregard moved his headquarters from lower Meeting Street to Broad and then finally, by December, north of Calhoun. The hotels closed. The businesses, banks, and newspapers relocated. The last service at St. Michael's was on November 19, a special service giving thanks for the Confederate victory in Tennessee at Chickamauga. When the congregation came out of the church, passing by the tomb of James Louis Petigru, a shell burst nearby, scattering them for cover. For the rest of the war the parish would meet at St. Paul's a couple of miles farther up the peninsula. Outraged that the Federals would fire on the city's churches, William Gilmore Simms attacked in verse:

> Ay, strike with sacrilegious aim
> The temple of the Living God;
> Hurl iron bolt, and seething flame
> Though aisles which holiest feet have trod;
> Tear up the altar, spoil the tomb,
> And raging with demoniac ire,
> Send down, in sudden crash of doom,
> That grand, old, sky-sustaining spire.

That last line was a fit metaphor for the hubris of the city, as if its own grand tradition of slavery held up the roof of heaven. If so, the sky was falling.[65]

On Christmas Day 1863, 150 shells poured into the city, igniting the largest fires of the entire siege, which were finally put out after great effort by the Negro fire companies. At year's end, twenty-seven thousand Union troops were encamped on Morris and Folly Islands, and Beauregard looked for a final assault. Despite all of this effort and attention, Charleston was already becoming irrelevant. Union troops staged another invasion of James Island, but it was a feint meant to draw troops away from Florida, where the real offensive threatened Jacksonville. The siege went on, shells fell on the city every day, the lower end of the peninsula became a ghost town, the defending regiments used up their supplies and went hungry, and still the shelling continued, only now the Union hardly even meant to take the city. The besiegers threatened the city in order to pin down as many Confederates as possible. In April, Beauregard left: Lee needed his help for the more urgent crisis in Virginia. The shelling in May was desultory, only fifteen shells a day, but the cumulative effect of months and months was devastating. The bombed-out cityscape below Calhoun Street was a land of the dead. Where giant masonry and steel buildings once stood, "shapeless wrecks" now crouched under the glare of the summer sun. Glass and broken bricks fertilized the streets, and the "grass and lank weeds were growing long." Rats and rabbits rooted in the rubble. Troops from both sides in Charleston were secretly shuttled away to more important scenes. In June, far to the north, Ulysses S. Grant dug into trenches outside Petersburg, where the Army of the Potomac faced the entrenched Army of Northern Virginia. In July, a skirmish on James Island proved that the depleted Union troops couldn't dislodge the depleted Confederates from Fort Johnson. It was the last attempt—if it could even be called an attempt—to advance on the city. Far more important than anything happening in Charleston were events in Georgia: Sherman, commanding the Armies of the Tennessee, Cumberland, and Ohio, took Atlanta in September and then started his march to Savannah. Still the thinned ranks of Union artillerists shelled Charleston, while the thinned ranks of Confederates manned their posts.[66]

By November 1864, Beauregard was back in charge in Charleston, but by then the endgame had commenced. Sherman accepted Savannah's surrender on December 21, and he offered the city to President Lincoln as a Christmas present. By January he was marching through South Carolina. When Sherman reached the Congaree River just outside Columbia, Beauregard ordered the evacuation of Charleston. The Confederates filled the big guns at the Battery with powder and blew them up. They blew up the ironclads at the wharves. They burned the bridge across the Ashley River. The train depot exploded accidentally, killing and maiming many refugees fleeing the city. The soldiers piled all the bales of cotton and lit them up, and the fire spread and wasn't put out until Union troops arrived on the morning of February 18.[67]

Steaming across the harbor with a proud brisk wave rolling off her bow was the *Planter*, recently refitted in Philadelphia, captained by Robert Smalls. Smalls had gone north with his ship, where he was a sensation, lecturing to societies, learning to read and write, charming everyone. He met President Lincoln and had campaigned for him in the 1864 election. Now he was ferrying the American flag and Union troops to take possession of Charleston. The exploded, scuttled wrecks of the Confederacy's ironclads, the *Palmetto State*, *Chicora*, and the *Charleston*, monstrous dragons leaking smoke and oil, were a sober greeting as the African America soldiers stepped onto Mill's Wharf and entered the abandoned city at about 10:00 a.m.: the Twenty-First U.S. Colored Troops and "several companies" of the storied Fifty-Fourth Massachusetts were among the first. Smoke was still drifting in the air from the fires; in fact, it was the Union soldiers and the black citizens who put them out. The Twenty-First paraded up Meeting Street in military order flying a flag emblazoned with "Liberty," and behind them came the Fifty-Fourth singing "John Brown's Body," surrounded by broken buildings. The slaves who woke up that morning free men and women cheered the black soldiers heartily. A few weeks later, Smalls came back, escorting the Union's General Saxton on an official inspection, and he had a chance to drift through the streets, astounded by the ruin of the city of his youth, the city of his bondage. His first job as a boy had been at the Planters Hotel. Its door was "splintered," and the broken glass windows were boarded up: an apt symbol for the way of life its name was meant to evoke. He and his wife, Hannah, had first lived above a stable on East Bay: it was obliterated entirely. At twenty-six, now able to read and write, entrepreneurial, wealthy, in possession of his master's house in Beaufort, in command of a navy ship, and an important part of the colossal effort that had freed the slaves, Robert Smalls represented a new South not only to the freed men and women of Charleston, who marveled at him as he walked the streets, but to the whites of the North who celebrated him in their newspapers.[68]

Just a couple of weeks after Charleston fell, after images of its destruction smoldered in the pages of northern magazines and in the correspondent reports in northern newspapers, Abraham Lincoln was inaugurated for his second term in office. "If God wills that [the war] continue," he said, near the conclusion of that short speech, "until all the wealth piled up by the bondman's two hundred and fifty years of unrequited toil shall be sunk, and until every drop of blood drawn with the lash shall be paid by another drawn with the sword, as was said three thousand years ago, so still it must be said, 'The judgments of the Lord are true and righteous altogether.'" He might have been thinking about Charleston, where the chandeliers and roofs and the very floorboards of the planters' mansions were spilled out into the streets, where the faces of the houses were no more than masks, their windows opening onto blue sky from both directions. This opulent city, the very symbol of the elegance and grace of a civilization, was little more than broken windows and masonry. Two hundred years of stolen labor and the laying on of the lash had been repaid by twenty long months of mortar shells, Greek fire, and 200-pound Parrott rifles.

On April 14, 1865, the *Planter*, with Smalls at the helm and its three decks packed with "three thousand blacks and whites, military and civilians, male and female," took the same route it had three years earlier, when Smalls and his family and friends escaped slavery. A contemporary account described "men and women of every grade of color possible to Southern civilization, the latter decorated with bandanas and turbans of flashy colors; comely and buxom girls attired in neat chintz; cadaverous and ragged beings holding about them their tattered garments; boys and girls whose jubilation exhibited itself in the most astonishing display of ivory." A different crowd than those ladies and gentlemen who had ferried out to dance in Beauregard's ball just two years earlier. This time through the harbor, Smalls did not try to sneak past Fort Sumter: the *Planter* moored at the wharf, and the passengers crowded into the fort, which was little more than a circle of rubble, for a ceremonial raising of the American flag. Less than a week earlier, Robert E. Lee had surrendered the Army of Northern Virginia to Ulysses S. Grant and the Army of the Potomac. The war was over. Abraham Lincoln had been invited to Charleston for the flag raising, but it was deemed still too dangerous for him to visit the South. Robert Anderson, the Union major who had surrendered the fort to Beauregard in 1861, now a general, spoke emotionally: "After four long, long years of war, I restore to its proper place this flag which floated here in peace. I thank God that I have lived to see this day." Henry Ward Beecher observed that "it is not the same flag." Before the war, "four million people had no flag. Today it rises and four million people cry out, behold our flag! No more slavery!" But Robert Smalls had little time for solemnities. He answered reporters' questions for an hour, entertaining them with his wit and surprising them with his intelligence, though why they should be surprised by that late date is a mystery.[69]

That evening, Abraham Lincoln, while attending the theater in Washington, was shot in the head by John Wilkes Booth. Booth was only twenty-seven years old. He was born in Maryland just one year after John C. Calhoun's famous "positive good" speech in the Senate, a fine example of the lost generation of white southerners. His part in this great American tragedy was written by Calhoun and Hammond and Hamilton and Rhett. Slavery, Booth insisted, was "one of the greatest blessings . . . that God ever bestowed on a favored nation," an opinion hardly expressed anywhere, let alone in a border state, before Calhoun made it respectable. Thus was Abraham Lincoln construed a tyrant by a man who advocated the enslavement of four million Americans.[70]

When finally General Sherman toured the ruins, he commented, "Anyone who is not satisfied with war should go and see Charleston, and he will pray louder and deeper than ever that the country may in the long future be spared any more war." As an afterthought, he suggested the city be left in ruins as an example, "so that centuries may pass away before that false doctrine" of secession "is again preached in our Union."[71]

CONCLUSION

||

Robert Smalls's flight from slavery in the *Planter* was spectacular, but aside from the theft of a $60,000 boat, thousands of other slaves lived the same adventure. In November 1861, Union troops occupied several islands protecting Port Royal Sound from the Atlantic Ocean, and in so doing they liberated about seven thousand slaves on the lucrative sea island cotton plantations. Shortly thereafter, another three thousand escaped to these sanctuaries on the very edge of the Confederacy. On January 1, 1863, Lincoln used his powers as commander in chief to liberate the slaves in all of the rebellious states as a matter of military expediency, but of course the Emancipation Proclamation could only be enforced where the Union held Confederate territory, so many slaves accelerated their attempts to cross the lines of battle. By early 1865, federal troops occupied islands up and down the Carolina coast, including Folly and Morris Islands near Charleston, and about thirty thousand slaves somehow made it to safety on these islands. By August, four months after Lee's surrender, the Union settled forty thousand freedmen and women on confiscated plantations along the coast under a program that came to be known by the popular phrase, "forty acres and a mule." By 1866, one in ten of South Carolina's former slaves owned and farmed their own land, and the other 90 percent had expectations of doing the same.

Very few of these had the advantages that Robert Smalls exploited —the marketable skill of a steamship pilot, prominent and influential contacts in Republican politics, or his extraordinary entrepreneurial drive—and they had to depend upon the government policies that would or would not dictate radical change in the terms of their farming. Even while the war was still being fought, civilian volunteers sailed down from the North to the sea islands to set up schools and to supervise the slaves in the management of what became, essentially, their own cotton plantations, experimenting in how to reorganize all of southern society, giving slaves a crash course in independent living. Not the least of these innovations were the several South Carolina regiments that mustered their ranks from freed slaves, including Higgenson's 1st South Carolina Volunteers. All soldiers earned money, many husbanded their savings to buy and stock farms when the war ended, some learned to read and write, and from their ranks emerged a number of leaders who would captain their communities and enter politics during Reconstruction. After the war, one of First South Carolina's soldiers became the state treasurer, and two sergeants, Prince Rivers and Henry Hayne, both served in the legislature. The demobilized soldiers, so far as Higgenson knew, were "generally prospering." The scheme that John Laurens had fought so hard to bring about in 1780 was finally made reality eighty years later.[1]

Reconstruction was nothing short of revolution: economic, social, and political upheaval. Though President Andrew Johnson, a Tennessean who sympathized with the dispossessed white planters, put a halt to the confiscation and redistribution of plantation land, the countryside nevertheless suffered a sea change as white owners and black workers adjusted to a system of contract labor. Those in domestic service demanded wages. A group of elite blacks sprang up in business and the professions—ministers, lawyers, doctors, teachers—some from the small class of free people of color whose existence grew more and more precarious during the first half of the century, others from the army, some from the North. Robert Smalls, for instance, prospered in the years after the war. Under the same program that redistributed hundreds of coastal plantations to the people who actually tilled the fields, Smalls bought the Beaufort home in which his mother had slaved for so many years. After the war, its previous owners sued to repossess their property, but the U.S. Supreme Court upheld the practice of confiscation, and so Smalls and his family lived in the two-story clapboard house at the corner of Prince and North Streets for the next ninety years. In the most remarkable of ironies, Smalls became the patron of his former owners, the McKee family, supporting them financially, finding the white children jobs, even taking the widowed mother into the house on Prince Street and caring for the destitute woman until her death in 1904. Smalls ran a steamship service, bought a general store, organized a railroad in Charleston, sat on the boards of corporations, solicited investors.[2]

One of Higgenson's soldiers told him that he was going to leave the South when the war ended: "dese yer Secesh," he reasoned, "will neber be cibilized in my time." Nor were they. Social changes shocked whites, especially in those areas of South Carolina—mostly along the coast—that were garrisoned by black Union soldiers. Whites who had spent their entire lives learning that the races were not equal suddenly had to share sidewalks with blacks. The sight of black men and black women wearing decent and even fancy clothes that had hitherto been the exclusive domain of the white caste, riding in carriages, shopping in stores elbow to elbow with white citizens seemed to the defeated Confederates a deliberate affront to their dignity. Ironically, in some respects, emancipation led to a greater separation of the races than obtained before. Whites maintained their sense of superiority by keeping exclusive company, and blacks, naturally enough, were happy to form societies beyond the surveillance of whites. Very quickly a color line emerged, privileging whites in public restaurants, conveyances, theaters, and so on. As blacks came into more political power after 1868, they fought these restrictions in the courts and in the legislature, but it was an ever-vigilant crusade, because whites resisted in practice the nondiscrimination demanded in law. The Ku Klux Klan emerged with the express purpose of resisting Reconstruction and maintaining white supremacy by terrorizing blacks and white Republicans. In South Carolina, whites refused to join mixed militia units, so the ninety thousand militiamen were all black. Miscegenation declined, which is not a surprise when we consider the adjusted power relation, the lack of opportunity for exploitation, and the fact that "young [white] gentlemen did not want mulatto children sworn to them at a cost of three hundred dollars apiece."[3]

But perhaps the most dramatic changes were in the realm of politics. Insomuch as South Carolina's politics had been dominated always by a handful of powerful families—essentially an oligarchy in the guise of a republic—the war effected a revolution. South Carolina became a democracy. In 1868, 85 percent of eligible black voters—sixty-nine thousand—voted unanimously for a new state constitution. In the same election, barely half of the fifty thousand white voters exercised their franchise; a slight majority voted against a constitutional convention. The Fifteenth Amendment, ratified in 1870, guaranteed the right to vote to all male citizens, turning the state's old ruling class into a tiny minority. In Robert Smalls's Beaufort, for instance, 80 percent of the electorate was African American, and those voters looked to Republican candidates and men from their own ranks for their leaders. Even so, politics were far more complex than one might suppose, as factions emerged among the Republicans, and these factions disputed the distribution of patronage jobs that inevitably followed victories at the polls. Increasingly, black candidates demanded more power from their white scalawag and carpetbagger allies. By 1872, blacks occupied 106 of 156 seats in Columbia as well as four of South Carolina's five seats in the U.S. House of Representatives.[4]

The Republican administration developed a scheme of high property taxes—as much as 25 percent—to support an array of public works, including, most significantly, free schools, a service that whites found particularly unnatural and distasteful. No doubt the large amounts of money flowing through government encouraged the corruption that the postwar Republican regimes are often faulted for, but even so it cannot be denied that African Americans made stunning progress while the Republicans were in power and while they were protected by federal troops. Reconstruction most emphatically exploded the positive good theory's contention that blacks were unsuited for independence and self-determination.

But, the revolution attempted by Reconstruction was abruptly halted by Rutherford B. Hayes, a Republican who owed his presidency to another devil's bargain. Most of the Southern states had been "redeemed" by 1876, which means that the exclusively white Democratic Party had gained the upper hand, reestablished white supremacy, and rolled back the civil and political rights of African Americans, through various dubious political practices and terror. The only Southern states still dominated by the Republicans were South Carolina, Louisiana, and Florida, and the electoral results in those states were contested, throwing the election into dispute. Whoever won those states would win the election. The Democrats promised to drop their challenge of the votes if Hayes promised to withdraw Union troops from the South, which he promptly did, betraying men like Robert Smalls who had delivered South Carolina into his camp.

The revolution was over. Reconstruction had lasted fewer than twelve years, hardly long enough to loosen the ideological siege on the minds of white Southerners but at least long enough to begin it. Hyman Rubin conducted a thorough study of white Republicans in South Carolina during Reconstruction, and his findings are surprising. Some of course were opportunists, tying their fortunes to the ascendant party. Some had been closet Unionists or even abolitionists, afraid to voice their convictions in the police state that preceded the war. But others were Confederates converted to the civil rights movement and willing to suffer ostracization and terror attacks by the Klan for the sake of social justice. They were truly heroic figures and in time might have pluralized white Southern politics.[5]

But twelve years was not time enough, and with the election of the Democrat Wade Hampton as governor in 1876, South Carolina joined the rest of the South in returning to the white supremacist mentality that had reigned since the 1830s. Jim Crow, Charleston's legacy, passed on through the generations. The South voted as a virtual solid block for Democratic candidates in the next seventeen presidential elections. The only significant exception was in 1928, when about half of the South went for Republican Herbert Hoover, and then they were likely motivated by anti-Catholic bigotry, for the Democrats had nominated Al Smith, whom the Klan denounced as un-American. Not until 1948 did the Democratic Party begin to lose its grip on the South, and that was because the party of Roosevelt and Harry S. Truman increasingly became associated with civil rights.

At the Democratic National Convention in 1948, Hubert Humphrey succeeded in pushing through a civil rights platform, and once again South Carolina took center stage in American politics. Just as it had seceded from the Democratic Party in 1860, South Carolina again abandoned the Democrats in order to preserve white supremacy. Governor Strom Thurmond led the exodus and was rewarded with the Dixiecrats' nomination for president. Thurmond was a character, every inch of him worthy of the worst antebellum South Carolina politicians. When he was twenty-two years old, he had sex with a six-teen-year-old black girl working for his parents, and the baby born of the affair was secreted away until his death, seventy-eight years later. He met his first wife when he was governor and she was a college student: he hired her as his personal secretary, a successful if unorthodox strategy of courtship. She died of a brain tumor and was replaced by Miss South Carolina of 1965, a twenty-two-year-old woman who also worked in his office. Thurmond was sixty-six and a U.S. senator when they married. In the 1948 presidential election, the fiery Thurmond famously declared, "There's not enough troops in the army to force the Southern people to break down segregation and admit the Nigra race into our theaters, into our swimming pools, into our homes, and into our churches." Strategically, he neglected to mention "our beds." The speech betrays the same nationalist ideology that Calhoun had foisted on the Lost Generation, including the notion that whites living in Southern states constituted a distinct and separate "people." Thurmond carried South Carolina, Alabama, Mississippi, and Louisiana and nearly lost the election for Truman.

It was the beginning of the end of the Democratic Party in the South. The Democrats promoted democracy and social justice; Southern whites eroded from its ranks, finding more congenial company among the Republicans. Thurmond backed Republican Dwight D. Eisenhower in the 1952 election and won his first seat in the Senate as a write-in candidate against the Democratic nominee. South Carolina, like most Southern states, had a one-party system, and usually the only contests that mattered were the Democratic primaries, so Thurmond's victory as a write-in was doubly remarkable. In response to *Brown v. Board of Education*, Thurmond penned *The Southern Manifesto*, a treatise modeled on the constitutional arguments of John C. Calhoun's defense of slavery. Thurmond excoriated the U.S. Supreme Court for overreach, arguing that it was legislating from the bench. Fully believing what he said, Thurmond appealed to "elemental humanity and common sense," indicatng that he thought that the principle of Jim Crow was positively good for both whites and blacks. Sounding like Calhoun warning against incendiary, fanatical, Northern abolitionists, he appealed for unanimity in the South against "the explosive and dangerous condition . . . inflamed by outside meddlers." He insisted that the Constitution protected the individual states' rights to enforce white supremacy. He pledged to "prevent the use of force" to execute the court's decision. And his peroration, ostensibly an appeal to nonviolence, nevertheless raises the malevolent specter of terror that would soon stalk the South: "In this trying period, as we all seek to right this wrong, we appeal to our people not to be provoked by the agitators and troublemakers invading our States and to scrupulously refrain from disorder and lawless acts."[6] Thurmond's most dramatic moment came a year later, when he filibustered the Senate for over twenty-four hours—the longest harangue on record—to delay vote on the first civil rights bill since Reconstruction. He was defeated, and try as he might, he could not prevent the great advances in civil rights enacted in the next decade—and championed by the Democratic president from Texas, Lyndon Johnson.

But Thurmond could bolt the party, which he did just before Johnson's election in 1964, two years after Ronald Reagan switched from the Democrats to the Republicans. Reagan exploded onto the national scene in his famous televised campaign speech for Barry Goldwater, what his devotees today call affectionately and simply, "The Speech." Reagan's conversion was not motivated by bigotry, nor was Goldwater cut from the same cloth as Thurmond; nevertheless, Goldwater opposed the Civil Rights Act of 1964, which won him the Deep South, from Louisiana to South Carolina, the only states besides Goldwater's own Arizona that voted Republican. Richard Nixon could read these signs, and he made his deal with the devil in 1968, a modern version of the deal that Sherman cut with Rutledge in 1787 and Hayes with the Democrats in 1876. It is now known by the moniker, "the Southern strategy," a cynical courtship of white Southern voters by appealing to their racism. But in 1968 Nixon lost the Deep South to George Wallace, who ran on bigotry, and he hardly needed the South's help in 1972, when he routed George McGovern. Courting racists did not really start paying dividends for the Republicans until Ronald Reagan's 1980 victory over Jimmy Carter. Reagan's first appearance after winning the Republican nomination was in Philadelphia, Mississippi, notorious for the 1964 murders of civil rights activists James Chaney, a black man from Meridian; and Andrew Goodman and Michael Schwerner, two New York "agitators and troublemakers invading our states," to apply Thurmond's phrase. Standing not far from the earthen dam where those martyrs were buried, Reagan announced his support for "states' rights," tacitly aligning himself with segregationists and wooing Southern whites into the party of Abraham Lincoln. Let us hope that the election of 2012 has taught the Republican Party to put to rest the legacy of this republic's original sin, has convinced them that the "Southern" strategy is over, that no longer can a minority of racists leverage the domestic policy of United States.

But the shadow of the 1830s seems to linger. Nearly everywhere—and certainly in South Carolina—cynical politicians are trying once again to disqualify black voters. As in the days of Denmark Vesey, torture is thought by many to be a legitimate means of extracting testimony. As in the days of Calhoun, federal laws are openly flouted. Shortly after President Obama's reelection in November 2012, South Carolina legislators introduced a bill called, ironically enough, "The Freedom of Health Care Protection Act." Just as Calhoun had tried to nullify the federal tariffs in the 1830s, this act seeks to "render null and void certain unconstitutional laws enacted by the Congress of the United States taking control over the health insurance industry and mandating that individuals purchase health insurance." It doesn't matter what the Supreme Court said about it: the South Carolina legislature will determine what is and is not constitutional, and they would exercise this judgment through nullification. Several other states are considering similar measures. Conservative talk radio is now full of nullification, those gleeful pundits somehow encouraged by the tragic history of South Carolina. Sounding like Strom Thurmond's threats to prevent the execution of *Brown v. Board of Education*, the Freedom of Health Care Protection Act would make it a felony for anyone to execute certain provisions of Obamacare in South Carolina. Similarly, Charleston County Sheriff Al Cannon recently declared that he will not enforce any federal law that he thinks violates the Second Amendment right to bear arms. Other "rural lawmen and lawmakers" have "vowed to ignore" federal laws that they think violate "constitutional rights."[7] Everywhere we hear the old bogus talk of defiance, resistance to tyranny, and devotion to the Constitution.

The damage slavery did to the American mind has not fully healed even now. The flag of our federal government may still fly over Fort Sumter, where rangers of the National Park Service teach history to school children, requiems over the dead. Ten-year-olds have made jungle gyms of the Parrott rifles and the cannon on Charleston's Battery. Brightly clad adults pose to get their pictures taken. Fort Johnson on the edge of James Island is gone. The old batteries at Secessionville are lost in the woods, strange ridges of high ground grown over with trees and thickets. The impenetrable walls of Wagner, where so many squandered lives were lost, have melted into the sands of Morris Island. Time has leveled so many of the old siege sites, and the others are diminished by the regiments of tourists marching through them with their noses stuck in guidebooks.

But the siege guns still echo. James Hamilton, John C. Calhoun, and William Gillmore Simms still walk our streets, and their voices are getting louder. If we let them go on pretending much longer that they are the voices of reason, they'll gain ground and ground again until they shame all conscience into silence. The demagogues will divide one people in two.

NOTES

||

INTRODUCTION

1. William J. Grayson, *James Louis Petigru: A Biographical Sketch* (New York: Harper & Brothers, 1866), 169. *Charleston Courier*, March 11, 1863.

2. *Charleston Courier*, March 11, 1863. Letter, Francis Middleton to Harriott Middleton, March 15, 1863; Letter, Isabella Cheves to her children, November 1862, both in: *Harriott Kinloch Middleton Family Correspondence, 1861–1865*, South Carolina Historical Society. For self-satisfaction, see "Preface" to *Memorial of the Late James L. Petigru, Proceedings of the Bar of Charleston, S.C., March 25, 1863* (New York: Richardson and Company, 1866), 5–6. For magnanimity, see Grayson, *James Louis Petigru*, 151.

3. Letter, Henry Laurens to John Laurens, August 14, 1776. *The Papers of Henry Laurens*, ed. Philip Hamar and George Rogers, vol. 11 (Columbia: University of South Carolina Press, 1968–2003), 224–25. References to these volumes will be cited as *PHL*. "Notice" in Preface, in Henry Laurens, *South Carolina Protest against Slavery* (New York: G. P. Putnam, 1861), 5–6.

4. "Extract from a Private Letter," *New York Tribune*, November 27, 1860, quoted in Lillian A. Kibler, "Unionist Sentiment in South Carolina in 1860," *Journal of Southern History* 4 (August 1938): 362, 360. All discussions of the political crisis take it for granted that South Carolina wanted to secede; the only question was whether it would or would not wait for other slave states to join her. See also Freehling, *The Road to Disunion*, vol. 2, *Secessionists Triumphant, 1854–1861* (New York: Oxford University Press, 1990), 375–94. *New York Tribune*, December 11, 1860. Kibler, "Unionist Sentiment," 361. *Census of the City of Charleston, South Carolina, For the Year 1861*, prepared by Frederick A. Ford (Charleston: Evans and Cogswell, 1861), 7–11.

5. William H. Pease and Jane H. Pease, *James Louis Petigru: Southern Conservative, Southern Dissenter* (Athens: University of Georgia Press, 1995), 136. See also Petigru to Susan King, July 12, 1849, in James Petigru Carson, *Life, Letters, and Speeches of James Louis Petigru, the Union Man of South Carolina* (Washington, DC: W. H. Lowdermilk & Co., 1920), 278.

6. Pease and Pease, *James Louis Petigru*, 156.

7. Letter, JLP to Edward Everett, January 26, 1861, Petigru Correspon-

dence, Library of Congress, quoted in Pease and Pease, *James Louis Petigru*, 156; and in Maury Klein, *Days of Defiance: Sumter, Secession, and the Coming of the Civil War* (New York: Alfred A. Knopf, 1997), 145–46. See also Carson, *Petigru*, 364. After secession, Petigru was somewhat supportive of the establishment of the Confederate States of America, but only because he believed that South Carolina had irrevocably dissolved the Union and that the other southern states were sure to inhibit the headlong idiocy of South Carolina's local leaders. In this he was clearly right. In the vain flush of its declared independence, South Carolina was spoiling for a fight, and Governor Pickens precipitously planned to bombard Fort Sumter. The new national government delayed, trying desperately to negotiate a bloodless resolution with Lincoln, and the arrival of the Confederate general, Beauregard, to command the district put the southern forces into competent hands that were loathe to fire cannon on the flag of the United States. In fact, Beauregard knew well the Union commander at Charleston, Major Anderson, and was reluctant to fire on him. See E. Milby Burton, *The Siege of Charleston, 1861–1865* (Columbia: University of South Carolina Press, 1970), 26–28.

8. "Preface" to *Memorial*, 3–4.

9. Ibid., and Pease and Pease, *James Louis Petigru*, 156.

10. James Oscar Farmer Jr., *The Metaphysical Confederacy: James Henly Thornwell and the Synthesis of Southern Values* (Macon, GA: Mercer University Press, 1986), 26. Emma Holmes, *The Diary of Miss Emma Holmes, 1861–1866*, ed. John F. Marszalek (Baton Rouge: Louisiana State University Press, 1979), 55. Mary Chesnut, *Mary Chesnut's Civil War*, ed. C. Vann Woodward (New Haven, CT: Yale University Press, 1981), 379.

11. W. Chris Phelps, *The Bombardment of Charleston, 1863–1865* (Gretna, LA: Pelican, 2002), 11, 19–21, 27–28. Quotation from p. 28.

CHAPTER 1

1. James Oglethorpe, "An Account of the Negroe Insurrection in South Carolina," in *Colonial Records of the State of Georgia*, vol. 22, pt. 2 (Athens, GA: Franklin Printing and Publishing Col, 1904–1989), 232–36.

2. Ibid., 232–33, and Peter Wood, *Black Majority: Negroes in Colonial South Carolina From 1670 through the Stono Rebellion* (New York: Alfred A. Knopf, 1974), 309–14.

3. *The St. Augustine Expedition of 1740: A Report to the South Carolina General Assembly Reprinted from the Colonial Records of South Carolina* (Columbia: South Carolina Department of Archives, 1954), 40. A comprehensive report of an invetigative commitee appears in J. H Easterby, *Journal of the Commons House of Assembly* vol. 3 (Columbia: Historical Commission of South Carolina, 1951) (July 1, 1741), 78–247.

4. Robert Pringle to James Henderson, December 17, 1740, in *The Letterbook of Robert Pringle*, ed. Walter B. Edgar, vol. 1 (Columbia: University of South Carolina Press, 1972), 277, quoted in Robert Olwell, *Masters, Slaves, & Subjects: The Culture of Power in the South Carolina Low Country, 1740–1790* (Ithaca, NY: Cornell University Press, 1998), 27.

5. Robert M. Weir, *Colonial South Carolina: A History* (Millwood, NY: KTO Press, 1983), 196. James Oglethorpe, "Account of the Negroe Insurrection in South Carolina," 234. Olwell, *Masters, Slaves, & Subjects*, 23, 26–27. Whites stole labor from each slave at the rate of between eight and ten pounds sterling annually (Olwell, *Masters, Slaves, & Subjects*, 188).

6. James Barry Hawkins, *Alexander Garden: The Commissary in Church and State* (Ph.D. diss., Duke University, 1981), 166–67. Arnold A. Dollimore, *George Whitefield: The Life and Times of the Great Evangelist of the Eighteenth-Century Revival*, vol. 1 (Edinburgh: Banner of Truth Trust, 1970), 491–92.

7. Unless otherwise noted, this summary of Charles Town's early days is based on Walter J. Fraser Jr., *Charleston! Charleston!: The History of a Southern City* (Columbia: University of South Carolina Press, 1989), 1–38. Alexander S. Salley, ed. *Narratives of Early Carolina 1960–1708* (New York: Barnes and Noble, 1939, 1967), 116–20.

8. In 1696, thirty families from Maine tried to do just that near Biggin Swamp on the Cooper River. They refused to buy slaves and reproduce the plantation system already established. After a dozen years the experiment failed. See Edward Ball, *Slaves in the Family* (New York: Farrar, Straus and Giroux, 1998), 92.

9. See J. E. Buchanan, *The Colleton Family and the Early History of South Carolina and Barbados 1646–1775* (Ph.D. diss., University of Edinburgh, 1989), UMI, 39. One of the proprietors of the Carolina colony was John Colleton, a Barbadian planter. Buchanan demonstrates that making money, not the siphoning off of surplus white population or other possible emigration pressures, motivated the expedition to Carolina. See also Meaghan N. Duff, *Designing Carolina: The Construction of an Early American Social and Geographical Landscape, 1670–1719* (Ph.D. diss., The College of William and Mary in Virginia, 1998), UMI, 26–27. Weir, *Colonial South Carolina*, 61. Gary Livingston Hewitt, *Expansion and Improvement: Land, People and Politics in South Carolina and Georgia, 1690–1745* (Ph.D. diss., Princeton University, 1996), UMI, 38.

10. Unless otherwise noted, the following discussion of the origins of racial prejudice in America is a summary of Winthrop D. Jordan, *The White Man's Burden: Historical Origins of Racism in the United States* (New York: Oxford University Press, 1974), 29–54. Quotations from 32 and 33.

11. See David H. Corkran, *The Carolina Indian Frontier* (Columbia: University of South Carolina Press, 1970), 1–19. Quotation from Weir, *Colonial*

South Carolina, 27; Hewitt, *Expansion and Improvement*, 25–27; Richard Seabrook Keating, *From Conflict to Culture: A Literary Study of Colonial South Carolin's Economic Societies, 1670–1750* (PhD diss., University of North Carolina at Chapel Hill, 1993), 27.

12. Unless otherwise noted, for this description of Charles Town in the 1730s, see Fraser, *Charleston! Charleston!*, 26, 45–66. H. Roy Merrens, ed., *The Colonial South Carolina Scene: Contemporary Views, 1697–1774* (Columbia: University of South Carolina Press, 1977), 20–21. Weir, *Colonial South Carolina*, 145. For "over 500," Fraser, *Charleston! Charleston!*, 63.

13. Fraser, *Charleston! Charleston!*, 46, 61, and 55.

14. Olwell, *Masters, Slaves, & Subjects*, 34–35.

15. Fraser, *Charleston! Charleston!*, 58–63. See David S. Shields, *Civil Tongues & Polite Letters in British America* (Chapel Hill: University of North Carolina Press, 1997), 55–64, 104–26. For a résumé of Charles Town's societies and clubs, see Frederick P. Bowes, *The Culture of Early Charleston* (Chapel Hill: University of North Carolina Press, 1942), 119–21. Shields, *Civil Tongue*, 159.

16. Jordan, *White Man's Burden*, 15–18. For the stereotypes involved in colonization, see Edward Said's groundbreaking *Orientalism* (New York: Vintage Books, 1978).

17. See Wood, *Black Majority*, 19.

18. Jordan, *White Man's Burden*, 53, 52.

19. J. H. Easterby, ed., *Journal of the Commons House of Assembly*, vol. 2 (Columbia Historical Commission of South Carolina, 1951–), December 11, 1739, 97–98. See Olwell, *Masters, Slaves, & Subjects*, 25.

20 Dollimore, *George Whitefield*, 116, 202–3. These phrases are from a sermon published in 1739 and quoted in Dollimore, *George Whitefield*, 116.

21. Hawkins, 60-69, 65, 141.

22. Hawkins, *Alexander Garden*, 145–47.

23. George Whitefield. *George Whitefield's Journals, 1737–1741: To Which Is Prefixed His Short Account (1746) and Further Account (1747)*, facsimile reproduction edition of William Wale in 1905 with an Introduction by William V. Davis (Gainesville, FL: Scholars Facsimile and Reprints, 1969), 151. See Hawkins, *Alexander Garden*, 145–47.

24. Alan Gallay, "Planters and Slaves in the Great Awakening," in *Masters and Slaves in the House of the Lord: Race and Religion in the American South 1740–1870*, ed. John B. Boles (Lexington: University Press of Kentucky, 1988), 20. Alexander Garden, *Regeneration and the Testimony of the Spirit: Being the Substance of Two Sermons lately Preached in the Parish Church of St. Philip's, Charles-Town, in South Carolina: Occasioned by Some Erroneous Notions of Certain Men Who Call Themselves Methodists* [1740; reprint, Boston: T. Fleet, 1741]. Quotation in Gallay, "Planters and Slaves," 21n6. Jeffrey Robert Young identifies Garden's let-

ter as the first "public justification of slavery" in the Deep South (*Domesticating Slavery: The Master Class in Georgia and South Carolina, 1670–1837* [Chapel Hill: University of North Carolina Press, 1999], 31).

25. Unless otherwise noted, this sketch of Bryan derives from the excellent study, Harvey H. Jackson, "Hugh Bryan and the Evangelical Movement in Colonial South Carolina," *William and Mary Quarterly* 43 (October 1986): 594–614. This quotation is from 596.

26. Hugh Bryan and Mary Hutson, *Living Christianity Delineated in the Diaries and Letters of Two Eminently Pious Persons Lately Deceased, viz. Mr. Hugh Bryan and Mrs. Mary Hutson* (Boston: Hastings, Etheridge, and Bliss, 1809), 50. *South Carolina Gazette*, January 1–8, 1741.

27. See Jackson, "Hugh Bryan," 603n21.

28. Cf. Easterby, *Journal of the Commons House of Assembly*, vol. 3, 380–82, and Jackson, "Hugh Bryan," 606. Eliza Lucas Pinckney, *The Letterbook of Eliza Lucas Pinckney, 1739–1762*, ed. Elise Pinckney (Chapel Hill: University of North Carolina Press, 1972), 30. "Extract of a Letter from South Carolina," *Boston Weekly Post-Boy*, May 3, 1742, quoted in Jackson, "Hugh Bryan," 608.

29. Easterby, *Journal of the Commons House of Assembly*, vol. 3, 461. Pinckney, *Letterbook of Eliza Lucas Pinckney*, 30.

30. Easterby, *Journal of the Commons House of Assembly*, vol. 3, 462.

31. Alexander Garden, *Six Letters to the Rev. Mr. George Whitefield* (Boston: T. Fleet, 1740), 52.

32. Olwell, *Masters, Slaves, & Subjects*, 120–21.

33. See Wood, *Black Majority*, 157–66.

34. Garden, *Six Letters*, 53. Gallay sees these years—during the Great Awakening—as the start of paternalism in the South, which pushes the ideology back much further than Eugene Genovese does in *In Red and Black: Marxian Explorations in Southern and Afro-American History* (New York: Pantheon Books, 1971) and *Roll, Jordan, Roll: The World the Slaves Made* (New York: Pantheon Books, 1974). See Gallay's "The Origins of Slaveholders' Paternalism: George Whitefield, the Bryan Family, and the Great Awakening in the South," *Journal of Southern History* 53 (August 1987): 369–94. This is a slightly expanded version of his "Planters and Slaves in the Great Awakening."

35. Olwell, *Masters, Slaves, & Subjects*, 30.

36. Ibid., 32.

CHAPTER 2

1. Letter to James Crokatt, June 3, 1747, in *PHL*, vol. 1, 3.

2. *PHL*, vol. 1, 12–22.

3. David Duncan Wallace, *The Life of Henry Laurens, with a Sketch of the*

Life of Lieutenant-Colonel John Laurens (New York: G. P. Putnam and Sons, 1915), 1–2.

4. Letter to William Flower, July 10, 1747, in *PHL*, vol. 1, 23.

5. Unless otherwise noted, this summary of the Laurenses' history derives from Wallace's *Life of Henry Laurens*, 1–14. Wallace depends largely on a few of Henry Laurens's letters, in particular one of February 25, 1774, to the Laurences of Poitiers, France (which Wallace reprints on 12-14 n.3); as well as municipal records in New York and Huguenot sources. Edwin G. Burrows and Mike Wallace, *Gotham: A History of New York City to 1898* (New York: Oxford University Press, 1998), 95. David Duncan Wallace puts the family's move in either 1715 or 1716. As I will explain below, the Yemassee War makes the earlier date highly unlikely.

6. David Duncan Wallace, *Life of Henry Laurens*, 11.

7. Letter, Laurens to Messieurs and Madame Laurence, February 25, 1774, *PHL*, vol. 9, 309–11. Weir, *Colonial South Carolina*, 248–56; quotation from 253. For "every virtuous pursuit," see David Ramsay, *Ramsay's History of South Carolina, from Its First Settlement in 1670 to the Year 1808*, vol. 2 (Newberry, SC: W. J. Duffie, 1858), 253. See also Daniel J. McDonough, *Christopher Gadsden and Henry Laurens: The Parallel Lives of Two American Patriots* (Sellinsgrove, PA: Susquehanna University Press, 2000), 16.

8. Wallace, *Life of Henry Laurens*, 14.

9. Cf. Samuel C. Smith, "Henry Laurens: Christian Pietist," *df* 100 (April 1999), 161.

10. For the best discussion of Laurens's religious beliefs, see Smith, "Henry Laurens: Christian Pietist," 143–70.

11. The inventory is a bit sketchy on the value of a number of items, but a conservative tally tops £5500. I excluded the three slaves that were left to Henry, presumably Colonel and one of the mother/daughter pairs, who together were valued at £600; see *PHL*, vol. 1, 369–81 and 57. The earliest recorded use of "store" in the modern sense was in Pennsylvania in 1740 (cf. the *Oxford English Dictionary*). For "as they seem," HL to Richard Grubb, June 23, 1747, *PHL*, vol. 1, 8.

12. HL to Alexander Watson, August 24, 1748, *PHL*, vol. 1, 171 and 173n6.

13. Because of British politics, the tax actually took the form of a sales tax on the purchase of imported slaves rather than an import duty, but the effect was the same. In 1744, the tax was allowed to lapse, yet in the depressed economy only four insignificant cargoes of slaves were brought to Charles Town (Elizabeth Donnan, *Documents Illustrative of the History of the Slave Trade to America*, vol. 4 [Washington, DC: Carnegie Institution of Washington, 1930–1935], 296. The tax was reenacted for three years in 1746 without controversy.

14. Winthrop D. Jordan, *The White Man's Burden: Historical Origins of Racism in the United States* (New York: Oxford University Press, 1974), 22. Ruth Scarborough, *The Opposition to Slavery in Georgia Prior to 1860* (Nashville, TN: George Peabody College for Teachers, 1933; reprinted in 1968), 23–57.

15. Cf. Donnan, *Documents*, vol. 3, 485–87. *PHL*, vol. 1, 229n2.

16. On the reopening of the slave trade, Donnan remarks that "here arises one of the puzzles in the South Carolina legislation" (*Documents*, vol. 4, 301n1). J. H. Easterby, ed., *Journal of the Commons House of Assembly* vol. 9 (Columbia: Historical Commission of South Carolina, 1951–), 311. For the tax policy in the Commons House, see Weir, *Colonial South Carolina*, 125.

17. Easterby, *Journal of the Commons House of Assembly*, vol. 9, 363 and 355.

18. Robert Pringle, Letter to Andrew Pringle, March 23, 1743, in *Letterbook of Robert Pringle*, ed. Walter B. Edgar, vol. 3 (Columbia: University of South Carolina Press, 1972), 517, typed copy in South Carolina Historical Society; quoted in *PHL*, vol. 1, 176n.

19. Easterby, *Journal of the Commons House of Assembly*, vol. 9. Jack Greene extensively examines this struggle, though he does not consider the issue of slavery, in *The Quest for Power: The Lower Houses of Assembly in the Southern Royal Colonies, 1689–1776* (Chapel Hill: University of North Carolina Press, 1963), 51–72.

20. For Achilles, see *PHL*, vol. 1, 1 and note 3; and Laurens to Gadsden, December 28, 1747, in *PHL*, vol. 1, 93–95. For John Laurens's view of slavery, see HL to JL, September 21, 1779, quoted in Wallace, *Life of Henry Laurens*, 451. For James's view, see Wallace, *Life of Henry Laurens*, 192.

21. *PHL*, vol. 1, 178n6. HL to George Austin, February 11, 1749, in *PHL*, vol. 1, 208–9. HL to Foster Cunliffe, January 20, 1749, in *PHL*, vol. 1, 202. HL to James Pardoe, February 21, 1749, in *PHL*, vol. 1, 213.

22. See, for example, HL to Richard Farr, February 18, 1749, in *PHL*, vol. 1, 211–12. For Laurens's script, see HL to George Austin, February 11, 1749, in *PHL*, vol. 1, 208.

23. For Crokatt's scruples, see HL to Isaac Hobhouse, March 16, 1749, in *PHL*, vol. 1, 227. Laurens attributes Crokatt's decision to his being "fully employ'd with Business on Commission & chuses to be confin'd in that way," which may have been the case. But such polite excuses typically allowed a merchant to decline business without accusing a colleague of sinful activity. Laurens himself similarly obfuscated nearly a quarter of a century later, after he quit the slave trade. For an example of how insubstantial such images of solidity could be, see HL to Henry Carver, March 6, 1749, in *PHL*, vol. 1, 217–18. For Pardoe's business, see HL to George Austin, February 11, 1749, in *PHL*, vol. 1, 208, and HL to James Pardoe, January 23, 1749, in *PHL*, vol. 1, 206.

24. *South Carolina Gazette*, July 29 and August 5, 1751, quoted in Donnan, *Documents*, vol. 4, 302n10. The prices and numbers of slaves sold are cal-

culated from the firm's "wastebook"; see Donnan, *Documents*, vol. 4, 307–9. For standard fees, see Leila Sellers, *Charleston Business on the Eve of the American Revolution* (Chapel Hill: University of North Carolina Press, 1934), 140, and Wallace, *Life of Henry Laurens*, 75.

25. Warner O. Moore Jr., *Henry Laurens: A Charleston Merchant in the Eighteenth Century, 1747–1771* (Ph.D. diss., University of Alabama, 1974), 300–304. HL to Charles Gwynn, June 12, 1755, in *PHL*, vol. 1, 263. This letter actually was posted after Laurens discovered what had happened to the *Emperor*. HL to Wells, Wharton, & Doran, May 27, 1755, in *PHL*, vol. 1, 259; their correspondence with the ship's captain, Charles Gwynn, "one of the most famous and most successful of the captains of Bristol privateers," seems to indicate that Austin and Laurens had chartered the ship, for Laurens speculates that he might outfit it as a privateer in case war breaks out with France (*PHL*, vol. 1, 259–61 [the quotation is from 259n6]). For the average price of slaves in the summer of 1755, see HL to Richard Prankerd & Co., July 5, 1755, in *PHL*, vol. 1, 287. For Gwynn's sales, see HL to John Knight, June 26, 1755, in *PHL*, vol. 1, 270–71. For Laurens's losses, see HL to Devonsheir, Reeve, & Lloyd, July 4, 1755, in *PHL*, vol. 1, 286. HL to Charles Gwynn, June 12, 1755, in *PHL*, vol. 1, 263, and HL to Peter Furnell, June 12, 1755, in *PHL*, vol. 1, 262.

26. For these calculations, see Wallace, *Life of Henry Laurens*, 75, 78, and Sellers, *Charleston Business*, 140. Ball puts the estimate at £156,000. Prices of slaves in good years rose as high as £550 currency and even higher.

27. Wallace, *Life of Henry Laurens*, 58n.

28. Ibid., 95.

29. Letter, HL to Joseph Brown, October 28, 1765, in *PHL*, vol. 5, 29–32. See Wallace, *Life of Henry Laurens*, 116–22.

30. Wallace, *Life of Henry Laurens*, 125–30.

31. Edward Ball's 1998 *Slaves in the Family*, which won the National Book Award, digs through the murky and repressed history of the Ball family. Wallace, *Life of Henry Laurens*, 60–66. HL to George Appleby, September 26, 1769, in *PHL*, vol. 7, 15–151.

32. HL to Alexander Garden, February 19, 1774, in *PHL* vol. 9, 295. See also HL to Ann Foster, October 24, 1771, in *PHL*, vol. 8, 16. Wallace, *Life of Henry Laurens*, 464.

CHAPTER 3

1. For a thorough discussion of the Somerset case, see Steven M. Wise, *Though the Heavens May Fall: The Landmark Trial That Led to the End of Human Slavery* (Cambridge, MA: De Capo, 2005). The quotation is from p. 4. The *Chronicle* quotation is quoted in *PHL*, vol. 8, 436n.

2. HL to John Lewis Gervais, May 29, 1772, in *PHL*, vol. 8, 353.

3. JL to James Laurens, April 17, 1772, Kendall Collection, quoted in Gregory Massey, *John Laurens and the American Revolution* (Columbia: University of South Carolina Press, 2000), 32–33.

4. JL to HL, March 29, 1775, in *PHL* vol. 10, 93–94.

5. Wallace, *Life of Henry Laurens*, 205–6.

6. Ibid., 209.

7. JL to HL, September 4, 1775, in *PHL*, vol. 10, 361–62.

8. *South Carolina General Gazette Extraordinary*, October 16, 1775, in *PHL*, vol. 10, 460–67.

9. HL to JL, October 21, 1775, in *PHL*, vol. 10, 489–90.

10. JL to HL, November 24, 1775, in *PHL*, vol. 10, 512. JL to James Laurens, November 16 and 18, 1775, Kendall Collection, quoted in Massey, *John Laurens and the American Revolution*, 55.

11. Massey, *John Laurens and the American Revolution*, 41, 47–48. Wallace, *Life of Henry Laurens*, 466.

12. JL to James Laurens, October 25, 1776, quoted in *PHL*, vol. 11, 277n6 (the letter is in the Kendall Collection). JL to HL, October 26, 1776, in *PHL*, vol. 11, 277. HL to JL, October 8, 1773, in *PHL*, vol. 9, 120–21.

13. For honor and shame, see, for example, W. J. Cash's excoriation of southern notions of honor in *The Mind of the South* (New York: Vintage Books, 1960; first published in 1941) and James McBride Dabbs's *Who Speaks for the South?* (New York: Funk & Wagnalls, 1964), which defends it. Cf. David Hackett Fischer, "Two Minds of the South: Ideas of Southern History in W. J. Cash and James McBride Dabbs," in *W. J. Cash and the Minds of the South*, ed. Paul D. Escott (Baton Rouge: Louisiana State University Press, 1992), 134–66. HL to JL, August 14, 1776, in *PHL*, vol. 11, 228.

14. Massey, *John Laurens and the American Revolution*, 65.

15. *PHL*, vol. 11, 224n4.

16. See John P. Kaminski, ed., *A Necessary Evil?: Slavery and the Debate over the Constitution* (Madison, WI: Madison House, 1995), 2–3. Pauline Maier, *American Scripture: Making the Declaration of Independence* (New York: Alfred A. Knopf, 1997), 122.

17. Joseph Ellis calls the grievance a "complete fiction" but suggests that Jefferson's "romantic view of America's uncontaminated origins" compelled him to believe his own fabrication. It also had the salutary effect of absolving Americans of any blame for the continuance of slavery: "This was less a clarion call to end slavery than an invitation to wash one's hands of the matter" (*American Sphinx: The Character of Thomas Jefferson* [New York: Vintage Books, 1998], 35–74; quotations from 61).

18. HL to JL, August 14, 1776, in *PHL*, vol. 11, 222–36.

19. JL to HL, October 26 ,1776, in *PHL*, vol. 11, 275–77. Thomas Day, *Fragment of an Original Letter on the Slavery of the Negroes; Written in the Year 1776* (Philadelphia: Francis Bailey, 1784). Massey discusses Day and this letter (*John Laurens and the American Revolution*, 63). It is possible also that Henry Laurens was familiar with some Quaker antislavery tracts, which invoked the Golden Rule also (see James A. McMillin, *The Final Victims: Foreign Slave Trade to North America, 1783–1810* [Columbia: University of South Carolina Press, 2004], 5).

20. HL to JL, August 14, 1776, in *PHL*, vol. 11, 225.

21. Alexander Hamilton to JL, [April 1779], in *The Papers of Alexander Hamilton*, ed. Harold C. Syrett, vol. 2 (New York: Columbia University Press, 1961–1987), 34–35, quoted in Massey, *John Laurens and the American Revolution*, 81.

22. HL to John Lewis Gervais, October 8, 1777, in *PHL*, vol. 11, 546–47.

23. William Henry Drayton to JL, September 7, 1778, Thomas Addis Emmet Collection (EM 1213), New York Public Library; quoted in Massey, *John Laurens and the American Revolution*, 122.

24. JL to HL, December 15, 1777, in *PHL*, vol. 12, 157. See Massey, *John Laurens and the American Revolution*, 93–95. JL to HL, January 14, 1778, in *PHL*, vol. 12, 305.

25. HL to JL, January 8, 1778, in *PHL*, vol. 12, 271 and 274. HL to JL, January 22, 1778, in *PHL*, vol. 12, 328.

26. JL to HL, February 3, 1778, in *PHL*, vol. 12, 390–92. Rob Chernow, *Alexander Hamilton* (New York: Penguin Press, 2004), 23. Lafayette invited Washington to join him in a scheme to demonstrate how emancipation might work in western Virginia (see Jason Lane, *General and Madame de Lafayette* [New York: Taylor Trade Publishing, 2003], 78–79), and he ardently supported Frances Wright and her program for emancipation in the 1820s (see Lloyd Kramer, *Lafayette in Two Worlds: Public Cultures and Personal Identities in an Age of Revolutions* [Chapel Hill: University of North Carolina Press, 1996], 154–70). For Fleury's role, see JL to HL, February 3, 1778, in *PHL*, vol. 12, 398. JL to HL, February 3, 1778, in *PHL*, vol. 12, 390–92. Joseph Ellis dates Washington's first approval of the Black Regiment scheme in 1779, a year later than he actually expressed it (*His Excellency George Washington* [New York: Alfred A. Knopf, 2005], 162).

27. HL to JL, February 6, 1778, in *PHL*, vol. 12, 412–13. JL to HL, February 15, 1778, in *PHL*, vol. 12, 446.

28. Edward McCrady, *The History of South Carolina in the Revolution, 1775–1780* (New York: Macmillan, 1901), 330. John Rutledge to S.C. Delegates, March 18, 1779, in *PHL*, vol. 15, 67. Cf. *PHL*, vol. 15, 60n3. HL to George Washington, March 16, 1779, in *PHL*, vol. 15, 66.

29. Alexander Hamilton to John Jay, March 14, 1779, in *The Papers of Alexander Hamilton*, vol. 2, 18–19.

30. Committee Report, March 25, 1779, in *PHL*, vol. 15, 72. Massey is probably right when he credits military necessity as the persuasive factor, but even so it is important that South Carolina's representatives thought that slavery was expendable. Keith Krawczynski, *William Henry Drayton: South Carolina Revolutionary Patriot* (Baton Rouge: Louisiana State University Press, 2001), 309–11.

31. See Massey, *John Laurens and the American Revolution*, 135–36.

32. David Ramsay, *Ramsay's History of South Carolina: From Its First Settlement in 1670 to the Year 1808* (Spartanburg, SC: Reprint Co., 1959–1961), 309. See McCrady, *History of South Carolina in the Revolution*, 358–76.

33. John Laurens, "Account of the Operations in South Carolina," [May 1779], *Henry Laurens Papers*, South Carolina Historical Society, quoted extensively in Massey, *John Laurens and the American Revolution*.

34. McCrady, *History of South Carolina in the Revolution*, 373.

35. Massey, *John Laurens and the American Revolution*, 140. Massey seems to quote Christopher Gadsden, in a letter to Samuel Adams, expressing "disgust" and "resentment" at the notion of arming slaves, but the usually impeccable biographer is mistaken here, and the quotation is misattributed. JL to Alexander Hamilton, July 14, 1779, in *Papers of Alexander Hamilton*, vol. 2, 103. Dr. Ramsay to Hon. William Henry Drayton, September 1, 1779, in R. W. Gibbes, ed., *Documentary History of the American Revolution*, vol. 2, *1776–1782* (Spartanburg, SC: The Reprint Company, 1972; originally published in New York: D. Appleton, 1857), quoted in Massey, *John Laurens and the American Revolution*, 141.

36. David Ramsay to Benjamin Rush, February 3, 1779, Library Company of Philadelphia, Historical Society of Philadelphia; quoted in Arthur H. Shaffer, *To Be an American: David Ramsay and the Making of the American Consciousness* (Columbia: University of South Carolina Press, 1991), 165, 166–67. David Ramsay to Thomas Jefferson, May 3, 1786, in Robert L. Brunhouse, ed., "David Ramsay, 1749–1815: Selections from His Writings," *Transactions of the American Philosophical Society*, New Series, 55 no. 1, [1965]): 101; quoted in Shaffer, *To Be an American*, 167.

37. Massey, *John Laurens and the American Revolution*, 155, and Carl P. Borick, *A Gallant Defense: The Siege of Charleston, 1780* (Columbia: University of South Carolina Press, 2003), 40–41.

38. Borick, *Gallant Defense*, 36, 31–33.

39. Ibid., 32, 42–45, 54, 57.

40. Ibid., 54–55, 60–61, 64.

41. Ibid., 65, 81–85, 103–5.

42. Ibid., 114–17.

43. Ibid., 121–42.

44. Ibid., 135, 206, 219. See Ramsay, *History of South Carolina*, vol. 1, 181–209; David Duncan Wallace, *The Life of Henry Laurens, with a Sketch of the Life of Lieutenant-Colonel John Laurens* (New York: G. P. Putnam and Sons, 1915), 356.

45. See Wallace, *Life of Henry Laurens*, 355–89.

46. Massey, *John Laurens and the American Revolution*, 201.

47. E[ward] Rutledge to A[rthur] Middleton, February 8, 1782, "Correspondence of Arthur Middleton," *South Carolina Historical and General Magazine* 27 (January 1926): 4. See also Aedanus Burke to Arthur Middleton, January 25, 1782, "Correspondence of Hon. Arthur Middleton, Signer of the Declaration of Independence," annotated by Joseph W. Barnwell, *South Carolina Historical and General Magazine* 25 (October 1925): 194. See Jerome J. Nadelhaft, *The Disorders of War: The Revolution in South Carolina* (Orono: University of Maine at Orono Press, 1981), 75 and 240n16. Shaffer, *To Be an American*, 168.

48. *PHL*, vol. 12, 53.

CHAPTER 4

1. William Howard Adams, *Gouverneur Morris: An Independent Life* (New Haven, CT: Yale University Press, 2003), 126–27, 95.

2. These population ratios are figured from the 1790 census.

3. The summaries of these speeches, from which I have quoted, come from James Madison's notes on the convention proceedings, published in Max Farrand, ed., *The Records of the Federal Convention of 1787*, vol. 2 (New Haven, CT: Yale University Press, 1966), 220–23.

4. Much of this physical description was cobbled together by Richard Barry, *Mr. Rutledge of South Carolina* (Salem, NH: Ayer Publishing, 1942; reprinted in 1993), 22–23. For "quick Apprehension" see James Haw, *John & Edward Rutledge of South Carolina* (Athens: University of Georgia Press, 1997), 15. Diary of John Adams, September 1, 3, October 10, 1774, in Paul H. Smith, ed., *Letters of Delegates to Congress, 1774–1789*, vol. 1 (Washington, DC: Library of Congress, 1976–2000), 6, 8, 168; quoted in Haw, *John & Edward Rutledge of South Carolina*, 62. For "blue-gray," Barry, *Mr. Rutledge of South Carolina*, 23.

5. See Barry, *Mr. Rutledge of South Carolina*, 4–8.

6. See ibid., 7, and Haw, *John & Edward Rutledge of South Carolina*, 4.

7. See Barry, *Mr. Rutledge of South Carolina*, 48. For a description of Charleston's legal scene and Rutledge's place in it, see Haw, *John & Edward Rutledge of South Carolina*, 12–16.

8. See Haw, *John & Edward Rutledge of South Carolina*, 22.

9. See Barry, *Mr. Rutledge of South Carolina*, 73.

10. Ibid., 304 and 329.

11. See Walter J. Fraser Jr., *Charleston! Charleston!: The History of a Southern City* (Columbia: University of South Carolina Press, 1989), 162–68.

12. James A. McMillin, *The Final Victims: Foreign Slave Trade to North America, 1783–1810* (Columbia: University of South Carolina Press, 2004), 8.

13. Marvin R. Zanhiser, *Charles Cotesworth Pinckney, Founding Father* (Chapel Hill: University of North Carolina Press, 1967), 75. *Charleston Evening Gazette*, October 1, 1785, 2.

14. See Fraser, *Charleston! Charleston!*, 170–73.

15. Barry, *Mr. Rutledge of South Carolina*, 72.

16. Zahniser, *Charles Cotesworth Pinckney, Founding Father*, 76–77.

17. Haw, *John & Edward Rutledge of South Carolina*, 184–85.

18. Arthur H. Shaffer, *To Be an American: David Ramsay and the Making of the American Consciousness* (Columbia: University of South Carolina Press, 1991), 171.

19. Haw, *John & Edward Rutledge of South Carolina*, 167. David Ramsay to Benjamin Rush, February 3, 1779, in Robert L. Brunhouse, "David Ramsay, 1749–1815: Selections from His Writings," *Transactions of the American Philosophical Society*, New Series, 55, pt. 4 (1965): 59.

20 For Rutledge's views, see Barry, *Mr. Rutledge of South Carolina*, 329. Shaffer, *To Be an American*, 173–74. Richard Hutson to Isaac Hayne, January 27, 1766; Hutson to Hayne, January 29, 1767; and Hutson to Mr. Croll, August 22, 1767, in *Richard Hutson Letterbook, 1765–1777* at the South Carolina Historical Society.

21. Cf. Jeffery H. Morrison, *John Witherspoon and the Founding of the American Republic* (Notre Dame, IN: University of Notre Dame Press, 2005), 76. Shaffer, *To Be an American*, 30–31.

22. Shaffer, *To Be an American*, 79. *Charleston Evening Gazette*, October 1, 1785, 2.

23. *Charleston Evening Gazette*, October 1, 1785, 2 and 3.

24. This tardiness shows how keeping the capital in Charleston benefitted the oligarchy, because delegates from Upcountry had a slow and difficult journey to reach the coast.

25. *Charleston Evening Gazette*, October 3, 1785, 2.

26. *Ibid.*, October 18, 1785, 1.

27. Haw, *John & Edward Rutledge of South Carolina*, 200.

28. *Charleston Evening Gazette*, October 18, 1785, 3. David Ramsay, *Ramsay's History of South Carolina*, 248–49.

29. *Charleston Evening Gazette*, October 18, 1785, 3. *Charleston Morning Post*, March 23, 1787, 2.

30. Thomas Jefferson to Edward Rutledge, July 14, 1787, in *The Writings of Thomas Jefferson*, ed. Paul L. Ford, 10 vols. (New York: G. P. Putnam's Sons,

1892–1899), vol. 4, 410; quoted in Zahniser, *Charles Cotesworth Pinckney*, 82. Haw, *John & Edward Rutledge of South Carolina*, 72. Zahniser, *Charles Cotesworth Pinckney*, 82.

31. David Ramsay to HL, February 26, 1787, in *PHL*, vol. 16, 703. Ernest M. Lander Jr., "The South Carolinians at the Philadelphia Convention, 1787," *South Carolina Historical Magazine* 57, no. 3 (July 1956): 134.

32. For this biographical sketch of the Pinckneys and unless otherwise noted, see Frances Leigh Williams, *A Founding Family: The Pinckneys of South Carolina* (New York: Harcourt Brace Jovanovich, 1978), 3–18.

33. Marty D. Matthews, *Forgotten Founder: The Life and Times of Charles Pinckney* (Columbia: University of South Carolina Press, 2004), 11.

34. See Zahniser, *Charles Cotesworth Pinckney*, 30–31. Zahniser bases this description on Josiah Quincy's testimony in *Memoir of the Life of Josiah Quincy* (Boston: Cummings, Hillard, 1825), 103; and, apparently, on James Earl's 1795 portrait in the Gibbes Museum of Art.

35. Matthews, *Forgotten Founder*, 19, 23. Arthur Middleton to Charles Pinckney, October 30, 1782, *South Carolina Historical Magazine* 27 (1926): 27, quoted in Matthews, *Forgotten Founder*, 23.

36. Christopher Collier and James Lincoln Collier, *Decision in Philadelphia: The Constitutional Convention of 1787* (New York: Random House, 1986), 69.

37. Zahniser, *Charles Cotesworth Pinckney*, 89.

38. Barry, *Mr. Rutledge of South Carolina*, 315–17. Jeffrey St. John, *Constitutional Journal: A Correspondent's Report from the Convention of 1787* (Ottawa, IL: Jameson Books, 1987), 10.

39. Farrand, *Records of the Federal Convention of 1787*, vol. 1, 486.

40. Barry, *Mr. Rutledge of South Carolina*, 331 and 329. Barry imprecisely documented his description of this dinner, and, like his entire biography, its purpose is to lionize Rutledge. Nevertheless, his lively book remains the most cited authority on Rutledge and is generally reliable.

41. Madison (back in 1787) and most historians thought Connecticut sought assurances about the carrying trade, but Forrest McDonald makes a persuasive case that the land claims were, indeed, what Sherman and Ellsworth wanted to secure (*E Pluribus Unum" The Formation of the American Republic, 1776–1790* [Indianapolis: Liberty Press, 1979, c1965], 291–94).

42. Joseph C. Morton, *Shapers of the Great Debate at the Constitutional Convention of 1787: A Biographical Dictionary* (Westport, CT: Greenwood Press, 2006), 194–95. Farrand, *Records of the Federal Convention of 1787*, vol. 2, 364.

43. Farrand, *Records of the Federal Convention of 1787*, vol. 2, 364–65.

44. Helen Hill Miller, *George Mason, Gentleman Revolutionary* (Chapel Hill: University of North Carolina Press, 1975), 55–58 and 214. Even so, we should

temper our praise of Mason. As Virginians debated whether or not to ratify the Constitution, Mason did attack the protection of the slave trade until 1808, but he also complained that the document did not outlaw federal meddling in slavery itself (*The Papers of George Mason 1725–1792*, vol. 3: *1787–1792*, ed. Robert A. Rutland [Chapel Hill: University of North Carolina Press, 1970], 1066).

45. Jeff Broadwater, *George Mason, Forgotten Founder* (Chapel Hill: University of North Carolina Press, 2006), 36. Noting the difference between Mason's rhetoric and his actions (for instance, he never manumitted his own slaves), Broadwater explains that "the revolution ought not to be seen as a missed opportunity to put slavery on the road to an early death." He thinks that slavery was, in fact, inevitable in the new republic (38). Obviously, I disagree with that conclusion.

46. Farrand, *Records of the Federal Convention of 1787*, vol. 2, 370.

47. Ibid., 371.

48. Ibid., 373–74.

49. Jonathan Elliot, ed. *The Debates in the Several State Conventions of the Adoption of The Federal Constitution, as recommended by the General Convention at Philadelphia in 1787*. Vol. 5 (Philadelphia: J. B. Lippincott Company, 1836), 314–15 and 286.

50. Ibid., 286.

51. Lawrence S. Rowland, "The South Carolina Lowcountry during the ratification of the United States Constitution," in *With Liberty and Justice: Essays on the Ratification of the Constitution of the United States* (Columbia: United States Constitution Bicentennial Commission, 1988), 1–8. Quotation from 1–2. See *Journal of the Convention of South Carolina Which Ratified the Constitution of the United States May 23, 1788* (United States Constitution Bicentennial Commission of South Carolina, 1988), facsimile edition.

52. See especially the speeches of James Lincoln and Patrick Dollard. Elliot, *The Debates in the Several State Conventions*, 337–38.

53. Ibid., 308.

54. Ibid., 321–24.

55. Ibid., 322.

56. Letter, William Mason to William Bentley, December 3, 1788, in Shaffer, *To Be an American*, 181.

57. Ibid., 177.

58. Ibid., 182–83.

59. See Ibid., 287n58.

60. Ibid., 177.

CHAPTER 5

1. Unless otherwise noted, this summary of Denmark Vesey's early life draws from the most authoritative modern source, Douglas R. Egerton, *He Shall Go Out Free: The Lives of Denmark Vesey* (Madison, WI: Madison House, 1999), 3–74. Nearly everything we know about Vesey and the outline of Egerton's work comes from a short sketch of his life in James Hamilton Jr., *An Account of the Late Intended Insurrection among a Portion of the Blacks of This City* (Charleston, SC: A. E. Miller, 1822), 17.

2. See Egerton, *He Shall Go Out Free*, 75. Archibald Grimké, *Right on the Scaffold, or, The Martyrs of 1822* (Washington, DC: The Academy, 1901), 3.

3. Frederick Douglass, *Narrative of the Life of Frederick Douglass, an American Slave Written by Himself* (Boston: Anti-Slavery Office, 1845), 35–36. Loren Schweninger, "Slave Independence and Enterprise in South Carolina, 1780–1865," *South Carolina Historical Magazine* 93 (April 1992): 107, 110, and 111. See also Allison Carll-White, "South Carolina's Forgotten Craftsmen," *South Carolina Historical Magazine* 86 (January 1985): 33. It is a problem in studies of this nature that black voices are often silent or muted, especially so in the case of Denmark Vesey, in which all of the words uttered by African Americans are either omitted or filtered through white court officers. I recommend to anyone interested in the nineteenth-century experience of slavery in South Carolina the recent book *I Belong to South Carolina: South Carolina Slave Narratives*, ed. Susanna Ashton (Columbia: University South Carolina Press, 2010), which gives voice to seven Americans who lived it firsthand.

4. Walter J. Fraser Jr., *Charleston! Charleston!: The History of a Southern City* (Columbia: University of South Carolina Press, 1989), 178–87.

5. Lacy K. Ford, *Deliver Us from Evil: The Slavery Question in the Old South* (New York: Oxford University Press, 2009), 121–22.

6. James A. McMillin, *The Final Victims: Foreign Slave Trade to North America, 1783–1810* (Columbia: University of South Carolina Press, 2004), 31–32.

7. For Charleston's role in the rise of paternalism, see Alan Gallay, "The Origins of Slaveholders' Paternalism: George Whitefield, the Bryan Family, and the Great Awakening in the South," *Journal of Southern History* 53 (August 1987): 369–94. For Ford's indispensable discussion of paternalism (and the scholarship on that subject), see Ford, *Deliver Us from Evil*, 144–72. As is evident from my discussion of the white reaction to the Stono Rebellion, I quibble with Ford on his point about recognizing the humanity of slaves. The pre-paternalistic model of slavery, which so emphasizes corporal punishment and unrelenting discipline, implicitly (and often explicitly) recognizes the common humanity of slaves: they are captives of war who are motivated by the same desire for freedom and hatred of oppression that beat in the hearts of their white captors. Slaves were thought to be fully human, and it was their natural

love of liberty that made them so dangerous.

8. Ford, following most scholars, believes that the domestication of slavery was a strategy to soften the institution, to make it (at least apparently) compatible with American republicanism. In other words, it was an ideology designed to indemnify owners against charges of cruelty and render slavery a perpetual institution. It is on this point that my argument differs from those historians, like Ford, Freehling, Genovese, Rose, Young, and Berlin, to whom we all are indebted for our understanding of American slave ideology. See William W. Freehling, *The Road to Disunion*, vol. 1: *Secessionists at Bay, 1776–1854* (New York: Oxford University Press, 1990), 59–97; Jeffrey Robert Young, *Domesticating Slavery: The Master Class in Georgia and South Carolina, 1670–1837* (Chapel Hill: University of North Carolina Press, 1999); Willie Lee Rose, "The Domestication of Domestic Slavery," in *Slavery and Freedom*, ed. William W. Freehling (New York: Oxford University Press, 1982), 18–36; Larry E. Tise, *Proslavery: A History of the Defense of Slavery in America, 1800–1840* (Athens: University of Georgia Press, 1987); Ira Berlin, *Many Thousands Gone: The First Two Centuries of Slavery in North America* (Cambridge, MA: Harvard University Press, 1998); Robert Olwell, *Masters, Slaves, & Subjects: The Culture of Power in the South Carolina Low Country, 1740–1790* (Ithaca, NY: Cornell University Press, 1998); Eugene D. Genovese, *Roll, Jordan, Roll: The World the Slaves Made* (New York: Pantheon Books, 1974). For a succinct discussion of slavery and the concept of "progress," see Genovese, *The Slaveholders' Dilemma: Freedom and Progress in Southern Conservative Thought, 1820–1860* (Columbia: University of South Carolina Press, 1992).

9. For manumissions and population distribution, see Ira Berlin, *Slaves without Masters: The Free Negro in the Antebellum South* (New York: Oxford University Press, 1974), 25. For Baptist and Methodist moral pressure, see Benjamin Joseph Klebenar, "Manumission Laws and the Responsibility for Supporting Slaves," *Virginia Magazine of History and Biography* 63 (October 1965): 448–51. For Washington and Lafayette, see Joseph Ellis, *His Excellency George Washington* (New York: Alfred A. Knopf, 2005), 162–65. For "Manumission begets," see Berlin, *Slaves without Masters*, 30–31.

10. For slave owners' prerogatives and manumission in the Upper South, see Berlin, *Slaves without Masters*, 29, 31. For Baltimore, see Stephen Whitman, "Manumission and the Transformation of Urban Slavery," *Social Science History* 19 (Autumn 1995): 334–36; quotation from 336. For the Charleston free black community, see Carll-White, "South Carolina's Forgotten Craftsmen," 33.

11. Egerton, *He Shall Go Out Free*, 73–74.

12. Ibid., 92–93, 95. Bernard E. Powers Jr., *Black Charlestonians: A Social History, 1822–1885* (Fayetteville: University of Arkansas Press, 1994), 41–42

and 52. The ease and eagerness with which the brown elites distinguished themselves from other African Americans should be tempered to some degree. For example, the one man expelled from the group was George Logan, who, after seventeen years of membership, was found to have colluded in the selling of a free black man back into slavery (see Robert L. Harris Jr., "Charleston's Free Afro-American Elite: The Brown Fellowship Society and the Humane Brotherhood," *South Carolina Historical Magazine* 82 [October 1981]: 290).

13. Powers, *Black Charlestonians*, 38. Also see Klebenar, "Manumission Laws and the Responsibility for Supporting Slaves," for a general discussion of increased regulations in all southern states after 1800; and Whitman, "Manumission and the Transformation of Urban Slavery," 336.

14. Powers, *Black Charlestonians*, 60.

15. For Petigru and subterfuges, see ibid., 60 and 39. For indentured servitude, see Robert Olwell, "Becoming Free: Manumission and the Genesis of a Free Black Community in South Carolina, 1740–1790," *Slavery & Abolition* 17, no. 1 (April 1996): 7–8. For the quasi-free in Charleston and South Carolina, see Schweninger, "Slave Independence and Enterprise in South Carolina," 120–21 and 124.

16. Egerton, *He Shall Go Out Free*, 80, 110–11.

17. See ibid., 112, 121–22, and the *Charleston Courier*, June 9 and 11, 1818. For a summary of Vesey's supposed theology, see Egerton, *He Shall Go Out Free*, 114–20; as I will discuss below, our knowledge of these meetings comes from court testimony that I consider unreliable.

18. Hamilton, *Account of the Late Intended Insurrection*, 4, and Egerton, *He Shall Go Out Free*, 155. For the names of the ships, see Edward A. Pearson, *Designs against Charleston: The Trial Record of the Denmark Vesey Slave Conspiracy of 1822* (Chapel Hill: University of North Carolina Press, 1999), 104. Michael Johnson has thoroughly discredited that volume as an accurate version of the unpublished court records; nevertheless, Pearson's long introduction provides helpful original research, and the trial records in his volume, despite being too unreliable for scholarly use, remain the only accessible version for the casual reader. Pearson gives the slave, Peter, the last name of Desverneys, while Egerton and Johnson call him Peter Prioleau, after his master.

19. Hamilton, *Account of the Late Intended Insurrection*, 3–7; Egerton, *He Shall Go Out Free*, 156.

20. Virginia Louise Glenn, *James Hamilton, Jr., of South Carolina: A Biography* (Ph.D. diss., University of North Carolina, Chapel Hill, 1964), 2–6, 11.

21. Ibid., 30, 13–14.

22. Ibid., 19–20.

23. Hamilton, *Account of the Late Intended Insurrection*, 5.

24. Ibid., 6, and Egerton, 158.

25. The two narratives are James Hamilton Jr.'s *Account* (cited above) and the *An Official Report of the Trials of Sundry Negroes, Charged with an Attempt to Raise an Insurrection in South Carolina: Preceded by an Introduction and Narrative and, in an Appendix, a Report of the Trials of Four White Persons on Indictments for Attempting to Excite the Slaves to Insurrection*, edited by Lionel H. Kennedy and Thomas Parker (Charleston: J. R. Schenck, 1822). The Vesey Rebellion is the most hotly disputed event among the entire history recounted in this volume. At one extreme are historians and biographers like Douglas R. Egerton, who believes just about everything reported in the voluminous trial record, and at the other, scholars such as Michael P. Johnson, who does not think there ever was any plot to rebel. Johnson's is the minority opinion, corroborated mainly by Richard C. Wade ("The Vesey Plot: A Reconsideration," *Journal of Southern History*, 30 [1964]: 143–61). As will become evident in my narrative, I find Johnson entirely convincing. See his "Denmark Vesey and His Co-Conspirators," *William and Mary Quarterly*, 3rd Series, 58 (October 2001): 915–56. His disputants in this famous debate rebutted his arguments in the next issue of the magazine, volume 59 (January 2002), and Egerton again disputed Johnson in "Of Facts and Fables: New Light on the Denmark Vesey Affair," *South Carolina Historical Magazine* 105 (January 2004): 8–35, cowritten with Robert L. Paquette. For the most recent installment in this debate (and a helpful summary of the current controversy), see Philip F. Rubio, "'Though He Had a White Face, He Was a Negro in Heart': Examining the White Men Convicted of Supporting the 1822 Denmark Vesey Slave Insurrection Conspiracy," *South Carolina Historical Magazine* 113 (January 2012): 52n6.

26. Johnson, "Denmark Vesey and His Co-Conspirators," 952.

27. Hamilton, *Account of the Late Intended Insurrection*, 6–7.

28. Ibid., 7.

29. See Pearson, *Designs against Charleston*, 106–7, Egerton, *He Shall Go Out Free*, 160–61, and Hamilton, *Account of the Late Intended Insurrection*, 6–7.

30. Pearson, *Designs against Charleston*, 174.

31. Joe's testimony is published in Pearson, *Designs against Charleston*, 168–72 and the Kennedy and Park, *Official Report of the Trials of Sundry Negroes*.

32. For a contradictory interpretation of this testimony, see James O'Neil Spady, "Power and Confession: On the Credibility of the Earliest Reports of the Denmark Slave Conspiracy," *William and Mary Quarterly* 68, no. 2 (April 2011): 287–304. Spady, like Egerton, argues that Vesey and the others were involved in a real conspiracy.

33. See Pearson, *Designs against Charleston*, 168n10.

34 For the corps, Hamilton, *Account of the Late Intended Insurrection*, 9. For white reactions, Egerton, *He Shall Go Out Free*, 164–65.

35. Hamilton, *Account of the Late Intended Insurrection*, 12. For Bennett's view of Rolla, Egerton, *He Shall Go Out Free*, 161.

36. Johnson, "Denmark Vesey and His Co-Conspirators," 934.

37. For details about the unreliable methods of the committee and the court, see Johnson, "Denmark Vesey and His Co-Conspirators," 934, 942, and 945.

38. Hamilton, *Account of the Late Intended Insurrection*, 11. William Johnson Jr., "Melancholy Effect of Popular Excitement," *Charleston Courier*, June 22, 1822. Michael Johnson discusses this article extensively ("Denmark Vesey and His Co-Conspirators," 935–37). William Johnson Jr., *To the Public of Charleston* (Charleston: C. C. Sebring, 1822), 5–6.

39. Donald G. Morgan, *Justice William Johnson: The First Dissenter* (Columbia: University of South Carolina Press, 1954). See also Irwin F. Greenberg, "Justice William Johnson: South Carolina Unionist, 1823–1830," *Pennsylvania History* 36 (July 1969): 307–34. William Johnson, *To the Public*, 11–12, 14.

40. Egerton thinks William Paul informed on Vesey (*He Shall Go Out Free*, 173). Hamilton, *Account of the Late Intended Insurrection*, 17.

41. Kennedy and Parker, *Official Report of the Trials of Sundry Negroes*, 29–31.

42. See Pearson, *Designs against Charleston*, 191. Hamilton, *Account of the Late Intended Insurrection*, 16.

43. Martha Proctor Richardson to James Screven, July 6, 1822, Arnold and Screven Papers, Southern Historical Collection, University of North Carolina, quoted in Egerton, *He Shall Go Out Free*, 190.

44. For the murder penalty, see Johnson, "Denmark Vesey and His Co-Conspirators," 966. Hayne to Bennett, July 3, 1822, Document E (copy), Governor's Messages, 1328, General Assembly Papers, South Carolina Department of Archives and History, quoted in Johnson, "Denmark Vesey and His Co-Conspirators," 938.

45. Hamilton, *Account of the Late Intended Insurrection*, 19–20.

46. Kennedy and Parker, *Official Report of the Trials of Sundry Negroes*, 99.

47. Hamilton, *Account of the Late Intended Insurrection*, 20–22.

48. Ibid.

49. Ibid., 28 and 47. Michael Johnson applied the term "star" and "superstar," and he calculated the percentages of testimony based on the number of lines in the official record ("Denmark Vesey and His Co-Conspirators," 945–47).

50. Egerton, *He Shall Go Out Free*, 171–72.

51. Hamilton, *Account of the Late Intended Insurrection*, 30. Kennedy and Parker, *Official Report of the Trials of Sundry Negroes*, 26.

52. Kennedy and Parker, *Official Report of the Trials of Sundry Negroes*, 22.

53. Hamilton, *Account of the Late Intended Insurrection*, 30.

54. *Charleston Courier*, February 5, 1820. For how ubiquitous was this argument, see Freehling, *Road to Disunion*, vol. 1, 150–52.

55. This speech was published as a pamphlet: William Smith, *Speech of the Hon. Wm. Smith of South Carolina, Delivered in the Senate of the United States, December 8th, 1820: Containing a View of the Constitutions, Laws & Regulations of the Several States, on the Subject of Their Colored Population, Vagrants, &c.* (Washington, DC: Gales & Seaton, 1823), 13.

56. William Smith, [Speech on the Missouri Question], *Annals of Congress*, 15th Cong., 2nd Sess. (January 26, 1820): 268 and 269. Freehling, *Road to Disunion*, vol. 1, 150–51, emphasis added.

57. Rufus King, *Substance of Two Speeches, Delivered in the Senate of the United States, on the Subject of the Missouri Bill* (New York: Kirk and Mercein, 1819), 19, 26. Nevertheless, the moral argument was still subsumed by northern dissatisfaction with the three-fifths rule. Five white Virginians, King demonstrated, wielded the same electoral power as seven white men in northern states (24). See Freehling, *Road to Disunion*, vol. 1, 148.

58. Kennedy and Parker, *Official Report of the Trials of Sundry Negroes*, 19.

59. For Hamilton's bill, see Robert Tinkler, *James Hamilton of South Carolina* (Baton Rouge: Louisiana State University Press, 2004), 48. For Atlantic maritime culture, see W. Jeffery Bolster, *Black Jacks: African-American Seamen in the Age of Sail* (Cambridge, MA: Harvard University Press, 1997), and Peter Linebaugh and Marcus Rediker, *The Many-Headed Hydra: Sailors, Slaves, Commoners, and the Hidden History of the Revolutionary Atlantic* (Boston: Beacon Press, 2000).

60. Greenberg, "Justice William Johnson," 310–11. Alan F. January, "The South Carolina Association: An Agency for Race Control in Antebellum Charleston," *South Carolina Historical Magazine* 78 (July 1977): 191–201. See also Philip M. Hamer, "Great Britain, the United States, and the Negro Seaman Acts, 1822–1848," *Journal of Southern History* 1 (February 1935): 3–28. Lyon G. Taylor, "James Louis Petigru: Freedom's Champion in a Slave Society," *South Carolina Historical Magazine* 83 (October 1982): 274. Greenberg, "Justice William Johnson," 316–17.

CHAPTER 6

1. Angelina Grimké, *Walking by Faith: The Diary of Angelina Grimké, 1828–1835*, ed. Charles Wilbanks (Columbia: University of South Carolina Press, 2003), 2–3. See Wilbanks's introduction, xvi.

2. Grimké, *Walking by Faith*, 5, 15, 18, 23.

3. Ibid., 10.

4. Irving H. Bartlett, *John C. Calhoun: A Biography* (New York: W. W. Norton, 1993), 20, 22–25.

5. Quoted in ibid., 19.

6. J. H. Hammond, *An Oration on the Life, Character and Services of John Caldwell Calhoun* (Charleston, SC: Walker & James, 1850), 18. Bartlett, *John C. Calhoun*, 19, 43–56, quotation from p. 56.

7. Bartlett, *John C. Calhoun*, 74 and 79.

8. John C. Calhoun, *The Papers of John C. Calhoun*, vol. 1, ed. Robert L. Meriwether (Columbia: University of South Carolina Press, 1959): 312.

9. Bartlett, *John C. Calhoun*, 279–85, quotation from 283.

10. Ibid., 62.

11. See ibid., 67, "From the Frontispiece Volume Ten of the Calhoun papers. National Portrait Gallery."

12. John C. Calhoun, Great Britain, Reported to the House of Representatives, June 3, 1812, *American State Papers: Foreign Relations* vol. 3, 567. Emphasis added.

13. See Bartlett, *John C. Calhoun*, 145–49.

14. *Papers of John C. Calhoun*, vol. 10, 474.

15. Ibid., 10, 470 and 460.

16. Ibid., 10, 454, 448, 454, 486, 490, 510.

17. Ibid., 10, 446, 500, 513–14.

18. Ibid., 10, 492, 496.

19. Ibid., 10, 496.

20. Ibid.

21. Charles M. Wiltse, *John C. Calhoun Nullifier, 1829–1839* (Indianapolis: Bobbs-Merrill, 1949), 11.

22. H. W. Brands, *Andrew Jackson, His Life and Times* (New York: Doubleday, 2005), 424.

23. Bartlett, *John C. Calhoun*, 154.

24. Ibid., 155.

25. Ibid., 150.

26. Ibid., 171.

27. Wiltse, *John C. Calhoun Nullifier*, 61.

28. Ibid., 60, 62.

29. The Jefferson Day dinner story is retold in a hundred histories. For a full account, including the newspaper reactions, see Wiltse, *John C. Calhoun Nullifier*, 67–73. Brands, *Andrew Jackson, His Life and Times*, 446.

30. William Freehling, *The Road to Disunion*, vol. 1, *Secessionists at Bay, 1776–1854* (New York: Oxford University Press, 1990), 272–73. The Calhoun quotation, quoted by Freehling, is from a letter, John C. Calhoun to Virgil Maxcy, September 11, 1830, *Papers of Calhoun*, vol. 11, 229.

31. Freehling, *Road to Disunion*, vol. 1, 274–75.

32. *Proceedings of the State Rights Celebration, at Charleston, S.C., July 1st, 1830.* (Charleston: A. E. Miller, 1830), 2–3.

33. Ibid., 21, 32–33, and 56.

34. William Gilmore Simms, *The Letters of William Gilmore Simms*, ed. Mary Simms Oliphant, Alfred Taylor Odell, and T. C. Duncan Eaves, vol. 1 (Columbia: University of South Carolina Press, 1952), lix. John Caldwell Guilds, *Simms: A Literary Life* (Fayetteville: University of Arkansas Press, 1992), 6–7.

35. *Letters of William Gilmore Simms*, vol. 1, xl–xli.

36. *City Gazette*, August 27, 1830; Jon L. Wakelyn, *The Politics of a Literary Man: William Gilmore Simms* (Westport, CT: Greenwood Press, 1973), 24. James Louis Petigru's letters to William Elliott, who was from the Beaufort district, clearly indicate the highly radical politics of the planters in that region. See James Petigru Carson, *Life, Letters, and Speeches of James Louis Petigru, the Union Man of South Carolina* (Washington, DC: W. H. Lowdermilk & Co., 1920), 78–115. Wakelyn, *Politics of a Literary Man*, 26.

37. See Wiltse, *John C. Calhoun Nullifier*, 88.

38. Thomas Grimké, *Letter to the Honorable John C. Calhoun, Vice-President of the United States, Robert Y. Hayne, Senator of the United States, George McDuffie, of the House of Representatives of the United States, and James Hamilton, Jr. Governor of the State of South Carolina*, 2nd ed. (Charleston, SC: James S. Burges, 1832). Carson, *Life, Letters, and Speeches of James Louis Petigru*, 79.

39. Carson, *Life, Letters, and Speeches of James Louis Petigru*, 78.

40. Ibid., 81–82.

41. Bartlett, *John C. Calhoun*, 186. Letter, James Louis Petigru to William Elliott, September 7, 1831, in Carson, *Life, Letters, and Speeches of James Louis Petigru*, 85.

42. Freehling, *Road to Disunion*, vol. 1, 275–76, and Wakelyn, *Politics of a Literary Man*, 29.

43. *Papers of John C. Calhoun*, vol. 9, 613–32.

44. Carson, *Life, Letters, and Speeches of James Louis Petigru*, 93.

45. Letter, JLP to William Elliott, September 28, 1832, in Carson, *Life, Letters, and Speeches of James Louis Petigru*, 97.

46. May 8, 1832, *City Gazette*; cf. Wakelyn, *Politics of a Literary Man*, 32–33.

47. Letter, JLP to Hugh S. Legaré, October 29, 1832, in Carson, *Life, Letters, and Speeches of James Louis Petigru*, 103–4. Letter, JLP to William Elliott, September 20, 1832, in Carson, *Life, Letters, and Speeches of James Louis Petigru*, 97. Letter, JLP to Hugh S. Legaré, October 29, 1832, in Carson, *Life, Letters, and Speeches of James Louis Petigru*, 104.

48. Freehling, *Road to Disunion*, vol. 1, 276. Letters, JLP to William Elliott, October 3, 1832, and September 28, 1832, in Carson, *Life, Letters, and Speeches of James Louis Petigru*, 99 and 98.

49. Lyon G. Taylor, "James Louis Petigru: Freedom's Champion in a Slave Society," *South Carolina Historical Magazine* 83 (October 1982): 274,

279–80. Lacy Ford, "James Louis Petigru: The Last South Carolina Federalist," in Michael O'Brien and David Moltke-Hansen, *Intellectual Life in Antebellum Charleston* (Knoxville: University of Tennessee Press, 1986), 152–85.

50. Letter, JLP to Hugh S. Legaré, December 21, 1832, in Carson, *Life, Letters, and Speeches of James Louis Petigru*, 112.

51. Wakelyn, *Politics of a Literary Man*, 35.

52. Carson, *Life, Letters, and Speeches of James Louis Petigru*, 107. Letter, WGS to James Lawson, November 25, 1832. *Letters of William Gilmore Simms*, vol. 1, 46.

53. Letter, WGS to James Lawson, January 19, 1833, *Letters of William Gilmore Simms*, vol. 1, 50.

54. *Remonstrance and Protest of the Union and States Rights party*, in Carson, *Life, Letters, and Speeches of James Louis Petigru*, 108.

55. Letter, JLP to Hugh S. Legaré, December 21, 1832, in Carson, *Life, Letters, and Speeches of James Louis Petigru*, 113.

56. Brands, *Andrew Jackson, His Life and Times*, 476–78.

57. Ibid., 480–81.

58. Carson, *Life, Letters, and Speeches of James Louis Petigru*, 115.

59. See Freehling, *Road to Disunion*, vol. 1, 285.

60. Brands, *Andrew Jackson, His Life and Times*, 481.

61. Letter, JLP to Hugh S. Legaré, October 29, 1832, in Carson, *Life, Letters, and Speeches of James Louis Petigru*, 104.

62. Letter, WGS to James Lawson, November 27, 1833, in *Letters of William Gilmore Simms*, vol. 1, 54.

63. See Douglas R. Egerton, *He Shall Go Out Free: The Lives of Denmark Vesey* (Madison, WI: Madison House, 1999), 32–33.

64. Grimké, *Walking by Faith*, 57–58.

65. Ibid., 58.

66. Ibid., 135.

CHAPTER 7

1. "America's First Direct Mail Campaign," *Pushing the Envelope* (blog), July 29, 2010, http://postalmuseumblog.si.edu/2010/07/americas-first-direct-mail-campaign.html.

2. *Charleston Courier*, July 30, 1835, July 2 and 31, 1835, 2. Letter, England to Cullen, February 23, 1836, in *Records of the American Catholic Historical Society of Philadelphia* 8 (1897), 219–20.

3. Gilbert Hobbs Barnes, *The Antislavery Impulse: 1830–1844* (Gloucester, MA: Peter Smith, 1973), 61. "To the Public," *The Liberator* 1, no. 1 (January 1, 1831): "Declaration of the National Anti-Slavery Convention," *The Liberator* 13, no. 50 (December 14, 1833): 198.

4. Ignatius Alysius Reynolds, ed., *The Works of the Right Rev. John England, First Bishop of Charleston*, vol. 5 (Baltimore: John Murphy & Co., 1849), 53–55.

5. Ibid., vol. 3, 98. See Peter K. Guilday, *The Life and Times of John England*, vol. 1 (New York: America Press, 1927), 38–40, 50.

6. Christian Brother, *A Century of Catholic Education: Brother Burke and His Associates*. (Dublin: Browne and Nolan, 1916), quoted in Guilday, *Life and Times of John England*, vol. 1, 58n.

7. Reynolds, *Works of the Right Rev. John England*, vol. 5, 55. Pastoral letter, December 31, 1796, quoted in Cornelius G. Buttimer, "Gaelic Literature and Contemporary Life in Cork, 1700–1840," in *Cork: History and Society, Interdisciplinary Essays on the History of an Irish County*, ed. Patrick O'Flanagan and Cornelius Buttimer (Dublin: Geography Publications, 1993), 601–2.

8. Reynolds, *Works of the Right Rev. John England*, vol. 1, 5. John England, *Diurnal of the Right Rev. John England, D. D. First Bishop of Charleston, South Caroling, 1820–1823* (Philadelphia: American Catholic Historical Society, 1895), 4. Patrick Carey, *An Immigrant Bishop: John England's Adaptation of Irish Catholicism to American Republicanism* (Yonkers, NY: U.S. Catholic Historical Society, 1982), 13.

9. Carey, *Immigrant Bishop*, 15–16, 18.

10. James S. Donnelly Jr., *The Land and the People of Nineteenth-Century Cork: The Rural Economy and the Land Question* (Boston: Routledge and Kegan Paul, 1975), 16–17, 24–25. *Cork Mercantile Chronicle*, September 2, 1816, quoted in Carey, *Immigrant Bishop*, 19. *Cork Mercantile Chronicle*, June 24, July 1, and July 4, 1814; from Carey, *Immigrant Bishop*, 49.

11. This story is pieced together from two sources: Reynolds, *Works of the Right Rev. John England*, vol. 1, 7, and Peter Clarke, "John England: Missionary to American, Then and Now," in *Patterns of Episcopal Leadership*, ed. Gerald P. Fogarty, SJ (New York: Macmillan, 1989), 70.

12. Clarke, "John England," 70.

13. Carey, *Immigrant Bishop*, 22. Guilday, *Life and Times of John England*, vol. 1, 117. *Cork Mercantile Chronicle*, August 30, 1815, quoted in Carey, *Immigrant Bishop*, 71. Guilday, *Life and Times of John England*, vol. 1, 122. Reynolds, *Works of the Right Rev. John England*, vol. 1, 11. Clarke, "John England," 70. Carey, *Immigrant Bishop*, 49.

14. Richard Madden, *Catholics in South Carolina: A Record* (New York: University Press of America, 1985), 28. John England, *Diurnal*, Charleston Diocesan Archives, 45.

15. The copy of the constitution I am using is that in Reynolds, *Works of the Right Rev. John England*, vol. 5, 91–108. That is the second edition, published in 1839, but, as Guilday points out, it is nearly identical to the draft ver-

sion submitted to the Vatican for approval back in 1822. The first edition was first published in 1826 and is extremely rare. The second edition is the edition by which historians discuss John England's role in the American church. See Guilday, *Life and Times of John England*, vol. 1, 343–44.

16. *U.S. Catholic Miscellany*, March 24, 1824, 178–79.

17. *Records of the American Catholic Historical Society of Philadelphia* 8 (1897), 328–29, quoted by Clarke, "John England," 394.

18. Letter, England to Cullen, August 18, 1834, reprinted in Guilday, *Life and Times of John England*, vol. 2, 320. Scipio de' Ricci, *Female Convents. Secrets of Nunneries Disclosed*, comp. Mr. De Potter, ed. Thomas Roscoe (New York: D. Appleton & Co., 1834), xxii, quoted in Ray Allen Billington, *The Protestant Crusade, 1800–1860* (New York: Macmillan, 1938), 68. Report of Bishop England to the Cardinal Prefect of Propaganda, *Records of the American Catholic Historical Society of Philadelphia* 8 (1897), 323.

19. Letter, England to Gaston, January 30, 1837, *Records of the American Catholic Historical Society of Philadelphia* 19 (1908), 161–62.

20. Letter, England to Dr. Cullen, February 23, 1836, *Records of the American Catholic Historical Society of Philadelphia* 8 (1897), 219.

21. Letter, England to Gaston, January 30, 1837, *Records of the American Catholic Historical Society of Philadelphia* 19 (1908), 161–62. Letter, England to Cullen, February 23, 1836, *Records of the American Catholic Historical Society of Philadelphia* 8 (1897), 218–19.

22. Letter, England to Cullen, February 23, 1836, *Records of the American Catholic Historical Society of Philadelphia* 8 (1897), 230–32.

23. Letter, England to Cullen, February 23, 1836, *Records of the American Catholic Historical Society of Philadelphia* 8 (1897), 219–20.

24. Letter to the Editor, *Charleston Courier*, July 30, 1835. Letter, England to Cullen, February 23, 1836, *Records of the American Catholic Historical Society of Philadelphia* 8 (1897), 232.

25. Letter, England to Cullen, February 23, 1836, *Records of the American Catholic Historical Society of Philadelphia* 8 (1897), 220. Letter, England to the Presiding Officer of the S.C. Association, July 29, 1835, reprinted in *Charleston Courier*, July 30, 1835.

26. *Charleston Courier*, August 4, 1835. Letter, England to Cullen, February 23, 1836, *Records of the American Catholic Historical Society of Philadelphia* 8 (1897), 221.

27. Letter, England to Cullen, February 23, 1836, *Records of the American Catholic Historical Society of Philadelphia* 8 (1897), 222.

28. Letter, Angelina Grimké to Sarah Grimké, September 27, 1835, in Angelina Grimké and Sarah Grimké, *The Public Years of Sarah and Angelina Grimké: Selected Writings, 1835–1839*, ed. Larry Ceplair (New York: Columbia

University Press, 1989), 28. Angelina Grimké, *Walking by Faith: The Diary of Angelina Grimké, 1828–1835*, ed. Charles Wilbanks (Columbia: University of South Carolina Press, 2003), 210.

29. See, for example, Patrick H. Breen, "A Prophet in His Own Land: Support for Nat Turner and His Rebellion within Southampton's Black Community," in *Nat Turner: A Slave Rebellion in History and Memory*, ed. Kenneth Greenberg (New York: Oxford University Press, 2003), 104. "The Insurrection," *The Liberator* 1, no. 36 (September 3, 1831): 143.

30. Eva Sheppard Wolf, *Race and Liberty in the New Nation: Emancipation in Virginia from the Revolution to Nat Turner's Rebellion* (Baton Rouge: Louisiana State University Press, 2006), 196. *Speech of Thomas J. Randolph in the House of Delegates of Virginia, on the Abolition of Slavery* (Richmond, VA: Samuel Shepherd and Company, 1832), 3, 6. See Wolf, *Race and Liberty in the New Nation*, 198 and 230. By contrast, Allison Goodyear Freehling holds that the debate did not finally settle anything in Virginia between the proponents and opponents of abolition (see *Drift toward Dissolution: The Virginia Slavery Debate, 1831–1832* [Baton Rouge: Louisiana State University Press, 1982]).

31. For "positive law" see Erik S. Root, *All Honor to Jefferson?: The Virginia Slavery Debates and the Positive Good Thesis* (Lanham, MD: Lexington Books, 2008). Thomas Roderic Dew, *Abolition of Negro Slavery*, in *The Ideology of Slavery: Proslavery Thought in the Antebellum South, 1830–1860*, ed. Drew Gilpin Faust (Baton Rouge: Louisiana State University Press, 1981), 27–28. For an analysis of Dew's economic theory, see Eugene D. Genovese, *The Slaveholders' Dilemma: Freedom and Progress in the Southern Conservative Thought, 1820–1860* (Columbia: University of South Carolina Press, 1992), 18.

32. "Christian Heroism," *The Liberator* 5, no. 38 (September 19, 1835): 150.

33. Letter, AG to William Lloyd Garrison, August 30, 1835. First published in *The Liberator* 5, no. 38 (September 19, 1835): 150. It is more conveniently available in *Public Years of Sarah and Angelina Grimké*, 25–27, quotations from 25–26.

34. *Public Years of Sarah and Angelina Grimké*, 26. Letter, Andrew Jackson to Amos Kendall, August 9, 1835, quoted in William Freehling, *The Road to Disunion*, vol. 1, *Secessionists at Bay, 1776–1854* (New York: Oxford University Press, 1990), 291.

35. "Speech at Pennsylvania Hall," May 16, 1838, in *Public Years of Sarah and Angelina Grimké*, 319.

36. Within a year, Grimké developed her "doctrine of non-resistance" and advocated that "every member of an Anti-Slave Society should belong to a Peace Society" (Letter, Angelina Grimké to The Ladies Anti-Slavery Society, Concord, New Hampshire, March 16, 1836, in *Public Years of Sarah and Angelina Grimké*, 32).

37. Grimké, *Walking by Faith*, 212. *Public Years of Sarah and Angelina Grimké*, 27 and 30n.

38. See, for example, Gerda Lerner, *The Grimké Sisters from South Carolina; Pioneers for Women's Rights and Abolition*, Revised and Expanded Edition (Chapel Hill: University of North Carollina, 1967, 1998, 2004).

39. Stephen Howard Browne, *Angelina Grimké: Rhetoric, Identity, and the Radical Imagination* (East Lansing: Michigan University Press, 1999), 7 and 16.

CHAPTER 8

1. *Washington Globe*, April 24, 1833, quoted in Richard E. Ellis, *Union at Risk: Jacksonian Democracy, States' Rights, and the Nullification Crisis* (New York: Oxford University Press, 1989), 190.

2. William Freehling, *The Road to Disunion*, vol. 1, *Secessionists at Bay, 1776–1854* (New York: Oxford University Press, 1990), 292.

3. Letter, Arthur P. Hayne to Andrew Jackson, November 11, 1835, Jackson Papers in the Library of Congress, quoted and summarized by Freehling, *Road to Disunion*, vol. 1, 292–93.

4. Henry J. Nott to James Hammond, March 8, 1835, Hammond Papers, Library of Congress; *United States Telegraph*, September 4, 1835; and James Hammond to M. M. Noah, August 19, 1835, Hammond Papers, Library of Congress, quoted in Freehling, *Road to Disunion*, vol. 1, 295; *United States Telegraph*, September 4, 1835; James Hammond to M. M. Noah, August 19, 1835, Hammond Papers, Library of Congress; all quoted in Freehling, *Road to Disunion*, vol. 1, 293–95.

5. S. M. Grimké, *An Epistle to the Clergy of the Southern States* (New York: s.n., 1836), 15.

6. Drew Gilpin Faust, *James Henry Hammond and the Old South: A Design for Mastery* (Baton Rouge: Louisiana State University, 1982), 7, 11, 16, 225. William Gilmore Simms, *The Letters of William Gilmore Simms*, ed. Mary Simms Oliphant, Alfred Taylor Odell, and T. C. Duncan Eaves (Columbia: University of South Carolina Press, 1952), cxii.

7. Carol Bleser, ed., *The Hammonds of Redcliffe* (New York: Oxford University Press, 1981), 6. Faust, *James Henry Hammond and the Old South*, 29, 33, 70–71, 230. The portrait, reproduced as a frontispiece in Faust, is in the South Caroliniana Library.

8. Faust, *James Henry Hammond and the Old South*, 70–75.

9. Register of Debates, 24th Cong., 1st Sess. (January 21, 1836): 2244. Quoted in Freehling, *Road to Disunion*, vol. 1, 311.

10. Freehling, *Road to Disunion*, vol. 1, 315–16. See also Eugene Genovese, *The Slaveholders' Dilemma: Freedom and Progress in the Southern Conservative Thought, 1820–1860* (Columbia: University of South Carolina Press, 1992).

11. Register of Debates, 24th Cong., 1st Sess. (February 1, 1836), 2448, 2460, and 2456. Freehling discusses this speech at some length, although he mistakenly attributes it to the 2nd session (*Road to Disunion*, vol. 1, 319–21).

12. Register of Debates, 24th Cong., 1st Sess. (January 21, 1836), 2248–49.

13. Register of Debates, 24th Cong., 1st Sess. (February 1, 1836), 2458.

14. Ibid., 2457.

15. Faust, *James Henry Hammond and the Old South*, 87, 241–43. Hammond Diary, January 31, 1844, Library of Congress, quoted in Faust, *James Henry Hammond and the Old South*, 242.

16. Faust, *James Henry Hammond and the Old South*, 100–101.

17. Charles M. Wiltse, *John C. Calhoun Nullifier, 1829–1839* (Indianapolis: Bobbs-Merrill, 1949), 278.

18. John C. Calhoun, *The Papers of John C. Calhoun*, eds. W. Edwin Hemphill, Clyde N. Wilson, and Shirley Bright Cook, vol. 13 (Columbia: University of South Carolina Press, 1987), 91, 102–3. This speech is also available in the *Register of Debates*, 24th Cong., 1st Sess., cols. 765–78.

19. *Papers of John C. Calhoun*, vol. 13, 98, 105, 103, 107.

20. Ibid., 104.

21. Freehling, *Road to Disunion*, vol. 1, 326. *Papers of John C. Calhoun*, vol. 13, 100, 104, 108.

22. Freehling, *Road to Disunion*, vol. 1, 327–31.

23. Ibid., 332, 336.

24. Henry Laurens Pinckney, *Address to the Electors of Charleston District, South Carolina, on the Subject of the Abolition of Slavery* (Washington, DC: n.p., 1836), 4–6.

25. *John C. Calhoun: Selected Writings and Speeches*, ed. H. Lee Cheek Jr., Conservative Leadership Series (Washington, DC: Regnery Publishing, 2003), 693, 686, and *Papers of John C. Calhoun*, vol. 13, 396. Wiltse, *John C. Calhoun Nullifier*, 278, emphasis added.

26. *Papers of John C. Calhoun*, vol. 13, 390–98.

27. Christine Kinealy, *Daniel O'Connell and the Anti-Slavery Movement: 'The Saddest People the Sun Sees'* (London: Pickering & Chatto, 2011), 27–28, 52–53. John England, *Letters of the Late Bishop England to the Hon. John Forsyth: On the Subject of Domestic Slavery: To Which Are Prefixed Copies, in Latin and English, of the Pope's Apostolic Letter concerning the African Slave Trade: with Some Introductory Remarks, etc.* (Baltimore: J. Murphy, 1844), 13, 18.

28. John Forsyth, "Address to the People of Georgia," *Augusta Constitutionalist*, September 5 and 12, 1840. R. Frank Saunders Jr. and George A. Rogers, "Bishop John England of Charleston: Catholic Spokesman and Southern Intellectual, 1820–1842," *Journal of the Early Republic* 13, no. 3 (Autumn

1993): 319. England, *Letters of the Late Bishop England to the Hon. John Forsyth*, 13.

29. Letter, John England to Judge Gaston, September 4, 1840, in *Records of the American Catholic Historical Society of Philadelphia* 19 (1908), 180. England, *Letters of the Late Bishop England to the Hon. John Forsyth*, 15.

30. Ignatius Alysius Reynolds, ed., *The Works of the Right Rev. John England, First Bishop of Charleston*, 5 vols. (Baltimore: John Murphy & Co., 1849), vol. 3, 110–12.

31. "The Slave Trade," in Reynolds, *Works of the Right Rev. John England*, vol. 3, 112. First published in the *United States Catholic Miscellany*, March 14, 1840.

32. "The Slave Trade," in Reynolds, *Works of the Right Rev. John England*, vol. 3, 112. First published in the *United States Catholic Miscellany*, March 14, 1840. Reynolds, *Works of the Right Rev. John England*, vol. 3, 190–91.

33. "Death of the Right Reverend Dr. England," *Charleston Patriot*, April 12, 1842, reprinted in Reynolds, *Works of the Right Rev. John England*, vol. 1, 21. For dysentery, see William George Read, *Memoir of the Rt. Rev. John England* (Baltimore: John Murphy, 1842), 18. "Death of Bishop England," *Charleston Courier*, April 12, 1842, reprinted in Reynolds, *Works of the Right Rev. John England*, vol. 1, 22.

34. Freehling, *Road to Disunion*, vol. 1, 302.

35. For a discussion of how the antislavery Baptists and Methodists came to support slavery within a couple of generations in southern states, see Christine Leigh Heyrman, *Southern Cross: The Beginnings of the Bible Belt* (Chapel Hill: University of North Carolina Press, 1998).

36. "The time will come" quoted in John W. Higham, "The Changing Loyalties of William Gilmore Simms," *Journal of Southern History* 9 (May 1943): 214. Frances Trollope, *Domestic Manners of the Americans*, 2 vols. (London: Whittaker, Tracher, Co., New York reprint, 1832). William Gilmore Simms, "*Domestic Manners of the Americans* by Mrs. Trollope," *American Quarterly Review* 12 no. 23, (September 1, 1832): 109. Wakelyn suggests that Simms, who distrusted mobocracy, attacked Trollope by championing a republican ideology that "he hardly believed" and that "Simms was already close-minded on the subject of slavery" (Jon L. Wakelyn, *The Politics of a Literary Man: William Gilmore Simms* [Westport, CT: Greenwood Press, 1973], 52). But, as my interpretation suggests, it seems more plausible that Simms was himself transitioning from the gradualist emancipatory view to the perpetual view.

37. Faust, *James Henry Hammond and the Old South*, 36–37. For the review, see Faust, *James Henry Hammond and the Old South*, 55.

38. William P. Trent, *William Gilmore Simms* (New York: Haskell House, 1968), 91.

39. See Vincent King, "'Foolish Talk 'Bout Freedom': Simms's Vision of America in *The Yemassee*," *Studies in the Novel* 35, no. 2 (2003): 141.

40. Anthony Dyer Hoefer, "'The Slaves That They Are' and the Slaves That They Might Become: Bondage and Liberty in William Gilmore Simms's *The Yemassee*," *MELUS* 34, no. 3 (Fall 2009): 129. Charles S. Watson, *From Nationalism to Secessionism: The Changing Fiction of William Gilmore Simms* (Westport, CT: Greenwood Press, 1993), 17.

41. William Gilmore Simms, *The Yemassee: A Romance of Carolina*, ed. John Caldwell Guilds, Selected Fiction of William Gilmore Simms Arkansas Edition (Fayetteville: University of Arkansas Press, 1994), xix–xxx.

42. *Letters of William Gilmore Simms*, vol. 1, 90–93.

43. Trent, *William Gilmore Simms*, 96–99.

44. Ibid., 99.

45. William Gilmore Simms, "Miss Martineau on Slavery," *Southern Literary Messenger* (Richmond), 3, no. 9 (November 1837): 643.

46. Ibid., 641–57. Quotations are from 656 and 657. Higham, "Changing Loyalties of William Gilmore Simms," 215.

47. *Letters of William Gilmore Simms*, vol. 1, cxiii. Trent, *William Gilmore Simms*, 155. *Letters of William Gilmore Simms*, vol. 1, cxii.

48. See Alan Henry Rose, "The Image of the Negro in the Pre-Civil-War Novels of John Pendleton Kennedy and William Gilmore Simms," *Journal of American Studies* 4 (February 1971): 217. See *Letters of William Gilmore Simms*, vol. 1, 308–14. John Caldwell Guilds, *Simms: A Literary Life* (Fayetteville: University of Arkansas Press, 1992), 132. *Letters of William Gilmore Simms*, vol. 1, 312, 318. *Magnolia* 1 (September 1842): 200, quoted in Guilds, *Simms: A Literary Life*, 138.

49. Guilds, *Simms: A Literary Life*, 134–38, 141.

50. "Editorial Bureau: Our New Monthly," *Southern and Western Monthly Magazine and Review* 1 (January 1845): 67, 67–68, quoted in Guilds, *Simms: A Literary Life*, 146–47. "Northern" is Guilds, *Simms: A Literary Life*, 147. "small but fairly capable" is Guilds, *Simms: A Literary Life*, 150.

51. Simms, "Gen. Hammond's Letters on Slavery," *Southern and Western Monthly Magazine and* Review 2 (July 1845): 72. William Gilmore Simms, Thomas Dew, James Hammond, and William Harper, *The Pro-Slavery Argument as Maintained by the Most Distinguished Writers of the Southern States, Containing the Several Essays, on the Subject, of Chancellor Harper, Governor Hammond, Dr. Simms, and Professor Dew* (Charleston, SC: Walker, Richards, 1852), 100–175. Calhoun quotation in Faust, *James Henry Hammond and the Old South*, 278.

52. See the description of Stowe's book in Doris Kearns Goodwin's *Team of Rivals: The Political Genius of Abraham Lincoln* (New York: Simon & Schuster, 2005), 161–62. For the anecdote, see Daniel L. Vollaro, "Lincoln, Stowe, and

the Little Woman/Great War Story: The Making, and Breaking, of a Great American Anecdote," *Journal of the Abraham Lincoln Association* 30, no. 1 (2009): 22. "Notices of New Works," *Southern Literary Messenger* 18 (October 1852): 630–38, quoted by Charles S. Watson, "Simms' Review of *Uncle Tom's Cabin*," *American Literature* 48 (November 1976): 368.

53. *Letters of William Gilmore Simms*, vol. 3, 222–23, 243n64. In this same letter to Hammond, Simms bemoaned the fact that the Charleston papers had not much noted his achievement.

54. Laylon Wayne Jordan, "Education for Community: C. G. Memminger and the Origination of Common Schools in Antebellum Charleston," *South Carolina Historical Magazine* 83 (April 1982): 110, 114.

55. 1860 U.S. Census, 448.

56. For a very useful summary of southern identity as constructed by northerners, from colonial times through the Civil War, see the first chapter of James C. Cobb, *Away Down South: A History of Southern Identity* (New York: Oxford University Press, 2007), 9–33. Laylon W. Jordan, "Schemes of Usefulness: Christopher Gustavus Memminger," in *The Intellectual Life in Antebellum Charleston*, ed. Michael O'Brien and David Moltke-Hansen (Knoxville: University of Tennessee Press, 1986), 213.

57. See chap. 23, "The Motivation," in William Freehling, *Road to Disunion*, vol. 2, *Secessionists Triumphant, 1854–1861* (New York: Oxford University Press, 1990), 352–74.

CHAPTER 9

1. *Charleston Courier*, April 24, 1860, 1–2. M. Halstead, *Caucuses of 1860. A History of the National Political Conventions of the Current Presidential Campaign: Being a Complete Record of the Business of All the Conventions with Sketches of Distinguished Men in Attendance upon Them. And Descriptions of the Most Characteristic Scenes and Memorable Events* (Columbus, OH: Pollett, Foster, 1860), 5.

2. *Charleston Courier*, April 24, 1860, 1–2. Halstead, *Caucuses of 1860*, 5. Ralph Wooster, "Membership of the South Carolina Secession Convention," *South Carolina Historical Magazine* 55 (1954): 186.

3. Eric H. Walther, *William Lowndes Yancey and the Coming of the Civil War* (Chapel Hill: University of North Carolina Press, 2006), 22–45. Halstead, *Caucuses of 1860*, 5.

4. William C. Davis, *Rhett: The Turbulent Life and Times of a Fire-Eater* (Columbia: University of South Carolina Press, 2001), 1–29, 47–48, 84–90. Quotations from 48, 88, 90.

5. Robert Barnwell Rhett, *A Fire-Eater Remembers: The Confederate Memoir of Robert Barnwell Rhett*, ed. William C. Davis (Columbia: University of South Carolina Press, 2000), 11.

6. Halstead, *Caucuses of 1860*, 6 and 9.

7. See William Freehling, *The Road to Disunion*, vol. 2, *Secessionists Triumphant, 1854–1861* (New York: Oxford University Press), 296–97.

8. Halstead, *Caucuses of 1860*, 48.

9. Walther, *William Lowndes Yancey and the Coming of the Civil War*, 35.

10. William Lowndes Yancey, *Speech of the Hon. William L. Yancey, of Alabama, Delivered in the National Democratic Convention, Charleston, April 28th, 1860, with the Protest of the Alabama Delegation*, from the Report of the "Charleston Mercury," pamphlet, no publisher, no date.

11. Yancey, *Speech of the Hon. William L. Yancey*, 13.

12. Ibid., 13.

13. Ibid., 14, 16. Halstead, *Caucuses of 1860*, 49.

14. Halstead, *Caucuses of 1860*, 49–50.

15. Ibid., 76.

16. Ibid., 75.

17. *Charleston Tri-Weekly Courier*, November 8 and 15, 1860. For Georgetown slaves, Thomas Wentworth Higginson, *Army Life in a Black Regiment* (New York: Barnes and Noble, 2009), 28.

18. John Amasa May and Joan Reynolds Faunt, *South Carolina Secedes* (Columbia: University of South Carolina Press, 1960), 94. May and Faunt, whose history was commissioned by South Carolina's all-white, Jim Crow legislature a hundred years later, consider it something to brag about that only the "highest type of men" served as delegates, suggesting that the state's politics were nearly as undemocratic even a hundred years later. For "wealthy, middle-aged," Wooster, "Membership of the South Carolina Secession Convention," 189–90.

19. "Extract from a private letter," *New York Tribune*, November 27, 1860, quoted in Lillian A. Kibler, "Unionist Sentiment in South Carolina in 1860," *Journal of Southern History* 4 (August 1938): 362, 360. The *Charleston Tri-Weekly Courier* extensively reported, and apparently approved, the cooperationist speeches in the state legislature just after Lincoln's election (see, for example, "Legislative Proceedings," Tuesday morning, November 13, 1860). All discussions of the political crisis take it for granted that South Carolina wanted to secede; the only question was whether it would or would not wait for other slave states to join her. See also Freehling, *Road to Disunion*, vol. 2, 375–94. *New York Tribune*, December 11, 1860. Kibler, "Unionist Sentiment in South Carolina in 1860," 361.

20. *Journal of the Convention of the People of South Carolina, Held in 1860–1861. Together with the Reports, Resolutions, &c.* (Charleston, SC: Evans & Cogswell, 1861), 3–4.

21. William J. Grayson, *James Louis Petigru: A Biographical Sketch* (New York: Harper & Brothers, 1866), 150.

22. *Charleston Mercury*, December 21, 1860.

23. *Charleston Mercury*, December 22, 1863.

24. Mary Chesnut, *Mary Chesnut's Civil War*, ed. C. Vann Woodward (New Haven, CT: Yale University Press, 1981), 4.

25. "Hostilities Commenced Bombardment of Fort Sumter," *Charleston Tri-Weekly Courier*, April 13, 1861, 1.

26. Ibid.. "The Issue," *Charleston Mercury*, April 12, 1861. "Bombardment of Fort Sumter," *Charleston Mercury*, April 13, 1861. For an excellent, thorough account of the attack on Fort Sumter and the events leading to it, see David Detzer, *Allegiance: Fort Sumter, Charleston, and the Beginning of the Civil War* (New York: Harcourt, 2001).

27. "Our Washington Dispatches," *New York Herald*, April 15, 1861. "A New Account of the Battle at Fort Sumter!," *Boston Daily Advertiser*, April 16, 1861, 1 and 4.

28. "Notice" in preface to Henry Laurens, *South Carolina Protest against Slavery* (New York: G. P. Putnam, 1861), 5–6.

29. Higginson, *Army Life in a Black Regiment*, 8. James Henry Gooding, *On the Altar of Freedom: A Black Soldier's Civil War Letters from the Front*, ed. Virginia Matzke Adams (Amherst: University of Massachusetts Press, 1991), 26.

30. See Patrick Brennan, *Secessionville: Assault on Charleston* (Campbell, CA: Savas Publishing Company, 1996), 9–10, and E. Milby Burton, *The Siege of Charleston 1861–1865* (Columbia: University of South Carolina Press, 1970), 78–80.

31. Burton, *Siege of Charleston*, 80–84.

32. Andrew Billingsley, *Yearning to Breathe Free: Robert Smalls of South Carolina and His Families* (Columbia: University of South Carolina Press, 2007), 54–55. E. Milby Burton, *Siege of Charleston*, 92–94.

33. Billingsley, *Yearning to Breathe Free*, 54–58.

34. Ibid., 31–33, 42, 44–45.

35. Ibid., 58.

36. Burton, *Siege of Charleston*, 94–95.

37. Billingsley, *Yearning to Breathe Free*, 58–59.

38. Ibid., 60–65.

39. Burton, *Siege of Charleston*, 96–98.

40. Accessible Archives, May 15, 2011.

41. For "high feathers," Meg Stevens to Bache, April 8, 1962, quoted in Brennan, *Secessionville*, p. 6; Benham's photograph is reproduced on p. 2. "The Secessionville Fight," *Charleston Mercury*, June 18, 1862. For "a shower of musket," see G. B. Fuller, letter, *Jackson Weekly Citizen*, July 5, 1862, quoted in Brennan, *Secessionville*, 176; for the scythe image, Orrin Bump, *Personal Account of Private Orrin Bump, 8th Michigan Infantry*, Bentley Historical Library, quoted in

Brennan, *Secessionville*, 170; other details of the battle are drawn from Brennan, *Secessionville*, chaps. 7 and 8. See also Burton, *Siege of Charleston*, 98–114.

42. For "Look!," see W. E. C., letter in the *Flint Wolverine Citizen*, July 5, 1862, quoted in Brennan, *Secessionville*, 270.

43. *Charleston Mercury*, June 17, 1862.

44. Stephen R. Wise, *Gate of Hell: Campaign for Charleston Harbor, 1863* (Columba: University of South Carolina Press, 1994), 18. A color plate of this portrait is reproduced in Robert N. Rosen, *Confederate Charleston: An Illustrated History of the City and the People during the Civil War* (Columbia: University of South Carolina Press, 1994), 12.

45. John Johnson, *The Defense of Charleston Harbor, including Fort Sumter and the Adjacent Islands, 1863–1865* (New York: Books for Libraries Press, 1970 [first published in 1889]), 28. For a summary of this engagement, see Burton, *Siege of Charleston*, 126–31. For the mood of the city, see Diary of Jacob Schirmer, January 31, 1863, in South Carolina Historical Society, quoted in Burton, *Siege of Charleston*, 129.

46. *Official Records of the Union and Confederate Armies in the War of the Rebellion*. (Washington, DC: Government Printing Office, 1880–1922), vol. 1, 32–33, quoted in Burton, *Siege of Charleston*, 54–55.

47. Letter, Isabella Cheves to her children, November [n.d.] 1862. Middleton, Harriott Kinloch, 1801–1878. *Harriott K. Middleton Family correspondence, 1861–1865*. (1168.02.06), South Carolina Historical Society. Alicia Middleton to Harriott Middleton, December 10 [?], 1862. Middleton, Harriott Kinloch, 1801–1878, *Harriott K. Middleton Family correspondence, 1861–1865* (1168.02.06), South Carolina Historical Society. Letter, December 6, 1862, Harriott Kinloch Middleton, 1801–1878, *Harriott K. Middleton Family correspondence, 1861–1865*, South Carolina Historical Society.

48. Higginson, *Army Life in a Black Regiment*, 32–33.

49. T. Harry Williams, *P.G.T. Beauregard: Napoleon in Gray* (Baton Rouge: Louisiana Statue University Press, 1955), 52.

50. Schirmer Family, December 24, 1862, *Schirmer Family Journals and Registers, 1806–1929*, South Carolina Historical Society.

51. Wise, *Gate of Hell*, 44. Francis Middleton to Harriott Middleton, February 22, 1863. Harriott Kinloch Middleton, 1801–1878. *Harriott K. Middleton Family Correspondence, 1861–1865*, South Carolina Historical Society.

52. Burton, *Siege of Charleston*, 98. Williams, *P.G.T. Beauregard*, 175.

53. The comparison was made in Charleston later that summer: the Union commander, General Gillmore, likened to the Persian king, Xerxes. Wise, *Gate of Hell*, 81.

54. See Brennan, *Secessionville*, 284.

55. See George B. Davis, Leslie J. Perry, and Joseph W. Kirkley, *The Of-*

ficial Military Atlas of the Civil War, comp. Calvin D. Cowles (New York: Arno Press, 1978). This volume is a reproduction of the original *Atlas to Accompany the Official Records of the Union and Confederate Armies* by the same authors (Washington, DC: Government Printing Office, 1891–1895). Charleston's defenses are depicted on plate 4, 1. A more accessible but less detailed map of Charleston's defenses can be found in Craig L. Symonds, *A Battlefield Atlas of the Civil War* (Baltimore: Nautical and Aviation Publishing Company of America, 1983), 4–5.

56. Wise, *Gate of Hell*, 81.

57. Burton, *Siege of Charleston*, 135–41; Johnson, *Defense of Charleston Harbor*, 78.

58. Johnson, *Defense of Charleston Harbor*, 88–97. Quotations from 95 and 103.

59. Gooding, *On the Altar of Freedom*, 38–40.

60. Billingsley, *Yearning to Breathe Free*, 82, 84–85.

61. For the sap rollers, see Wise, *Gate of Hell*, 180. Burton, *Siege of Charleston*, 135–45, 154–80. Gooding, *On the Altar of Freedom*, 57–58.

62. Johnson, *Defense of Charleston Harbor*, 273. Quotation from W. Chris Phelps, *The Bombardment of Charleston, 1863–1865* (Gretna, LA: Pelican, 2002), 23.

63. Phelps, *Bombardment of Charleston*, 27–28, 35–36; Johnson, *Defense of Charleston Harbor*, 132n; Gooding, *On the Altar of Freedom*, 56.

64. Phelps, *Bombardment of Charleston*, 27–35.

65. Ibid., 46–47, 60–61.

66. Ibid., 93–100.

67. Ibid., 137–40.

68. Billingsley, *Yearning to Breathe Free*, 89–90. Luis Fenollosa Emilio, *History of the Fifty-Fourth Regiment of Massachusetts Volunteer Infantry, 1863–1865*, 2nd ed. (Boston: Boston Book Company, 1894), 282–85. Joel Williamson, *After Slavery: The Negro in South Carolina during Reconstruction, 1861–1877* (Hanover, NH: University Press of New England, 1965, 1990), 22.

69. Billingsley, *Yearning to Breathe Free*, 91–92.

70. John Wilkes Booth, *"Right or Wrong, God Judge Me": The Writings of John Wilkes Booth*, ed. John Rhodehamel and Louise Taper (Urbana: University of Illinois Press, 2001), 7.

71. Phelps, *Bombardment of Charleston*, 137–40.

CONCLUSION

1. For good discussions of the war's end and Reconstruction in South Carolina, see Joel Williamson, *After Slavery: The Negro in South Carolina during Reconstruction, 1861–1877* (Hanover, NH: University Press of New England, 1965, 1990); James Lowell Underwood and W. Lewis Burke Jr., eds., *At Free-*

dom's Door: African American Founding Fathers and Lawyers in Reconstruction South Carolina (Columbia: University of South Carolina Press, 2000); Eric Foner, *Forever Free: The Story of Emancipation and Reconstruction* (New York: Alfred A. Knopf, 2005); and Eric Foner, *Reconstruction: America's Unfinished Revolution, 1863–1877* (New York: Harper & Row, 1988). For the figure of forty thousand small-holding farmers, see Williamson, *After Slavery*, 62–63. Thomas Wentworth Higginson, *Army Life in a Black Regiment* (New York: Barnes and Noble, 2009), 211.

    2. Billingsley, *Yearning to Breathe Free*, 98–99, 104.

    3. Higginson, *Army Life in a Black Regiment*, 211. Williamson, *After Slavery*, 94–95, 263, 278, 287–88, 295. Foner, *Reconstruction*, 425–26.

    4. Williamson, *After Slavery*, 360.

    5. For white Republicans in South Carolina, see Hyman Rubin III, *South Carolina Scalawags* (Columbia: University of South Carolina Press, 2006). For white dissenters in the antebellum period, Reconstruction, and later, see Carl N. Degler, *The Other South: Southern Dissenters in the Nineteenth Century* (New York: Harper & Row, 1974).

    6. *Congressional Record*, 84th Cong. Second Sess., vol. 102, part 4 (March 12, 1956). (Washington, DC: Governmental Printing Office, 1956), 4459–60.

    7. *Freedom of Health Care Protection Act*. H. 3101, South Carolina General Assembly, 120th Sess., 2013–2014. Christina Elmore and Glenn Smith, "Sheriff Cannon Says He Will Ignore Any Gun Control Measures He Deems Unconstitutional," *Charleston Post and Courier*, January 18, 2013. Online. January 23, 2013.

BIBLIOGRAPHY

||

Adams, William Howard. *Gouverneur Morris: An Independent Life.* New Haven, CT: Yale University Press, 2003.

"America's First Direct Mail Campaign." *Pushing the Envelope* (blog). July 29, 2010. http://postalmuseumblog.si.edu/2010/07/americas-first-direct-mail-campaign.html.

Ball, Edward. *Slaves in the Family.* New York: Farrar, Straus and Giroux, 1998. Print.

Barnes, Gilbert Hobbs. *The Antislavery Impulse: 1830–1844.* Gloucester, MA: Peter Smith, 1973.

Barry, Richard. *Mr. Rutledge of South Carolina.* Salem, NH: Ayer Publishing, 1942; reprinted in 1993.

Bartlett, Irving H. *John C. Calhoun: A Biography.* New York: W. W. Norton, 1993.

Berlin, Ira. *Many Thousands Gone: The First Two Centuries of Slavery in North America.* Cambridge, MA: Harvard University Press, 1998.

———. *Slaves without Masters: The Free Negro in the Antebellum South.* New York: Oxford University Press, 1974. Print.

Billingsley, Andrew. *Yearning to Breathe Free: Robert Smalls of South Carolina and His Families.* Columbia: University of South Carolina Press, 2007.

Billington, Ray Allen. *The Protestant Crusade, 1800–1860.* New York: Macmillan, 1938.

Bleser, Carol, ed. *The Hammonds of Redcliffe.* New York: Oxford University Press, 1981.

Boles, John B., ed. *Masters and Slaves in the House of the Lord: Race and Religion in the American South, 1740–1870.* Lexington: University Press of Kentucky, 1988.

Bolster, W. Jeffery. *Black Jacks: African-American Seamen in the Age of Sail.* Cambridge, MA: Harvard University Press, 1997.

Booth, John Wilkes. *"Right or Wrong, God Judge Me": The Writings of John Wilkes Booth.* Edited by John Rhodehamel and Louise Taper. Urbana: University of Illinois Press, 2001.

Borick, Carl P. *A Gallant Defense: The Siege of Charleston, 1780*. Columbia: University of South Carolina Press, 2003.

Bowes, Frederick P. *The Culture of Early Charleston*. Chapel Hill: University of North Carolina Press, 1942. Print.

Brands, H. W. *Andrew Jackson, His Life and Times*. New York: Doubleday, 2005.

Breen, Patrick H. "A Prophet in His Own Land: Support for Nat Turner and His Rebellion within Southampton's Black Community." In *Nat Turner: A Slave Rebellion in History and Memory*, edited by Kenneth Greenberg, 103–18. New York: Oxford University Press, 2003.

Brennan, Patrick. *Secessionville: Assault on Charleston*. Campbell, CA: Savas Publishing Company, 1996. Print.

Broadwater, Jeff. *George Mason, Forgotten Founder*. Chapel Hill: University of North Carolina Press, 2006.

Brother, Christian. *A Century of Catholic Education: Brother Burke and His Associates*. Dublin: Browne and Nolan, 1916.

Browne, Stephen Howard. *Angelina Grimké: Rhetoric, Identity, and the Radical Imagination*. East Lansing: Michigan University Press, 1999.

Bryan, Hugh, and Mary Hutson. *Living Christianity Delineated in the Diaries and Letters of Two Eminently Pious Persons Lately Deceased, Viz. Mr. Hugh Bryan and Mrs. Mary Hutson*. Boston: Hastings, Etheridge, and Bliss, 1809. Print.

Buchanan, J. E. *The Colleton Family and the Early History of South Carolina and Barbados 1646–1775*. PhD diss., University of Edinburgh, 1989. Print.

Burke, Aedanus. Letter to Arthur Middleton. January 25, 1782. "Correspondence of Hon. Arthur Middleton, Signer of the Declaration of Independence." Edited by Joseph W. Barnwell. *South Carolina Historical and General Magazine* 25 (1925): 194. Print.

Burrows, Edwin G., and Mike Wallace. *Gotham A History of New York City to 1898*. New York: Oxford University Press, 1999.

Burton, E. Milby. *The Siege of Charleston, 1861–1865*. Columbia: University of South Carolina Press, 1970.

Burton, Orville Vernon. *The Age of Lincoln*. New York: Hill and Wang, 2007.

Buttimer, Cornelius G. "Gaelic Literature and Contemporary Life in Cork, 1700–1840." In *Cork: History and Society, Interdisciplinary Essays on the History of an Irish County*, edited by Patrick O'Flanagan and Cornelius Buttimer, 585–654. Dublin: Geography Publications, 1993.

Calhoun, John C. Great Britain, Reported to the House of Representatives, June 3, 1812, *American State Papers: Foreign Relations* 3: 567–70.

———. *John C. Calhoun: Selected Writings and Speeches*. Edited by H. Lee Cheek Jr. Conservative Leadership Series. Washington, DC: Regnery Publishing, 2003.

———. *The Papers of John C. Calhoun*. Edited by W. Edwin Hemphill, Clyde N. Wilson, and Shirley Bright Cook. 25 vols. Columbia: University of South Carolina Press, 1959–2003.

Carey, Patrick. *An Immigrant Bishop: John England's Adaptation of Irish Catholicism to American Republicanism*. Yonkers, NY: U.S. Catholic Historical Society, 1982.

Carll-White, Allison. "South Carolina's Forgotten Craftsmen." *South Carolina Historical Magazine* 86 (January 1985): 32–38.

Carson, James Petigru. *Life, Letters, and Speeches of James Louis Petigru, the Union Man of South Carolina*. Washington, DC: W. H. Lowdermilk & Co., 1920.

Cash, W. J. *The Mind of the South*. New York: Vintage Books, 1960. Print.

Chernow, Rob. *Alexander Hamilton*. New York: Penguin Press, 2004. Print.

Chesnut, Mary. *Mary Chesnut's Civil War*. Edited by C. Vann Woodward. New Haven, CT: Yale University Press, 1981. Print.

Cheves, Isabella. Letter to Her Children. November 1862. *Harriott K. Middleton Family Correspondence, 1861–1865*. South Carolina Historical Society. Print.

Clarke, Peter. "John England: Missionary to American, Then and Now." In *Patterns of Episcopal Leadership*, edited by Gerald P. Fogarty, SJ, 68–84. New York: Macmillan, 1989.

Cobb, James C. *Away Down South: A History of Southern Identity*. New York: Oxford University Press, 2007.

Collier, Christopher, and James Lincoln Collier. *Decision in Philadelphia: The Constitutional Convention of 1787*. New York: Random House, 1986.

Corkran, David H. *The Carolina Indian Frontier*. Columbia: University of South Carolina Press, 1970. Print.

Dabbs, James McBride. *Who Speaks for the South?* New York: Funk & Wagnalls, 1964. Print.

Davis, George B., Leslie J. Perry, and Joseph W. Kirkley. *The Official Military Atlas of the Civil War*. Compiled by Calvin D. Cowles. New York: Arno Press, 1978. Print.

Davis, William C. *Rhett: The Turbulent Life and Times of a Fire-Eater*. Columbia: University of South Carolina Press, 2001.

Day, Thomas. *Fragment of an Original Letter on the Slavery of the Negroes; Written in the Year 1776*. Philadelphia: Francis Bailey, 1784. Print.

Degler, Carl N. *The Other South: Southern Dissenters in the Nineteenth Century.* New York: Harper & Row, 1974.

Detzer, David. *Allegiance: Fort Sumter, Charleston, and the Beginning of the Civil War.* New York: Harcourt, 2001.

Dew, Thomas Roderic. *Abolition of Negro Slavery.* In *The Ideology of Slavery: Proslavery Thought in the Antebellum South, 1830–1860*, edited by Drew Gilpin Faust, 21–77. Baton Rouge: Louisiana State University Press, 1981.

Dollimore, Arnold A. *George Whitefield: The Life and Times of the Great Evangelist of the Eighteenth-Century Revival.* Vol. 1. Edinburgh: Banner of Truth Trust, 1970. Print.

Donnan, Elizabeth. *Documents Illustrative of the History of the Slave Trade to America.* 4 vols. Washington, DC: Carnegie Institution of Washington, 1930–1935.

Donnelly, James S., Jr. *The Land and the People of Nineteenth-Century Cork: The Rural Economy and the Land Question.* Boston: Routledge and Kegan Paul, 1975.

Douglass, Frederick. *Narrative of the Life of Frederick Douglass, an American Slave Written by Himself.* Boston: Anti-Slavery Office, 1845.

Duff, Meaghan N. *Designing Carolina: The Construction of an Early American Social and Geographical Landscape, 1670–1719.* PhD diss., The College of William and Mary, 1998. Print.

Easterby, J. H., ed. *Journal of the Commons House of Assembly.* 14 vols. Columbia: Historical Commission of South Carolina, 1951–.

Egerton, Douglas R. *He Shall Go Out Free: The Lives of Denmark Vesey.* Madison, WI: Madison House, 1999.

Egerton, Douglas R., and Robert L. Paquette. "Of Facts and Fables: New Light on the Denmark Vesey Affair." *South Carolina Historical Magazine* 105 (January 2004): 8–35.

Elliot, Jonathan, ed. *The Debates in the Several State Conventions of the Adoption of the Federal Constitution, as Recommended by the General Convention at Philadelphia in 1787.* Vol. 5. Philadelphia: J. B. Lippincott Company, 1836.

Ellis, Joseph. *American Sphinx: The Character of Thomas Jefferson.* New York: Vintage Books, 1998. Print.

———. *His Excellency George Washington.* New York: Alfred A. Knopf, 2005. Print.

Ellis, Richard E. *Union at Risk: Jacksonian Democracy, States' Rights, and the Nullification Crisis.* New York: Oxford University Press, 1989.

Emilio, Luis Fenollosa. *History of the Fifty-Fourth Regiment of Massachusetts Volunteer Infantry, 1863–1865*, 2nd ed. Boston: Boston Book Company, 1894.

England, John. *Diurnal of the Right Rev. John England, D.D. first Bishop of Charleston, South Carolina, 1820–1823*. Philadelphia: American Catholic Historical Society, 1895.

———. "Letters from the Right Reverend John England, D.D., to William Gaston, LL.D." *Records of the American Catholic Historical Society of Philadelphia* 18 (1907), 367–88.

———. *Letters of the Late Bishop England to the Hon. John Forsyth: On the Subject of Domestic Slavery: To Which Are Prefixed Copies, in Latin and English, of the Pope's Apostolic Letter concerning the African Slave Trade: with Some Introductory Remarks, etc.* Baltimore: J. Murphy, 1844.

"Extract from a Private Letter." *New York Tribune*, November 27, 1860. Quoted in Lillian A Kibler, "Unionist Sentiment in South Carolina in 1860." *Journal of Southern History* 4 (August 1938): 362, 360. Print.

"Extract of a Letter from South Carolina." *Boston Weekly Post-Boy*, May 3, 1742. Print.

Farmer, James O., Jr. *The Metaphysical Confederacy: James Henly Thornwell and the Synthesis of Southern Values*. Macon, GA: Mercer University Press, 1986. Print.

Farrand, Max, ed. *The Records of the Federal Convention of 1787*. 2 vols. New Haven, CT: Yale University Press, 1966.

Faust, Drew Gilpin. *James Henry Hammond and the Old South: A Design for Mastery*. Baton Rouge: Louisiana State University Press, 1982.

Ferrara, Marie. "Moses Henry Nathan and the Great Charleston Fire of 1861." *South Carolina Historical Magazine* 104 (2003): 258–80. Print.

Fischer, David Hackett. "Two Minds of the South: Ideas of Southern History in W. J. Cash and James McBride Dabbs." In *W. J. Cash and the Minds of the South*, edited by Paul D. Escott, 134–66. Baton Rouge: Louisiana State University Press, 1992. Print.

Foner, Eric. *The Fiery Trial: Abraham Lincoln and American Slavery*. New York: W. W. Norton, 2010.

Ford, Frederick A., comp. *Census of the City of Charleston, South Carolina, for the Year 1861*. Charleston, SC: Evans & Cogswell, 1861. Print.

Ford, Lacy K. *Deliver Us from Evil: The Slavery Question in the Old South*. New York: Oxford University Press, 2009.

———. "James Louis Petigru: The Last South Carolina Federalist." In Michael O'Brien and David Moltke-Hansen, *Intellectual Life in Antebel-*

lum Charleston, 152-85. Knoxville: University of Tennessee Press, 1986.

Forsyth, John. "Address to the People of Georgia." *Augusta Constitutionalist*, September 5 and 12, 1840.

Franklin, Benjamin. *Memoirs of the Life and Writings of Benjamin Franklin*. Vol. 1. Philadelphia: T. S. Manning, 1808. Print.

Fraser, Walter J., Jr. *Charleston! Charleston!: The History of a Southern City*. Columbia: University of South Carolina Press, 1989. Print.

Freehling, Allison Goodyear. *Drift toward Dissolution: The Virginia Slavery Debate, 1831–1832*. Baton Rouge: Louisiana State University Press, 1982.

Freehling, William. *The Road to Disunion*. 2 vols. New York: Oxford University Press, 1990. Print.

Gallay, Alan. "The Origins of Slaveholders' Paternalism: George Whitefield, the Bryan Family, and the Great Awakening in the South." *Journal of Southern History* 53 (August 1987): 369–94. Print.

———. "Planters and Slaves in the Great Awakening." In *Masters and Slaves in the House of the Lord: Race and Religion in the American South 1740–1870*, edited by John B. Boles, 19–37. Lexington: University Press of Kentucky, 1988.

Garden, Alexander. *Regeneration and the Testimony of the Spirit: Being the Substance of Two Sermons Lately Preached in the Parish Church of St. Philip's, Charles-Town, in South Carolina: Occasioned by Some Erroneous Notions of Certain Men Who Call Themselves Methodists*. Boston: T. Fleet, 1741. Print.

———. *Six Letters to the Rev. Mr. George Whitefield*. Boston: T. Fleet, 1740.

Genovese, Eugene. *In Red and Black: Marxian Explorations in Southern and Afro-American History*. New York: Pantheon Books, 1971. Print.

———. *Roll, Jordan, Roll: The World the Slaves Made*. New York: Pantheon Books, 1974. Print.

———. *The Slaveholders' Dilemma: Freedom and Progress in the Southern Conservative Thought, 1820–1860*. Columbia: University of South Carolina Press, 1992.

Gibbes, R. W., ed. *Documentary History of the American Revolution*. Vol. 2, *1776–1782*. Spartanburg, SC: The Reprint Company, 1972. Print.

Gillespie, Joanna Bowen. *The Life and Times of Martha Laurens Ramsay, 1759–1811*. Columbia: University of South Carolina Press, 2001.

Glenn, Virginia Louise. *James Hamilton, Jr., of South Carolina: A Biography*. PhD diss., University of North Carolina, Chapel Hill, 1964.

Gooding, James Henry. *On the Altar of Freedom: A Black Soldier's Civil War*

Letters from the Front. Edited by Virginia Matzke Adams. Amherst: University of Massachusetts Press, 1991.

Goodwin, Doris Kearns. *Team of Rivals: The Political Genius of Abraham Lincoln*. New York: Simon & Schuster, 2005.

Grayson, William J. *James Louis Petigru: A Biographical Sketch*. New York: Harper & Brothers, 1866. Print.

Greenberg, Irwin F. "Justice William Johnson: South Carolina Unionist, 1823–1830." *Pennsylvania History* 36 (July 1969): 307–34.

Greene, Jack. *The Quest for Power: The Lower Houses of Assembly in the Southern Royal Colonies, 1689–1776*. Chapel Hill: University of North Carolina Press, 1963. Print.

Grimké, Angelina. *Walking by Faith: The Diary of Angelina Grimké, 1828–1835*. Edited by Charles Wilbanks. Columbia: University of South Carolina Press, 2003.

Grimké, Angelina, and Sarah Grimké. *The Public Years of Sarah and Angelina Grimké: Selected Writings, 1835–1839*. Edited by Larry Ceplair. New York: Columbia University Press, 1989.

Grimké, Archibald. *Right on the Scaffold, or, The Martyrs of 1822*. Washington, DC: The Academy, 1901.

Grimké, S. M. *An Epistle to the Clergy of the Southern States*. New York: s.n., 1836.

Grimké, Thomas. *Letter to the Honorable John C. Calhoun, Vice-President of the United States, Robert Y. Hayne, Senator of the United States, George McDuffie, of the House of Representatives of the United States, and James Hamilton, Jr. Governor of the State of South Carolina*. 2nd ed. Charleston, SC: James S. Burges, 1832.

Guilday, Peter K. *The Life and Times of John England*. 2 vols. New York: America Press, 1927.

Guilds, John Caldwell. *Simms: A Literary Life*. Fayetteville: University of Arkansas Press, 1992.

Halstead, M. *Caucuses of 1860. A History of the National Political Conventions of the Current Presidential Campaign: Being a Complete Record of the Business of All the Conventions with Sketches of Distinguished Men in Attendance upon Them. And Descriptions of the Most Characteristic Scenes and Memorable Events*. Columbus, OH: Pollett, Foster, 1860.

Hamer, Philip M. "Great Britain, the United States, and the Negro Seaman Acts, 1822–1848." *Journal of Southern History* 1 (February 1935): 3–28.

Hamilton, Alexander. *The Papers of Alexander Hamilton*. Edited by Harold

C. Syrett. 27 vols. New York: Columbia University Press, 1961–1987.

Hamilton, James, Jr. *An Account of the Late Intended Insurrection among a Portion of the Blacks of This City*. Charleston, SC: A. E. Miller, 1822.

Hammond, James. [Slavery in the District of Columbia]. Register of Debates. 24th Congress. 1st Session. (1 February 1836): 2448–66. Online.

———. *An Oration on the Life, Character and Services of John Caldwell Calhoun*. Charleston, SC: Walker & James, 1850.

Harris, Robert L., Jr. "Charleston's Free Afro-American Elite: The Brown Fellowship Society and the Humane Brotherhood." *South Carolina Historical Magazine* 82 (October 1981): 289–310.

Haw, James. *John & Edward Rutledge of South Carolina*. Athens: University of Georgia Press, 1997.

Hawkins, James B. *Alexander Garden: The Commissary in Church and State*. PhD diss., Duke University, 1981. Print.

Hewitt, Gary L. *Expansion and Improvement: Land, People and Politics in South Carolina and Georgia, 1690–1745*. PhD diss., Princeton University, 1996. Print.

Heyrman, Christine Leigh. *Southern Cross: The Beginnings of the Bible Belt*. Chapel Hill: University of North Carolina Press, 1998.

Higginbotham, A. Leon, Jr. *In the Matter of Color: Race and the American Legal Process*. New York: Oxford University Press, 1978. Print.

Higginson, Thomas Wentworth. *Army Life in a Black Regiment*. New York: Barnes and Noble, 2009.

Higham, John W. "The Changing Loyalties of William Gilmore Simms." *Journal of Southern History* 9 (May 1943): 210–23.

Hoefer, Anthony Dyer. "'The Slaves That They Are' and the Slaves That They Might Become: Bondage and Liberty in William Gilmore Simms's *The Yemassee*." *MELUS* 34, no. 3 (Fall 2009): 115–32.

Holmes, Emma. *The Diary of Miss Emma Holmes, 1861–1866*. Edited by John F. Marszalek. Baton Rouge: Louisiana State University Press, 1979. Print.

I Belong to South Carolina: South Carolina Slave Narratives. Edited by Susanna Ashton. Columbia: University of South Carolina Press, 2010.

Jackson, Harvey H. "Hugh Bryan and the Evangelical Movement in Colonial South Carolina." *William and Mary Quarterly* 43 (October 1986): 594–614. Print.

January, Alan F. "The South Carolina Association: An Agency for Race Control in Antebellum Charleston," *South Carolina Historical Magazine* 78 (July 1977): 191–201.

Jefferson, Thomas. *The Writings of Thomas Jefferson.* Collected and edited by Paul L. Ford. 10 vols. New York: G. P. Putnam's Sons, 1892–1899.

Johnson, John. *The Defense of Charleston Harbor, including Fort Sumter and the Adjacent Islands, 1863–1865.* New York: Books for Libraries Press, 1970. Print.

Johnson, Michael. "Denmark Vesey and His Co-Conspirators." *William and Mary Quarterly*, 3rd Series, 58 (October 2001): 915–56.

Johnson, Michael P., and James L. Roark, eds. *No Chariot Let Down: Charleston's Free People of Color on the Eve of the Civil War.* New York: W.W. Norton & Co., 1984. Print.

Johnson, William, Jr. "Melancholy Effect of Popular Excitement," *Charleston Courier*, June 22 ,1822.

———. *To the Public of Charleston.* Charleston: C. C. Sebring, 1822.

Jordan, Laylon Wayne . "Education for Community: C. G. Memminger and the Origination of Common Schools in Antebellum Charleston." *South Carolina Historical Magazine* 83 (April 1982): 99–115.

———. "Schemes of Usefulness: Christopher Gustavus Memminger." In *The Intellectual Life in Antebellum Charleston*, edited by Michael O'Brien and David Moltke-Hansen, 211–29. Knoxville: University of Tennessee Press, 1986,

Jordan, Winthrop D. *The White Man's Burden: Historical Origins of Racism in the United States.* New York: Oxford University Press, 1974. Print.

Journal of the Convention of the People of South Carolina, Held in 1860–1861. Together with the Reports, Resolutions, &c. Charleston: Evans & Cogswell, 1861. Print.

Journal of the Convention of South Carolina Which Ratified the Constitution of the United States May 23, 1788. United States Constitution Bicentennial Commission of South Carolina, 1988. Facsimile edition.

Kaminski, John P., ed. *A Necessary Evil?: Slavery and the Debate over the Constitution.* Madison, WI: Madison House, 1995. Print.

Keating, Richard Seabrook. *From Conflict to Culture: A Literary Study of Colonial South Carolina's Economic Societies, 1670–1750.* PhD diss. University of North Carolina at Chapel Hill, 1993.

Kennedy, Lionel H., and Thomas Parker, eds. *An Official Report of the Trials of Sundry Negroes, Charged with an Attempt to Raise an Insurrection in South Carolina: Preceded by an Introduction and Narrative and, in an Appendix, a Report of the Trials of Four White Persons on Indictments for Attempting to Excite the Slaves to Insurrection.* Charleston: J. R. Schenck, 1822.

Kibler, Lillian A. "Unionist Sentiment in South Carolina in 1860." *Journal of Southern History* 4 (1938): 346–66. Print.

Kinealy, Christine. *Daniel O'Connell and the Anti-Slavery Movement: 'The Saddest People the Sun Sees.'"* London: Pickering & Chatto, 2011.

King, Rufus. *Substance of Two Speeches, Delivered in the Senate of the United States, on the Subject of the Missouri Bill.* New York: Kirk and Mercein, 1819.

King, Vincent. "'Foolish Talk 'Bout Freedom': Simms's Vision of America in *The Yemassee.*" *Studies in the Novel* 35, no. 2 (2003): 139–48.

Klebenar, Benjamin Joseph. "Manumission Laws and the Responsibility for Supporting Slaves." *Virginia Magazine of History and Biography* 63 (October 1965): 443–53.

Klein, Maury. *Days of Defiance: Sumter, Secession, and the Coming of the Civil War.* New York: Alfred A. Knopf, 1997. Print.

Kramer, Lloyd. *Lafayette in Two Worlds: Public Cultures and Personal Identities in an Age of Revolutions.* Chapel Hill: University of North Carolina Press, 1996. Print.

Krawczynski, Keith. *William Henry Drayton: South Carolina Revolutionary Patriot.* Baton Rouge: Louisiana State University Press, 2001. Print.

Lander, Ernest M. Jr. "The South Carolinians at the Philadelphia Convention, 1787." *South Carolina Historical Magazine* 57, no. 3 (July 1956): 134–55.

Lane, Jason. *General and Madame de Lafayette.* New York: Taylor Trade Publishing, 2003. Print.

Laurens, Henry. *Papers of Henry Laurens.* Edited by G. C. Rogers Jr., David R. Chesnutt, and C. James Taylor. 16 vols. Columbia: University of South Carolina Press, 1968.

———. *A South Carolina Protest against Slavery.* New York: G. P. Putnam, 1861.

"Legislative Proceedings." *Tri-Weekly Courier* [Charleston, SC], Tuesday morning, November 13, 1860. Print.

Lerner, Gerda. *The Grimké Sisters from South Carolina: Pioneers for Women's Rights and Abolition.* Revised and Expanded Edition. Chapel Hill: University of North Carolina, 1967, 1998, 2004.

Letter. December 6, 1862. *Harriott K. Middleton Family Correspondence, 1861–1865.* South Carolina Historical Society. Print.

Letter, Henry Laurens to John Laurens, August 14, 1776. *The Papers of Henry Laurens.* Edited by Philip Hamar and George Rogers. Vol. 11, 224–25. Columbia: University of South Carolina Press, 1968–2003.

Letter to Messieurs and Madame Luarence. February 25, 1774. In *The*

Papers of Henry Laurens. Edited by G. C. Rogers Jr., David R. Chesnutt, and C. James Taylor. Vol. 9, 309–11. Columbia: University of South Carolina Press, 1968. Print.

Letter to William Flower. July 10, 1747. In *The Papers of Henry Laurens.* Edited by G. C. Rogers Jr., David R. Chesnutt, and C. James Taylor. Vol. 1, 23. Columbia: University of South Carolina Press, 1968. Print.

Linebaugh, Peter, and Marcus Rediker. *The Many-Headed Hydra: Sailors, Slaves, Commoners, and the Hidden History of the Revolutionary Atlantic.* Boston: Beacon Press, 2000.

Madden, Richard. *Catholics in South Carolina: A Record.* New York: University Press of America, 1985.

Maier, Pauline. *American Scripture: Making the Declaration of Independence.* New York: Alfred A. Knopf, 1997. Print.

Mason, George. *The Papers of George Mason 1725–1792.* Vol. 3: *1787–1792.* Edited by Robert A. Rutland. Chapel Hill: University of North Carolina Press, 1970.

Massey, Gregory. *John Laurens and the American Revolution.* Columbia: University of South Carolina Press, 2000.

Matthews, Marty D. *Forgotten Founder: The Life and Times of Charles Pinckney.* Columbia: University of South Carolina Press, 2004.

May, John Amasa, and Joan Reynolds Faunt. *South Carolina Secedes.* Columbia: University of South Carolina Press, 1960. Print.

McCrady, Edward. *The History of South Carolina in the Revolution, 1775–1780.* New York: Macmillan, 1901. Print.

McDonald, Forrest. *E Pluribus Unum: The Formation of the American Republic, 1776–1790.* Indianapolis: Liberty Press, 1979, c1965.

McDonough, Daniel J. *Christopher Gadsden and Henry Laurens: The Parallel Lives of Two American Patriots.* Sellinsgrove, PA: Susquehanna University Press, 2000. Print.

McMillin, James A. *The Final Victims: Foreign Slave Trade to North America, 1783–1810.* Columbia: University of South Carolina Press, 2004.

Meleney, John C. *The Public Life of Aedanus Burke: Revolutionary Republican in Post-Revolutionary South Carolina.* Columbia: University of South Carolina Press, 1989. Print.

Merrens, H. Roy, ed. *The Colonial South Carolina Scene: Contemporary Views, 1697–1774.* Columbia: University of South Carolina Press, 1977. Print.

Middleton, Francis. Letter to Harriott Middleton. February 22, 1863. *Harriott K. Middleton Family Correspondence, 1861–1865.* South Carolina Historical Society. Print.

Miller, Helen Hill. *George Mason, Gentleman Revolutionary*. Chapel Hill: University of North Carolina Press, 1975.

Moore, Warner O., Jr. *Henry Laurens: A Charleston Merchant in the Eighteenth Century, 1747–1771*. PhD diss., University of Alabama, 1974.

Morgan, Donald G. *Justice William Johnson: The First Dissenter*. Columbia: University of South Carolina Press, 1954.

Morrison, Jeffery H. *John Witherspoon and the Founding of the American Republic*. Notre Dame, IN: University of Notre Dame Press, 2005.

Morton, Joseph C. *Shapers of the Great Debate at the Constitutional Convention of 1787: A Biographical Dictionary*. Westport, CT: Greenwood Press, 2006.

Nadelhaft, Jerome J. *The Disorders of War: The Revolution in South Carolina*. Orono: University of Maine at Orono Press, 1981.

"Notice" in Preface. In Henry Laurens, *South Carolina Protest against Slavery*, 5–6. New York: G. P. Putnam, 1861. Print.

Oglethorpe, James. "An Account of the Negroe Insurrection in South Carolina." In *Colonial Records of the State of Georgia*, vol. 22, pt. 2, 232–36. Athens, GA: Franklin Printing and Publishing Col, 1904–1989. Print.

Olwell, Robert. "Becoming Free: Manumission and the Genesis of a Free Black Community in South Carolina, 1740–1790." *Slavery & Abolition* 17, no. 1 (April 1996): 1–19.

————. *Masters, Slaves, & Subjects: The Culture of Power in the South Carolina Low Country, 1740–1790*. Ithaca, NY: Cornell University Press, 1998.

Pearson, Edward A. *Designs against Charleston: The Trial Record of the Denmark Vesey Slave Conspiracy of 1822*. Chapel Hill: University of North Carolina Press, 1999.

Pease, William H. and Jane H. *James Louis Petigru: Southern Conservative, Southern Dissenter*. Athens: University of Georgia Press, 1995.

Phelps, W. Chris. *The Bombardment of Charleston, 1863–1865*. Gretna, LA: Pelican, 2002.

Pinckney, Eliza L. *The Letterbook of Eliza Lucas Pinckney, 1739–1762*. Edited by Elise Pinckney. Chapel Hill: University of North Carolina Press, 1972. Print.

Pinckney, Henry Laurens. *Address to the Electors of Charleston District, South Carolina, on the Subject of the Abolition of Slavery*. Washington, DC: n.p., 1836.

Powers, Bernard E., Jr. *Black Charlestonians: A Social History, 1822–1885*. Fayetteville: University of Arkansas Press, 1994.

Preface. *Memorial of the Late James I.. Petigru: Proceedings of the Bar of Charleston, S.C., March 25, 1863*, 3–4. New York: Richardson and Company, 1866. Print.

Pringle, Robert. Letter to Andrew Pringle. March 23, 1743. In *Letterbook of Robert Pringle*, edited by Walter B. Edgar, vol. 3, 571. Columbia: University of South Carolina Press, 1972. Print.

———. Letter to James Henderson. December 17, 1740. In *The Letterbook of Robert Pringle*, edited by Walter B. Edgar, vol. 1. Columbia: University of South Carolina Press, 1972. Print.

Proceedings of the State Rights Celebration, at Charleston, S.C., July 1st, 1830. Charleston, SC: A. E. Miller, 1830.

Quincy, Josiah. *Memoir of the Life of Josiah Quincy*. Boston: Cummings, Hillard, 1825.

Radford, John P. "Testing the Model of the Pre-industrial City: The Case of Ante-Bellum Charleston, South Carolina." *Transactions of the British Geographical Society* 4 (1979): 392–410. Print.

Ramsay, David, "David Ramsay, 1749–1815: Selections from His Writings." Robert L. Brunhouse, ed., *Transactions of the American Philosophical Society*, New Series, 55, no. 4 (1965), 1–250.

———. *Ramsay's History of South Carolina: From Its First Settlement in 1670 to the Year 1808*. Spartanburg, SC: Reprint Co., 1959–1961. Print.

———. *Ramsay's History of South Carolina, from Its First Settlement in 1670 to the Year 1808*. Vol. 2. Newberry, SC: W. J. Duffie, 1858.

Randolph, Thomas J. *Speech of Thomas J. Randolph in the House of Delegates of Virginia, on the Abolition of Slavery*. Richmond, VA: Samuel Shepherd and Company, 1832.

Read, William George. *Memoir of the Rt. Rev. John England*. Baltimore: John Murphy, 1842.

Reynolds, Ignatius Alysius, ed. *The Works of the Right Rev. John England, First Bishop of Charleston*. 5 vols. Baltimore: John Murphy & Co., 1849.

Rhett, Robert Barnwell. *A Fire-Eater Remembers: The Confederate Memoir of Robert Barnwell Rhett*. Edited by William C. Davis. Columbia: University of South Carolina Press, 2000.

Ricci, Scipio de'. *Female Convents. Secrets of Nunneries Disclosed*. Compiled by Mr. De Potter. Edited by Thomas Roscoe. New York: D. Appleton & Co., 1834.

Root, Erik S. *All Honor to Jefferson?: The Virginia Slavery Debates and the Positive Good Thesis*. Lanham, MD: Lexington Books, 2008.

Rose, Alan Henry. "The Image of the Negro in the Pre-Civil-War Novels of John Pendleton Kennedy and William Gilmore Simms." *Journal of American Studies* 4 (February 1971): 217–26.

Rose, Willie Lee. "The Domestication of Domestic Slavery." In *Slavery and Freedom*, edited by William W. Freehling, 18–36. New York: Oxford University Press, 1982.

Rosen, David. "Willing Freedom: Law, Culture, and the Manumission of Slaves in North and South Carolina." In *The Politics of Culture*, edited by Brett Williams, 45–62. Washington, DC: Smithsonian Institution Press, 1991. Print.

Rosen, Robert N. *Confederate Charleston: An Illustrated History of the City and the People during the Civil War*. Columbia: University of South Carolina, 1994. Print.

Rowland, Lawrence S. "The South Carolina Lowcountry during the ratification of the United States Constitution." In *With Liberty and Justice: Essays on the Ratification of the Constitution of the United States*, 1–8. Columbia: United States Constitution Bicentennial Commission, 1988.

Rubin, Hyman, III. *South Carolina Scalawags*. Columbia: University of South Carolina Press, 2006.

Rubio, Philip F. "'Though He Had a White Face, He Was a Negro in Heart': Examining the White Men Convicted of Supporting the 1822 Denmark Vesey Slave Insurrection Conspiracy." *South Carolina Historical Magazine* 113 (January 2012): 50–67.

Rutledge, Edward. Letter to Arthur Middleton. February 8, 1782. "Correspondence of Arthur Middleton." *South Carolina Historical and General Magazine* 27 (1926): 4. Print.

Said, Edward W. *Orientalism*. New York: Vintage Books, 1979. Print.

Salley, Alexander S., ed. *Narratives of Early Carolina 1650–1708*. New York: Barnes and Noble, 1939, 1967. First published by Charles Scribner's Sons, 1911.

Saunders, R. Frank, Jr., and George A. Rogers. "Bishop John England of Charleston: Catholic Spokesman and Southern Intellectual, 1820–1842." *Journal of the Early Republic* 13, no. 3 (Autumn 1993): 301–22.

Schirmer, Jacob. *Diary of Jacob Schirmer*. South Carolina Historical Society. Print.

Schirmer Family. December 24, 1862. *Schirmer Family Journals and Registers, 1806–1929*. South Carolina Historical Society. Print.

Schweninger, Loren. "Slave Independence and Enterprise in South Carolina, 1780–1865." *South Carolina Historical Magazine* 93 (April 1992): 101–25.

Sellers, Leila. *Charleston Business on the Eve of the American Revolution*.

Chapel Hill: University of North Carolina Press, 1934.

Shaffer, Arthur H. *To Be an American: David Ramsay and the Making of the American Consciousness*. Columbia: University of South Carolina Press, 1991. Print.

Shields, David S. *Civil Tongues & Polite Letters in British America*. Chapel Hill: University of North Carolina Press, 1997. Print.

Simms, William Gilmore. "*Domestic Manners of the Americans* by Mrs. Trollope." *American Quarterly Review* 12 (September 1, 1832): 109-133.

———. "Gen. Hammond's Letters on Slavery." *Southern and Western Monthly Magazine and Review* 2 (July 1845): 72.

———. *The Letters of William Gilmore Simms*. 6 vols. Edited by Mary Simms Oliphant, Alfred Taylor Odell, and T. C. Duncan Eaves. Columbia: University of South Carolina Press, 1952.

———. "Miss Martineau on Slavery." *Southern Literary Messenger* (Richmond) 3, no. 9 (November 1837): 641–57.

———. *The Yemassee: A Romance of Carolina*. Edited by John Caldwell Guilds. Selected Fiction of William Gilmore Simms Arkansas Edition. Fayetteville: University of Arkansas Press, 1994.

Simms, William Gilmore, Thomas Dew, James Hammond, and William Harper. *The Pro-Slavery Argument as Maintained by the Most Distinguished Writers of the Southern States, Containing the Several Essays, on the Subject, of Chancellor Harper, Governor Hammond, Dr. Simms, and Professor Dew*. Charleston, SC: Walker, Richards, 1852.

Smith, Paul H. ed. *Letters of Delegates to Congress, 1774–1789*. 26 vols. Washington, DC: Library of Congress, 1976–2000.

Smith, Samuel C. "Henry Laurens: Christian Pietist." *South Carolina Historical Magazine* 100 (April 1999): 143–70.

Smith, William. *Speech of the Hon. Wm. Smith of South Carolina, Delivered in the Senate of the United States, December 8th, 1820: Containing a View of the Constitutions, Laws & Regulations of the Several States, on the Subject of Their Colored Population, Vagrants, &c*. Washington, DC: Gales & Seaton, 1823.

———. [Speech on the Missouri Question.] *Annals of Congress*, 15th Congress, 2nd Session, January 26, 1820: 259–75.

South Carolina Gazette. January 1–8, 1741. Print.

South Carolina General Gazette Extraordinary. October 16, 1775. Print.

Spady, James O'Neil. "Power and Confession: On the Credibility of the Earliest Reports of the Denmark Vesey Slave Conspiracy." *William and Mary Quarterly* 68, no. 2 (April 2011): 287–304.

The St. Augustine Expedition of 1740: A Report to the South Carolina General Assembly Reprinted from the Colonial Records of South Carolina. Columbia: South Carolina Department of Archives, 1954. Print.

St. John, Jeffrey. *Constitutional Journal: A Correspondent's Report from the Convention of 1787.* Ottawa, IL: Jameson Books, 1987.

Symonds, Craig L. *A Battlefield Atlas of the Civil War.* Baltimore: Nautical and Aviation Publishing Company of America, 1983. Print.

Taylor, Lyon G. "James Louis Petigru: Freedom's Champion in a Slave Society." *South Carolina Historical Magazine* 83 (October 1982): 272–86.

Tinkler, Robert. *James Hamilton of South Carolina.* Baton Rouge: Louisiana State University Press, 2004.

Tise, Larry E. *Proslavery: A History of the Defense of Slavery in America, 1800–1840.* Athens: University of Georgia Press, 1987.

Trent, William P. *William Gilmore Simms.* New York: Haskell House, 1968.

Underwood, James Lowell, and W. Lewis Burke Jr., eds. *At Freedom's Door: African American Founding Fathers and Lawyers in Reconstruction South Carolina.* Columbia: University of South Carolina Press, 2000.

United States. War Department. *The War of the Rebellion: A Compilation of the Official Records of the Union and Confederate Armies.* Washington, DC: Government Printing Office, 1880–1901. Print.

Vollaro, Daniel L. "Lincoln, Stowe, and the Little Woman/Great War Story: The Making, and Breaking, of a Great American Anecdote." *Journal of the Abraham Lincoln Association* 30, no. 1 (2009): 18–34.

Wade, Richard C. "The Vesey Plot: A Reconsideration." *Journal of Southern History* 30 (1964): 143–61.

Wakelyn, Jon L. *The Politics of a Literary Man: William Gilmore Simms.* Westport, CT: Greenwood Press, 1973.

Wallace, David Duncan. *The Life of Henry Laurens, with a Sketch of the Life of Lieutenant-Colonel John Laurens.* New York: G. P. Putnam and Sons, 1915.

Walther, Eric H. *William Lowndes Yancey and the Coming of the Civil War.* Chapel Hill: University of North Carolina Press, 2006.

Watson, Charles S. *From Nationalism to Secessionism: The Changing Fiction of William Gilmore Simms.* Westport, CT: Greenwood Press, 1993.

———. "Simms' Review of *Uncle Tom's Cabin.*" *American Literature* 48 (November 1976): 365–68.

Weir, Robert M. *Colonial South Carolina: A History.* Millwood, NY: KTO Press, 1983. Print.

Whitefield, George. *George Whitefield's Journals, 1737–1741: To Which Is Pre-*

fixed His Short Account (1746) and Further Account (1747). Vol. 5. Gainesville, FL: Scholars' Facsimiles & Reprints, 1969. Print.

———. *Regeneration of the Testimony of the Spirit: Being the Substance of Two Sermons Lately Preached in the Parish Church of St. Philip's, Charleston, in South-Carolina. Occasioned by Some Erroneous Notions of certain Men Who Call Themselves Methodists*. 1740; rpt. in Boston, 1741.

Whitman, Stephen. "Manumission and the Transformation of Urban Slavery." *Social Science History* 19 (Autumn 1995): 333–70.

Williams, Frances Leigh. *A Founding Family: The Pinckneys of South Carolina*. New York: Harcourt Brace Jovanovich, 1978.

Williams, T. Harry. *P.G.T. Beauregard: Napoleon in Gray*. Baton Rouge: Louisiana State University Press, 1955. Print.

Williamson, Joel. *After Slavery: The Negro in South Carolina during Reconstruction, 1861–1877*. Hanover, NH: University Press of New England, 1965, 1990.

Wilson, Theodore B. *The Black Codes of the South*. Tuscaloosa: University of Alabama Press, 1965. Print.

Wiltse, Charles M. *John C. Calhoun Nullifier, 1829–1839*. Indianapolis: Bobbs-Merrill, 1949.

Wise, Stephen R. *Gate of Hell: Campaign for Charleston Harbor, 1863*. Columbia: University of South Carolina, 1994. Print.

Wise, Steven M. *Though the Heavens May Fall: The Landmark Trial That Led to the End of Human Slavery*. Cambridge, MA: De Capo, 2005.

Wolf, Eva Sheppard. *Race and Liberty in the New Nation: Emancipation in Virginia from the Revolution to Nat Turner's Rebellion*. Baton Rouge: Louisiana State University Press, 2006.

Wood, Peter. *Black Majority: Negroes in Colonial South Carolina from 1670 through the Stono Rebellion*. New York: Alfred A. Knopf, 1974. Print.

Wooster, Ralph. "Membership of the South Carolina Secession Convention." *South Carolina Historical Magazine* 55 (1954): 189–90. Print.

Yancey, William Lowndes. *Speech of the Hon. William L. Yancey, of Alabama, Delivered in the National Democratic Convention, Charleston, April 28th, 1860, with the Protest of the Alabama Delegation*. From the Report of the "Charleston Mercury." Pamphlet. No publisher. No date.

Young, Jeffrey Robert. *Domesticating Slavery: The Master Class in Georgia and South Carolina, 1670–1837*. Chapel Hill: University of North Carolina Press, 1999.

Zanhiser, Marvin R. *Charles Cotesworth Pinckney, Founding Father*. Chapel Hill: University of North Carolina Press, 1967.

INDEX

||